Healthcare Human Resource Management

Second Edition

Walter J. Flynn | Robert L. Mathis | John H. Jackson

CENGAGE
Learning

Australia • Brazil • Japan • Korea • Mexico • Singapore • Spain • United Kingdom • United States

**Healthcare Human Resource Management:
Second Edition**

Healthcare Human Resource Management, Second Edition
Walter J. Flynn | Robert L. Mathis | John H. Jackson
© 2007, 2004 Cengage Learning. All rights reserved.

For product information and technology assistance, contact us at
Cengage Learning Customer & Sales Support, 1-800-354-9706

For permission to use material from this text or product,
submit all requests online at **cengage.com/permissions**
Further permissions questions can be emailed to
permissionrequest@cengage.com

This book contains select works from existing Cengage Learning resources and was produced by Cengage Learning Custom Solutions for collegiate use. As such, those adopting and/or contributing to this work are responsible for editorial content accuracy, continuity and completeness.

Compilation © 2015 Cengage Learning

ISBN: 978-1-305-74579-7

WCN: 01-100-101

Cengage Learning

20 Channel Center Street
Boston, MA 02210
USA

Cengage Learning is a leading provider of customized learning solutions with office locations around the globe, including Singapore, the United Kingdom, Australia, Mexico, Brazil, and Japan. Locate your local office at:
www.international.cengage.com/region.
Cengage Learning products are represented in Canada by Nelson Education, Ltd.

For your lifelong learning solutions, visit **www.cengage.com /custom.**

Visit our corporate website at **www.cengage.com.**

BRIEF CONTENTS

Contents

CHAPTER 5 *Job Design and Analysis*   82

PREFACE

WHY A BOOK ON HEALTHCARE HUMAN RESOURCE MANAGEMENT

As the authors of this textbook, we have long recognized the unique aspects of healthcare human resource management (HRM) and the need for a textbook specifically focused on this area. Collectively, we have experience in healthcare HRM as practitioners, consultants, and professors. Here we provide both the HRM student and the practitioner a comprehensive, focused source of information on this important body of knowledge and specialized field of practice.

PRIMARY AUDIENCES FOR THIS BOOK

There are several audiences that will find this book to be a useful resource, including college and university students and faculty members, various HR practitioners in healthcare organizations, and healthcare professionals and managers in numerous fields where HR management (HRM) issues affect organizational and individual performance.

COLLEGE/UNIVERSITY STUDENTS AND FACULTY MEMBERS

The importance of human relations skills and HRM knowledge for application in the healthcare industry has grown due to the significant recruitment and retention issues that exist for healthcare workers. Graduates of healthcare-related administration/management degree programs must have a solid knowledge base of HRM topics to be successful in their careers. The types of courses that are well suited for this text include:

- Undergraduate courses in HR management for healthcare administration majors.
- Undergraduate courses in human resources for management with an emphasis on the healthcare industry.

- Graduate courses in human resources for Healthcare Administration programs.
- College curriculums for management tracks for degrees in:
  - Nursing
  - Respiratory Care
  - Radiological Technology
  - Allied Health
  - Public Health
  - Health Promotion
- Distance learning programs related to the above.

HEALTHCARE HR PROFESSIONALS AND HEALTHCARE MANAGEMENT PRACTITIONERS

HR management issues will continue to be a major focus for all individuals with management responsibilities in healthcare organizations. Both the academic and practical experience of the authors have contributed to the book's balance between the theoretical and the practical aspects of healthcare HR. This balance makes the textbook not only useful for the academic setting, but equally useful as a reference for healthcare managers, supervisors, and professionals with HR responsibilities. Even highly experienced healthcare HR professionals will find the presentations of both theory and actual healthcare organizational HR practices insightful and informative.

ORGANIZATION OF THIS BOOK

The textbook includes fourteen chapters; each chapter discusses a particular HRM topic. Each chapter can be used in instruction as a stand-alone presentation, or in conjunction with the other chapters. Regardless of the approach, this book provides a comprehensive source of information on both theory and practice in healthcare HRM.

Chapter 1 discusses the nature and challenges of healthcare HR management through an overview of the current and future states of the healthcare industry. The chapter also describes the various types of organizations that make up the healthcare industry, including physician practices, hospitals, and dental clinics.

Chapter 2 presents a unique review of the HR competencies that are important for healthcare HR professionals. The chapter discusses healthcare organizational structures and the placement of HR departments within the organizational structure, and HR budgets and staffing. The Joint Commission on Accreditation of Healthcare Organizations (JCAHO) is also described along with the key quality standards that impact healthcare HRM.

Chapter 3 describes the importance of strategic HRM. The chapter discusses the process and relevance of effective HR planning against the backdrop of the most challenging HRM issues that confront healthcare organizations, especially staffing and retaining skilled healthcare workers.

Chapter 4 discusses the legal issues affecting the healthcare workplace, with particular focus on Equal Employment Opportunity regulations and issues. Chapter 5 reviews the importance of job design and analysis as it affects all aspects of HRM in healthcare organizations.

Chapter 6 presents a comprehensive discussion on the critical topics for healthcare organizations of recruitment and selection. The chapter includes a discussion on strategic recruiting and an overview of various recruitment methods that are proving successful in the healthcare industry.

Chapter 7 explores employee retention, presenting many of the acknowledged "best practices" that are achieving retention results in healthcare organizations. Given both the current state and the anticipated future critical shortage of healthcare workers, employee retention is one of the most important responsibilities that healthcare HR professionals and healthcare managers have.

Chapter 8 provides a comprehensive discussion on training and development in healthcare organizations. The JCAHO standards dealing with orientation and training also are highlighted in the chapter, as they relate to the verification and development of healthcare worker competencies.

Chapter 9 focuses on the topic of performance management. This chapter includes a review of both the theoretical and practical aspects of establishing performance criteria and developing and conducting performance appraisals for healthcare workers.

Chapters 10 and 11 deal with the interrelated healthcare HR management topics of employee and labor relations. Chapter 10 focuses on a variety of concerns that affect how healthcare organizations manage their workers. Chapter 11 deals specifically with the complexities of managing healthcare workers who are covered under collective bargaining agreements.

Chapters 12 and 13 present healthcare compensation, benefits, and variable pay practices. Chapter 12 details the various compensation programs and processes, including executive pay plans, utilized in healthcare organizations. Chapter 13 discusses the benefits and variable pay programs that make up the total compensation provided to healthcare workers.

Chapter 14 describes the safety, health, and security issues in healthcare organizations and how they affect HRM. The safety, health, and security concerns present in healthcare environments are emphasized as part of healthcare HRM.

TEXTBOOK FEATURES AND HIGHLIGHTS

To enhance the readability and healthcare focus, there are a number of features in the book, including:

Examples Specific to the Healthcare Focus

The healthcare environment is the focus of each HRM topic covered. "Best Practice" examples appear throughout the text, enriching the discussion of current theory.

Healthcare HR Insights

Each chapter begins with a "Healthcare HR Insight," which is an example of programs, solutions, and/or initiatives undertaken by various healthcare organizations relevant to the topic covered in the chapter. Special attention has been given by the authors to ensure that healthcare institutions of different types are represented in the Healthcare HR Insights.

Ethics and Compliance Practices

The importance of maintaining the highest standards in organizational and personal ethical standards has never been more important in healthcare organizations due to the trust that the healthcare consumers place in those organizations. In addition, government entities at all levels are increasing their level of oversight through more regulation and compliance requirements. Due to the need for healthcare organizations to effectively manage their ethics and compliance activities, each chapter contains an "Ethics and Compliance" feature. Each feature presents commentary on an aspect of organizational or personal/professional ethics and/or legal compliance linked to a topic presented in the chapter.

Joint Commission on Accreditation of Healthcare Organizations (JCAHO)

JCAHO is a quality review organization that accredits healthcare organizations relative to a set of quality standards. These standards include such areas as patient care, governance, life safety code, etc. Due to the influence of JCAHO on healthcare HR management, Chapter 2 presents a detailed review of the various JCAHO standards that directly pertain to HR. In addition, many of the chapters contain additional commentary on how JCAHO standards influence the practice of HR in JCAHA accredited organizations.

Study Aides

Figures, including illustrations, process maps, charts, and tables, are used throughout the chapters to assist readers in examining the topics discussed.

Glossary: Key Vocabulary and Concepts

Key vocabulary and concepts are contained in the glossary. For ease of reference these terms also appear in bold print in the text to alert readers that a definition is included in the glossary.

Chapter Ending Cases

At the end of each chapter, case studies are offered to allow readers to analyze a case scenario that is relevant to the chapter content. The cases describe actual situations that have been experienced by healthcare organizations, but the names have been disguised. The problems and issues to be analyzed are framed by discussion questions at the end of the case.

SUPPLEMENTAL MATERIALS

In order to facilitate and enhance the use of the book by faculty members and instructors, an Instructor's Manual, Test Bank, and Web site are available:

Instructor's Manual contents include:

- Chapter outlines;
- Overhead transparency masters derived from key textbook figures;
- Teaching suggestions;
- Chapter Ending Cases include a discussion guide, analysis of the questions and recommended solutions.

Test Bank contents include:

- Multiple-choice
- True-false
- Short essay questions

All questions include answers with reference to pages in the text.

The above ancillary products–the *Instructor's Manual*, and *Test Bank*–are conveniently packaged together on an instructor's CD-ROM along with short video clips that feature HR issues within the healthcare industry.

ACKNOWLEDGEMENTS

There are a number of individuals who assisted the authors in the development of this book and we would like to acknowledge them. One who deserves special recognition is Kathy Flynn, who was so supportive and encouraging throughout the development of this edition.

Some of the other individuals whose ideas and assistance were invaluable include Patrick Langan, Ken Brockman, Allyson Flynn, Joseph Flynn, Kelly Flynn, Michael Flynn, Marian Furlong, Nancy Good, Jennifer Greenburg, Randee Lyons, Steve Mullerleile, Jeff Mutz, Lori Southwood, Angie Williams, and Shenea Wisniewski.

Additionally, the reviewers were so important to the creation of a quality text:

Janice Brown
Bellevue University

Mary Jane Mastorovich
Georgetown University

Ann Luggen
Northern Kentucky University

Delight Wreed
Bellevue University

The authors thank Joe Sabatino, Acquisitions Editor, and Mardell Glinski-Schultz, Development Editor, for their guidance and support. We also appreciate the support of our Production Editor, Joanna Grote.

ABOUT THE AUTHORS

Walter J. Flynn, SPHR, MBA

Mr. Flynn was born in Kentucky and currently resides in Minnesota. He is the CEO of and partner in the human resources consulting firm of Langan and Flynn, LLC, based in Eagan, Minnesota. His firm specializes in working with healthcare organizations in all areas of human resources management. Mr. Flynn has published numerous articles covering a wide array of HR topics.

Mr. Flynn's education includes an M.B.A. from Xavier University, Cincinnati, Ohio; a B.S. from Northern Kentucky University; and advanced work in Quality Management, Diversity Awareness, and Strategic Management. In addition, he has attained the Senior Professional Human Resources (SPHR) designation from the Society for Human Resources Management (SHRM).

In addition to his current consulting experience, he has over 25 years of HR practice and leadership experience including: Vice President of Human Resources for Cincinnati's Children's Hospital, Personnel Director for the Central Trust Co., and Managing Consultant for R. J. Kemen and Associates. He currently holds faculty appointments at The University of Minnesota and Concordia University of St. Paul, Minnesota, and has held faculty appointments at the University of Cincinnati, Northern Kentucky University (where he continues to provide guest lectures), and Thomas More College.

Dr. Robert L. Mathis

Dr. Robert Mathis is a Professor of Management at the University of Nebraska at Omaha (UNO). Born and raised in Texas, he received a BBA and MBA from Texas Tech University and a Ph.D. in management and organization from the University of Colorado. At UNO he received the university's "Excellence in Teaching" award.

Dr. Mathis has co-authored several books and published numerous articles covering a variety of topics over the last twenty-five years. On the professional level, Dr. Mathis has held numerous national offices in the Society for Human Resource Management and in other professional organizations, including the Academy of Management. He also served as President of the Human Resource Certification Institute (HRCI) and is certified as a Senior Professional in Human Resources (SPHR) by HRCI.

He has had extensive consulting experiences with organizations of all sizes in a variety of areas. Firms assisted have been in telecommunications, telemarketing, financial, manufacturing, retail, health care, and utility industries. He has extensive specialized consulting experience in establishing or revising compensation plans for small and medium-sized firms. Internationally, Dr. Mathis has consulting and training experience with organizations in Australia, Lithuania, Romania, Moldova, and Taiwan.

Dr. John H. Jackson

Dr. John H. Jackson is a Professor of Management at the University of Wyoming. Born in Alaska, he received his BBA and MBA from Texas Tech University. He then worked in the telecommunications industry in human resources management for several years. After leaving that industry, he completed his doctoral studies at the University of Colorado and received his Ph.D. in management and organization.

During his academic career, Dr. Jackson has authored six other college texts and more than fifty articles and papers, including those appearing in *Academy of Management Review, Journal of Management, Human Resources Management,* and *Human Resource Planning.* He has consulted with a variety of organizations on HR and management development matters and served as an expert witness in a number of HR-related cases.

At the University of Wyoming he served three terms as department head in the Department of Management and Marketing. Dr. Jackson received the university's highest teaching award and worked with two-way interactive television for MBA students. He designed one of the first classes in the nation on "Business, Environment, and Natural Resources." Two of the governors of the state of Wyoming have appointed him to the Wyoming Business Council and the Workforce Development Council. Dr. Jackson is also president of Silverwood Ranches, Inc.

Healthcare Human Resource Management

THE NATURE AND CHALLENGES OF HEALTHCARE HR MANAGEMENT

Learning Objectives

After you read this chapter, you should be able to:

- Identify the types of healthcare organizations.

- Describe the current and future states of the healthcare industry.

- List and briefly describe human resource management activities.

- Explain the unique aspects of managing human resources in healthcare organizations.

- Discuss several of the human resource challenges existing in healthcare.

Healthcare HR Insights

The American Hospital Association Commission on Workforce for Hospitals and Health Systems recently concluded an extensive study on the shortage of healthcare workers in the United States. Their findings and recommendations were published in a report titled *In Our Hands: How Hospital Leaders Can Build a Thriving Workforce*. With input from healthcare CEOs, physicians, educators, labor leaders, nursing and other allied professionals, and even students, the Commission recommends and challenges healthcare organizational leaders to consider five areas of focus. These areas are vital for a healthcare workforce that will be able to meet the healthcare needs of the aging baby boom generation. These focus areas include:

- Fostering meaningful work
- Improving workplace partnerships
- Broadening the recruiting base
- Collaborating with others
- Building societal support for healthcare careers

Examples of healthcare organizations around the country that are achieving significant results in the recruitment and retention of employees are numerous. At Mountainview Medical Center in White Sulfur Springs, Montana, the nurse position was redefined to deal with a nursing shortage. This streamlined duties and made the work less fragmented. By fostering meaningful work, the center was able to improve patient care and increase morale without spending a lot of additional funds.

At Legacy Health System in Portland, Oregon, they are broadening the base of potential healthcare workers with their "YES Program" (Youth Employment in Summer). It is designed to introduce Latino and African-American students to the healthcare workplace and ultimately encourage them to complete high school and to pursue a healthcare-related career through post-secondary education.

Story County Medical Center in Nevada, Iowa, is a model organization in collaborating with others. Story County Medical Center was asked to help develop a curriculum for a health occupations class for area high school students. Not only did they develop the curriculum, they ended up teaching the class, providing hands-on experiences and offering a CNA (Certified Nurse Assistant) certification. During their involvement with the program, over 100 students have taken the course and many have received their CNA certifications.

The American Hospital Association (AHA) has framed the argument for building societal support through a number of recommendations to Congress, state legislators, and government agencies, who write and interpret laws that impact health policy in the United States. An example of a key recommendation brought forward by AHA that could directly affect the availability of healthcare workers is the recommendation that government- and employer-based retirement laws and policies need to change to encourage older workers to remain in the workplace.[1]

NATURE OF HEALTHCARE ORGANIZATIONS

In the United States over 500,000 establishments make up the healthcare industry. The healthcare industry is very diverse, including organizations that provide medical care, residential care and treatment, and various forms of therapies and health services. Physician offices and clinics comprise the largest category of establishments.

Healthcare organizations can be divided into several categories. Some of these—such as hospitals—employ hundreds of people in large building complexes. Others—such as home healthcare providers—involve few employees, and the "facility" is wherever the patient is. In between are many organizations that make up the healthcare spectrum.

- *Physician Offices and Clinics*—Physicians and surgeons practice individually or in groups of practitioners who have the same or different specialties. Group practice has become the recent trend, including clinics, freestanding emergency care centers, and ambulatory surgical centers.

- *Hospitals and Medical Centers*—Hospitals provide complete healthcare, ranging from diagnostic services to surgery and continuous nursing care. Hospitals can be small, freestanding rural facilities, or they can be part of a vast, multi-facility, geographically dispersed, integrated system. Some hospitals specialize in treatment such as burn care, cancer, or pediatrics, while others are full-service providers.

- *Nursing and Residential Care Facilities*—Nursing facilities provide inpatient nursing, rehabilitation, and health-related personal care to those who need continuous healthcare, but do not require hospital services. Other facilities, such as nursing and convalescent homes, help patients who need less assistance but also need special rehabilitation services.

- *Home Healthcare*—Skilled nursing or medical care is sometimes provided in the home, under a physician's supervision. Home healthcare services are provided mainly to the elderly.

- *Outpatient Care Services*—Among the establishments in this group are kidney dialysis centers, drug treatment clinics and rehabilitation centers, blood banks, and providers of childbirth preparation classes.

- *Medical and Diagnostic Laboratories*—These laboratories provide analytic and diagnostic services to medical care providers or directly to patients following a physician's direction. Workers may analyze blood, take X rays, or perform other clinical tests. In dental laboratories, workers make dentures, artificial teeth, and orthodontic appliances.

- *Offices and Clinics of Other Health Practitioners*—This segment includes offices of chiropractors, ophthalmologists, optometrists, and podiatrists, as well as occupational and physical therapists, psychologists, audiologists, speech-language pathologists, dietitians, and other miscellaneous health practitioners. This segment also includes alternative-medicine practitioners, such as acupuncturists, homeopaths, hypnotherapists, and naturopaths.

- *Dental Offices and Clinics*—Almost 20 percent of healthcare establishments in the United States are dental offices. Most employ only a few workers who provide general or specialized dental care, including dental surgery and orthodontia.
- *Other Ambulatory Healthcare Services*—Included in this segment are such services as ambulance services, blood and organ banks, pacemaker monitoring, and smoking cessation programs.

Employment in Healthcare

No matter what form of healthcare or type of facility is involved, employees are needed to deliver care. Healthcare is one of the largest industries in the United States, providing almost 13 million jobs. The healthcare industry can be characterized as a labor-intensive industry with a wide diversity of position types requiring a broad cross-section of skill sets, professional training, and academic preparation. Many healthcare positions require at least four-year college degrees.

Figure 1-1 shows the composition of healthcare employment by type of organization. Hospitals account for less than 2 percent of all health service facilities, yet they employ nearly 40 percent of all healthcare workers.[2]

Types of Healthcare Jobs

The delivery of healthcare requires workers in a variety of job categories with different levels of education, training, and experience. In addition to the myriad

FIGURE 1-1   Employment in Healthcare

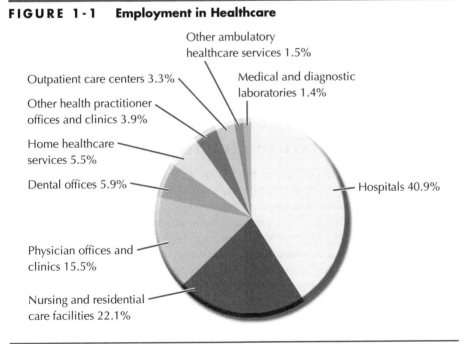

Other ambulatory healthcare services 1.5%

Medical and diagnostic laboratories 1.4%

Outpatient care centers 3.3%

Other health practitioner offices and clinics 3.9%

Home healthcare services 5.5%

Dental offices 5.9%

Hospitals 40.9%

Physician offices and clinics 15.5%

Nursing and residential care facilities 22.1%

Source: U.S. Department of Labor: Bureau of Labor Statistics, 2005.

of medical and clinical positions present in healthcare delivery, there are also significant requirements for workers with skills in the following fields:

- Management and administration
- Legal and compliance services
- Physical plant operations
- Safety and security
- Information technology
- Fund raising and community affairs
- Food and nutritional services

The scope of jobs in healthcare depicted in Figure 1-2 shows a healthcare position hierarchy. It also depicts two other relationships: the levels and the number of positions required in each job category.

Healthcare Position Hierarchy   It is useful to understand the various levels of positions to appreciate the distribution of power and responsibility within healthcare organizations. Large health systems are especially hierarchical with significant numbers and levels of jobs, while clinics and physician groups have very flat organizational structures with few levels. Purposely not depicted on this illustration are physicians, who by definition would fall in the clinical professional category. However, depending on the nature and size of a healthcare organization, physicians could also be associated with any level of executive, senior, or middle management or supervision, and their power associated with their knowledge makes them difficult to classify in a typical managerial position chart.

Distribution of Positions   The graphical depiction of a pyramid is a model for considering the labor requirements of the various levels in a healthcare organization. At the top of the pyramid is executive management, which would represent the fewest number of individuals required across the industry. At the base of the pyramid are service workers, who would represent the category of workers requiring the largest numbers of individuals.

THE CURRENT STATE OF HEALTHCARE

The current state of the delivery of healthcare in the United States is important to the discussion of healthcare human resources (HR) management and how healthcare organizations manage their employees.

Healthcare and change have been synonymous since the late 1960s with the passage of Medicare legislation and the continued rise in healthcare costs. Federal and state governmental involvement in healthcare, coupled with ever-increasing costs, has been a primary impetus behind the changes in healthcare in recent years. Managed care and the growth of government regulation have driven the changes. Also, there have been continuing pressures to reduce the cost of delivering healthcare in all forms.[3]

The U.S. healthcare system is one of the best in the world. Access to care (although sometimes unevenly distributed) and advances in technology,

FIGURE 1-2   Healthcare Position Hierarchy

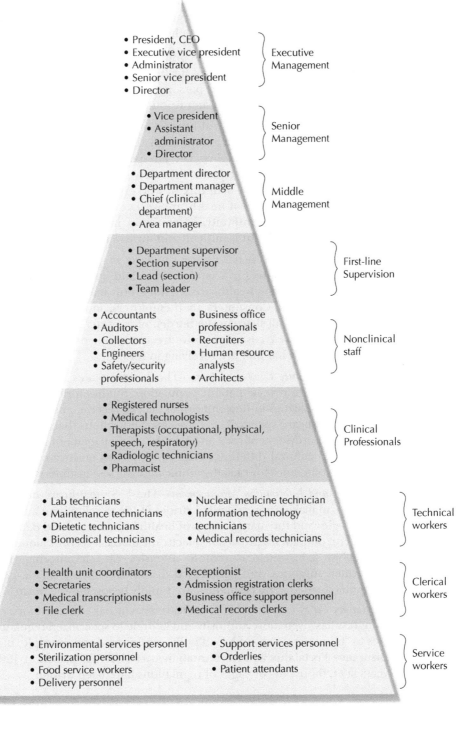

therapies and pharmaceuticals continually contribute to a longer and higher quality of life for the U.S. population. Yet certain realities and issues provide a compelling backdrop against which the accomplishments of the healthcare system must be balanced. The following list details some of the key areas for awareness in the environment in which healthcare operates:

- *Growing Resource Needs*—Healthcare organizations are faced with an aging population (increasing the number of healthcare consumers), growing numbers of uninsured and underinsured persons, the need for costly technology, and other pressures that require greater resources.

- *Multifaceted Workforce Crisis*—Healthcare organizations are not just contending with a short supply of workers, although there are significant shortages of nursing personnel, certain physician sub-specialists, and other professional caregivers; there are other equally difficult aspects of the crisis. At the top of the list are changes in the skill mix of workers needed to meet new service requirements, high levels of healthcare worker dissatisfaction, and a tremendous need for labor continuity, especially in intensive care positions, in a period where recruitment is difficult and turnover is high.

- *Ensuring Patient Safety and Reducing Variability in Service, Quality, and Cost*—Consumer expectations for a safe, positive, and cost-effective experience in accessing and receiving healthcare are not evenly met throughout the healthcare delivery system. Consumers, their employers, and Federal, state and local governments, who all share in the burden of ever-increasing healthcare costs, are challenging these costs if negative treatment outcomes occur, or if unsafe or rude care are what they are receiving in return.[4]

- *Providing Culturally Competent Care*—The United States' increasing diversity results in a more diverse patient population. Studies indicate that there are significant disparities in how minorities access, receive, and benefit from the nation's healthcare system. There are clear indications that a lack of diversity in the direct providers of care and healthcare management and their lack of sensitivity to cultural differences can produce less positive or even negative healthcare outcomes for racially/ethnically diverse consumers.[5]

- *Technology and Information Management*—The U.S. healthcare delivery system continues to make unprecedented strides in the development and use of new technologies and the management of health information and data. Complete (inpatient, outpatient, physician) electronic medical records along with other technology gains such as remote intensive care monitoring, robotically performed surgeries, and gene-based disease treatments (made possible by computer-assisted gene mapping), are rapidly becoming the norm.[6]

- *Regulatory Policy*—As the U.S. healthcare system has become more complex, Congress has given more authority and latitude to specialized regulatory agencies to "fill in the detail" of broad policy decisions. As an example, the Health Insurance Portability and Accountability Act (HIPAA) passed in 1996. Eight years later, thousands of pages of regulations have been written.[7]

THE FUTURE OF HEALTHCARE

Predicting the future of the healthcare industry is difficult. The pace of change is so rapid and unpredictable forces and events can dramatically alter the direction and course of trends we may have felt confident to predict. As an example, the events of September 11, 2001 have had a dramatic impact on many aspects of the healthcare delivery system in the U.S. and who could have possibly predicted that event and its outcomes?

However, as depicted in Figure 1-3, there are certain trends and "drivers" of the future of healthcare that can be predicted with a degree of certainty, primarily because they have so much momentum that regardless of unforeseen or catastrophic events it would be difficult to alter their course.

- *Continued Financial Pressures*—The federal government, third party payers, consumers, and employers will continue to pressure the healthcare industry to stabilize costs. And perhaps as importantly, they will provide more value in all aspects of the care delivery continuum for the healthcare dollars being spent.

- *Demographic Changes*—The U.S. population is growing, and growing older. The implications for healthcare are enormous. The number of Medicare enrollees will grow from about 42 million today to 77 million in 2030. By 2010, 70 million Americans will have two or more chronic conditions.[8]

- *Technology, Costs, and Competition*—Unlike the application of technology in other fields, changes in healthcare technology have increased the cost of care by allowing more to be done for more people. Advancements in technology also allow for a shift in healthcare delivery from inpatient to outpatient settings to free-standing care centers and physician offices. The result has been growth to excess in capacity which in turn has created more competition. Unlike other industries, however, so far the competition has not resulted in price competition to any great extent.

- *Public Opinion*—The public is growing increasingly more frustrated with the U.S. healthcare system. In a recent poll, only 6 out of 10 Americans said that

FIGURE 1-3   The Current and Future States of Healthcare

HEALTHCARE	
CURRENT STATE	➡ FUTURE STATE
• Growing resource needs	• Continued financial pressure
• A multifaceted workforce crisis	• Demographic changes
• Patient safety and reduced variability in service, quality, and cost	• Technology, costs, and competition
	• Public opinion
• Culturally competent care	• More accountability
• Technology and information management	• Health planning policy initiatives
• Regulatory policy	

the healthcare system was meeting their needs and the needs of their family. Only 2 out of 10 believed the system was meeting the needs of most Americans. In a survey conducted by the Gallup Organization, healthcare is only one of six industries to receive more negative evaluations than positive evaluations. The other five industries included the legal field and the pharmaceutical industries.[9] Rising costs and the uninsured were named as two of the biggest issues facing the system today. Predictions are that unless these issues are dealt with, the public's opinion of the healthcare industry will worsen.

- *More Accountability*—Federal, state, and local governments, along with employer and consumers groups, are already demanding more accountability from healthcare organizations and individual providers. The future will predictably include a call for more information on the quality of doctors and hospitals. Hospital and physician price information should also be publicly available, as well as information on the actual net cost of any procedure, treatment, or test.

- *Health Planning Policy Initiatives*—The United States will have to deal with the uneven supply of healthcare resources. Historically the marketplace has allocated resources, resulting in a mismatching between demand and supply. Rural America has especially suffered from a lack of access to healthcare. Future predictions are that decisions on planned allocation versus universal coverage will most likely have to occur.[10]

HR CHALLENGES IN HEALTHCARE

The current state of healthcare and predictions about the industry require healthcare organizational leaders who can manage in an ever-changing and challenging environment. HR leadership is especially critical because many of the current realities and future eventualities for the healthcare industry have, at their core, significant human resource management implications.

The list of challenges is both daunting and exciting. HR professionals have the opportunity to make contributions to their organizations and to their industry by providing solutions for the most difficult issues and problems the industry faces. Two of the most prominent challenges include the *recruitment and retention* of the correct number of qualified staff and *managing the changes* that affect human resources.

Recruitment and Retention

The enormous demand for healthcare workers is likely to continue or even increase for a number of key healthcare positions. The nursing shortage has been well-chronicled in the popular media with an estimated national shortfall of over 600,000 registered nurses (RNs) by the year 2012. However, the recruitment and staffing issues are clearly not exclusive to nursing; all healthcare professions have been and will be affected. The projected growth of healthcare occupations in comparison to the growth of non-healthcare occupations is 2 to 1.

FIGURE 1-4   Projected Growth of Selected Health Professions 2000–2010

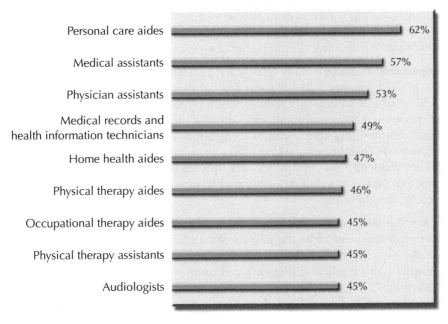

Many health professions are expected to have rapid job growth by 2010

Profession	Growth
Personal care aides	62%
Medical assistants	57%
Physician assistants	53%
Medical records and health information technicians	49%
Home health aides	47%
Physical therapy aides	46%
Occupational therapy aides	45%
Physical therapy assistants	45%
Audiologists	45%

Source: U.S. Census Bureau, 2005.

To further illustrate the magnitude of the growth in health occupations, Figure 1-4 shows the projected growth of nine selected healthcare-related positions. Note that many of these positions require a minimum of a two year associate's degree and two of the positions, Physician Assistant and Audiologist, require specialized training beyond a four year bachelor's degree.

HR professionals in all segments of the industry will be faced with the challenge of recruiting and retaining the right number of competent employees for their organizations. The following trends will have a direct impact on the supply and demand for healthcare workers.

Hospitals, Residential Care, and Rehabilitation Facilities   During the next 15 years, the U.S. healthcare system, particularly inpatient institutions, will face two critical problems related to the healthcare workforce. First and foremost, there will not be enough workers, and second, those who will be available will not have the skills needed in the health system that is emerging. The issues, again, are the demographics of the aging population demanding more care and the overall size of the healthcare delivery system.

The demand for nurses and allied health workers will also be driven by significant growth in three other parts of the healthcare system, as follows.

Ambulatory Care   Healthcare continues to move from inpatient to outpatient or ambulatory care. Thus care providers, which include clinics, physician offices, home health agencies, and free standing surgery and diagnostic centers, will see requirements for ambulatory care providers expand.

Health Service Businesses   Alternative care delivery is rapidly gaining momentum, creating a variety of health service businesses. Managed care companies, "health concierge" companies, and grocery and drug stores will be looking for individuals with clinical training and a knack for customer service.

Independent Practice   Many healthcare professionals are moving to independent practice to meet the demand for alternative care. High demand skills include nutrition and weight management, physical therapy, pain management and personal care combined with therapy. Independent practitioners are utilizing the training they received from hospitals and clinics and establishing fee-for–service businesses marketed directly to the consumer.

The challenge to healthcare HR professionals to recruit and retain competent employees includes dealing with some very compelling issues, among which are the following:

- Over the last two decades there has been a dramatic decline in the United States in the interest in training nurses and allied health professionals and in the capacity to do so. As an example, as recently as the 1980s many large hospitals and medical centers offered their own nursing training programs, awarding "diploma RN" degrees. These programs are either no longer in existence or they have been dramatically downsized and folded into two or four-year degree programs at colleges.

- Attractive career paths have emerged outside of the life sciences, particularly in technology, which offer comparable or better wages, friendlier work environments, and greater opportunities for advancement.

- As career opportunities for women have broadened over the last 50 years, many women who would have historically chosen health careers have pursued other non–health-related career paths.

- The healthcare workplace, due to budget issues, staffing shortage, and increased workloads caused by greater demand and fewer workers, has grown more stressful and less able to attract and retain workers.

- The pressures on the healthcare workplace have caused increased friction between management and employees, resulting in predictions of widespread unionization in the healthcare industry over the next decade as a means for healthcare workers to bargain for better working conditions.[11]

Managing Change

The healthcare industry and change have been and are synonymous. Without question managing the changes that impact the healthcare workplace is one of the most important challenges facing healthcare HR professionals. Figure 1-5

FIGURE 1-5   Major Healthcare HR Change Elements

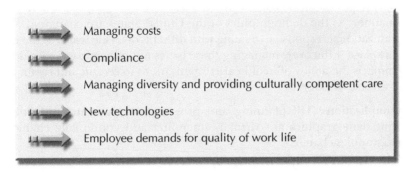

Managing costs

Compliance

Managing diversity and providing culturally competent care

New technologies

Employee demands for quality of work life

provides an overview of five of the more compelling elements of change impacting the healthcare workplace that have significant HR implications and require HR change management.

Discussion has highlighted the continuous pressure on the cost of healthcare delivery, rapid and constant technology advances, consumers demanding improvement in clinical performance, and other environmental and market forces. These changes have had a significant effect on the management of human resources in healthcare organizations.

Managing Costs   In response to cost-containment issues, healthcare organizations have undertaken a seemingly endless stream of budget cutting initiatives, restructuring to gain efficiencies, curtailment of low-demand or low-margin services, and other initiatives designed to meet cost reduction objectives.

- **HR Implications:** Given the fact that 50 percent to 60 percent of the total operating costs of most healthcare organizations resides in employee pay and benefits, managing costs almost always means managing the number, skill mix, or wages of employees.

Compliance with Quality Standards   With the increasing pressure on the healthcare delivery system to improve clinical performance, performing to quality standards is a critical challenge. Whether meeting the Joint Commission for the Accreditation of Healthcare Organizations (JCAHO) quality standards, responding to third-party payer clinical outcome reviews, or dealing with a state health department audit, healthcare organizations are required to continually improve the quality and responsiveness of their delivery of services.

- **HR implications:** The tasks of orienting, training, and continually monitoring employees' performance relative to safety, quality, and care standards are critical requirements for HR planning and programming. Inevitably each year, new regulations, standards, or requirements require updated training, new policies, and other programming in order to maintain employees' competencies in this critical area.

Managing Diversity and Providing Culturally Competent Care Healthcare providers must ensure that each person, regardless of race, ethnicity, gender, age, and ability to pay medical bills, receive medical care in a competent, sincere, and equal manner. As the demographics of the United States are changing, so must the organizational response to dealing with difficult diversity issues in the healthcare workplace. Effectively managing these issues not only impacts care delivery, it also impacts the ability of healthcare organizations to recruit and retain a competent, diverse workforce.

- **HR implications:** HR planning and programming to match provider and patient demographics are virtually unending and continually changing as demographics change.

Preparing Healthcare Workers for New Technologies New technologies are leading to significant advances in the delivery and quality of services. These advances are also contributing to productivity gains and more cost-effective care. Advances include new drugs, new imaging technologies, genetic mapping and testing, and the transfer of medical information from paper to computer.

- **HR implications:** As these advances are implemented, healthcare workers must receive orientation and training to effectively and safely operate with new technologies. The skill sets of future healthcare workers must include not only clinical and administrative capabilities, but also computer knowledge and related capabilities to facilitate their use of ever-improving healthcare technology.

Quality of Work Life Healthcare workers, like workers in other industries, are experiencing significant difficulty in juggling work and family responsibilities. However, in healthcare work environments that frequently demand 24 hours a day, 7 days per week coverage, this is especially true. The patients, residents, and clients of healthcare providers require care outside what is considered a "normal" work day of 8:00 A.M. to 5:00 P.M. And even if healthcare workers are not required to do shift work, they are still continually confronted with work and schedule demands that conflict with family and other personal life responsibilities.

- **HR implications:** HR policy development is required to continually monitor and initiate solutions such as flexible scheduling programs, on-site day care and other efforts to aid employees in this difficult area.

JOINT COMMISSION ON ACCREDITATION OF HEALTHCARE ORGANIZATIONS

Every industry possesses unique characteristics that affect the management of human resources. This is especially true in the healthcare industry. One of the most unique characteristics of the healthcare industry is that healthcare worker errors can potentially result in death or injury to patients, clients, or residents.

This characteristic requires healthcare employers to have the highest standards in assuring staff competence, safe practice, ethical treatment, and confidentiality.

JCAHO is an accreditation organization concerned with quality whose members subscribe to a standards-based review process. Compliance with quality standards as demonstrated through onsite reviews by JCAHO is critical to ensure that the consumers of healthcare are receiving consistent levels of safe, quality care.

ETHICAL PRACTICES AND COMPLIANCE

Ethical practices and compliance are critical. With mounting pressure for cost containment, there is growing frustration from the consumers and payers of healthcare. This results in declining public opinion and increasing demand for more accountability throughout the healthcare system in the United States. A glaring example of what can happen when healthcare organizations fail to act responsibly with regard to ethical practices is the HealthSouth Corporation (HealthSouth).

HealthSouth, an operator of rehabilitation hospitals in the United States, agreed to pay over $300 million to settle Medicare fraud claims. In addition, founder Richard Scrushy personally was criminally charged and tried, and although he was eventually acquitted, 15 other executives of HealthSouth avoided trial by pleading guilty. The list of ethical and compliance issues cited is extensive, including overcharging patients and the Medicare System, defrauding insurance companies, allowing unlicensed personnel to perform treatments, performing false accounting practices, and executives spending lavishly on entertainment and travel.[12]

Healthcare organizations, whether they are a sole practitioner family practice physician, community nursing home, or major metropolitan medical center, must continually be aware of the public trust they hold. In fact, one could argue that the entire healthcare system is built on trust. There is trust that competent people are performing care and medical duties appropriately, that labs are producing accurate results, that physicians are carefully studying test results and using their best judgement in diagnoses, and that nursing homes that have been entrusted with the care of aging loved ones do so with respect and dignity.

Healthcare HR professionals have important and critical roles in the organizational processes of developing, updating, communicating training about, and enforcing ethics programs. In fact, promoting ethics was cited as a top-10 trend among HR professionals in the Society for Human Resource Management (SHRM) 2004–2005 Workplace Forecast. This underscores that pressure on healthcare organizations and their HR professionals to develop and facilitate ethics policies will continue for the foreseeable future. As a corollary, helping organizations shape and steer values has always been an HR reponsibility.[13] Based on the HealthSouth experience, the stakes are very high for healthcare organizations and the need for HR to take a strategic role in ethical practices and compliance programming is obvious.

JCAHO has standards for a wide array of hospital functions and performance areas. These performance areas are grouped by patient-focused and organization-focused functions. Additional areas surveyed are referred to as structures such as governance, management, medical staff, and nursing. JCAHO expects healthcare providers to use a collaborative and multidisciplinary approach to improve performance, pursue quality initiatives, and develop staff competencies. The multidisciplinary approach is evident because standards for all the functions are reviewed. Many human resource standards are linked to the standards for other departmental and division functions. As an example, staff education is shared among HR and other departments.

Within each of the organizational function areas, a number of standards deal with the responsibilities of HR management:

- Planning for effective staffing
- Providing competent staff
- Orienting, training, and educating staff
- Evaluating competence and managing performance.[14]

Each one of these responsibilities has standards associated with it that include policy, practice, and documentation of compliance requirements. Throughout the text, the JCAHO standards and their impact on HR practices in hospital or medical center facilities will be cited.

THE HR FUNCTION IN HEALTHCARE

The HR management function in healthcare organizations continues to gain prominence relative to the other functional areas of healthcare organizations.[15] This trend has evolved for two critical reasons: First, it is due to the clear need to provide HR support more efficiently and effectively. Second, healthcare HR professionals are increasing their training, skills, understanding, and competency, all of which increases their ability to contribute to their organizations.

HR MANAGEMENT ACTIVITIES

The central focus for healthcare HR management is to contribute to organizational success. As Figure 1-6 depicts, HR management usually is composed of several groups of interlinked activities. However, the performance of these HR activities is done in the context of a specific organization, which is represented by the inner rings in Figure 1-6. A brief description of the major HR activities follows.

- *HR Planning and Analysis*—Through *HR planning*, managers attempt to anticipate forces that will influence the future supply of and demand for employees. Having a *human resource information system (HRIS)* to provide accurate and timely information for HR planning is crucial.

- *EEO Compliance*—Compliance with equal employment opportunity (EEO) laws and regulations affects all other HR activities. For instance, strategic HR

FIGURE 1-6   HR Management Activities

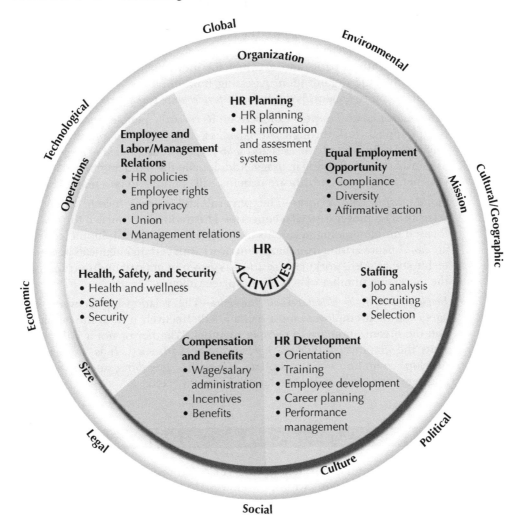

plans must ensure availability of a *diversity* of individuals to meet *affirmative action* requirements. In addition, when recruiting, selecting, and training individuals, all managers must be aware of EEO requirements, including accommodations of individuals with disabilities.

- *Staffing*—The aim of staffing is to provide an adequate supply of qualified individuals to fill the jobs in an organization. By studying what workers do, *job analysis* provides the foundation for the staffing function. From this analysis, *job descriptions* and *job specifications* can be prepared and used to *recruit* applicants for job openings. The *selection process* is then concerned with choosing the most qualified individuals to fill jobs in the organization.

- *HR Development*—Beginning with the *orientation* of new employees, HR training and development also includes *job-skill training*. As jobs evolve and change, ongoing *retraining* is necessary to accommodate technological changes. Encouraging *development* of all employees, including supervisors and managers, is necessary to prepare organizations for future challenges. *Career planning* identifies paths and activities for individual employees as they develop within the organization. Assessing how employees perform their jobs and make improvements is the focus of *performance management*.

- *Compensation and Benefits*—Compensation rewards people for performing organizational work through *pay, incentives,* and *benefits*. Employers must develop and refine their basic *wage* and *salary* systems. Also, *incentive programs* such as gainsharing are growing in usage. Additionally, the rapid increase in the costs of benefits, especially healthcare benefits, will continue to be a major issue.

- *Health, Safety, and Security*—The physical and mental health, safety, and security of employees are vital concerns. The traditional concern for *safety* has focused on eliminating accidents and injuries at work. Additional concerns are *health* issues arising from hazardous work with certain chemicals and newer technologies. Also, workplace *security* has grown in importance, in response to the increasing number of acts of workplace violence.

- *Employee and Labor–Management Relations*—The relationship between managers and their employees must be handled effectively if both the employees and the organization are to prosper together. Whether or not a *union* represents the employees, *employee rights* must be addressed. It is important to develop, communicate, and update *HR policies, procedures,* and *rules* so that managers and employees alike know what is expected.

CASE

For more than a half-century, two acute-rehabilitation facilities existed within 10 miles of each other in a large metropolitan area. Over several years, competition intensified for patients, physicians, and staff. The competition resulted in duplication of services and increased costs, one of which was higher wages and benefits needed in order for each hospital to compete for skilled healthcare workers. Acknowledging the financial issues of the two organizations, the two Boards of Trustees initiated merger discussions.

The two Boards prepared a "Rationale for Merger" document that indicated that a merger could result in several benefits, as follows:

- More efficient utilization of healthcare resources through
  - A single workforce, with coordinated services, requiring less duplication in positions
  - A single operating budget, reducing the need for two management structures
  - A reduction or elimination in operational redundancy and program duplication
- Proactive leadership to gain community support and to increase the ability of the

combined organization to negotiate favorable reimbursement contracts

Another area the Boards had to consider was the structural impact of the merger, including:

- Consolidation of two Boards into one, two management hierarchies into one, and union contracts
- Combination of pay and benefits programs
- The merger of two different organizational cultures, with all of the "politics" and personal anxieties common in mergers

This was an important decision for the two organizations. The impact on the community, patients, and employees would be far-reaching and compelling. Much of the planning had HR dimensions.

Questions

1. Describe the leadership role of human resources in a successful merger of these two organizations?
2. What are the key human resource challenges and opportunities to a merger of this magnitude?

END NOTES

1. Adapted from "In Our Hands How Hospital Leaders Can Build a Thriving Workforce," *AHA Commission on Workforce for Hospitals and Health systems* (April 2002); "Workforce Ideas in Action 2, Case Examples," *American Hospital Association* (September 2003); "HR Pulse," *American Society for Healthcare Human Resources Administration* (Spring 2003).
2. U.S. Department of Labor, Bureau of Labor Statistics, 2005.
3. Lawrence D. Prybil, "Challenges and Opportunities Facing Health Administration Practice and Education," *Journal of Healthcare Management* (July/August 2003), 223–231.
4. Kate Austin, "Survey: Public More Aware of Quality, Patient Safety Issues," *AHA News* (November 29, 2004) 1, 3.
5. Peter A. Weil, "A Race/Ethnic Comparison of Career Attainments in Healthcare Management," *Health Executive* (January/February 2004), 24–25.
6. Molly J. Coye, "The Technology Imperative," *Futurescan, Healthcare Trends and Implications 2005–2010,* Health Administration Press (2005), 16–21.
7. Carmela Coyle, "The State of the Nation's Health Policy," *Futurescan, Healthcare Trends and Implications 2005–2010,* Health Administration Press (2005), 6–10.
8. Carmela Coyle, "The State of the Nation's Health Policy." *Futurescan, Healthcare Trends and Implications 2005–2010,* Healthcare Administation Press, (2005), 6–10.
9. Richard Blizzard, "Healthcare Suffers Chronic Image Problem," Gallup Poll News Service, *http://www.gallup.com/poll* (10/31/2004).
10. Edward H. O'Neil, "The Workforce Challenge and Opportunity," *Futurescan, Healthcare Trends and Implications 2005–2010,* Health Administration Press (2005), 32–35.
11. Futurescan Survey results, Unionization of Professional Employees—Survey of 1,200 CEO Members of the American College of Healthcare Executives, *Futurescan, Healthcare Trends and Implications 2005–2010,* Health Administration Press (2005), 33.
12. David Voreacos, "Tenacity Exposes Company Fraud," *Pittsburgh Tribune Review* (January 27, 2005), A1.
13. "Leadership: How HR Can Facilitate Ethics," *HR Focus* (April 2005), 1.
14. "Issues in Human Resources for Hospitals," *Joint Commission Resources,* Oakbrook Terrace, IL (2004), 3–5.
15. "CEO Survey Reveals Top Issues for Hospitals," *Health Financial Management* (February 2005), 25.

HEALTHCARE HR COMPETENCIES, STRUCTURES, AND QUALITY STANDARDS

Learning Objectives

After you have read this chapter, you should be able to:

- Define the competencies required for healthcare HR professionals.

- Describe the importance of attaining HR management credentials.

- Explain the relationship between the type of healthcare organization and the level of senior HR position.

- Discuss how the healthcare industry compares to other industries in terms of HR staffing and expenditures.

- Explain the importance of HR programs to the delivery of safe, competent healthcare.

Healthcare HR Insights

Effective HR management is increasingly being seen as critical to the success of healthcare organizations. HR leaders are able to contribute strategically if they understand how their organization works and develop the HR programs and policies that support the "business" of the organization.

Robert Grossman, the author of a recent article in *HR Magazine,* poses the following for HR practitioners: "Demand a seat at the table. Become a strategic business partner. Be proactive. It's all good advice. But like a mother's reminders to take your vitamins or wear galoshes, these mantras seem to have turned off—rather than motivated—many HR professionals. It's easy to see why: It's one thing to talk about becoming a business partner; doing it is a whole other matter. Experts say the surest way for HR professionals to become strategic partners is to learn more about the business they serve. And actually 'doing the business' is often the best way to learn it."[1]

As an example, Grossman described a formal job rotation program for executive development for HR leaders at St. John's Health System in Warren, Michigan. Participating in a formal rotation program is definitely a unique and enriching opportunity. St. John Health is clearly a forward thinking healthcare organization for their programming in this regard, and the "healthcare HR insight" is their recognition of the importance of having HR professionals who know their business. HR professionals who invest the time and learning, whether they work in a clinic, home healthcare agency, pharmacy, or dental practice, to truly understand how care is delivered and how patients are served, will be more credible "business partners" with their management colleagues and more effective in meeting the needs of the employees.[2]

To fulfill their mission, healthcare organizations must have competent HR leaders, effective HR structures and programs, and an understanding of the relationship between the delivery of quality care and effective HR policies and practices.[3] This chapter will provide an overview of these areas and establish the framework for how HR activities are managed.

COMPETENCIES FOR HEALTHCARE MANAGEMENT AND HR

Research, study, and discussion on the topics of management competencies and HR management competencies have been extensive and far ranging. For example, the general HR literature tends to refer to competencies through the acronyms SKAs or KSAs, sometimes referred to as skills, knowledge, and ability. More practical definitions exist relating to the approach of defining competencies in the context of a cluster of related knowledge, skills, and attitudes that impact a major part of a manager's job. As an example, the need for communication skills

FIGURE 2-1 **Five Core Competencies Critical to High-Performing HR Leaders**

that include the abilities to coach and counsel employees, as well as make professional presentations to large audiences.

In a study commissioned by the University of Michigan Business School in conjunction with the Society of Human Resource Management (SHRM), five core competencies for HR professionals were identified. As depicted in Figure 2-1, these five core competencies were determined to be critical to the high-performing HR leader:

* *Strategic Contribution*—It is important to be available and to add value to the performance of the business.
* *Personal Credibility*—Personal credibility involves being able to deliver what is promised, establishing a successful track record, and developing effective written and verbal skills.
* *HR Delivery*—Designing and implementing the HR processes that effectively deliver the HR services required by the organization is another requirement.
* *Business Knowledge*—Understanding the organization's business, the industry, including how revenue is generated, and the business processes that accomplish its mission and are key to revenue generation give vital insight to HR leaders.
* *HR Technology*—This involves understanding and leveraging technology to enhance the delivery of HR services and adding value to customers through technology.[4]

Behavioral Competencies and Emotional Intelligence

Closely related to the management and HR competencies previously described are specific behavioral competencies that can also be identified as contributors to the success of healthcare HR and organizational leaders. As described below, these include behaviors such as collaboration, innovation, continuous learning

FIGURE 2-2   Emotional Intelligence

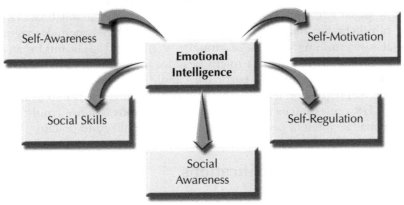

and personal development, the ability to take reasonable risks, and work/life balance.

- *Collaboration*—The ability to share authority, responsibility and control must be developed.
- *Innovation*—The ability to generate new or different processes and solutions, including the ability to think outside of existing paradigms is a characteristic to cultivate.
- *Continuous Learning*—This is seeking opportunities to expand knowledge or skills and then to apply what has been learned to the work environment.
- *Risk Taking*—The ability to take reasonable risks as well as being comfortable with the possibility of failure is an important characteristic.
- *Work/Life Balance*—HR leaders need to pursue the appropriate balance between work and personal life.[5]

Emotional intelligence is another critical set of HR management skills equally relevant to the successful contribution of healthcare HR professionals to their organization. *Emotional intelligence* is defined as proficiencies in intrapersonal and interpersonal skills in the areas of self-awareness, self-regulation, self-motivation, social awareness, and social skills as shown in Figure 2-2.[6]

A common theme in the skill sets and competencies of effective healthcare HR professionals are strong intra- and interpersonal communications. The nature of healthcare requires HR professionals to be effective communicators in one-on-one interviews, small group discussions and meetings, and in presentations to large groups. Being socially aware and having the ability to treat people with respect and dignity and to communicate effectively with them is also a critical component of emotional intelligence. As an example, an HR manager in a busy family practice clinic in a urban setting must deal with employment and employee situations involving diverse applicants and employees. In order to be effective she must be competent in recognizing and dealing with their unique communication needs.

HR professionals typically have a great deal of organizational power because of the nature of their responsibilities and the scope of their authority. They regularly make decisions that can affect the lives, careers, and financial well-being of others. For instance, a typical duty for an Employment Manager at a hospital is determining who, out of a number of qualified applicants for an open position, is referred to the department head for final consideration. The power to reject or further consider a particular candidate should be used objectively and fairly. Self-regulation as a part of emotional intelligence is important to ensure that HR professionals make appropriate decisions that are consistent with effective management of people as well as with HR policy and practice.

HR Management Certifications

One of the characteristics of a professional field is having a means to acknowledge or certify the knowledge and competence of members of the profession. The most well-known certification program for HR generalists is administered by the Human Resource Certification Institute (HRCI), which is affiliated with the SHRM. Figure 2-3 describes the credential levels and the criteria that must be met to achieve either the Professional in Human Resources (PHR) or Senior Professional in Human Resources (SPHR) designations. Studying and preparing for the PHR or SPHR exams is an excellent opportunity to increase the HR knowledge base of a healthcare HR professional. Just as accounting professionals pursue CPAs, HR professionals should consider pursuing certification through HRCI or other certification organizations, to document their HR knowledge.

Other HR Certifications Additional certification programs for HR Specialists and generalists are sponsored by various other organizations. For specialists, some well-known programs include the following:

- Certified Compensation Professionals (CCP), sponsored by the WorldatWork Association

FIGURE 2-3 **HR Certification—Human Resource Certification Institute Certification Types**

PHR CERTIFICATION	SPHR CERTIFICATION
• Complete at least 2 years of exempt-level (professional) HR experience (recommended: 2–4 years).	• Complete at least 2 years of exempt-level (professional) HR experience (recommended: 6–8 years).
• Pass the PHR certification exam.	• Pass the SPHR exam.
• Students may take and pass exam, and then receive certification after 2 years of experience.	

Details on these certifications are available from the Human Resources Certification Institute, at *http://www.hrci.org.*

- Certified Employee Benefits Specialist (CEBS), sponsored by the International Foundation of Employee Benefits Plans
- Certified Benefits Professional (CBP), sponsored by the WorldatWork Association
- Certified Performance Technologist (CPT), co-sponsored by the American Society for Training & Development and the International Society for Performance Improvement
- Certified Safety Professional (CSP), sponsored by the Board of Certified Safety Professionals
- Occupational Health and Safety Technologist (OHST), given by the American Board of Industrial Hygiene and the Board of Certified Safety Professionals
- Certified Professional Outsourcing (CPO), provided by New York University and the Human Resource Outsourcing Association.[7]

HR Departments and Healthcare Organizational Charts

Consistent with the wide variety of titles and levels of responsibilities corresponding to the differences in the sizes and types of healthcare organizations, the actual organizational placement of healthcare HR departments varies widely. A trend is emerging in healthcare, that today, the HR leader reports directly to the CEO due to the importance of the HR issues facing healthcare organizations. A reporting relationship of this nature is designed to provide more access and better flow of communications between the two functions. In addition, and as importantly, if HR leaders report directly to the CEO, they will typically also be considered a part of the senior leadership team and participate in broader organizational decision making and have more access to their counterparts in other senior leadership positions with the so-called "seat at the table" of decision making.

Figure 2-4 depicts the organizational chart of a 60-doctor specialty practice with freestanding clinics and over 200 employees, located in Minneapolis, Minnesota. It shows how the HR function might report in a healthcare organization. As depicted on the chart, the Human Resources Director reports directly to the CEO and is at the same organizational level as other key leadership positions.

Measuring Healthcare HR Management

Another way to evaluate the strategic importance of HR in healthcare organizations is to statistically evaluate their organizational influence. Statistical analysis and comparisons are useful to understanding the broader context of the overall healthcare industry's commitment to HR.

FIGURE 2-4 Specialty Physician Practice Organizational Chart

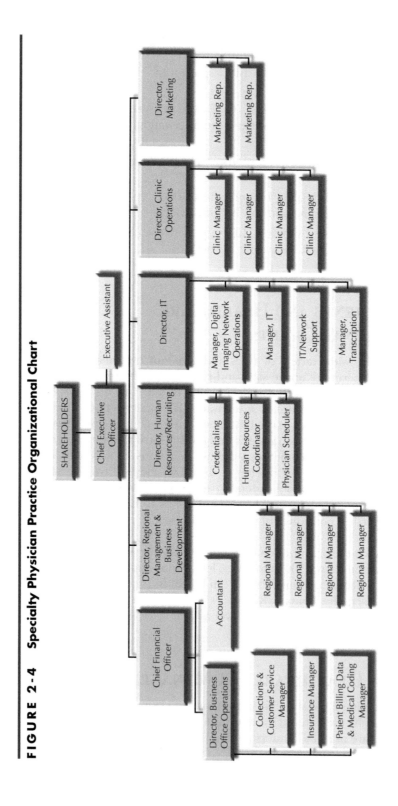

FIGURE 2-5   HR Staffing and Budgets Across Industries

MEDIAN HR STAFF PER 100 EMPLOYEES	
EMPLOYERS	RATIO
Transportation/Warehousing and Utilities (High)	1.6
All Industries	1.0
Healthcare	.8
Wholesale Trade (Low)	.7
MEDIAN ANNUAL HR EXPENDITURES PER EMPLOYEE	
EMPLOYERS	EXPENDITURES
Transportation/Warehousing and Utilities (High)	$ 2,092.00
All Industries	$ 965.00
Healthcare	$ 602.00
Federal and State Government	$ 545.00

Staffing Ratios and Budgets   HR activities, budgets, and staffing are regularly surveyed by the Bureau of National Affairs (BNA). BNA has surveyed and reported on HR staffing levels over the past several years. Figure 2-5 depicts the BNA comparison of the healthcare HR staffing ratios with other industries. Notice that for all industries the median ratio of HR department staff to total employee headcount is 1 HR staff member for every 100 employees in an organization. The amount of HR expenditures per employee offers another important insight as to the organizational commitment to the HR function.[8]

Taken at face value, these statistics might suggest a lesser HR commitment across the board by healthcare organizations compared to non-healthcare organizations. However, as noted earlier in the chapter, the healthcare industry varies both in size of organizations and in how healthcare is provided. This variety makes it difficult to capture who in a healthcare organization is performing HR duties. As an example, in a large medical center there is typically a full complement of HR leaders and specialists to handle the total continuum of HR activities. These individuals would be easily accounted for in the BNA survey data. In contrast, in a small rural nursing home the HR function might be the responsibility of an assistant administrator who "wears many hats," including HR. That individual would most likely not be recorded in a BNA survey as an HR staff member, nor would that person's salary be accounted for as a HR expenditure.

HR Metrics

HR Metrics or measurements should be disseminated to senior managers regarding HR competencies, the alignment of HR policies and systems with organizational strategy, workforce capabilities, and management quality.[9] The connection between HR measurement and organizational strategy and performance is vital.

FIGURE 2-6   Examples of Strategic and Operational HR Metrics

STRATEGIC	OPERATIONAL
• Revenue generated per full-time employee (FTE) • Net income per FTE • Ratio of managers to nonmanagers • Labor costs as percentage of total operating costs • Return on investment of human capital expenditures • HR department expenses as percentage of total expenses • Payroll/benefits costs as percentage of revenues	• Annual turnover rate • Benefits costs as percentage of payroll • Training expenditures per FTE • Average time to fill openings • Workers' compensation costs per FTE • Number of applicants per opening • Absenteeism by employee level/department

---

If HR wants to play a strategic role in organizations, it needs to develop its ability to measure how human resources decisions affect the business and how business decisions affect human capital.[10] HR metrics are specific measures tied to HR performance indicators. A metric can be developed using costs, quantity, quality, timeliness, and other designated goals or measures. Examples of some key strategic and operational HR metrics are shown in Figure 2-6.[11]

These useful and practical ratios and measures for assessment provide important insights as to the effectiveness of the organizational HR efforts. However, it is important to choose those HR Metrics that are relevant to the organization and measure those items that will aid the organization in improving results. It is also important to note that the types of ratios and measures depicted in Figure 2-6 are useful only when used in comparison to other data. *Comparison methodology* includes both internal and external data.

Internal data can be compared in several ways:

- By time (monthly, quarterly, or annually)
- By department compared to other departments or to the total organization
- By position (Dental Assistants, RNs, Pharmacists, etc.)

External data can be compared in several ways:

- By industry (total healthcare)
- By an industry segment (nursing homes, community hospitals, clinics)
- By a position group (professionals, managers, etc.)

The key to the effective use of HR metrics is to consistently conduct measurements and then take action based on the data. As an example, if a home healthcare agency is having difficulty in recruiting and retaining aides in a particular geographic area, it can study the success of their recruitment efforts in areas that are not experiencing the same issues and adopt the more successful approaches. In the absence of a comparative analysis, the agency may not recognize the issues or realize that successful alternatives exist.

HR and Quality Patient Care

Another consideration in establishing the framework for effectively managing the healthcare HR function is understanding the linkage between quality patient care delivery and HR programs. The process of ensuring healthcare consumers in the United States that a particular provider of care is competent and safe takes many forms. It includes governmental oversight through the Medicare reimbursement program; local, county, and state health departments oversight; independent agencies who supply quality review information on health insurance plans and their preferred providers; and quality review organizations that perform comprehensive standard-based assessments of their subscribing members.

Competitive Position   Healthcare organizations are experiencing significant change in response to ever-increasing costs, technology advances, and recruitment and retention issues. To ensure quality care and organizational viability, healthcare organizations must hire and retain a competent workforce.

Providing high-quality healthcare and achieving a competitive position in their respective marketplaces are clearly linked for healthcare providers. Business and industry groups have required health plans to disclose quality of care information on providers and to evaluate the effectiveness of a providers' care in certain disease categories and care modalities. The pressure from the healthcare plans on the providers to disclose outcomes information, consumer satisfaction information, and other metrics of safe patient care is having a significant impact on the healthcare industry at every level of delivery—from sole practitioner physicians to multistate integrated healthcare systems.

JOINT COMMISSION (JCAHO) AND HEALTHCARE MANAGEMENT

The dominant quality review organization for hospitals, long-term care and assisted living facilities, clinical laboratories, ambulatory care organizations, behavioral healthcare organizations, and home care agencies is the Joint Commission on Accreditation of Healthcare Organizations (JCAHO). The JCAHO accredits more than 15,000 healthcare organizations in the United States. In this section a review of how the JCAHO quality standards have affected HR programming and how healthcare organizations meet those standards is presented.

JCAHO Process

The JCAHO surveys healthcare organizations in a broad range of administrative and clinical functions. Under each of these functions is a series of standards that must be defined and operationalized by the healthcare organizations that subscribe to JCAHO. The standards are action statements that provide specific expectations for quality achievement on a detailed basis within each function. JCAHO reviewers survey healthcare organizations to determine their accomplishment on the various standards for all of the functions. An organization that attains a satisfactory survey receives accreditation from the JCAHO. Accreditation carries with it an indication that, within the functions surveyed, the organization is substantially meeting the standards. Surveyed organizations oftentimes will achieve overall accreditation, but will be given recommendations in certain areas to undertake improvement. These recommendations are referred to as *Type 1s*. The receipt of a Type 1 requires the organization to develop remediation plans to correct the issue. The organization is encouraged to pay close attention to Type 1 issues, because an excessive number of Type 1s can affect the accreditation status. Also, JCAHO survey data are critically reviewed by insurance companies, healthcare oversight groups, and individual consumers of healthcare.

Methodology of JCAHO Review The JCAHO surveyors attempt to be as comprehensive in their review of an organization's attainment of quality as possible. The JCAHO surveyors consider a variety of data points as evidence of quality and performance to determine the organization's accomplishment on a particular standard. Sources of evidence of performance for HR standards include the following:

- Interviews with staff members, department directors, and senior managers
- Performance evaluations or competency assessment processes
- Employee personnel records and file documentation
- Organizational and departmental policies and procedures
- Staff development plans and education records
- Committee reports and meeting minutes
- Description of licensure, certificates, and credential verifications

Due to the importance JCAHO has placed on the HR standards, HR professionals typically play key roles in the preparation for a JCAHO survey and in the actual on-site review.

The JCAHO's statement on the HR function indicates that through its Management of Human Resources, Improving Organization Performance (PI), Leadership (LD), and other accreditation standards, the JCAHO helps healthcare organizations take a systematic approach to addressing staffing needs.[12] Figure 2-7 depicts the HR leadership responsibilities. The JCAHO's statement on HR management notes that the broad goals of the HR function are to identify and provide the right number of competent staff to meet the needs of the patients, clients, or residents served by the healthcare provider. As indicated in

---

FIGURE 2-7 JCAHO Requirements for HR

- Defining staff qualifications & performance expectations
- Providing adequate numbers of competent staff   } Healthcare Leaders'
- Ongoing assessments of staff competence   HR Responsibilities
- Orienting, training, and educating staff

Figure 2-7, healthcare leaders are responsible for the following broad processes to fulfill this goal:

- *Planning*—This defines the qualifications, competencies, and staffing necessary to fulfill the provider's mission.

- *Providing Competent Staff*—The staff includes both employees of the organization and those contracted to provide service or care. Applicants' credentials must be assessed and confirmed prior to employment or service delivery.

- *Assessing, Maintaining, and Improving Staff Competence*—This includes ongoing periodic competence assessment and performance evaluation of staff to ensure the continuing ability of staff to perform.

- *Promoting Self-Development and Learning*—Leaders encourage self-development and continued learning.

JCAHO HR Standards and Serious Adverse Events

HR standards are not the exclusive domain of HR professionals in healthcare organizations. The JCAHO evaluates the extent to which these standards are met through a multidisciplinary approach. As such, HR professionals and operational managers must work collaboratively to meet the standards. These standards serve as a valuable set of guiding principles for HR policy and practice for healthcare organizations that are reviewed by JCAHO. Healthcare HR professionals play a very key role in ensuring the delivery of safe, competent healthcare by developing programming to meet these standards and by documenting performance to the standards.[13]

The Role of HR Issues in Serious Adverse Events   Since the mid-1990s JCAHO has been collecting data on serious adverse events in the healthcare setting; these are also referred to as *sentinel events*. A sentinel event is further defined as an unexpected occurrence involving death or serious physical or psychological injury or the risk thereof. The term *sentinel* is used by JCAHO because they signal the need for immediate reporting, investigation, and remediation to ensure that there is no further occurrence.

By studying the causes, trends, settings, and outcomes of sentinel events, the JCAHO has been able to provide valuable information designed to help prevent the circumstances that lead to such events. Over 2,000 such events have been closely studied and evaluated, and HR issues have consistently played a major role. The primary causes that organizations have identified as leading to sentinel events include:

- Insufficient employee orientation and training—56%

- Insufficient employee staffing—22%

- Employee competency and credentialing issues—16%[14]

Throughout this book, JCAHO standards and how they impact the HR function in healthcare organizations will be brought into the discussion. For those organizations that do not subscribe to JCAHO, these standards can still provide a useful template for how quality standards apply to all HR management within healthcare organizations.

ETHICAL PRACTICES AND COMPLIANCE

HR plays a number of critical roles in ensuring ethical practices and compliance in healthcare organizations. The continuum includes a full spectrum from strategic to operational issues, as examined in the following list:

- HR can help ensure that ethics is a top organizational priority. HR leaders must be the organizational ethics champions or ensure that some other capable person in the organization is championing ethics with full support.

- HR must stay abreast of ethics issues. This includes following legal requirements and initiatives, looking at the entire social and business environment, and spotting potential organizational conflicts of interest and other ethics problems before they become full-blown scandals.

- HR is responsible for developing the proper policies and practices as well as the training that supports compliance with ethical expectations.

- HR should be responsible for advising on and helping to establish the appropriate organizational structures and reporting relationships, which are key to maintaining the integrity of corporate compliance.

- HR can help to ensure that organizational firewalls exist between key departments when conflicts of interest or organizational improprieties could exist, such as establishing separation between those who administer compensation and those who operationally run payroll.

Currently, ethics has become a high priority in healthcare organizations, and HR should be at the forefront in policy formation, programming, and operational support for compliance. The nature of business and healthcare administration dictates that conflicts will continue to exist, and these conflicts will exert an evolutionary pressure on matters related to organizational ethics. Healthcare organizations, effectively aided by their HR leaders, must continue to be proactive and vigilant in addressing conflicts of interest and other ethical issues.[15]

CASE

On January 1, St. Michael's Hospice had 100 employees on their payroll. Throughout the month, 2 employees were terminated for poor performance and 3 other employees voluntarily resigned. On January 31, the hospital had 110 employees on payroll.

Turnover rate analysis:

A. Total number of staff at beginning of the period

B. Total number of staff at end of the period

C. Total number of terminations, quits, etc.

Computation:

$A + B \div 2 = D$ (average month's staffing)

$C \div D$ = turnover rate

During the first quarter, St. Michael's Hospice had employment activity producing 30 new hires. They determined that interview time amounted to 500 hours for the quarter on the part of the HR Recruiter who is paid an annual salary of $50,000.00. The HR records clerk spent 100 hours in scheduling appointments, performing reference checks, and completing new hire paperwork. The clerk is compensated on an hourly basis at a rate of $20.00 an hour. Recruitment advertising costs for the period were $15,000.00. Applicant travel expenses equaled $6,000.00. In addition, they incurred $2,800.00 in employment agency fees.

Questions

1. What was St. Michael's Hospice's turnover rate for the month of January?
2. Compute the average HR cost-per-hire, utilizing St. Michael's Hospice data from the previous paragraph.

END NOTES

1. Robert J. Grossman, "Putting HR in Rotation," *HR Magazine* (March 2003), 50–57.
2. "Key Competencies HR Managers Must Have To Stay Current," IOMA's Human Resource Department Management Report (August 2003), 3–5.
3. Adopted from an article by Robert Riney, "Cultivating Our Human Capital," *HR Pulse* (Spring 2003), 11–14.
4. Adapted from "Competencies Overview, Human Resource Competency Toolkit," *http://www.shrm.org/competencies/competencies.asp;* Kevin Sweeney, "Growing Numbers of HR Professionals Influence business Direction," *Benefits Finance* (November 2003), 1, 13. Susan Meisinger, "HR Resolutions for the New Year," *HR Magazine* (January 2005).
5. Donald H. Hutton, "Competencies You Can't Afford to Ignore," *Healthcare Executive* (November/December 2004), 28.
6. Daniel Gorman, *Working With Emotional Intelligence* (New York: Bantam Books, 1998).
7. Glenn Davidson, "Who Knows This Stuff?" *HRO TODAY* (December 2003), 62.
8. HR Department Benchmarks and Analysis Survey 2004, a BNA/SHRM collaboration.
9. "Getting Real—and Specific With Measurements." *HR FOCUS* (January 2005), 11, 13.
10. Edward E. Lawler, III, Alec Leverson, and John W. Boudreau, "HR Metrics and Analytics: Use and Impact," *Human Resource Planning* (2004, Issue 4), 27–35.
11. Jac Fitz-Enz and Barbara Davidson describe in detail how to measure HR activities by areas in *How to Measure Human Resources* (New York: McGraw-Hill, 2002).
12. Issues in Human Resources for Hospitals Joint Commission Resources, 2004, 3.
13. Management of Human Resources Function Manual, Medical Consultants Networks, Inc., 2002.
14. Joint Commission on Accreditation of Healthcare Organizations: Root Causes of Sentinel Events (1995–2004). Found at *http://www.jcaho.org.*
15. Adapted from Mark R. Vickers, "Business Ethics and HR Role: Past, Present, and Future," *Human Resource Planning* (2005, 1), 26–33; and John Rossheim "Human Resources Is Tapped to Address New Compliance Complexities." *Workforce Management* (July 2004), 74–76.

STRATEGIC HR MANAGEMENT

Learning Objectives

After you have read this chapter you should be able to:

- Describe why a strategic view of Human Resources (HR) is important.

- Discuss HR as an organizational core competency.

- Explain how healthcare HR planning contributes to the attainment of organizational strategies and objectives.

- Define HR planning in healthcare organizations.

- Identify three HR management challenges found in healthcare organizations.

Healthcare HR Insights

A recent headline in a Kentucky newspaper reads "The Hospital Building Boom"; the article states that there are over ten major projects planned for the greater Cincinnati and northern Kentucky area that will be completed by 2008. Some of the new construction is designed to replace older, outdated, and inefficient buildings, but much of the new construction is facilitating a shifting of services from one location to another or is designed to allow for the installation of new technologies. The new construction will add intensive care, operating rooms, maternity suites, cardiac care, doctors' offices, and state-of-the-art equipment to serve hundreds of thousands of patients for decades to come.[1]

Even though this article was written about southern Ohio and northern Kentucky, it could have been written about many areas of the United States. Healthcare facility building and expansion is occurring throughout the country. Population growth in different parts of the country, shifts in population from urban to suburban areas, new technologies and treatment approaches, and historically low interest rates which are significantly lowering the cost of financing building expansion have all contributed to the growth in new facilities around the country.

Interestingly, what the article did not discuss was the HR implications these new projects hold. The HR planning necessary to staff these new facilities with sufficient numbers of qualified employees is key to the ability of the healthcare organizations building these new facilities to make them viable. The HR insight is the recognition that it is clearly important for healthcare organizations to have state-of-the-art facilities and equipment, but equally important is the need for a competent workforce to utilize those facilities and equipment properly in order to provide quality patient care.

Many factors determine whether or not an organization will be successful. Effectiveness, efficiency, and the ability to adapt to changes in the market, as well as other issues, are involved. Adept management will decide where the organization needs to go, how to get there, and then regularly evaluate to see if it are on track. Strategic objectives, the external environment, internal business processes, and determining how effectiveness will be measured and defined should all be addressed in the strategic management process.

HR management is (or should be) involved with all these points. For example, how can effective HR help improve productivity in an assisted living facility or dental practice? How can it enhance innovativeness in a medical center? These kinds of questions are indicative of strategic thinking.[2]

Strategic HR management maximizes the effectiveness of employees and results in the achievement of an organizational mission and a competitive advantage in the market. This advantage may occur through the HR department's formal contributions to organization-wide planning efforts, or by simply being knowledgeable about issues facing the organization and being prepared to make effective HR-related recommendations.

MANAGEMENT OF HUMAN ASSETS IN ORGANIZATIONS

Organizations must manage four types of assets in their search for success:

- *Physical*—Buildings, land, furniture, computers, vehicles, equipment, etc.
- *Financial*—Cash, financial resources, financial securities, etc.
- *Intangible*—Specialized research capabilities, patents, information systems, designs, operating processes, etc.
- *Human*—Individuals with talents, capabilities, experience, professional expertise, relationships, etc.

All these assets are crucial to varying degrees. However, human assets are the "glue" that holds all the other assets together and guide their use to achieve organizational goals and results.[3] Certainly the doctors, nurses, receptionists, technical professionals, and other employees at a clinic or hospital allow all the other assets of their organization to be used to provide customer or patient services. By recognizing the importance of human assets, healthcare organizations are increasingly emphasizing human capital.

Human Capital and HR

Human capital is not the people in organizations—it is what those people bring and contribute to organizational success.[4] **Human capital** is the collective value of the capabilities, knowledge, skills, life experiences, and motivation in an organization's workforce.

Sometimes it is called *intellectual capital* to reflect the thinking, knowledge, creativity, and decision making that people in organizations contribute. For example, an academic medical complex like the Mayo Clinic has significant intellectual capital, including technical and research employees who create new biomedical devices, formulate pharmaceuticals that can be patented, and develop new software for specialized therapeutic uses. All these organizational contributions indicate the value of Mayo's human capital.

Human Resources as a Core Competency

The development of specific business strategies must be based on the areas of strength that an organization has. Referred to as *core competencies,* these strengths are the foundation for creating a competitive advantage for an organization. These are the things the organization does well. A **core competency** is a unique capability in the organization that creates high value and differentiates the organization from its competition. In many organizations, human capital is—or should be—a core competency.

Certainly, many organizations have showcased their human capital as differentiating them from their competitors.[5] Almost every healthcare organization has a website, advertising, or marketing brochures emphasizing some special competency of their employees or the expertise and credentials of their clinical providers. As an example, one ophthalmology practice in a Dallas suburb advertised in a radio commercial that their doctors and staff had performed more LASIK procedures then any other ophthalmology group in their area, clearly focusing on their human resources as providing special strategic value for their organization.

The people in an organization become a core competency through the HR activities of attracting and retaining employees with unique professional and technical capabilities, investing in training and development of those employees, and compensating them in ways that retain them and keep them competitive with their counterparts in other organizations. For example, smaller community hospitals have attracted patient referrals because they emphasize a more personal, caring attitude rather than the impersonal approach characteristic of large medical centers. They emphasize their staff members as an advantage. Figure 3-1 shows some possible areas where human resources might become part of a core competency.

Another critical core competency area to be considered is its organizational culture, constituted by the shared values and beliefs of a workforce. Healthcare managers must consider the culture of their organization because otherwise excellent strategies can be negated by a culture that is incompatible with those strategies.[6] As an example, if a home care agency's strategy is to position itself as especially sensitive to the needs of the patients it serves, but employees are not rewarded or supported in their efforts to provide highly sensitive care, the culture may be incompatible with the agency's strategy.

In addition, the culture of the organization, as viewed by the people in it, affects attraction and retention of competent employees. Numerous examples

FIGURE 3-1   Examples of Healthcare Human Resource Areas for Core Competencies

can be given of key technical, professional, and administrative employees leaving organizations because of cultures that seem to devalue people and create barriers to the use of individual capabilities.[7]

HR MANAGEMENT ROLES

Several roles can be fulfilled by healthcare HR management. The nature and extent of these roles depends on both what upper management wants HR management to do and on what competencies the HR staff have demonstrated. Three roles are typically identified for HR:

- *Administrative:* Focusing on HR clerical administration and recordkeeping
- *Operational and Employee Advocate:* Managing most HR activities and serving as employee "champion"
- *Strategic:* Becoming a contributor to organizational results and the "keeper" of organizational ethics

As noted in Chapter 1, the administrative role has been the dominant part of HR. However, as Figure 3-2 indicates, a significant transformation in HR is occurring. The HR pyramid is now being turned upside down, so that significantly less HR time and fewer HR staff are used for clerical administration. Notice in Figure 3-2 that the percentage of emphasis on the operational and employee advocate role is remaining constant.

However, the greatest shift is for HR to devote more emphasis to strategic HR management.[8] A look at each of the roles of HR and how they can be used to contribute to positive human capital follows.

FIGURE 3-2   Changing Roles of HR Management

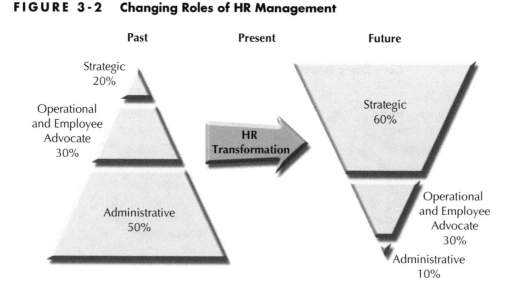

Past   Present   Future

Strategic
20%

Operational
and Employee
Advocate
30%

HR
Transformation

Strategic
60%

Administrative
50%

Operational
and Employee
Advocate
30%

Administrative
10%

Administrative Role of HR   The administrative role of HR management has been heavily oriented to paperwork processing and record keeping. However, this role has given HR management in some healthcare organizations the reputation of being staffed by paper shufflers who primarily tell managers and employees what *cannot* be done. If limited to the administrative role, HR staff are seen primarily as clerical and lower-level contributors, or even obstacles, in the organization. Two major shifts driving the transformation of the administrative role are greater use of technology and outsourcing.

To improve the administrative efficiency of HR and the responsiveness of HR to employees and managers, more HR functions are becoming available electronically or are being done on the Internet. Web-based technology is reducing the amount of HR administrative time and staff needed. Technology is being used in all HR activities, from employment application and employee benefits enrollment to e-learning using Internet-based resources. Later in this chapter there is more discussion on the nature, types, and uses of HR technology.

Increasingly, many HR administrative functions are being outsourced. One survey found that about 50 percent of all HR work is being outsourced, and HR outsourcing revenues for vendors have jumped $15 billion in just two years. According to various surveys by outsourcing firms, the areas most commonly outsourced are employee assistance/counseling, pension/retirement planning, benefits administration, training, and payroll services.[9]

The primary reasons why HR functions are outsourced is to save money on HR staffing, to take advantage of specialized vendor expertise and technology, and to be able to focus on more strategic HR activities. As a result, it is forecasted that a significant percentage of HR administrative staff jobs are or will be eliminated in the next few years. These jobs are being outsourced to firms both in the United States and worldwide.

Operational and Employee Advocate Role for HR   Traditionally, HR has been viewed as the "employee advocate" in healthcare organizations. As the voice for employee concerns, HR professionals traditionally have been seen as "the morale officers" who do not understand the business realities of organizations and do not contribute measurably to the strategic success of the business. Despite this view, someone must be the "champion" for employees and employee issues.

HR professionals spend considerable time on HR "crisis management" dealing with employee problems that are both work and non-work related. As an example, HR generalists at a nursing home may spend a considerable portion of their efforts on overseeing both the nursing home's and the employees' compliance with Family and Medical Leave Act requirements. Employee advocacy helps ensure fair and equitable treatment for employees regardless of personal background or circumstances. Sometimes the HR advocate role may create conflict with operating managers. However, that role is important in making the organization a better place to work. In addition, without the advocate role, employers would face even more lawsuits and regulatory complaints than they do now.

The operational role requires HR professionals to identify and implement needed programs and policies in the organization in cooperation with operating managers. HR implements plans suggested by or developed with other managers, as well as those identified by HR professionals. At a large urban hospital, the Director of Nursing suggested that the HR recruiters set up tours for area high school students to encourage the students to consider health careers. The implementation of the tours has proven to be an excellent program that has resulted in many students choosing academic programs leading to healthcare-related careers. Even though priorities may change as labor markets and economic shifts occur, the operational HR role emphasizes support for executives, managers, and employees when addressing and resolving HR problems and issues.

Operational activities are tactical in nature. Compliance with Equal Employment Opportunity (EEO) and other laws must be ensured, employment applications are processed, current openings are filled through interviews, supervisors are trained, safety problems are resolved, and wages and salaries are appropriately given. These efforts require coordinating the management of HR activities with actions of managers and supervisors throughout organizations.

Strategic Role for HR   Differences between the operational and strategic approaches in a number of HR areas exist.[10] The strategic HR role requires that HR professionals be proactive in addressing business realities and in focusing on future needs, such as workforce planning, compensation strategies, and improving the value of HR for top management.

Many executives, managers, and HR professionals increasingly see the need for HR management to become a greater strategic contributor to the "business" success of organizations. Even organizations that are not-for-profit, such as governmental and social service entities, must manage their human resources in a "business-oriented" manner to be successful.

THE HR STRATEGIC PLANNING PROCESS

Strategic planning must include having the people necessary to carry out the organizational strategic plan. Based on the strategic plan, **HR strategic planning** is the process of analyzing and identifying the need for and availability of human resources in order to accomplish the organizational objectives.[11]

The steps in the HR planning process are shown in Figure 3-3. Notice that the HR planning process begins with considering the organizational *objectives* and *strategies*. Then both *external* and *internal assessments* of HR needs and supply sources must be performed, and *forecasts* must be developed. Key to assessing internal HR is having information accessible through a human resource information system (HRIS). Once the assessments are complete, mismatches between *HR supply* and *HR demand* must be identified. HR strategies and plans to address the imbalance, both short and long term, must be developed. In healthcare organizations, forecasting HR supply and demand is made even more challenging

FIGURE 3-3   HR Strategic Planning Process

by the need to consider more than the absolute numbers of employees needed. As an example, if a radiology practice is opening a new facility, management has to determine the correct number of radiologic technologists, special procedures technologists, receptionists, and business-office staff to provide timely quality care.

HR strategies are the means used to aid the organization in managing the supply and demand for employees. These strategies provide overall direction for how HR activities will be developed and managed. Finally, specific *HR plans* are developed to provide more specific direction for the management of HR activities.

Scanning the External Environment

At the heart of strategic planning is the knowledge gained from scanning the external environment for changes. **Environmental scanning** is the process of studying the environment of the organization to pinpoint opportunities and threats. Scanning especially affects HR planning because each organization must draw from the same labor market that supplies all other employers. Indeed, one measure of organizational effectiveness is the ability of an organization to compete in the labor market for a sufficient supply of human resources with the appropriate capabilities.

Many factors can influence the supply of labor available to an employer. Some of the more significant environmental factors include workforce composition and work patterns, geographic competitive concerns, economic conditions, and government influences.

Workforce Composition and Work Patterns Changes in the composition of the workforce, combined with the varied work patterns of the healthcare environment, have created healthcare workplaces and organizations that are very different from those of the past. The traditional work schedule, in which employees work full-time, 8 hours a day, 5 days a week at the employer's place of operations, is in transition. Healthcare organizations have been leaders in experimenting with and implementing many different possibilities for change: the 4-day, 40-hour week; the 4-day, 32-hour week; the 12-hour shifts, 3-days a week; and flexible scheduling.

The healthcare industry has also been especially aggressive in adopting approaches to flexibility in staffing, especially as part of its recruitment and retention efforts. Changes of this nature must be considered in HR planning. Also, a growing number of healthcare employers are allowing workers to use different working arrangements. Some employees work partly at home and partly at an office and share office space with other *office nomads*. As an example, many hospitals, clinics, and physician practices have all or part of their medical transcription work performed by employees who work out of their homes. *Telecommuting* is the process of going to work via electronic computing and telecommunications equipment.

Other employees have *virtual offices:* their offices are wherever they are, whenever they are there. An office for a visiting nurse could be an unoccupied treatment room, a conference room, or even his or her car. The shift to such arrangements means that work is done anywhere, anytime, and that people are judged more on results than on "putting in time." Greater trust, less direct supervision, and more self-scheduling are all job characteristics of those with virtual offices and other less traditional arrangements.

Geographic and Competitive Concerns Employers must consider the following geographic and competitive concerns in making HR plans:

- Population growth/decline in the area
- All other employers in the area
- Employee/applicant resistance to geographic relocation
- Direct competitors in the area

Economic Conditions   The general business cycle also affects HR planning. Such factors as interest rates, inflation, and economic growth help determine the availability of workers and figure into organizational plans and objectives. Decisions on wages, overtime, and hiring or laying off workers all hinge on economic conditions.

Government Influences   A major element that affects labor supply is the government. Today, healthcare managers are confronted with an expanding and often bewildering array of government rules as the regulation of HR activities has steadily increased. Government regulations have especially affected the healthcare industry in such areas as patient safety, medical records confidentiality, and funding. As a result, HR planning must be done by individuals who understand the legal requirements of various government regulations, including those that may impact staffing levels and requirements for professional certifications.

Internal Assessment of Organizational Workforce

Analyzing the jobs that will need to be done and the skills of people currently available to do them is the next part of HR planning. The needs of the organization must be compared with the labor supply available. The starting point for evaluating internal strengths and weaknesses is the evaluation of the jobs currently being done in the organization.

In the rapidly changing healthcare environment, the evaluation of jobs is especially important. As an example, the shift from inpatient to ambulatory care has had a significant impact on how care is provided and what jobs are necessary to provide that care. Healthcare providers, whether in acute care hospitals, nursing homes, or physician practices, have had to continually reassess their jobs. The following questions are addressed during the internal assessment:

- What jobs now exist?
- How many individuals are performing each job?
- What are the reporting relationships of jobs?
- How essential is each job?
- Can jobs be "redesigned" or duties changed?
- What jobs will be needed to implement the organizational strategy?
- What are the characteristics of anticipated jobs?

Organizational Capabilities Inventory   Doing HR planning requires an understanding of current jobs and the new jobs that will be necessary to carry out organizational plans. The managers can prepare an "inventory" of current employees and their capabilities. The basic source of data on employees is the HR records in the organization. By using different databases, HR planners can identify the employees' capabilities, knowledge, and skills. Then these inventories could be used to determine long-range needs for recruiting, selection, and HR development.[12]

Human Resource Information Systems   Computers have simplified the task of analyzing vast amounts of data, and they can be invaluable aids in HR management, from payroll processing to record retention. With computer hardware, software, and databases, organizations can keep records and information better, as well as retrieve data more easily. An HRIS is an integrated system designed to provide information used in HR decision making. An HRIS has many uses in an organization. The most basic is the automation of payroll and benefit activities. With an HRIS, employees' time records are entered into the system, and the appropriate deductions and other individual adjustments are reflected in the final paychecks. As a result of HRIS development and implementation in many organizations, several payroll functions are being transferred from accounting departments to HR departments. Another common use of HRIS is EEO/affirmative action tracking.

The dramatic increase in the use of the Internet is raising possibilities and concerns for HR professionals, particularly when establishing an HRIS. Use of Web-based information systems has allowed HR departments in healthcare organizations to become more administratively efficient and to be able to deal with more strategic and longer-term HR planning issues.[13]

Two issues of concern for HR are *security* and *privacy of HRIS*. Controls must be built into the system to restrict indiscriminate access to HRIS data on employees. For instance, health insurance claims might identify someone who has undergone psychiatric counseling or treatment for alcoholism, and access to such information must be limited both for employee privacy reasons and for compliance with Health Insurance Portability and Accountability Act (HIPAA) requirements. Likewise, performance appraisal ratings of employees must be guarded.

Forecasting

The information gathered from external environmental scanning and assessment of internal strengths and weaknesses is used to predict or forecast HR supply and demand in light of organizational objectives and strategies. **Forecasting** uses information from the past and present to identify expected future conditions. Of course, projections for the future are subject to error. Changes in the conditions on which the projections are based might even completely invalidate them, which is the chance forecasters take. Fortunately, experienced people are able to forecast with enough accuracy to benefit organizational long-range planning. Figure 3-4 depicts the process of HR forecasting.

Approaches to forecasting HR range from a manager's best guess to a rigorous and complex computer simulation of the labor force. Simple assumptions might be sufficient in certain instances, but complex models might be necessary for others. HR forecasting should be done over three planning periods: *short range, intermediate,* and *long range*. The most commonly used planning period is short range, usually a period of six months to one year. This level of planning is routine in many healthcare organizations because very few assumptions about the future are necessary for such short-range plans. Also, in many healthcare organizations, a six month to one year period typically corresponds with a budget cycle, which requires some level of forecasting in order to establish or project payroll and benefit expense budgets.

FIGURE 3-4   HR Forecasting

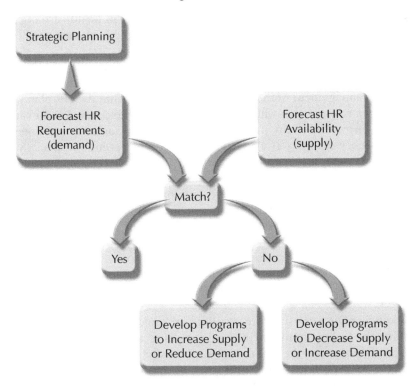

Demand Versus Supply of Human Resources   Forecasting the number of people needed can be done using two frameworks. One approach considers specific openings that are likely to occur and uses that information as the basis for planning. The openings (or demands) are created when employees leave positions because of promotions, transfers, or terminations. The analysis always begins with the top positions in the organization, because from those there can be no promotions to a higher level.

Once the need for human resources has been forecasted, then availability or supply must be identified. Forecasting the availability of human resources considers both external and internal supplies. The external supply of potential employees available to the organization must be estimated. Here are some of the factors that may be considered:

- Individuals entering and leaving the workforce
- Individuals graduating from schools and colleges
- Economic forecasts for the next few years
- Technological developments and shifts

ELEMENTS OF SUCCESSFUL HR PLANNING

There are several critical success factors to HR planning in healthcare organizations. The HR plan should be strategically aligned, purposeful, measurable, and documented. Each of these areas is discussed next.

The HR plan must be aligned with the broader organizational strategies and objectives. This requires HR leaders to be fully knowledgeable and involved in the strategic management of the organization to ensure that the HR plan will be developed in a manner that will meet organizational objectives. As an example, many large surgical specialty practices have found that owning and operating same-day surgery facilities is an excellent source of revenue, especially with declining reimbursement payments. The strategic decision by the surgeons to operate a same-day surgery center must be supported by an HR plan that would include the staffing, compensation, and employee relations of surgical nurses and technicians for the facility. The success and viability of the surgery center would, in large part, be dependent on the successful implementation of the HR plan.

The HR plan must be developed so that there is no ambiguity about its purpose and what it is to accomplish. In implementing and sustaining the elements of an HR plan, it is important that it is developed in such a way that progress can be tracked.

Referencing the same-day surgery clinic example, the HR plan component for staffing the facility should include trigger points relating to patient volumes. As the facility increases the number of surgeries performed, the employment, orientation, and training of new staff must be appropriately identified and sequenced to ensure that staffing levels and competencies correspond to the growth in the patient care delivery needs of the facility.

The HR plan should be written and updated annually. HR leaders should be responsible for presenting the plan to the other executives and Board of Directors. Periodic updates regarding the progress of the plan should also be provided. In the surgery center example, the implementation of the staffing component of the HR plan would carry significant costs that should be discussed with and agreed to by the Board.

Key Inputs to the Healthcare HR Strategic Plan   A strategic plan cannot be created in a vacuum. For the HR plan to be useful, it must take into account a number of important internal and external organizational inputs. A look at each of these areas from Figure 3-5 follows:

- *Organizational Mission*—The purest definition of *mission* is answering the question, "Why does the organization exist?" Healthcare organizations rarely struggle with this question; in fact, one of the true strengths of a healthcare provider is the clarity of its care delivery mission. An example of a healthcare organizational mission statement for a home care agency:
  - "At Atlas Homecare we are committed to serving the special needs of our clients through a sensitive and caring approach to the services we provide."

FIGURE 3-5   Inputs to Healthcare HR Strategic Plan

- *Organizational Objectives and Strategies*—In many instances, organizational objectives and strategies include significant HR considerations, especially regarding workforce planning, executive and management staffing, and compensation. The HR plan should cover the regular and routine HR aspects of supporting organizational functioning such as staffing and employee relations. It should also consider new initiatives or objectives of the organization, such as in the example of a hospital opening a new nursing unit for oncology patients, the HR needs of which would include staffing, compensation, and employee orientation and training for the unit.

- *Environmental Assessment*—As detailed earlier in the chapter, evaluating the environment is extremely important to the management of healthcare human resources. The HR plan must fully and comprehensively consider external environmental issues and opportunities, such as other healthcare organizations that may be expanding or downsizing that could potentially affect the supply of healthcare workers.

- *Organizational Resources and Capabilities*—The HR plan must consider the volume or productivity requirements of the organization. For instance, measurement of patient census, patient days, admissions, and average length of stay are used in developing staffing plans in order to match human resources with organizational capabilities.

- *Financial Realities*—Financial decisions, including budgetary allocations and capital expenditures, affect every aspect of HR management. The HR plan must be financially realistic, while maintaining consistent levels of support for such HR activities as staffing, compensation, and benefit administration. Financial resources needed for new human resources initiatives, such as the upgrade of the HR information system, must also be considered.
- *Considering the Plans of Other Functional Areas*—Effective HR planning should be both supportive of and compatible with the planning of all the other functional areas within the organization, such as patient care, surgery, or finance. The actual development of the HR plan should be in line with the development of the plans for the other areas.

ETHICAL PRACTICES AND COMPLIANCE

There are significant strategic aspects to ethical practices and compliance in healthcare organizations. Ethics and legal compliance require well-formulated planning leading to the implementation of effective policies. The planning should include four key elements:

1. Develop a written code of conduct that is distributed to all employees.
2. Provide ethics and compliance training that is relevant to each employee's position, responsibilities, and duties.
3. Create an internal ethics hotline which any employee can use anonymously to report potential ethics or compliance issues without fear of reprisal.
4. Make sure someone is in charge of ethics and compliance plans and programs.

Achieving ethical practices and compliance in healthcare organizations is important and meaningful work that requires planning, accountability, and implementation.[14] HR professionals play a key role in all aspects of these efforts.

HR MANAGEMENT CHALLENGES

The environment faced by HR management is challenging because changes are occurring rapidly across a wide range of issues. A study by the Hudson Institute, titled *Workforce 2020,* has highlighted some of the more important workforce issues that are identified in the following sections.[15]

Workforce Availability and Quality

Workforce availability and quality issues are not unique to the healthcare industry. In many parts of the United States, significant workforce shortages exist due to an inadequate supply of workers with the skills needed to perform the jobs being added. News reports have regularly described tight labor markets, and the shortage of many types of workers continues in many areas. Today, *contingent workers* (temporary workers, independent contractors, leased employees, and part-timers) represent a significant portion of the workforce. Many employers operate with a core group of regular employees with critical skills and then expand and contract the workforce through the use of contingent workers. This practice requires determining staffing needs and deciding in advance which employees and positions should form the core group and which should be more flexible. Although contingent workers can provide the flexibility a healthcare organization may require, they may not have the same commitment or loyalty as regular employees.[16]

Economic and Technological Change

Several economic changes have altered employment and occupational patterns in the United States. A major change is the shift of jobs from manufacturing and agriculture to service industries, healthcare, and telecommunications. This shift has meant that some organizations have had to reduce the number of employees, while others have had to attract and retain employees with different capabilities than previously were needed.[17] This is especially true for healthcare. As noted in Chapter 1, almost 13 million individuals are employed within healthcare, and the addition of new healthcare jobs is predicted to continue.

Occupational Shifts

Projections of the growth and decline in jobs illustrate the economic and employment shifts currently occurring. It is interesting to note that most of the fastest-growing occupations (percentage wise) are related to information technology or healthcare. The increase in technology jobs is due to the rapid increase in the use of information technology, such as databases, system design and analysis, and desktop publishing.

Diversity

Diversity is seen in demographic differences in the workforce. The shifting makeup of the U.S. labor force is illustrated in Figure 3-6. Many organizations are hiring employees from a more diverse pool of potential workers. Organizations have been seeing the effects of changing demographic trends for several years. A more detailed look at some of the key changes follows, as noted by the U.S. Department of Labor:[18]

- The rapid growth of women in the workforce is expected to slow, but still will increase faster than that of men. As a result, the share of women in the workforce is projected to increase from 47 percent in 2000 to 48 percent by 2010.

FIGURE 3-6 **Civilian Labor Force by Sex, Race, and Hispanic Origin, 2000 and Projected 2010**

GROUP	2000	2010
Men	53.4%	52.1%
Women	46.6%	47.9%
	100%	100%
White	83.5%	81.2%
Black	11.8%	12.7%
Asian and Other[1]	4.7%	6.1%
	100%	100%
Hispanic Origin	10.9%	13.3%
Other than Hispanic Origin	89.1%	86.7%
	100%	100%

Source: Bureau of Labor Statistics, 2005
[1]Includes Asians, Pacific Islanders, American Indians, and Alaska Natives

- Minority racial and ethnic groups have shown, and are projected to continue to show, widely varied growth rates of population growth. Among race and ethnic groups, Asians and Hispanics are projected to increase most rapidly.

- By 2010, the Hispanic labor force is projected to be larger than the black labor force, primarily due to a faster population growth.

- Despite slower-than-average growth and a declining share of the total workforce, white non-Hispanics will continue to make up more than two-thirds of the workforce.

Women in the Workforce The influx of women into the workforce has major social and economic consequences. Healthcare has historically had a very high female employment participation rate. According to EEO-1 data, the highest percentage of women are employed in the Nursing & Residential Care Facilities, with Hospitals and Ambulatory Healthcare Service Facilities second and third, respectively.[19] Implications for healthcare HR management of more women working include the following:

- Greater flexibility in work patterns and schedules to accommodate women with family responsibilities, part-time work interests, or other family pressures

- More variety in benefits programs and HR policies, including child-care assistance and parental leave programs
- Greater employer awareness of gender-related legal issues such as sexual harassment and sex discrimination

Aging of the Workforce Most of the developed countries—including Australia, Japan, most European countries, and the United States—are experiencing an aging of their populations. Implications of the aging of the U.S. workforce include the following:

- The projected labor force will be affected by the aging of the baby-boom generation, persons born between 1946 and 1964. By 2010, the baby-boom cohort will be ages 46 to 64, and this group will show significant growth over the 2005 to 2010 period.[20]
- Retirement will change in character as organizations and older workers choose phased retirements, early retirement buyouts, and part-time work.
- Service industries, including the healthcare industry, are actively recruiting senior workers for many jobs.
- Retirement benefits will increase in importance, particularly pensions and healthcare coverage for retirees and near retirees.

Individuals with Disabilities in the Workforce With the passage of the Americans with Disabilities Act (ADA) in 1990, healthcare employers are required to protect the employment rights of persons with disabilities. At least 43 million Americans with disabilities are covered by the ADA. Implications of greater employment of individuals with disabilities include the following:

- Employers must define more precisely what are the essential tasks in jobs and what knowledge, skills, and abilities are needed to perform each job.
- Accommodating individuals with disabilities will become more common as employers provide more flexible work schedules, alter facilities, and purchase special equipment.
- Employment-related health and medical examination requirements must be revised to avoid discriminating against individuals with disabilities.

Balancing Work and Family For many workers in the United States, including healthcare workers, balancing the demands of family and work is a significant challenge. Although this balancing has always been a concern, the growth in the number of working women and dual-career couples has resulted in greater tensions for many workers. To respond to these concerns, many healthcare employers are facing pressures to provide "family-friendly" policies and benefits. The assistance given by employers ranges from maintaining references on child-care providers to establishing on-site childcare and eldercare facilities. Also, according to the Federal Family and Medical Leave Act, employers with at least 50 workers must provide up to 12 weeks of unpaid parental/family leave.

CASE

Sharonville Community Medical Center (SCMC) is a 25-bed hospital located in a rural area of the midwest. It is 75 miles away from the closest large city and serves a geographic region with a population base of approximately 14,000 people.

SCMC employs 200 employees, 40 of whom are in nursing positions, including 14 RNs and 26 LPNs.

SCMS's Board of Trustees is made up of various community and business leaders who are concerned about the hospital's future. As a community hospital, its operating and capital budget is supported through a small tax levy. Due to excellent fiscal control and planning, the financial condition of the hospital far exceeds its peer group. However, the Board commissioned a study of its workforce and was alarmed by the following findings:

- By the year 2010, 66 percent of the current nursing employees will be at retirement age.

- The primary source of nursing candidates has been from individuals with nursing training who live within a 30-mile radius of Sharonville. Eighty percent of the current nursing employees attended Sharonville High School, went away to college for nursing training, and returned to the area to pursue their careers. However, fewer recent graduates of Sharonville High School are entering nursing school. Those that do, are not returning to Sharonville as others before them did.

- SCMC does not have a current workforce replacement plan in place to deal with the nursing employee attrition expected over the next decade.

Questions

1. Define the role of HR in dealing with this critical workforce planning issue.
2. Apply the HR planning process in addressing this issue.

END NOTES

1. Tom Bonfield, "Special Report Health Care: What's Next? Hospital Building Boom," *Kentucky Enquirer* (June 19, 2005), A1, A10–11.
2. Laila Karamally, "Capturing the State of Human Resources in an Annual Report," *Workforce Management* (June 2004), 98, 100–101.
3. Lisa M. Aldisent, *Valuating People! How Human Capital Can Be Your Strongest Asset* (Chicago: Dearborn Trade Publishing, 2002).
4. Leslie A. Weatherly, "Human Capital—The Elusive Asset," *SHRM Research Quarterly* (March 2003).
5. Richare Fuier, "Human Capital Management (HCM)," *Human Resource Management International Digest* (2003, vol. 2), 2.
6. Pamela Bobcock, "Is Your Company Two-Faced?" *HR Magazine* (January 2004), 43–47.
7. Jeff Rosenthal and Mary Ann Masarech, "High-Performance Cultures: How Values Can Drive Business Results." *Journal of Organizational Excellence* (Spring 2003), 3–19.
8. *Tough Times, Tougher HR* (New York: Towers-Perrin, 2003).
9. "Internal HR: Outsourcing Growth," *Workforce Management* (December 2003), 89; and Beth McConnell, "Small Majority of Companies Outsource some HR Duties," *HR News* (August 14, 2003), *http://www.shrm.org/hrnews*.
10. Dina M. Cox and Channing H. Cox, "At The Table," *Workspan* (November 2003), 21–23.

11. Jonathan Tomplins, "Strategic Human Resources Management in Government: Unresolved Issues," *Public Personnel Management* (Spring 2002), 95–110.

12. Bill Macaleer and Jones Shannon, "Does HR Planning Improve Business Performance?" *Industrial Management* (January/February 2003), 15–20.

13. Carol Glover, "Tomorrow's World," *People Management* (February 26, 2004), 40–41.

14. Adapted from Steven Watkins, "Be Honest and Dependable: Make the Culture Ethical," *Investors Business Daily, National Edition* (January 14, 2005), A03; and Jonathan Pont, "Doing the Right Thing to Instill Business Ethics," *Workforce Management* (April 2005), 26.

15. Richard W. Judy and Carol D'Amico, *Workforce 2020: Work and Workers in the 21st Century* (Indianapolis, IN: Hudson Institute, 1997).

16. Michael Rybicki, "Temporary Worker, Permanent Loser," *Newsweek* (March 10, 2003), 18.

17. U.S. Bureau of Labor Statistics, 2004, *http://www.bls.gov.,* and U.S. Census Bureau.

18. Ibid.

19. U.S. Equal Employment Opportunity Commission, "Characteristics of Private Search Employment," (April 2003); *http://www.eeoc.gov.*

20. U.S. Bureau of Labor Statistics; *http://www.bls.gov.*

Legal Issues Affecting the Healthcare Workplace

Learning Objectives

After you have read this chapter, you should be able to:

- Describe the major laws affecting the healthcare workplace.

- Define what are lawful and unlawful preemployment inquiries.

- Discuss the components of an Affirmative Action Plan (AAP).

- Identify the important elements of a sexual harassment prevention program.

- Describe the steps to take in responding to an Equal Employment Opportunity (EEO) complaint.

- Compare and contrast legal responsibilities and ethics.

Healthcare HR Insights

At a major metropolitan medical center, a male research doctor was accused of systematically sexually harassing his entire staff of eight women. The alleged victims recounted episode after episode of behavior on his part that created a hostile work environment. His alleged comments included graphic descriptions of sex scenes in movies, discussion of the kinds of underwear the women preferred to wear, and using sexual overtones when talking about eating food.

The women complained to the medical center's HR department, which took the appropriate steps as described in the center's HR policies. After an investigation was conducted, the doctor was suspended and ultimately placed on a final disciplinary warning for the duration of his employment and given a conditional return to his duties. However, the women believed that the center failed to act decisively enough and filed suit against both the medical center and the doctor.

After an expensive discovery process, including multiple depositions, the medical center decided to settle the suit with a negotiated monetary award to the aggrieved women, including full payment of their attorneys' fees. The issues for the medical center did not stop there. In the afftermath of the settlement, over half of the women left the medical center or demanded reassignment. Those who continued to work with the doctor were given written assurances of receiving high priority in HR counseling relative to any future problems with the doctor.

Sexual harassment in the workplace continues to be an important and widespread problem, particularly in healthcare. In some studies upwards of 80 percent of nurses reported some form of sexual harassment. A survey of young doctors at a California medical school found that three-fourths of the women believe that they were sexually harassed during training.[1]

Healthcare HR professionals face many concerns beyond sexual harassment when ensuring equal treatment of all employees and compliance with numerous equal employment laws. Ensuring equal opportunity and fair treatment in the healthcare workplace is the responsibility of every healthcare leader who makes employment-related decisions. HR professionals in healthcare organizations shoulder a significant portion of the responsibility due to their role in the organization. Consequently, HR practitioners must be extremely knowledgeable about the laws that impact the workplace so they can provide leadership, compliance oversight, and consultation to the managers and staff.

EQUAL EMPLOYMENT OPPORTUNITY

Equal employment opportunity (EEO) is a broad concept holding that individuals should have equal treatment in all employment-related actions. Individuals who are covered under equal employment laws are protected from illegal discrimination, which occurs when individuals having a common characteristic are discriminated against based on that characteristic. Various laws have been passed to protect individuals who share certain characteristics, such as race, age, or gender. Those having the designated characteristics are referred to as members of a protected class. The following bases for protection have been identified by various federal laws:

- Race, ethnicity, origin, color (African Americans, Hispanic Americans, Native Americans, Asian Americans)
- Sex/gender (women, including those who are pregnant)
- Age (individuals over age 40)
- Individuals with disabilities (physical or mental)
- Military experience (Vietnam-era veterans)
- Religion (special beliefs and practices)
- Marital status (some states)
- Sexual orientation (some states and cities)

Major Employment Laws

Numerous federal, state, and local laws address EEO concerns. Figure 4-1 presents an overview of the major laws, regulations, and concepts. They are discussed in more detail in the remainder of this chapter.

Civil Rights Act of 1964, Title VII

The Civil Rights Act of 1964 was passed in part to bring about equality in all employment-related decisions. The Equal Employment Opportunity Commission (EEOC) was established to enforce the provisions of Title VII, the portion of the act that deals with employment. The key aspects of the Civil Rights Act of 1964 are discussed next.

Title VII Coverage Title VII, as amended by the Equal Employment Opportunity Act of 1972, covers most employers in the United States. Any organization meeting one of the criteria in the following list is subject to rules and regulations that specific government agencies have established to administer the act:

- All private employers of 15 or more persons who are employed 20 or more weeks a year
- All educational institutions, public and private
- State and local governments

FIGURE 4-1   Major Federal Equal Employment Opportunity Laws and Regulations

ACT	YEAR	PROVISIONS
Equal Pay Act	1963	Requires equal pay for men and women performing substantially the same work
Title VII, Civil Rights Act of 1964	1964	Prohibits discrimination in employment on basis of race, color, religion, sex, or national origin
Executive Orders 11246 and 11375	1965 1967	Require federal contractors and subcontractors to eliminate employment discrimination and prior discrimination through affirmative action
Age Discrimination in Employment Act (as amended in 1978 and 1986)	1967	Prohibits discrimination against persons over age 40 and restricts mandatory retirement requirements, except where age is a bona fide occupational qualification
Executive Order 11478	1969	Prohibits discrimination in the U.S. Postal Service and in the various government agencies on the basis of race, color, religion, sex, national origin, handicap, or age
Vocational Rehabilitation Act Rehabilitation Act of 1974	1973 1974	Prohibit employers with federal contracts over $2,500 from discriminating against individuals with disabilities
Vietnam Era Veterans Readjustment Act	1974	Prohibits discrimination against Vietnam-era veterans by federal contractors and the U.S. government and requires affirmative action
Pregnancy Discrimination Act	1978	Prohibits discrimination against women affected by pregnancy, childbirth, or related medical conditions; requires that they be treated as all other employees for employment-related purposes, including benefits
Immigration Reform and Control Act	1986 1990 1996	Establishes penalties for employers who knowingly hire illegal aliens; prohibits employment discrimination on the basis of national origin or citizenship
Americans with Disabilities Act	1990	Requires employer accommodation of individuals with disabilities
Older Workers Benefit Protection Act of 1990	1990	Prohibits age-based discrimination in early retirement and other benefits plans
Civil Rights Act of 1991	1991	Overturns several past Supreme Court decisions and changes damage claims provisions
Congressional Accountability Act	1995	Extends EEO and Civil Rights Act Provisions to U.S. congressional staff

- Public and private employment agencies
- Labor unions with 15 or more members
- Joint labor/management committees for apprenticeships and training

Title VII has been the basis for several extensions of EEO law. For example, in 1980, the EEOC interpreted the law to include sexual harassment. Further, a number of concepts identified in Title VII are the foundation for court decisions, regulations, and other laws discussed later in the chapter. Most healthcare organizations would fall under one or more of these categories; consequently they must comply with the provisions of Title VII.

Business Necessity and Job Relatedness As has been emphasized by regulations and court decisions, employers are expected to use job-related employment practices. In a Michigan case, a federal court ruled that a staffing agency was discriminating illegally by filling job requests from employers with such limitations as "males only," "no applicants with accents," and "no Detroit residents." The court ruled that such criteria were not job-related and that little business necessity could be shown for these requests being made by employers using the staffing service.[2]

A **business necessity** is a practice necessary for safe and efficient organizational operations. Business necessity has been the subject of numerous court decisions. Educational requirements often are based on business necessity. However, an employer who requires a minimum level of education must be able to defend the requirement as essential to the performance of the job. In healthcare organizations this defense is relatively easy to make based on the fact that many positions require licensures, certifications, or registrations that can only be obtained by educational attainment. However, for positions that do not have those types of requirements, healthcare organizations have the same burden to prove business necessity for any educational requirement. As an example, equating a degree or diploma with the possession of math or reading abilities would be considered questionable.

EEOC Compliance

Employers must comply with EEOC regulations and guidelines. To do so, management should have an EEO policy statement and maintain all required EEO-related records. This policy should be widely disseminated throughout the organization. All employers with fifteen or more employees are required to keep certain records that can be requested by the EEOC.

Preemployment Versus After-Hire Inquiries Figure 4-2 lists preemployment inquiries and identifies whether they may or may not be discriminatory. The following list further identifies circumstances that permit or prohibit certain preemployment inquiries:

- Employers acting under bona fide Affirmative Action Programs or acting under orders of Equal Employment law enforcement agencies of federal, state, or local governments may make some of the prohibited inquiries to the extent that the inquiries are required by such programs or orders.
- Employers having federal defense contracts are exempt to the extent that certain inquiries are required by federal law for security purposes.

FIGURE 4-2 Lawful and Unlawful Preemployment Inquiries

INQUIRIES BEFORE HIRING	LAWFUL	UNLAWFUL
1. Name	Name	Inquiry into any title which indicates race, color, religion, sex, national origin, handicap or ancestry
2. Address	Inquiry into place and length of current address	Inquiry into foreign address that would indicate national origin
3. Age	• Requiring proof of age in form of work permit issued by school authorities • Requiring proof of age by birth certificate or otherwise after hiring	Requiring birth certificate or baptismal record before hiring
4. Birthplace or National Origin		• Any inquiry into place of birth • Any inquiry into place of birth of parents, grandparents, or spouse
5. Race or Color		Any inquiry that would indicate race or color
6. Sex		Any inquiry that would indicate sex
7. Religion–Creed		• Any inquiry that would indicate or identify religious denomination or custom • Telling applicant of any religious identity or preference of the employer • Requesting religious leaders' recommendation/reference
8. Physical Limitations (requirements)	Inquiries necessary to determine applicant's ability to substantially perform job related functions and to determine accommodations, if any	• Disease diagnosis • Receipt of worker's compensation
9. Citizenship	• Whether a U.S. Citizen • Whether applicant can legally work in the United States	• If native-born or naturalized • Whether parents or spouse are native-born or naturalized • Proof of citizenship before offer
10. Photographs		Requiring photographs before hiring

(*Continued*)

FIGURE 4-2 Lawful and Unlawful Preemployment Inquiries (*Continued*)

INQUIRIES BEFORE HIRING	LAWFUL	UNLAWFUL
11. Arrests and Convictions	Inquiries into *conviction* of specific crimes related to the job for which the applicant applied	• Any inquiry which would reveal arrests without convictions • Convictions unrelated to the job responsibilities
12. Education	• Inquiry into nature and extent of academic, professional, or vocational training • Inquiry into language skills such as reading and writing of foreign languages, if job related	• Any inquiry asking specifically the nationality or racial or religious affiliation of a school • Inquiry as to what mother tongue is or how foreign language ability was acquired
13. Relatives	Names of relatives already employed by employer	Any inquiry about a relative that would be unlawful if made about the applicant
14. Organizations	Inquiry into organization memberships and offices held, excluding any organization, the name or character of which indicates the race, color, religion, sex, national origin, handicap or ancestry of its members	Inquiry into *all* clubs and organizations where membership is held
15. Military Service	• Inquiry into service in U.S. Armed Forces when such service is a qualification for the job • Requiring military discharge certificate after being hired	• Inquiry into military service in armed service of any country but United States • Requesting military service records • Type of discharge
16. Work Schedule	Inquiry into willingness to work required work schedule	Any inquiry into willingness to work any particular religious holiday
17. Other Qualifications	Any question required to reveal qualifications for the job applied for	Any non-job related inquiry which may reveal information permitting unlawful discrimination
18. References	General, personal, and work references not relating to race, color, religion, sex, national origin, handicap or ancestry	Request references specifically from any persons who might reflect race, color, religion, sex, national origin, handicap, or ancestry of applicant

Once an employer tells an applicant he or she is hired (the "point of hire"), inquiries that were prohibited earlier may be made. After hiring, medical examination forms, group insurance cards, and other enrollment cards containing inquiries related directly or indirectly to sex, age, or other bases may be requested. Photographs or other evidence of race, religion, or national origin also may be requested after hire for legal, compliance, and workplace security, but not before. Such data should be maintained in a separate personnel records system in order to avoid their use when managers and supervisors make appraisal, discipline, termination, or promotion decisions.

Bona Fide Occupational Qualification   Title VII of the 1964 Civil Rights Act states that employers may discriminate on the basis of sex, religion, or national origin if the characteristic can be justified as a "bona fide occupational qualification reasonably necessary to the normal operation of the particular business or enterprise."[3] Thus, a **bona fide occupational qualification (BFOQ)** is a legitimate reason why an employer can exclude persons on otherwise illegal bases of consideration. As an example, hiring only female caregivers in sensitive positions dealing with female patients would be justifiable.

Disparate Treatment and Disparate Impact   It would seem that the motives or intentions of the employer might enter into the determination of whether discrimination has occurred. However the outcome of the employer's actions, not the intent, is considered by the regulatory agencies or courts when deciding if illegal discrimination has occurred. Two concepts used to activate this principle are *disparate treatment* and *disparate impact.*

Disparate treatment occurs when protected-class members are treated differently from others. For example, if female applicants must take a special skills test not given to male applicants, then disparate treatment may be occurring. If disparate treatment has occurred, the courts generally have said that intentional discrimination exists.

Disparate impact occurs when there is substantial underrepresentation of protected-class members as a result of employment decisions that work to their disadvantage. The landmark case that established the importance of disparate impact as a legal foundation of EEO law is *Griggs v. Duke Power* (1971).[4] The decision of the U.S. Supreme Court established two major points:

1. It is not enough to show a lack of discriminatory intent if the employment tool results in a disparate impact that discriminates against one group more than another or continues a past pattern of discrimination.
2. The employer has the burden of proving that an employment requirement is directly job-related as a "business necessity." Consequently, the intelligence test and high school diploma requirements of Duke Power were ruled not to be related to the job.

Therefore, employers covered by Title VII must be able to document through numerical calculations and statistical analyses of the workforce that disparate treatment and disparate impact have not occurred.

Burden of Proof   Another legal issue that arises when discrimination is alleged is the determination of which party has the *burden of proof.* Based on the evolution of court decisions, current laws and regulations state that the plaintiff charging discrimination:[5] (1) must be a *protected-class member* and (2) must prove that *disparate impact* or *disparate treatment* existed. Once a court rules that a *prima facie* (preliminary) case has been made, the burden of proof shifts to the employer. The employer must then show that the bases for making employment-related decisions were specifically job-related and consistent with considerations of business necessity.

Employers are prohibited by EEO laws from retaliating against individuals who file discrimination charges. Retaliation occurs when employers take punitive actions against individuals who exercise their legal rights. For example, an organization was ruled to have engaged in retaliation when an employee who filed a discrimination complaint had work hours reduced, which resulted in a loss of pay, but no other employees' work hours were reduced.[6]

Civil Rights Act of 1991

The Civil Rights Act of 1991 requires employers to show that an employment practice is *job-related for the position* and is consistent with *business necessity*. The act clarifies that the plaintiffs bringing the discrimination charges must identify the particular employer practice being challenged and must show only that protected-class status played *some factor*. For employers, this means that an individual's race, color, religion, sex, or national origin *must play no factor* in their employment practices.

Compensatory/Punitive Damages and Jury Trials   The major impact of the 1991 act is that it allows victims of discrimination on the basis of sex, religion, or disability to receive both *compensatory* and *punitive damages* in cases of intentional discrimination. Compensatory damages typically include payments for emotional pain and suffering, loss of enjoyment of life, mental anguish, or inconvenience. However, limits were set on the amount of compensatory and punitive damages.

Reverse Discrimination

When equal employment opportunity regulations are discussed, probably the most volatile issue concerns the view that affirmative action leads to *quotas, preferential selection,* and *reverse discrimination.* At the heart of the conflict is the employer's role in selecting, training, and promoting protected-class members when they are underrepresented in various jobs in an organization. Those who are not members of any protected class have claimed that there is discrimination in reverse.

This reverse discrimination may exist when a person is denied an opportunity because of preferences given to a member of a protected class who may be less qualified. Specifically, some critics charge that white males are at a disadvantage today, even though they traditionally have held many of the better jobs. Affirmative action as a concept is under attack by some courts and employers, as well as by some individuals. Whether that trend continues will depend on future changes in the makeup of the U.S. Supreme Court and the results of presidential and congressional elections.

AFFIRMATIVE ACTION

To remedy areas in which it appears that individuals in protected classes have not had equal employment opportunities, some employers have developed affirmative action policies. Affirmative action occurs when employers identify problem areas, set goals, and take positive steps to guarantee equal employment opportunities for people in a protected class. Affirmative action focuses on hiring, training, and promoting protected-class members where they are *underrepresented* in an organization in relation to their availability in the labor markets from which recruiting occurs. Sometimes employers have instituted affirmative action voluntarily, but many times they have been required to do so because they are government contractors with more than 50 employees and more than $50,000 in government contracts annually.

Affirmative Action Requirements

Throughout the last 30 years, employers with federal contracts and other government entities have had to address additional areas of potential discrimination. Several acts and regulations have been issued that apply specifically to government contractors. These acts and regulations specify a minimum number of employees and size of government contracts. The requirements primarily come from federal Executive Orders 11246, 11375, and 11478.[7] Many states have similar requirements for firms with state government contracts.

Affirmative Action Plans (AAPs)

Under federal, state, and local regulations, many government contractors are required to compile affirmative action plans (AAPs) to report on the composition of their workforces. An AAP is a formal document that an employer compiles annually for submission to enforcement agencies. Generally, contractors with at least 50 employees and $50,000 in government contracts annually must submit these plans.

Courts have noted that any employer that is not a government contractor may have a *voluntary* AAP. Where an employer that is not a government contractor has a required AAP, a court has ordered the employer to have an AAP as a result of past discriminatory practices and violations of laws.

The contents of an AAP and the policies flowing from it must be available for review by managers and supervisors within the organization. Plans vary in length; some are long and require extensive staff time to prepare. Figure 4-3 depicts the components of an AAP.

Internal Background Review   In the internal background review the EEO and AAP *policy statements* are presented, including the employer's commitment to equal employment and affirmative action. Then the *workforce analysis* is done by detailing the makeup of the workforce as seen on an organization chart and by depicting departmental groupings, job titles and pay levels, and the lines of progression. This analysis details the status of employees by gender, race, and other bases. The final part of the internal background review is to prepare a

FIGURE 4-3   Components of an Affirmative Action Plan (AAP)

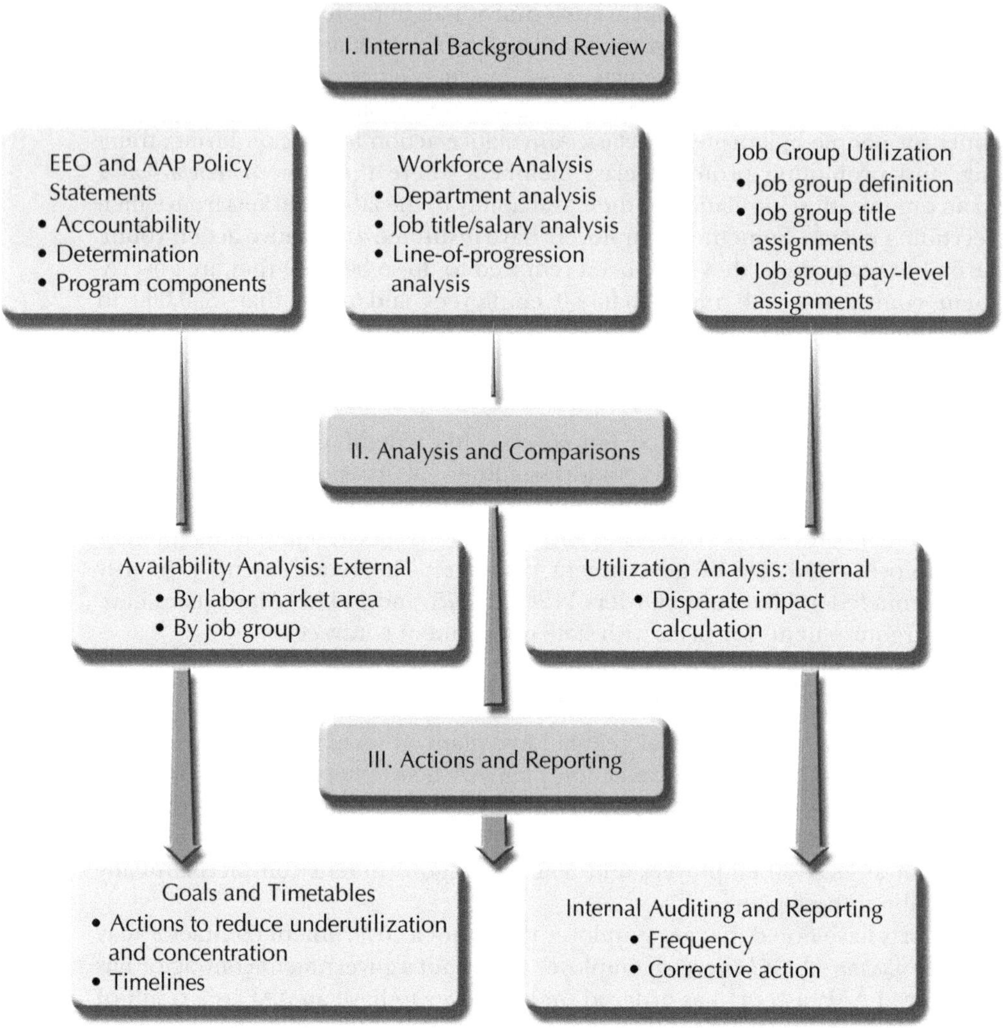

I. Internal Background Review

EEO and AAP Policy Statements
• Accountability
• Determination
• Program components

Workforce Analysis
• Department analysis
• Job title/salary analysis
• Line-of-progression analysis

Job Group Utilization
• Job group definition
• Job group title assignments
• Job group pay-level assignments

II. Analysis and Comparisons

Availability Analysis: External
• By labor market area
• By job group

Utilization Analysis: Internal
• Disparate impact calculation

III. Actions and Reporting

Goals and Timetables
• Actions to reduce underutilization and concentration
• Timelines

Internal Auditing and Reporting
• Frequency
• Corrective action

job group analysis. Unlike the workforce analysis, in which data are classified by organizational unit, the job group analysis looks at similar jobs throughout the organization, regardless of department. For instance, EEO *demographic* data on incumbents in all nursing jobs will be reported, regardless of department. For example, a hospital may have eight levels of nurses in 12 different units. All units would be considered together.

Analyses and Comparisons   As part of the second phase, two different types of analyses and comparisons are done. The first is an **availability analysis,** which identifies the number of protected-class members available to work in the appropriate labor markets in given jobs. This analysis can be developed with data from a state labor department, the U.S. Census Bureau, and other sources.

Another major section of an AAP is the **utilization analysis,** which identifies the number of protected-class members employed and the types of jobs they hold in an organization.

Once all of the data have been analyzed and compared, then *underutilization* statistics must be calculated by comparing the workforce analyses with the utilization analysis. It is useful to think of this as comparing the internal workforce against the available external labor force from which employees are hired.

Actions and Reporting   Using the underutilization data, *goals* and *timetables* for reducing the underutilization of protected-class individuals must then be identified. Actions that will be taken to recruit, hire, promote, and train more protected-class individuals are described. Also, the AAP must be updated and reviewed each year to reflect changes in the utilization and the availability of protected-class members. If an audit of an AAP is done by the Office of Federal Contract Compliance Programs (OFCCP), the employer must be prepared to provide additional details and documentation. Healthcare organizations that are recipients of federal research dollars through the National Institute of Health are subject to AAP audits by Health and Human Services (HHS).

Healthcare and Affirmative Action   In the past several years, one of the more important developments in the healthcare management field has been the recognition that as communities become more diverse, so must the healthcare organizations that serve them.[8] However, the field of healthcare management continues to be an underrepresented area and is becoming even more so despite efforts to promote racial diversity in the ranks of the industry leadership, according to the results of a study conducted by the American College of Healthcare Executives (ACHE).[9] The key findings of the study included:

- Sixty-two percent of the white males in the study sample held senior management positions (CEO, COO, or Senior Vice President); this compares to 51 percent of the white male respondents to a similar survey in 1997.

- White female executives made gains in the latest study, but the gap between white males and white females holding senior management positions widened. In the recent survey 40 percent of the female respondents held senior management jobs, up from 35 percent in 1997. However, the gap between white males and white females widened from 16 percent to 22 percent.

- In 1997, 43 percent of the black male respondents held senior management jobs; in the more recent survey the reported percentage was only 1 percent higher, at 44 percent. The gap between white male senior managers and black male senior managers stood at 8 percent in the 1997 study compared to 18 percent in the most recent study.

- Ninety-five percent of black male executives surveyed said inequities exist in healthcare management opportunities.

Affirmative action recruitment initiatives are supported by a broad coalition, including: ACHE, the Association of Hispanic Healthcare Executives, the Institute for Diversity in Health Management, and the National Association of Health Services. Initiatives include: Instituting outreach mechanisms to promising

ETHICAL PRACTICES AND COMPLIANCE

As the issues faced by healthcare HR professionals have increased in number and complexity, so have the pressures and challenges of acting ethically. Ethical issues pose fundamental questions about fairness, justice, truthfulness, and social responsibility. Concerns have been raised about the ethical standards used by managers and employees, including those in healthcare organizations.

For HR professionals, there are ethical ways in which they should act relative to a given HR issue. However, determining ethical actions is not always easy. Just complying with the laws does not guarantee ethical behavior. Business ethicists argue that laws and ethics intersect, as depicted, but are not the same.

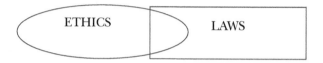

Dealing with discrimination in the healthcare workplace is clearly not just a legal issue. Healthcare employers can make legally correct decisions relative to employment promotion, pay increases, or other employment actions and yet violate ethical standards.

Although many large medical centers and university-based health organizations that receive federal funding must have an AAP and commit to pursuing affirmative action in attracting and recruiting qualified minority applicants, it is difficult to determine true compliance with that requirement. Organizations can merely go through the motions of affirmative action and focus on the documentation aspects of an AAP to prepare for OFCCP audits, or they can truly be very aggressive in efforts that produce results, whereby the numbers of protected group members are significantly increased.

Laws and regulations cannot cover every situation that HR professionals will face. Instead, healthcare HR professionals must also be guided by values and personal behavior codes of conduct that represent fairness and equal treatment.[10]

racially/ethnically diverse candidates in an attempt to attract them to healthcare, advocating racial and ethnic diversity in the appointment of search committees for healthcare positions, recruiting racially/ethnically diverse candidates at all levels to increase the pipeline of potential executive candidates, and recruiting candidates external to healthcare to broaden the pool of racially/ethnically diverse candidates.[11]

Healthcare organizations are increasingly recognizing that attracting and retaining a racially/ethnically diverse workforce is needed not only to be in compliance with appropriate federal, state, and local AAP requirements, but it is also of critical importance as the demographics of the country change. The importance of healthcare diversity participation and awareness will be discussed further in subsequent chapters.

GENDER DISCRIMINATION AND SEXUAL HARASSMENT

Title VII of the Civil Rights Act of 1964 prohibits discrimination in employment on the basis of gender. Other laws and regulations are aimed at eliminating such discrimination in specific areas.

Pregnancy Discrimination

The Pregnancy Discrimination Act (PDA) of 1978 requires that any employer with 15 or more employees treat maternity leave the same as other personal or medical leaves. Related to the PDA is the Family and Medical Leave Act (FMLA) of 1993, which requires that individuals be given up to 12 weeks of family leave without pay and also requires that those taking family leave be allowed to return to their jobs. The FMLA applies to both men and women.

In court cases it generally has been ruled that the PDA requires employers to treat pregnant employees the same as nonpregnant employees with similar abilities or inabilities. Therefore, an employer was ruled to have acted properly when terminating a pregnant employee for excessive absenteeism due to pregnancy-related illnesses because the employee was not treated differently than any other employees with absenteeism problems.[12] However, in another case, a dental employee who was fired five days after she told her manager that she was pregnant was awarded $18,460 by a court decision that ruled her employer violated the PDA.[13]

Two other areas somewhat related to pregnancy and motherhood also have been subjects of legal and regulatory action. The U.S. Equal Employment Commission has ruled that denial of health insurance coverage for prescription contraceptives under employer-provided health plans violates the PDA. A result of this ruling is that employers who have changed their health insurance plans to offer contraceptive coverage may face increases in benefit costs.

A number of states have passed laws that guarantee breast-feeding rights at work for new mothers. This is an important issue in healthcare given the large number of female employees in the industry. Many healthcare organizations, both in compliance with state statutes and consistent with their family friendly work policies, have gone to great lengths to facilitate female employees' desire to express milk while at work. Attempts to enact such legislation at the federal level, however, have not succeeded.

Equal Pay and Pay Equity

The Equal Pay Act of 1963 requires employers to pay similar wage rates for similar work without regard to gender. A *common core of tasks* must be similar, but tasks performed only intermittently or infrequently do not make jobs different enough to justify significantly different wages. Differences in pay may be allowed because of:

- Differences in seniority
- Differences in performance
- Differences in quality and/or quantity of production
- Factors other than sex, such as skill, effort, and working conditions

For example, a university was found to have violated the Equal Pay Act by paying a female professor a starting salary lower than salaries paid to male professors with similar responsibilities. In fact, the court found that the woman professor taught larger classes and had more total students than some of the male faculty members.[14]

Another pay-related concept is *pay equity,* which is that the pay for jobs requiring comparable levels of knowledge, skill, and ability should be similar, even if actual duties differ significantly. This concept has also been identified as *comparable worth* in some cases. But except where state laws require pay equity for public-sector employees, U.S. federal courts generally have ruled that the existence of pay differences between jobs held by women and jobs held by men is not sufficient to prove that illegal discrimination has occurred.

The Glass Ceiling

For years, women's groups have alleged that women encounter a glass ceiling in the workplace. The **glass ceiling** refers to discriminatory practices that have prevented women and other protected-class members from advancing to executive-level jobs.

A related problem is that women have tended to advance to senior management in a limited number of functional areas, such as human resources and corporate communications. Because jobs in these "supporting" areas tend to pay less than jobs in marketing, operations, or finance, the overall impact is to reduce women's career progression and income. However, just as the total employment of women fluctuates by industry, they are not evenly distributed across all industries as officials and managers. Figure 4-4 lists the 10 industries where women have the highest percentage of officials and managers. These industries are very similar to those based on the total employment of women.

Limits that keep women from progressing except in certain fields have often been referred to as *glass walls* or *glass elevators.* Some organizations, including healthcare organizations, have established formal mentoring programs in order to break down glass walls.

FIGURE 4-4   Top Ten Industries Based on the Employment of Women as Officers and Managers by Percentage

INDUSTRY	MANAGERS PERCENT WOMEN
Nursing & Residential Care Facilities	73.6
Hospitals	66.9
Ambulatory Health Care Services	62.8
Social Assistance	61.0
Clothing & Clothing Accessories Stores	59.3
Religious/Grant Making/ Prof/Like Organizations	52.0
Museums, Historical Sites & Like Institutions	51.6
Educational Services	50.2
General Merchandise Stores	49.4
Credit Intermediation & Related Activities	49.0

Source: EEO-1 Data, 2005.

Sexual Harassment

Healthcare employers are consistently challenged to provide a workplace free from sexual harassment. The very nature of healthcare delivery and the occupational need to discuss the body and body functions lends itself to discussions among physicians, employees, and patients which sometimes blurs the lines of appropriate speech and conduct.

Sexual harassment is a form of sex discrimination that violates Title VII of the Civil Rights Act of 1964. The two types of sexual harassment are defined as follows:

1. *Quid pro quo* harassment occurs when an employer or supervisor links specific employment outcomes to the individuals' granting sexual favors.

2. *Hostile environment* harassment occurs when the harassment has the effect of unreasonably interfering with work performance or psychological well-being or when intimidating or offensive working conditions are created.

FIGURE 4-5   **Potential Sexual Harassers**

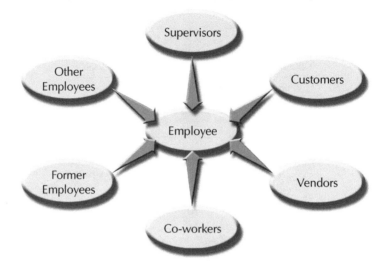

Unwelcome sexual advances, requests for sexual favors, and other verbal or physical conduct of a sexual nature constitutes sexual harassment when submission to or rejection of this conduct explicitly affects an individual's employment, unreasonably interferes with an individual's work performance, or creates an intimidating, hostile, or offensive work environment.

Sexual harassment can occur in a variety of circumstances, including but not limited to the following:

- The victim as well as the harasser may be a woman or a man. The victim does not have to be of the opposite sex.

- The harasser can be the victim's supervisor, an agent of the employer, a supervisor in another area, a coworker, or a nonemployee. (See Figure 4-5.)

- The victim does not have to be the person harassed but could be anyone affected by the offensive conduct.

- Unlawful sexual harassment may occur without economic injury to or discharge of the victim.

- The harasser's conduct must be unwelcome.

It is helpful for the victim to directly and clearly inform the harasser that the conduct is unwelcome and must stop. The victim should also use any employer complaint mechanism or grievance system available.

Linking any condition of employment—including pay raises, promotions, assignments of work and work hours, performance appraisals, meetings, disciplinary actions, and many others—to the granting of sexual favors can be the basis for a charge of *quid pro quo* ("something for something") harassment. Certainly, harassment by supervisors and managers who expect sexual favors as a condition for a raise or promotion is inappropriate behavior in a work environment. This view has been supported in a wide variety of cases.

The second type of sexual harassment involves the creation of a *hostile work environment*. In *Harris v. Forklift Systems, Inc.,* the U.S. Supreme Court ruled that in determining if a hostile environment exists, certain factors should be considered, such as whether the conduct is physically threatening or humiliating, rather than just offensive, whether the conduct interferes unreasonably with an employee's work performance, and/or whether the conduct affects the employee's psychological well-being.[15]

Healthcare employers should ensure **reasonable care** in their HR policies and practices by doing the following:

- Establishing a sexual harassment policy
- Communicating the policy regularly
- Training all employees, especially supervisors and managers, on avoiding sexual harassment
- Investigating and taking action when complaints are voiced

It is important that an employer take prompt action to first remove any potential for further harassment, and second, to investigate the harassment complaint and punish the identified harasser; these steps will aid an employer's defense. If harassment situations are taken seriously by employers, the ultimate outcomes are more likely to be favorable for them.

Prevention is the best tool to eliminate sexual harassment in the workplace. The first action an employer should take is to have a clearly stated policy on sex harassment prevention. A sample policy can be found on this book's Web site: *http://flynn.swlearning.com.* Employers are encouraged to take steps necessary to prevent sexual harassment from occurring. They should clearly communicate to employees that sexual harassment will not be tolerated. They can do so by establishing an effective complaint or grievance process and by taking immediate and appropriate action when an employee complains.

AGE DISCRIMINATION

The Age Discrimination in Employment Act (ADEA) of 1967, amended in 1978 and 1986, makes it illegal for an employer to discriminate in compensation, terms, conditions, or privileges of employment because of an individual's age. The later amendments first raised the minimum mandatory retirement age to 70 and then eliminated it completely. The ADEA applies to all individuals over age 40 working for employers with 20 or more workers. However, the act does not apply if age is a job-related occupational qualification.

Older Workers Benefit Protection Act (OWBPA)

The Older Workers Benefit Protection Act (OWBPA) is an amendment to the ADEA and is aimed at protecting employees when they sign liability waivers for age discrimination in exchange for severance packages. For example, an early retirement package that includes a waiver stating the employee will not sue for age discrimination if he or she takes the money for early retirement must:[16]

- Include a written, clearly understood agreement
- Offer something of value beyond what the employee will receive without the package
- Advise the employee to consult an attorney
- Allow the employee at least 21 days to consider the offer
- Allow the employee 7 days to revoke the agreement after signing it

AMERICANS WITH DISABILITIES ACT

The passage of the Americans with Disabilities Act (ADA) in 1990 represented an expansion in the scope of impact of laws and regulations on discrimination against individuals with disabilities. The ADA contains the following requirements dealing with employment.

- Discrimination is prohibited against individuals with disabilities who can perform the essential job functions, a standard that is somewhat vague.
- A covered employer must have reasonable accommodation for people with disabilities so that they can function as employees, unless undue hardship would be placed on the employer.
- Preemployment medical examinations are prohibited, except after a conditional employment offer is made.

As defined by the ADA, a *disabled person* is someone who has a physical or mental impairment that substantially limits that person in some major life activities, who has a record of such impairment, or who is regarded as having such impairment. A growing area of concern under the ADA is individuals with mental disabilities. Generally, employers have prevailed when charges of discrimination against a person with a mental disability have been brought against them. A mental illness is often more difficult to diagnose than a physical disability.

ADA Compliance

In complying with the ADA, healthcare employers must consider the following key aspects of the act:

- *Essential Job Functions*—The ADA requires that the essential job functions be identified in written job descriptions that indicate the amount of time spent performing various functions and their criticality. Most employers have interpreted this provision to mean that they should develop and maintain current and comprehensive job descriptions for all jobs.
- *Reasonable Accommodation*—A reasonable accommodation is a modification or adjustment to a job or work environment that enables a qualified individual with a disability to have equal employment opportunity. Employers are

required to provide reasonable accommodation for individuals with disabilities to ensure that legal discrimination does not occur.

- *Undue Hardship*—Reasonable accommodation is restricted to actions that do not place an undue hardship on an employer. An action places undue hardship on an employer if it imposes significant difficulty or expense. The ADA offers only general guidelines on when an accommodation becomes unreasonable and places undue hardship on an employer.

OTHER BASES OF DISCRIMINATION

There are several other bases of discrimination that various laws have identified as illegal. These are often a concern to employers and are outlined in the following sections.

Immigration Reform and Control Act (IRCA)

To deal with problems arising from the continued flow of immigrants to the United States, the Immigration Reform and Control Act (IRCA) was passed in 1986 to make it illegal for employers to discriminate in recruiting, hiring, or terminating based on an individual's national origin or citizenship. Recent revisions to the IRCA changed some of the restrictions on the entry of immigrants to work in U.S. organizations, particularly those organizations with high-technology and other "scarce skills" areas. Employers are required to examine identification documents for new employees, who also must sign verification forms about their eligibility to work legally in the United States.

Religious Discrimination

Title VII of the Civil Rights Act identifies discrimination on the basis of religion as illegal. However, religious schools and institutions can use religion as a bona fide occupational qualification (BFOQ) for employment practices on a limited scale.

Sexual Orientation

Some states and cities have passed laws prohibiting discrimination based on sexual orientation or lifestyle. Further, the issue of benefits coverage for "domestic partners," whether heterosexual or homosexual, has been the subject of some state and city statutes.

Veterans' Employment Rights

The employment rights of military veterans and reservists have been addressed by the passage of the Vietnam Era Veterans Readjustment Act. The act requires that affirmative action in hiring and advancing Vietnam-era veterans be undertaken by federal contractors and subcontractors with contracts of $10,000 or more.

Military Employment Rights

The employment rights of military veterans and reservists have been addressed in several laws. The two most important laws are the Vietnam Era Veterans Readjustment Assistance Act of 1974 and the Uniformed Services Employment and Reemployment Rights Act (USERRA) of 1994. Under the latter, employees are required to notify their employers of military service obligations. Employers must give employees serving in the military leaves of absence, and those employees have re-employment rights for up to five years. Other provisions protect the right to benefits of employees called to military duty.[17]

With the increasing use of reserves and National Guard troops abroad, the provisions of USERRA have had more impact on employers. This act does not require employers to pay employees while they are on military leave, although many employers do provide some compensation. Many requirements regarding benefits, disabilities, and reemployment are covered in the act as well.

ENFORCEMENT AGENCIES

Government agencies at several levels have powers to investigate illegal discriminatory practices. At the state and local levels, various commissions have enforcement authority. At the federal level, the two most prominent agencies are the EEOC and the OFCCP.

Federal and state agencies with EEO enforcement authority frequently must coordinate investigations of illegal discriminatory practices when charges are filed with both agencies by the same complainant.

Equal Employment Opportunity Commission (EEOC)

The EEOC is responsible for enforcing the employment-related provisions of the EEO act. The agency initiates investigations, responds to complaints, and develops guidelines to enforce various laws. The EEOC has enforcement authority for charges brought under a number of federal laws, including the responsibility to investigate equal pay violations, age discrimination, and discrimination based on disability. As Figure 4-6 shows, the greatest number of equal employment charges are based on race, sex, and national origin discrimination. That pattern has been constant for the past decade.

Office of Federal Contract Compliance (OFCCP)

The OFCCP, part of the Department of Labor, was established to ensure that federal contractors and subcontractors have nondiscriminatory practices. The major thrust of the OFCCP in healthcare organizations is to require that covered employers have affirmative action plans to counter prior discriminatory practices.

Many large healthcare providers, especially teaching and research hospitals that receive substantial Medicare reimbursement or National Institute of Health

FIGURE 4-6   EEO Charges for a Recent Year

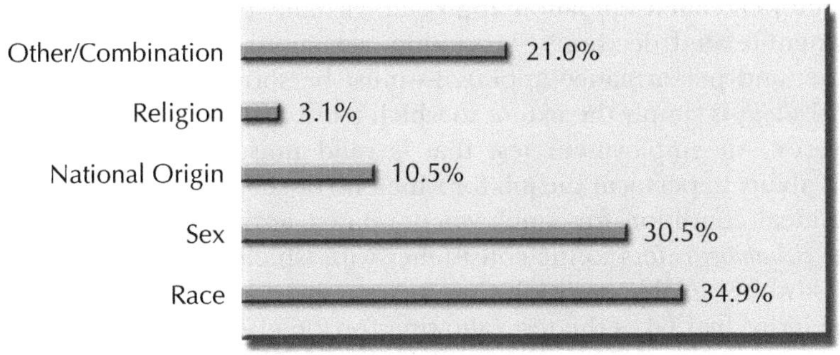

Source: *http://www.eeoc.gov.*

(NIH) grants, are periodically surveyed by OFCCP to determine their ongoing compliance with the Executive Orders.

State and Local Enforcement Agencies

In addition to federal laws and Executive Orders, many states and municipalities have passed laws prohibiting discrimination on a variety of bases, and state and local enforcement bodies have been established. Often, these laws are modeled after federal laws; however, state and local laws sometimes provide greater remedies, require different actions, or prohibit discrimination in areas beyond those addressed by federal law.

UNIFORM GUIDELINES ON EMPLOYEE SELECTION PROCEDURES

The Uniform Guidelines on Employee Selection Procedures were developed by the EEOC, the U.S. Department of Labor's OFCCP, the U.S. Department of Justice, and the Office of Personnel Management. The guidelines provide a framework used to determine whether employers are adhering to federal laws on discrimination. The guidelines apply to most employment-related decisions, not just to the initial hiring process. The major means of compliance identified by the guidelines are: (1) no disparate impact and (2) job-related validation.

"No-Disparate-Impact" Approach

Under the guidelines, disparate impact is determined by the four-fifths rule. If the selection rate for any protected group is less than 80 percent (four-fifths) of the selection rate for the majority group or less than 80 percent of the group's representation in the relevant labor market, discrimination exists. Thus, the guidelines have attempted to define discrimination in statistical terms.

Job-Related Validation Approach

Under the job-related validation approach, virtually every factor used to make employment-related decisions—recruiting, selection, promotion, termination, discipline, and performance appraisal—must be shown to be specifically job-related. *Validity* is simply the extent to which a test actually measures what it says it measures. An employment test that is valid must accurately measure the person's ability to perform the job for which he or she is being hired.

The ideal condition for employment-related tests is to be both valid and reliable. *Reliability* refers to the consistency with which a test measures an item. For a test to be reliable, an individual's score should be about the same every time the individual takes the test (allowing for the effects of practice). Unless a test measures a trait consistently (or reliably), it is of little value in predicting job performance.

The 1978 Uniform Selection Guidelines recognize three types of validation:

- Content validity
- Criterion-related validity (concurrent and predictive)
- Construct validity

Content validity is a logical, nonstatistical method used to identify the knowledge, skills, and abilities (KSAs) and other characteristics necessary to perform a job. A test has content validity if it reflects an actual sample of the work done on the job in question.

There are two approaches to **criterion-related validity.** When an employer measures *concurrent* validity, a test is given to current employees and the scores are correlated with their job performance. A high correlation suggests that the test can differentiate between the better-performing employees and those with poor performance records. To measure *predictive* validity, the most statistically defensible form of validity, test results of applicants are compared with their subsequent job performance. However, predictive validity requires: (1) a fairly large number of people (usually at least 30) and (2) a time gap between the test and the performance (usually one year). As a result, predictive validity is not practical in many situations. Because of these and other problems, other types of validity often are used.

Construct validity shows a relationship between an abstract characteristic inferred from research and job performance, such as "motivation." These are called *constructs.* Examples of psychological constructs are job satisfaction and learning.

ELEMENTS OF EEO COMPLIANCE

Healthcare employers must comply with a variety of EEO regulations and guidelines. To do so, management should have an EEO policy statement and maintain all required EEO-related records.

EEO Policy Statement

It is critical that all healthcare employers have a written EEO policy statement. This policy should be widely communicated by posting it on bulletin boards, printing it in employee handbooks, reproducing it in organizational newsletters, and reinforcing it in training programs. The contents of the policy should clearly state the organizational commitment to equal employment, and incorporate the listing of the appropriate protected classes.

EEO Records

All employers with 15 or more employees are required to keep certain records that can be requested by the Equal Employment Opportunity Commission, the Office of Federal Contract Compliance Programs (OFCCP), or other state and local enforcement agencies. Under various laws, employers also are required to post an "officially approved notice" in a prominent place where employees can see it. This notice states that the employer is an equal opportunity employer and does not discriminate.

EEO Records Retention All employment records must be maintained as required by the EEOC. Required records include application forms and records concerning hiring, promotion, demotion, transfer, layoff, termination, rates of pay or other terms of compensation, and selection for training and apprenticeship. Even application forms or test papers completed by unsuccessful applicants may be requested. The length of time documents must be kept varies, but generally *three years is recommended as a minimum.* Complete records are necessary to enable an employer to respond should a charge of discrimination be made.

Annual Reporting Form The basic report that must be filed with the EEOC is the annual report form EEO–1. The following employers must file this report:

- All employers with 100 or more employees, except state and local governments
- Subsidiaries of other companies where total employees equal 100
- Federal contractors with at least 50 employees and contracts of $50,000 or more
- Financial institutions with at least 50 employees in which government funds are held or saving bonds are issued

The form requires employment data by job category, classified according to various protected classes.

Applicant Flow Data Under EEO laws and regulations, employers may be required to show that they do not discriminate in the recruiting and selection of members of protected classes. Because collection of racial data on application blanks and other preemployment records is not permitted, the EEOC allows employers to use a "visual" survey or a separate *applicant flow form* that is not used in the selection process. This form is filled out voluntarily by the *applicant,* and the data must be maintained separately from other selection-related materials. These analyses may be useful in showing whether an employer has underutilized a protected class because of an inadequate applicant flow of protected class members, in spite of special efforts to recruit them. Also, these data are reported as part of affirmative action plans that are filed with the OFCCP.

EEOC Investigation Process

When a discrimination complaint is received by the EEOC or similar agency, it must be processed. To handle a growing number of complaints, the EEOC has instituted a system that categorizes complaints into three categories: *priority, needing further investigation,* and *immediate dismissal.* If the EEOC decides to pursue a complaint, it uses the process outlined here. In certain cases where a complaint is filed with both the EEOC and the State Civil Rights Agency, the EEOC may request the state agency to investigate first. However, regardless of the state agency's findings, the EEOC may continue its involvement in the investigation.

Compliance Investigative Stages In a typical situation, an EEO complaint goes through several stages before the compliance process is completed. First, the charges are filed by an individual, a group of individuals, or their representative. A charge must be filed within 180 days of when the alleged discriminatory action occurred. Then the EEOC staff reviews the specifics of the charge to determine if it has *jurisdiction,* which means that the agency is authorized to investigate that type of charge. If jurisdiction exists, a notice of the charge must be served on the employer within 10 days after the filing; the employer is asked to respond. Following the charge notification, the EEOC's major effort turns to investigating the complaint.

During the investigation, the EEOC may interview the complainants, other employees, company managers, and supervisors. Also, it can request additional records and documents from the employer. Assuming that sufficient cause is found that alleged discrimination occurred, the next stage involves mediation efforts by the agency and the employer. **Mediation** is a dispute resolution process in which a trained mediator assists the parties in reaching a negotiated settlement. The EEOC has found that use of mediation has reduced its backlog of EEO complaints and has resulted in faster resolution of complaints.

If the employer agrees that discrimination has occurred and accepts the proposed settlement, then the employer posts a notice of relief within the company and takes the agreed-on actions. If the employer objects to the charge and rejects conciliation, the EEOC can file suit or issue a **right-to-sue letter** to the complainant. The letter notifies the complainant that he or she has 90 days in which to file a personal suit in federal court.

In the court litigation stage, a legal trial takes place in the appropriate state or federal court. At that point, both sides retain lawyers and rely on the court to render a decision. The Civil Rights Act of 1991 provides for *jury trials* in most EEO cases. If either party disagrees with the court ruling, either can file appeals with a higher court. The U.S. Supreme Court becomes the ultimate adjudication body.

Employer Responses to EEO Complaints

The general steps in responding effectively to an EEO complaint are outlined in Figure 4-7 and are crucial for effective HR management. Employers who vigorously investigate their employees' discrimination complaints before they are taken to outside agencies can control many problems and expenses associated with EEO complaints. An internal employee complaint system and prompt, thorough responses to problem situations are essential tools in reducing EEO charges and in remedying illegal discriminatory actions.

FIGURE 4-7   Stages in Responding to EEO Complaints

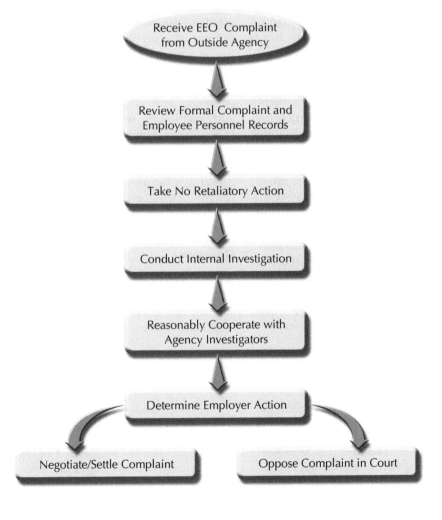

Harrison Family Practice Center (HFPC) is a 15 physician multispecialty clinic operating in five locations. In addition to the 15 physicians on staff, HFPC employs 80 individuals in clinical, administrative, and clerical support roles.

HFPC has an excellent reputation for providing quality care. The clinics' large patient base, combined with its ability to provide competent care, has resulted in financial stability and the ability to invest in state-of-the-art equipment and facilities. The management of HFPC includes a physician's CEO (elected to a five-year term by the board of directors), a practice administrator, and five department heads for the areas of clinic operations, labs, radiology, finance, and the business office.

Eight months ago, HFPC was involved in a sexual harassment lawsuit in which a former employee as the plaintiff prevailed and the jury awarded the plaintiff $500,000 in compensatory, punitive damages, and legal fees. The facts of the case included some disturbing issues about the work environment at HFPC. As disclosed during trial testimony, the plaintiff and her witnesses described an environment at HFPC where young, attractive females were continually subjected to sexual innuendos, suggestive comments, and jokes of a sexual nature by three of the HFPC physicians. Both current and past female employees of HFPC described behavior on the part of the defendants (three physicians) that was characterized as creating a hostile environment due to sexual harassment.

The attorneys for HFPC argued that the female plaintiff and others willingly participated in the sexual "banter" and had failed to advise the defendants that their behavior was making them uncomfortable or that they felt the physicians were creating a hostile environment. However, testimony from numerous terminated female employees indicated that they had disclosed their concerns to HFPC's administrative management, who did not take any action to stop the alleged harassment.

The trial and the verdict, although not front-page news, did receive some media coverage, and clearly HFPC's physicians and employees were well-aware of the proceedings. Many of them were deposed and/or interviewed by the plaintiff's or HFPC's attorneys. The trial and the verdict took a significant toll on the work attitudes of the physicians and employees and tarnished HFPC's otherwise unblemished reputation.

Questions

1. Describe the role of HR management in preventing sexual harassment.
2. Develop a plan for HFPC, going forward, to eliminate sexual harassment issues.

END NOTES

1. Adapted from Sharon M. Valente and Vern Bullough, "Sexual Harassment of Nurses in the Workplace," *Journal of Nursing Care Quality* (July/September 2004), 234–241; and "Woman Doctors Tell of Sex Harassment in Training," *Women's International Network News* (Spring 1993), 56; and Dorothy Kagehiro, "Sexual Harassment Litigation," *Employment Law Strategist* (September 11, 2004), 1.

2. "Court Orders Michigan Employment Agency to End Wholesale Discrimination," *Wall Street Journal* (May 2, 2000), 41.

3. Civil Rights Act of 1964, Title VII, Sec 703a.

4. *Gregg's v. Duke Power Co.,* 401 U.S. 424 (1971).

5. *Reevs v. Sanderson Plumbing Products, Inc.,* 530 U.S. 99-536 (June 12, 2000).

6. *O'Neal v. Ferguson Construction Co.,* 10th Ct. U.S. 99-2037 (January 24, 2001).

7. For details, see *http://www.dol.gov/esa/ofccp/.*

8. Peter Weil, "A Race/Ethnic Comparison of Career Attainments in Healthcare Management," *Healthcare Executive* (November/December 2003), 22–27.

9. David Burda "A Melting Pot It's Not," *Modern Healthcare* (August 11, 2003), 4, 6.

10. Caroll Lachnit, "Why Ethics is HR's Issue," *Workforce* (March 2002), 10.

11. Adapted from "Staffing Watch," *Hospitals and Health Networks* (January 2004), 24; and "Increasing and Sustaining Racial/Ethnic Diversity in Healthcare Management," Policy Statement American College of Healthcare Executives (March 2002).

12. *Arimindo v. Padlocker, Inc.,* 11th Cir, 99-4144 (April 20, 2000).

13. "Additional Pregnancy Bias Rulings," *Fair Employment Practices* (March 9, 2000), 78.

14. *EEOC v. Eastern Michigan University,* E.D. Michigan, 98-71806 (September 3, 1999).

15. *Harris v. Forklift Systems, Inc.,* 114S. Ct. 367 (1993).

16. "Provisions to Include Any ADEA Waivers," *HR Focus* (June 2002) 1.

17. Ruth I. Major, "Military Leave: An Employer's Obligation," *Franchising World* (January 2002), 52–53.

JOB DESIGN AND ANALYSIS

Learning Objectives

After you have read this chapter, you should be able to:

- Explain the relationship between productivity and job design.

- Describe the importance and typical uses of job analysis.

- List the common methods of job analysis.

- Identify the stages of the job analysis process.

- Define the elements of job descriptions and job specifications.

- Explain the relationship of Joint Commission on Accreditation of Healthcare Organizations (JCAHO) standards to job descriptions.

Healthcare HR Insight

From the beginning of the recent staffing shortage in healthcare, healthcare organizations of all types have had to be creative in order to attract and keep skilled workers. To do so requires a work environment that gives workers the time and tools to do what they do best, whether providing direct patient care, producing lab results, or evaluating diet plans.[1] Healthcare organizations that have successfully approached staff retention through job redesign initiatives include the following examples.

- An ambulatory surgery center in St. Paul, Minnesota, evaluated what was frustrating their surgical nurses and determined that nonpatient care duties, such as ordering supplies, were perceived as a negative. The center hired a purchasing specialist and shifted those duties away from the nurses, resulting in timelier ordering of supplies and nurses who could focus entirely on patient care duties.

- A hospital in Gainesville, Florida, installed a wireless phone system for the nurses' use in order to save nurses' time and allow them to interact more with patients. Now, instead of a call coming into a nursing station, and the clerk tracking the nurse down, the call goes directly to the nurse. Calls from physicians, the pharmacy, and labs don't have to wait.

- A skilled nursing facility in Cincinnati, Ohio, started utilizing social workers as an integral part of its patients' care teams. The faculty has successfully delegated many key family and hospital-to-nursing home transition communications and coordination duties that had been nursing duties to the social workers. This has freed nurses' time for direct patient care and has improved communication flow between the facility's residents, their families, and the hospitals caring for them.

All of these redesign initiatives required comprehensive job analysis in order to understand the work, the work flows, the inter- and intra-departmental interactions and communications, the outcomes, and other key aspects of the work.

Both employees and jobs in healthcare organizations are rapidly changing due to the service delivery expectations of the consumers of healthcare and the pressures to contain costs.[2] Two parts of dealing with those changes are job design and job analysis. Job design is logically arranging tasks and duties in a job to best get work done. A snapshot of what people are doing in their jobs currently is developed through formal job analysis, which aids in the development of job descriptions and job specifications. In addition, the information that comes from job analysis is the foundation for recruitment, selection, compensation, and many other HR activities.

ACCOMPLISHING STRATEGIC OBJECTIVES THROUGH JOB DESIGN

Analyzing what employees actually do in their jobs is vital to accomplishing the strategic objectives of healthcare organizations. Job design is a critical process, as is depicted in Figure 5-1.

As organizational objectives are planned and implemented, individual departments or functional areas are required to establish objectives that contribute to the accomplishment of the broader organizational objectives. These departmental objectives directly affect job design because job design ultimately outlines the duties and responsibilities that are required to accomplish the departmental objectives.

FIGURE 5-1   The Importance of Job Design

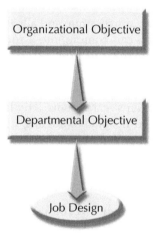

Productivity and Job Design

Job design refers to organizing tasks, duties, and responsibilities into a productive unit of work. It involves job content and the effect of jobs on employees. Identifying the components of a given job is an integral part of job design.

Job design can influence *performance* in many jobs, especially those where employee motivation can make a substantial difference. In healthcare organizations, job design can play an important role in the retention of key clinical employees. As an example, in response to the shortage of nurses and in an effort to reduce labor costs, clinics have adopted alternative staffing models by utilizing medical assistants instead of registered nurses to assist physicians in placing patients, taking histories and vitals, etc.[3]

Job design changes such as this can also affect *job satisfaction.* Jobs designed to take advantage of important job characteristics are more likely to be positively received by employees.[4] Such characteristics help distinguish between "good" and "bad" jobs. Many approaches to enhancing productivity and quality reflect efforts to expand some of the basic job characteristics.

Person/Job Fit   The person/job fit is a simple but important concept that involves matching the characteristics of people with the characteristics of jobs. Obviously, if a person does not fit a job, either the person can be replaced, or the job can be altered. In the past, it was much more common to try to make the "round" person fit the "square" job. However, "reshaping" people is not easy to do successfully.[5] By redesigning jobs, the person/job fit can be improved more easily. Jobs may be designed properly when they are first established or "reengineered" later.

FIGURE 5-2   Person-Job Fit

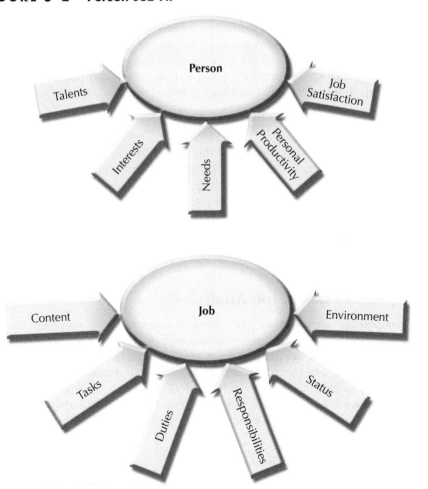

Nature of Job Analysis in Healthcare Organizations

The most basic building block of HR management, **job analysis,** is a systematic way to gather and analyze information about the content and human requirements of jobs and the context in which jobs are performed. Job analysis involves collecting information on the characteristics of a job that differentiate it from other jobs. Information that can be helpful in making that distinction includes the following:

- Work activities and behaviors
- Interactions with others
- Performance standards
- Financial and budgeting impact
- Equipment and technology used
- Working conditions
- Supervision given and received
- Necessary knowledge, skills, and abilities

Although the terms *job* and *position* are often used interchangeably, there is a slight difference in emphasis. A **job** is a grouping of common tasks, duties, and responsibilities. A **position** is a job performed by one person. Thus, if there are two people operating sterilization equipment, there are two positions (one for each person), but just one job (sterilization technician).

Task-Based Job Analysis

Job analysis based on what is done on the job, focuses on the tasks, duties, and responsibilities performed. A **task** is a distinct, identifiable work activity composed of motions, whereas a **duty** is a larger work segment composed of several tasks that are performed by an individual. Because both tasks and duties describe activities, it is not always easy or necessary to distinguish between the two. For example, if one of the employment supervisor's duties is to interview applicants, one task associated with that duty would be asking questions. The **job responsibilities** are obligations to perform certain tasks and duties.

Competency Based Job Analysis

The **competency approach** to job analysis focuses on the competencies that individuals need in order to perform jobs, rather than focusing on the tasks, duties, and responsibilities that compose a job. Instead of thinking of healthcare workers as having jobs that are relatively stable and that can be written up into typical job descriptions, it is more relevant to focus on the competencies used.[6] **Competencies** are basic characteristics that can be linked to enhanced performance by individuals or teams. Specific types of competencies include:

- Skill
- Ability
- Education
- Knowledge
- Training
- Licensure, certification, and/or registration

The competency approach also attempts to identify the hidden factors that are often critical to superior performance. For instance, many supervisors talk about employees' attitudes, but they have difficulty identifying what they mean by *attitude*. The competency approach uses some methodologies to help supervisors identify examples of what they mean by appropriate attitude and how those factors affect performance. Examples of common competencies often include the following:

- *General or Generic Competencies*—Characteristics required across all jobs in the organization, such as decision-making and problem-solving, professionalism and accountability, and customer service
- *Departmental Competencies*—Skills needed to provide care, treatment, or services within a department or unit and which apply to all employees in that department or unit; for example, providing care to residents with dementia on a unit in a skilled nursing home
- *Job-specific Competencies*—Competencies related to specific tasks, such as performing a specific procedure, and using particular equipment or technology
- *Cultural Competencies*—A set of attitudes, skills, and behaviors that allow an individual to work respectfully and effectively with patients and colleagues in a culturally diverse work environment[7]

Joint Commission Standards and Job Analysis

The JCAHO recognizes the importance of job design and job analysis in the development of staffing plans and organizational competence systems. Development of employees focuses on enhancing all their needed competencies, rather than preparing them for moving to specific jobs. In this way, they can develop capabilities useful in their jobs as changes occur.

Healthcare organizations that subscribe to the JCAHO standards and review process must establish staffing plans and a competency system. Both staffing plans and a competency system require significant attention to job design and analysis.

The **HR** and **leadership standards** relating to HR planning require the leaders of healthcare organizations to analyze their staffing needs and provide the appropriate types and sufficient number of staff to meet care needs. The HR and leadership standards relating to the establishment of a competency system expect the leaders of an organization to develop and maintain a system that ensures the following:

- Recruitment, employment, and retention of competent healthcare workers
- Ongoing assessment of staff competency
- Ability of the organization to maintain and increase staff knowledge in performance of their jobs

The foundation for these HR and leadership standards is job design and analysis. Job analysis—discovering how people's jobs are being done—is a critical element of maintaining staff competence, which is done by defining job qualifications, competencies, and performance expectations.

USES OF JOB ANALYSIS

Healthcare HR managers use job analysis as the foundation for a number of other HR activities. Job analysis provides an objective basis for hiring, evaluating, training, accommodating, and supervising persons with disabilities, as well as improving the efficiency of the organization. It is a logical process to determine the following:

- *Purpose*—The reason for the job
- *Essential Functions*—The job duties that are critical or fundamental to the performance of the job
- *Job Setting*—The work station and conditions where the essential functions are performed
- *Job Qualifications*—The minimal skills an individual must possess to perform the essential functions

The process of analyzing jobs in organizations requires planning of several factors. As Figure 5-3 indicates, some of these considerations include the analysis of how it is to be done, who provides data, and who conducts the analysis and uses the data so that job descriptions and job specifications can be prepared and reviewed. Once those decisions are made, then several results are linked to a wide range of HR activities. The most fundamental use of job analysis is to provide the information necessary to develop job descriptions and specifications.

In most cases, the job description and job specifications are combined into one document that contains several different sections. A brief overview of each follows next; a more detailed discussion appears later in the chapter.

A **job description** is a document that indicates the tasks, duties, and responsibilities of a job. It identifies what is done, why it is done, where it is done, and—briefly—how it is done.

Performance standards should flow directly from a job description, telling what the job accomplishes and how performance is measured in key areas of the job description. If employees know what is expected and how performance is to be measured, they have a much better chance of performing satisfactorily.

While the job description describes activities to be done in the job, the **job specifications** list the knowledge, skills, and abilities (KSAs) an individual needs to perform a job satisfactorily. KSAs include education, experience, work skill requirements, personal abilities, and mental and physical requirements. It is important to note that accurate job specifications identify what KSAs a person needs to do the job, not necessarily what qualifications the current employee possesses.

Job Families, Departments, and Organization Charts

Once all jobs in the organization have been identified, it is often helpful to group the jobs into job families and display them on an organization chart. There are

FIGURE 5-3   Decisions in the Job Analysis Process

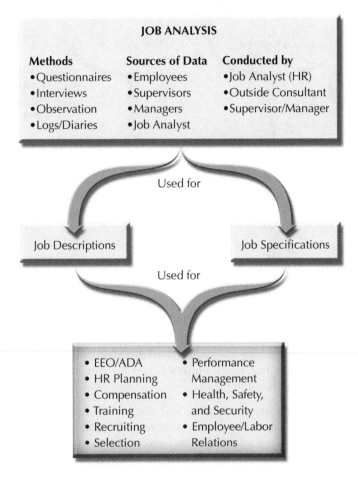

various ways of identifying and grouping job families. A **job family** is a grouping of jobs with similar characteristics. In identifying job families, significant emphasis is placed on measuring the similarity of jobs. A **department** depicts a distinct grouping of organizational responsibilities.

An **organization chart** depicts the relationships among jobs in an organization. Organization charts have traditionally been hierarchical and have shown the reporting relationships for authority and responsibilities. In most organizations, these charts can help clarify who reports to whom.

Job Analysis and HR Activities

The completion of job descriptions and job specifications, based on job analysis, is at the heart of many other HR activities, as Figure 5-4 indicates. But even if

FIGURE 5-4 Job Analysis and Other HR Activities

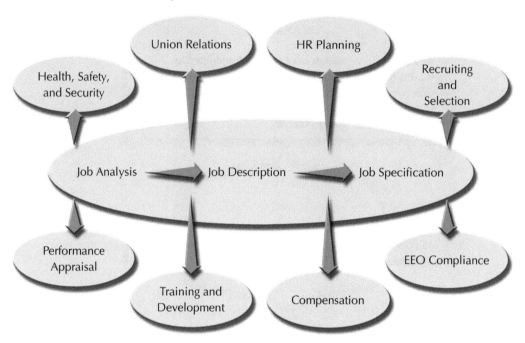

legal requirements did not force employers to do job analysis, effective HR management would demand it.

HR Planning HR planning requires auditing of current jobs. Current job descriptions provide the basic details necessary for this internal assessment, including such items as the jobs available, current number of jobs and positions, and reporting relationships of the jobs. By identifying the functions currently being performed and calculating the time being spent to perform them, managers and HR specialists can redesign jobs to eliminate unnecessary tasks and combine responsibilities where desirable.

Recruiting and Selection Equal employment opportunity (EEO) guidelines clearly require a sound and comprehensive job analysis to validate recruiting and selection criteria. Without a systematic investigation of a job, an employer may be using requirements that are not specifically job-related. Organizations use job analysis to identify job specifications necessary for obtaining qualified employees for anticipated job openings, whether recruited internally or externally.

EEO Compliance Many aspects of EEO compliance require accurate and verifiable job analysis information. Job analysis is critical in determining the essential functions of a job, and deciding what the necessary qualifications are for a job. This information is crucial for use in the selection process in a nondiscriminatory manner.[8]

Compensation   Job analysis information is vital when determining compensation. As part of identifying appropriate compensation, job analysis information is used to determine job content for *internal* comparisons of responsibilities and *external* comparisons with the compensation paid by competing employers. Information from job analysis can be used to give more weight, and therefore more pay, to jobs with more difficult tasks, duties, and responsibilities.

Training and Development   By defining which activities make up a job, the analysis helps the supervisor explain that job to new employees. Information from job descriptions and job specifications can also help in career planning by showing employees what is expected in jobs that they may choose in the future. Job specification information can point out areas in which employees might need to develop in order to further their careers.

Performance Appraisal   Using performance standards to compare what an employee is supposed to be doing with what the person actually has done, a supervisor can determine the employee's performance level. The **performance appraisal** process should then tie to the job description and performance standards.[9] Developing clear, realistic performance standards can also reduce communication problems in performance appraisal feedback among managers, supervisors, and employees.

Safety and Health   Job analysis information is useful in identifying possible job hazards and working conditions associated with jobs. From the information gathered, managers and HR specialists can work together to identify the health and safety equipment needed, specify work methods, and train workers.

Union Relations   Where workers are represented by a labor union, job analysis is used in several ways. First, job analysis information may be needed to determine whether the job should be covered by the union agreements. Second, it is common in unionized environments for job descriptions to be very specific about what tasks are and are not covered in a job. Finally, well-written and specific job descriptions can reduce the number of grievances filed by workers.

WORK SCHEDULES AND JOB ANALYSIS

A job consists of the tasks an employee does, the relationships required on the job, the tools the employee works with, and many other elements. Considerations that increasingly affect job design for both healthcare employers and employees are the time during which work is scheduled and the location of employees when working.

The pressures of employees' lives, coupled with the demands of their jobs, can lead to emotional imbalances that are collectively labeled *stress*. The main causes of job-related stress appear to be time pressures, fears of losing a job, deadlines, and fragmented work. The increasing use of technology means that many employees are "always on call" and can "burn out" on work. All exist in many aspects of the healthcare work environments. How employees view the demands of work have been identified in a study that found the following:[10]

- More than half of U.S. workers (52 percent) say they would be willing to have an extra day off a week instead of a day's pay.
- Over 80 percent wish they had more time to spend with family, and this view is shared among adults with and without children.
- About 60 percent feel pressure to work too much.

To respond to stress and other concerns, healthcare organizations are using different work schedule alternatives, flexible scheduling, and telework. Healthcare work schedules associated with different jobs vary widely. Some jobs must be performed during "normal" daily work hours and workdays, and some jobs require working nights, weekends, and extended hours.

Work Schedule Alternatives

The traditional work schedule in the United States, in which employees work 8 hours a day, 5 days a week at the employer's place of operation, is in transition. In healthcare organizations, workers' schedules are driven by patient care needs or the support requirements of healthcare delivery. Every conceivable permutation of work schedule exists throughout the healthcare industry, including the 4-day, 40-hour week; the 4-day, 32-hour week; the 3-day week; shift work and the compressed workweek; flexible scheduling; and job sharing.

Shift Work and the Compressed Workweek

Shift work is a commonly used work schedule design. Healthcare organizations such as acute care hospitals, nursing homes or hospice care providers need 24-hour coverage and therefore schedule three 8-hour shifts each day. Many of these employers provide some form of additional pay, called a *shift differential,* for working the evening or night shift. Shift work has been found to increase the number of workplace accidents, with employees who work the "graveyard" shift (11 P.M. to 7 A.M.) having 20 percent more accidents and five times as many work-related mistakes.[11] Also, shift work has long been known to cause difficulties for many employees with families. However, the types of providers noted above have no choice but to staff these shifts.

One type of shift work is the **compressed workweek,** in which a full week's work is accomplished in fewer than five eight-hour days. Compression simply alters the number of hours an employee works each day, usually resulting in more work hours each day and fewer workdays each week. The use of the compressed workweek illustrates how greater flexibility in work schedules is occurring.

Compressed workweeks have proven to be an especially successful staffing approach in healthcare organizations. Many hospitals or other types of healthcare facilities that require 24-hour weekend coverage utilize an approach scheduling and compensation referred to as the "Baylor Plan." The approach, named after the Baylor University Medical Center that first introduced it, schedules and compensates healthcare workers as full-time employees for working three 12-hour shifts starting on Friday on the second shift and concluding on Sunday on the third shift. This approach to scheduling has proven to be a successful recruitment and retention approach for healthcare workers for difficult to staff schedules.

Flexible Scheduling

Flexible work schedules allow healthcare organizations to make better use of workers by matching work demands to work hours. One type of flexible scheduling is **flextime,** in which employees work a set number of hours a day but vary starting and ending times. In another variation, employees work 30 minutes longer Monday through Thursday, take short lunch breaks, and leave work at 1 P.M. or 2 P.M. on Friday.

Flexible scheduling allows management to relax some of the traditional "time clock" control of employees, while still covering workloads. In the United States, over 30 percent of the full-time workforce vary their work hours from those in the traditional model, more than double the rate a decade ago. Also, over 60 percent of workers surveyed indicated that they had at least some control over their work schedules.[12]

Job Analysis and Legal Issues

Permeating the discussion of equal employment laws, regulations, and court cases in preceding chapters is the concept that legal compliance must focus on the jobs that individuals perform. The 1978 Uniform Selection Guidelines make it clear that HR requirements must be tied to specific job-related factors if employers are to defend their actions as a business necessity.

Americans with Disabilities Act (ADA)

ADA has increased the emphasis on job analysis, job descriptions, and job specifications. Healthcare organizations must identify how physical aspects of jobs are determined. Given that many service workers and technical/professional employees in healthcare perform significant physical work, the job analysis process must accurately define essential functions for two reasons: First, the job analysis process must appropriately define the physical requirements to ensure safe performance of the job duties for both the employee doing the job and the patients they care for. Second, the physical requirements of the essential functions must be accurately determined to facilitate nondiscriminatory hiring decisions.

In determining **essential functions,** the fundamental job duties of the employment position that an individual with a disability holds or desires must be evaluated. A useful approach is to answer the following questions:

1. What are the three or four major activities that actually constitute the job? Is each necessary? For example a medical receptionist must check-in-patients, collect insurance information, answer phones, and schedule patients for future appointments. In this case, each task is necessary.

2. What is the relationship among the tasks? Is there a special sequence that the tasks must follow?

3. Do the tasks necessitate sitting, standing, crawling, walking, climbing, running, stooping, kneeling, lifting, carrying, writing, operating, pushing, pulling, fingering, talking, listening, interpreting, analyzing, seeing, coordinating, or other physical activities?

4. How many other employees are available to perform the job function? Can that function be done by any other employees?

5. How much time is spent on the job performing each particular function? Are the tasks performed less frequently as important as those done more frequently?

6. Would removing a function fundamentally alter the job?

7. What happens if a task is not completed on time?

Having identified the essential job functions through a job analysis, an employer must be prepared to make reasonable accommodations. Again, the core job duties and KSAs must be considered, as Figure 5-5 highlights these considerations.

FIGURE 5-5   Determining Essential and Marginal Job Functions

CONSIDERATIONS	ESSENTIAL FUNCTIONS	MARGINAL FUNCTIONS
Percentage of time spent on task	Significant percentage of time, often 20 percent or more, is spent on task.	Generally less than 10 percent of time is spent on task.
Frequency of task	Task is performed regularly: daily, weekly, or monthly.	Task is performed infrequently or when substituting in part of another job.
Importance of task	Task affects other parts of job and other jobs.	Task is unrelated to job, and there are few consequences if not performed.

Job Analysis and Wage/Hour Regulations

Typically, job analysis identifies the percentage of time spent on each duty in a job. This information helps determine whether someone should be classified as exempt or non-exempt under the wage/hour laws.

As will be noted in Chapter 12, the Federal Fair Labor Standards Act (FLSA) and most state wage/hour laws indicate that the percentage of time employees spend on manual, routine, or clerical duties affects whether they must be paid overtime for hours worked in excess of 40 a week. To be exempt from overtime, the employees must perform their *primary duties* as executive, administrative, professional, or outside sales employees. *Primary* has been interpreted to mean occurring at least 50 percent of the time.

Other legal-compliance efforts, such as those involving workplace safety and health, can also be aided through the data provided by job analysis. In summary, it is extremely difficult for an employer to have a legal staffing system without performing formal job analysis.

ETHICAL PRACTICES AND COMPLIANCE

Meeting wage and hour regulations has been an especially difficult task for healthcare organizations. For instance, many different professional category clinical positions, such as RNs and pharmacists, in healthcare organizations could meet the wage and hour tests for exemption from the act; yet, a significant number of these organizations treat employees in these positions as non-exempt. This usually occurs because of the variability in hours that the RNs or pharmacists are required to work and the need to pay them overtime as an inducement to work beyond their regular shift, rather than because of a legal requirement to do so. Meeting the requirements of the Fair Labor Standards Act (FLSA) by appropriately designating whether the analyzed job is exempt under the act or non-exempt is extremely important. The revisions to the FLSA in 2004 provided much needed clarity for healthcare jobs that can be treated as exempt. Misclassification could result in significant back pay awards to the misclassified employees.

For many healthcare organizations it could be expedient and less costly to treat a non-exempt worker as exempt to avoid the additional record-keeping requirements and expense of paying overtime wages required by the FLSA. Additionally, unless an aggrieved worker files a complaint with the Wage and Hour Department of the Federal Labor Department or a similar state agency there is every likelihood the practice would go undetected. Many workers don't fully understand the wage and hour rules, and even if they did, might be reluctant to openly challenge their classification for fear of reprisal. However, this is clearly a case where healthcare HR professionals have the responsibility to act ethically and comply with the law to ensure that their organizations are classifying and paying their workers appropriately.

HUMAN REACTIONS TO JOB ANALYSIS

Behavioral Aspects of Job Analysis

Job analysis involves determining what the "core" job is. A detailed examination of jobs, although necessary, sometimes can be a demanding and disruptive experience for both managers and employees. These problems occur because job analysis may identify the differences between what duties currently are being performed in some jobs and what *should* be done. Consequently, a number of behavioral factors can affect job analysis, some of which are discussed next.

"Inflation" of Jobs and Job Titles

Employees and managers have some tendency to inflate the importance and significance of their jobs. Because job analysis information is used for compensation purposes, both managers and employees hope that "puffing up" jobs will result in higher pay levels and greater "status" for resumes and more possible promotion opportunities.

Titles of jobs often get inflated, too.[13] Some healthcare organizations give inflated titles in place of pay raises, and others do it to keep well-paid employees from leaving for "status" reasons. As an example, it is not unusual for healthcare organizations to use the titles *manager* or *director* for individuals that do not supervise other employees. Giving these individuals a title that denotes leadership is typically done for status reasons.

Employee and Managerial Anxieties

Both managers and employees have concerns about job analysis. Through the information developed in a job analysis, the job description is ideally supposed to identify the nature of a job. However, it is difficult to capture all facets of a job, particularly for jobs in which employees perform a variety of duties and operate with a high degree of independence, such as the assistant administrator at a small rural hospital who performs accounting, human resources, and facilities management duties.

Managerial Straitjacket   One primary concern of managers and supervisors is that the job analysis and job descriptions will unrealistically limit managerial flexibility. As healthcare workloads and demands change rapidly, managers and supervisors want to be able to move duties to other employees, cross-train employees, and have more dynamic, flexible ways to get work accomplished. If job descriptions are written restrictively, some employees may use an omission to limit managerial flexibility. The resulting attitude, "It's not in my job description," puts a straitjacket on a manager. In some healthcare organizations with unionized workforces, very restrictive job descriptions exist. Because of such difficulties, the final statement in many job descriptions is a *miscellaneous clause,* which consists of a phrase similar to "Performs other duties as assigned by the immediate supervisor." This statement covers unusual situations that may occur in an employee's job. However, duties covered by this phrase cannot be considered essential functions under the ADA.

Employee Fears   One fear that employees may have concerns the purpose of a detailed investigation of their job. Perhaps they feel that such a detailed look means someone thinks they have done something wrong. The attitude behind such a fear might be, "As long as no one knows precisely what I am supposed to be doing, I am safe."

Also, some employees may fear that an analysis of their jobs will put a strait-jacket on them, limiting their creativity and flexibility by formalizing their duties. However, analyzing a job does not necessarily limit job scope or depth. In fact, having a well-written, well-communicated job description can assist employees by clarifying their roles and the expectations within those roles.[14] One effective way to handle anxieties is to involve the employees in the revision process.

JOB ANALYSIS METHODS

Job analysis information can be gathered in a variety of ways. Common methods are observation, interviews, questionnaires, and specialized methods of analysis. Combinations of these approaches frequently are used, depending on the situation and the organization. Each of these methods is discussed in some detail in the following sections.

Observation

When the observation method is used, a manager, job analyst, or industrial engineer observes the individual performing the job and takes notes to describe the tasks and duties performed. Observation may be continuous or based on intermittent sampling. Use of the observation method is limited because many jobs do not have complete and easily observed job duties or complete job cycles. Thus, observation may be more useful for repetitive jobs and in conjunction with other methods.

Interviews

The interview method of gathering information requires that a manager or HR specialist visit each job site and talk with the employees performing each job. A standardized interview form is used most often to record the information. Frequently, both the employee and the employee's supervisor must be interviewed to obtain a complete understanding of the job. The interview method can be quite time-consuming, especially if the interviewer talks with two or three employees doing each job. Professional and managerial jobs often are more complicated to analyze and usually require longer interviews. For these reasons, combining the interview with one of the other methods is suggested.

Questionnaires

Job analysis questionnaires are a widely used method of gathering data on jobs. Survey instruments are developed and given to employees and managers to complete. The major advantage of the questionnaire method is that information on a large number of jobs can be collected inexpensively in a relatively short period of time. However, the questionnaire method assumes that employees can accurately analyze and communicate information about their jobs. Employees may vary in their perceptions of the jobs, and even in their ability to read and understand the questionnaire. For these reasons, the questionnaire method is usually combined with interviews and observations to clarify and verify the questionnaire information.

Computerized Job Analysis

As computer technology has expanded, researchers have developed computerized job analysis systems. An important feature of computerized job analysis sources is the specificity of data that can be gathered. All of this specific data is compiled into a job analysis database. A computerized job analysis system often can reduce the time and effort involved in writing job descriptions. These systems have banks of job duty statements that relate to each of the tasks and scope statements of the questionnaires.

THE JOB ANALYSIS PROCESS

The process of job analysis must be conducted in a logical manner, following appropriate management and professional psychometric practices. Therefore, a multistage process usually is followed, regardless of the job analysis methods used. The stages for a typical job analysis are outlined here, but they may vary with the methods used and the number of jobs included. Figure 5-6 illustrates the basic stages of the process.

Planning

It is crucial that the job analysis process be planned before gathering data from managers and employees. Probably the most important consideration is to identify the objectives of the job analysis. Maybe the main objective is to update job descriptions. Or, it may include revising the compensation programs in the organization based on the outcome. Another objective could be to redesign the jobs in a department or division of the organization or to change the structure in parts of the organization to align it better with new organizational strategies. As cost-containment and staffing issues have required revising strategies and plans, job analysis has proven to be an important tool to aid in implementing new initiatives or reducing staffing costs.

Preparation and Communication

Preparation consists of identifying the jobs under review. Another task in the identification phase is to review existing documentation. Existing job descriptions, organization charts, previous job analysis information, and other industry-related resources all may be useful to review. A crucial step is to communicate

FIGURE 5-6   Stages in the Job Analysis Process

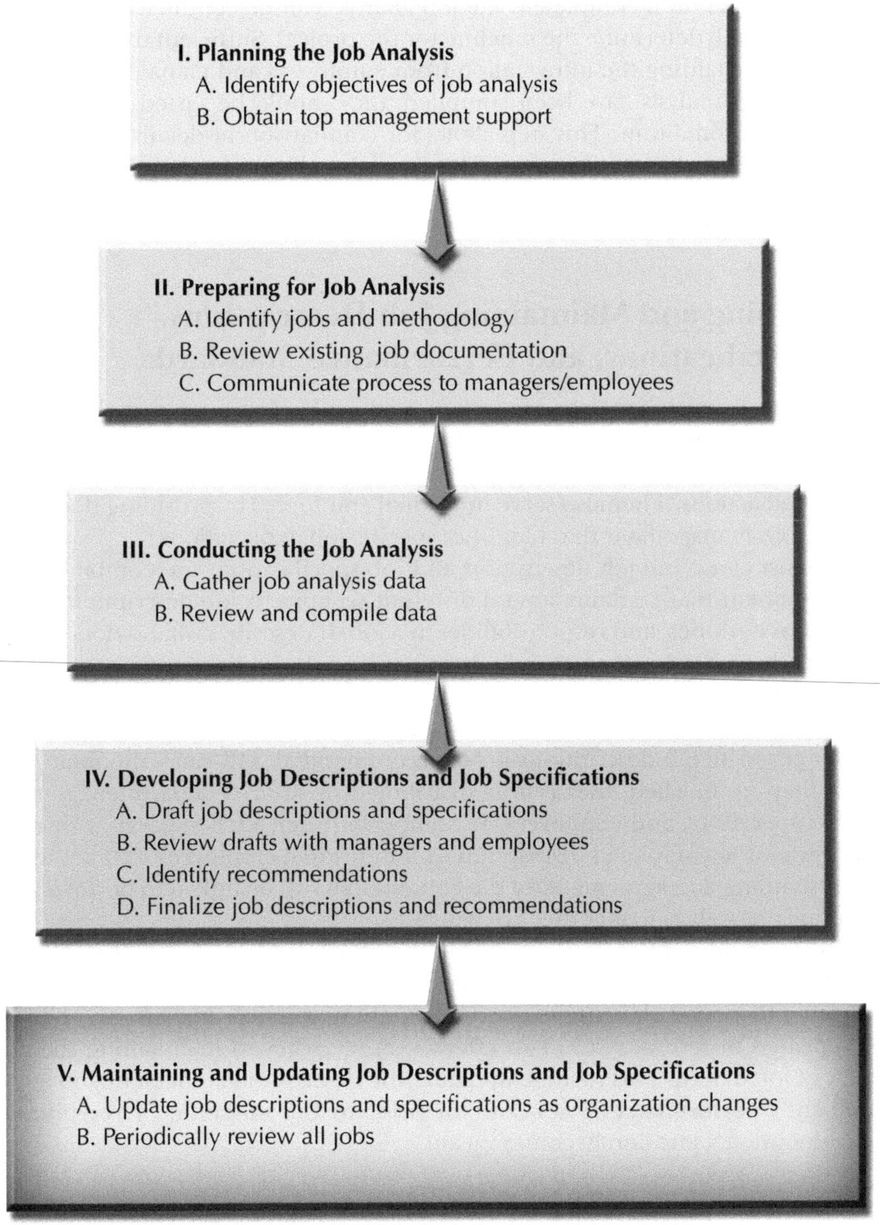

I. Planning the Job Analysis
    A. Identify objectives of job analysis
    B. Obtain top management support

II. Preparing for Job Analysis
    A. Identify jobs and methodology
    B. Review existing job documentation
    C. Communicate process to managers/employees

III. Conducting the Job Analysis
    A. Gather job analysis data
    B. Review and compile data

IV. Developing Job Descriptions and Job Specifications
    A. Draft job descriptions and specifications
    B. Review drafts with managers and employees
    C. Identify recommendations
    D. Finalize job descriptions and recommendations

V. Maintaining and Updating Job Descriptions and Job Specifications
    A. Update job descriptions and specifications as organization changes
    B. Periodically review all jobs

and explain the process to managers, affected employees, and other concerned people, such as union stewards. Explanations should address the natural concerns and anxieties people have when someone puts their jobs under close scrutiny and should anticipate issues likely to arise.

Conducting the Job Analysis

With the preparation completed, the job analysis can be conducted. The methods selected will determine the timeline for the project. Sufficient time should be allotted for obtaining the information from employees and managers. Once details from job analysis have been compiled, they should be sorted by job family and organizational unit. This step allows for comparison of details from similar jobs throughout the organization. The data also should be reviewed for completeness, and follow-up may be needed in the form of additional interviews of managers and employees.

Developing and Maintaining Job Descriptions, Job Specifications, and Performance Standards

The output from the analysis of a job is used to develop a job description, job specifications, and performance standards. Together, they summarize job analysis information into a readable format and provide the basis for legally defensible job-related actions. They also serve individual employees by providing documentation from management that identifies specific job expectations.

In most cases, the job description and job specifications are combined into one document that contains several different sections. A job description identifies the tasks, duties, and responsibilities in a job. It describes what is done, why it is done, where it is done, and briefly, how it is done. It should identify areas where clarification is needed.

Generally, healthcare organizations have found that having managers and employees write job descriptions is not recommended. HR can write them, and when they are finished, they can be distributed by the HR department to managers, supervisors, and employees. It is important that each supervisor or manager review the completed description with individual employees so that there is understanding and agreement on the content that will be linked to performance appraisals, as well as to all other HR activities.

Once job descriptions and specifications have been completed and reviewed by all appropriate individuals, a system must be developed for keeping them current. Otherwise, the entire process, beginning with job analysis, may have to be repeated in several years. Two effective approaches to maintaining the currency of job descriptions include updating the description coincidental to an incumbent's performance review and/or prior to the initiation of recruitment activities when a position becomes vacant.

JOB DESCRIPTION COMPONENTS

ADA focused attention on the importance of well-written job descriptions. Legal compliance requires that they accurately represent the actual jobs. Job titles should be descriptive of job functions performed. There is a real art to writing job descriptions that are sufficiently clear without being overly detailed. A typical job description, such as the one depicted in Figure 5-7, contains several major parts. Overviews of the most common components are presented next.

Identification

The first part of the job description is the identification section, in which the job title, reporting department, relationships, location, and FLSA status analysis may be given. Usually, it is advisable to note other information that is useful in tracking jobs and employees through a human resource information system.

General Summary

The second part is the general summary, which is a concise statement of the general responsibilities and components that make the job different from others. One HR specialist has characterized the general summary statement as follows: "In thirty words or less, describe the essence of the job."

Essential Functions and Duties

The third part of the typical job description lists the essential functions and duties. It contains clear, precise statements on the major tasks, duties, and responsibilities performed. Writing this section is the most time-consuming aspect of preparing job descriptions. The general format for an essential function statement is: (1) *action verb*, (2) *what it applies to*, (3) *how the information is obtained*, (4) *how, why and how often.*

The language of the ADA has stressed the importance of arranging job duties so that the most essential (in criticality and amount of time spent) be listed first and the supportive or marginal duties listed later. Within that framework, specific functional duties should be grouped and arranged in some logical pattern. If a job requires an accounting supervisor to prepare several reports, among other functions, statements relating to the preparation of reports should be grouped together. The *miscellaneous clause* typically listed last is included to assure some managerial flexibility.

Job Specifications

The next portion of the job description gives the qualifications needed to perform the job satisfactorily. The job specifications typically are stated as: (1) knowledge, skills, and abilities, (2) education and experience, and (3) physical requirements and working conditions. The components of the job specifications provide information necessary to determine what accommodations might and might not be possible under ADA regulations.

Job specifications can be developed from a variety of information sources. Obviously, the job analysis process provides the primary starting point. But any KSA included must be based on what is really needed to perform a job. Furthermore, the job specifications listed should reflect what is necessary for satisfactory job performance, not what the ideal candidate would have. In light of the ADA,

FIGURE 5-7 **Sample Job Description**

Title: Health Information Clerk   Pay Grade: Nonexempt, Hourly
Department: Medical Records   Date Approved: 3/15/2006
Supervisor: Medical Records Supervisor

Job Summary: Maintain patients' electronic medical records. Provide electronic files.

Job Accountabilities:

*E/M/NA	%Time	Description
E	35%	Maintains confidentiality of medical records. Controls access to electronic files.
M	30%	Batches patient information into the computer and retrieve patient demographic data.
E	20%	Inputs information such as progress notes, laboratory reports, X-ray results, and correspondence into patient charts.
E	5%	Creates new records.
E	5%	Releases patient information to requesting parties following established confidentiality procedures. Answers patient inquiries for laboratory results.
M	3%	Makes copies of dictated reports and forward as indicated.
M	2%	Answers telephones and greet patients. Schedules patient appointments.
		Performs other related duties as assigned or requested. The organization reserves the right to add or change duties at any time.

*Select E (Essential), M (Marginal) or NA (Non-Applicable) to denote importance of each job function to position.

it is crucial that the physical and mental dimensions of each job be clearly identified. If lifting, stooping, standing, walking, climbing, or crawling is required, it should be noted. Also, weights to be lifted should be specified, along with specific visual and hearing requirements of jobs.

Performance Standards and Competencies

Performance standards and competencies can flow directly from the job description and indicate what the job accomplishes and how performance is measured in

FIGURE 5-7   Sample Job Description (*continued*)

Job Specifications

Skills: Administrative
Understand and apply policies and procedures.   Prioritize different projects.
Assemble and organize numerical data.   Read handwritten text.
Answer telephones.

Education and Experience
Minimum education: Less than high school   Preferred education: High
                                                       school or equivalent
Preferred experience: 6–12 months   Preferred field-of-expertise:
                                                       Medical records

Physical Requirements

Physical Requirements	Rarely 0–12%	Occasionally 12–33%	Frequently 34–60%	Regularly 67–100%
Seeing—Reading reports, filing				X
Hearing—Communicating with coworkers				X
Standing/walking			X	
Climbing/stooping/kneeling			X	
Lifting/pulling/pushing			X	
Fingering/grasping/feeling— Writing, typing, and using telephone			X	

Skills: Computer Software ___X___   Scanning Equipment ___X___
       Fax ___X___

The above statements are intended to describe the general nature and level of work being
performed. They are not intended to be construed as an exhaustive list of all responsibilities,
duties, and skills required of personnel so classified and do not create an employment contract.

SIGNATURES

Employee: _____ Date: _____

Supervisor: _____ Date: _____

key areas of the job description. In compliance with JCAHO standards, many
healthcare organizations have adopted an approach of combining the job description with performance and competency assessment. The reason for including the performance standards and competencies is clear. If employees know what
is expected, how performance is to be measured, and what competencies are required, they have a much better chance of performing satisfactorily. Figure 5-8
shows job description duty statements and some performance standards used for
a Central Sterile Manager in a hospital as an example.

FIGURE 5-8 **Sample Job Duty Statements and Performance Standards**

Job Title: Central Sterile Manager
Supervisor: Director of Surgical Operations

DUTY	PERFORMANCE STANDARDS
Develop, review, evaluate, and ensure the implementation of a central sterilization process for the surgery department.	• Monitor and forecast workload of department and recommend staffing levels to director to meet workload requirement. • Prepare annual budget for department. • Ensure appropriate review and evaluation of hospital procedures and sterilization equipment as they pertain to infection control.
Identify sterilization problems and outcomes, and document and recommend corrective actions.	• Follow all related departmental policies, procedures, guidelines, and standards in carrying out technical functions. • Perform routine and specialized environmental checks per departmental guidelines. • Ensure new equipment meets standards of sterilization and infection control.

Disclaimer and Approvals

The final section on many job descriptions contains approval signatures by appropriate managers and a legal disclaimer. This disclaimer allows employers to change employees' job duties or request employees to perform duties not listed, so that the job description is not viewed as a "contract" between the employer and the employee.

Because healthcare organizations are changing and jobs vary in different organizations, managers and employees alike are finding that designing and analyzing jobs requires greater attention than in the past. Understanding the work done in the organization must be based on the analysis of facts and data, not just the personal perceptions of managers, supervisors, and employees.

CASE

Orange County Pediatric Medical Center (OCPMC) had acquired three physician practices in its service area to broaden its ability to provide primary care. Based on extensive studies, the Center was confident that it could reduce the costs of operations at these practices by consolidating and centralizing business activities. These business activities include accounting and finance, billing, purchasing and materials management, and facilities maintenance. Additionally, the Center would be able to spread the general costs of administration over the three facilities.

After nearly six months of operating these three new acquisitions, OCPMC's financial analysis found very poor budgetary results had occurred. All three practices were over budget by more than 10 percent, and projections were for even larger shortfalls. The most significant budgetary issue was labor costs.

In further analyzing the problem, the main issue appeared to be the staffing mix of MDs, RNs, and assistive (nonlicensed) personnel. When the practices were acquired, the staffing mix was a simple combination of MDs and nonlicensed medical assistants. When OCPMC took over the practices, it changed the staffing mix to include RNs. This was consistent with the staffing model in the other clinics OCPMC currently owned and operated. The budgetary problem was directly related to the increased expense of the RNs wages.

OCPMC decided to evaluate the care delivery processes and the skill sets necessary at these clinics to determine if the staffing mix could be changed. The HR department was requested to undertake a job analysis, consider alternative job designs, and make recommendations.

Questions

1. Outline the steps that should be taken to evaluate the work at the practices to determine the appropriate staffing mix.
2. What methods of job analysis would be most effective for this assignment?

END NOTES

1. Adapted from Anna Hayburst, Coleen Saylor, Diane Stuenkel, "Work Environmental Factors and Retention of Nurses," *Journal of Nursing Care Quality* (July/September 2005), 283–288; and Terese Hudson-Thrall, "Work Redesign," *Hospital and Health Networks* (March 2003), 34.
2. Michael E. Chernew, Peter D. Jacobson, Timothy P. Hofer, Keith D. Arnoson, and A. Mack Fendrick, "Barriers to Constraining Health Care Cost Growth," *Health Affairs* (November/December 2004), 122–128.
3. For more information on Clinic and Physician Group staffing models see *http://www.mgma.org.*
4. American Hospital Association, "Foster Meaningful Work," *Workforce Ideas in Action 2,* (September 2003), 3.
5. Adrian Savage, "Who Needs Superstars?" *Across the Board* (March/April 2004), 31–33.
6. "Strategies for Continuous Compliance—Meeting Challenging Competency Requirements." *Joint Commission: The Source 2* (January 2004), 3–4.
7. Joint Commission Resources, Inc., "Improving Healthcare Quality and Safety,"

Issues in Human Resources for Hospitals (2004), 21–25.
8. For a detailed explanation of the EEOC's Job Analysis Requirements, see *http://www.eeoc.gov/policy/docs/accommodation.html#reasonable.*
9. Kathy Gogne, "Using Performance Management to Support an Organization's Strategic Business Plan," *Employment Relations Today* (Winter 2002), 26–34.
10. "Poll Shows Americans Eager to Take Back Their Time," *Newsline* (October 6, 2003), accessed at *http://www.timeday.com.*
11. "Acacia Acquire Health in Extended Hours Operation: Understanding the challenges, Implementing Solutions" (2003), *http://www.circadian.com.*
12. Families and Work Institute (2002), *http://www.familiesandwork.com.*
13. Patrick Shannon and Bob Miller, "What's in a Title?" *WorldatWork Journal* (Fourth Quarter 2003), 26–34.
14. Merrie Spath, "Expanding Your Job Description," *Risk Management* (October 2002), 56.

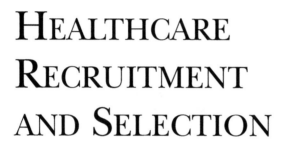

HEALTHCARE RECRUITMENT AND SELECTION

Learning Objectives

After you have read this chapter, you should be able to:

- Specify the decisions necessary as part of a strategic approach to recruitment.

- Describe the methods utilized for both internal and external recruitment.

- Discuss the criteria used to evaluate the effectiveness of organizational recruitment efforts.

- Compare and contrast job performance, selection criteria, and predictors.

- Identify the legal requirements of the selection process and outline that process.

- Explain the importance of conducting pre-employment background investigations.

The HR manager for a 200-bed long-term care facility in the southeast was delighted to report the vacancy rate for RNs for the quarter to the administrator. For the first time in over two years the rate was below 10 percent. Equally encouraging was that turnover was down and applicant numbers were up.

Registered nurse shortages have been cyclical in nature. Over the last half century the U.S. healthcare industry has been through at least three major cycles of RN shortages. Even the current shortage has shown some signs of slowing thanks to a number of retention initiatives, chief among which are higher wage rates for RNs and improvements in their quality of work-life, making the profession more attractive.[1] Also helping to add to the supply of new RNs, nursing schools have seen an increase in nursing faculty, allowing an increase in enrollments. Some of the evidence of the shortage slacking is noted below:

- Thousands of new RNs in their early- to mid-30s joined the healthcare work force, helping to boost RN employment in excess of two million.

- Overall, healthcare employers have been able to successfully attract and retain more nurses during recent years, making it one of the first periods during the recent shortage when gains have been noted.

- Other positive signs include: the time needed to fill a vacant position in small and midsize hospitals dropped by a significant margin; Minnesota, Florida, and Arizona have reported a drop in RN vacancy rates; and applications to nursing schools have jumped dramatically.[2]

But the industry continues to face challenges. The difference between this shortage cycle and those of the past is the aging population. The demand for healthcare due to the aging population will continue to increase as more of the current RNs leave the workforce due to retirement and other age-related reasons.

The Healthcare HR Insight illustrates that healthcare HR professionals must keep focused on dealing with staffing issues regardless of these positive signs, because they will return. Innovative recruitment and retention strategies will continue to be critical, even if there is a temporary lull in staffing shortages and requirements. There is no better time to re-strategize and improve processes than when some accomplishment has occurred and the press of immediate action subsides.[3]

RECRUITING AND LABOR MARKETS

There actually are not one but several **labor markets** that are the external sources from which healthcare employers attract employees. There are many ways to identify labor markets, including by geographical area, type of skill, and educational level. Some specific labor market segments might include managerial, clerical, professional and technical, and service and support. In healthcare, specific labor markets include major job markets, such as nurses, physicians, and administrative categories. Classified differently, some markets are local, others are regional, and others are national. There are international labor markets as well. To understand the labor markets in which recruiting takes place, one must consider three different concepts: *labor force population, applicant population,* and *applicant pool.*

The **labor force population** includes all individuals who are available for selection if all possible recruitment strategies are used in a particular market, such as the city of Louisville, Kentucky or the midwest region of the United States. This vast array of possible applicants may be reached in very different ways.

The **applicant population** is a subset of the labor force population that is available for selection using a particular recruiting approach. At least four recruiting decisions affect the nature of the applicant population:

- *Recruiting Method*—Advertising media chosen
- *Recruiting Message*—What is said about the job and how it is said
- *Applicant Qualifications Required*—Education level and amount of experience necessary
- *Administrative Procedures*—Time of year recruiting is done, follow-ups with applicants, and use of previous applicant files

The **applicant pool** consists of all people who are actually evaluated for selection. The applicant pool will depend on the reputation of the organization as a place to work, the screening done in the organization, and the information available to the applicant population. Assuming a suitable candidate is present, the final selection is made from the applicant pool.

HR professionals in the healthcare industry have been especially aware of the supply and demand of workers in the labor force population and the substantial impact supply issues have had on the staffing strategies of organizations in the industry. Internal labor markets also influence recruiting. A discussion of these and other strategic recruiting decisions follows.

PLANNING AND STRATEGIC DECISIONS REGARDING RECRUITING

The decisions that are made about recruiting help dictate not only the types and numbers of applicants, but also how difficult or successful recruiting efforts may be. Figure 6-1 shows an overview of these recruiting decisions. **Recruiting** involves identifying where to recruit, who to recruit, and what the job requirements will be. Another key consideration is deciding to what extent internal and external searches are to be made.

FIGURE 6-1   Strategic Recruiting Decisions

Internal Versus External Recruiting

Both advantages and disadvantages are associated with promoting from within the organization (internal recruitment) and hiring from outside the organization (external recruitment) to fill openings. Most healthcare organizations combine the use of internal and external methods. Historically, larger healthcare organizations, such as hospitals, medical centers, and long-term care facilities, have followed a policy of promotion from within. However, operating in rapidly changing environments and competitive conditions, healthcare organizations are placing a heavier emphasis on external sources in addition to their internal sources. Figure 6-2 lists the various recruiting methods, both internal and

FIGURE 6-2 Choosing a Recruiting Method: Possible Approaches

	SERVICE WORKER	OFFICE/CLERICAL	PROFESSIONAL/TECHNICAL	EXECUTIVE/MANAGERIAL
1. Promotion from within	*	*	*	*
2. Job posting and bidding	*	*	*	
3. Contacts and employee referrals	*	*	*	
4. Executive search firm			—	*
5. Internet recruiting sites	*	*	*	*
6. Media advertisements	*	*	*	
7. Public employment agency	*	*	—	
8. Private employment agency		*	*	—
9. Schools and colleges	*	*	*	*
10. Clinical rotations, preceptorships, and internships	—		*	
11. Fellowships			*	*
12. Volunteers	*	*	*	
13. Professional associations			*	*
14. Military service		—	*	—
15. Former employees		*	*	—
16. Special events		*	*	—
17. Temporary help		*	*	—

*A good recruiting method.

—A possible recruiting method.

external, that healthcare organizations utilize. It also notes which method is the most effective for each type of worker.

Flexible Staffing

Decisions as to who should be recruited hinge on whether to seek traditional full-time employees or use more flexible approaches. Healthcare organizations are finding a need to turn to creative staffing approaches to attract and retain workers. Part-time workers are the most traditional, flexible approach used in healthcare because a significant percentage of healthcare workers work part-time.[4] In fact, the nursing profession is seen by many individuals as a part-time profession.

Healthcare employers that use **temporary employees** can hire their own temporary staff or use agencies supplying temporary workers on a rate-per-day or per-week basis. There are an estimated 20,000 nurses who are "traveling nurses" who move from organization to organization on assignments lasting on average 13 weeks. In some cases, these traveling nurses are the difference between being able to keep hospital beds open or closing them and turning patients or residents away.[5] The use of more traditional temporary workers makes sense for healthcare organizations if their work is subject to fluctuations or as an opportunity to evaluate employees before placing them on the regular payroll. For example, HR departments in many large healthcare organizations have developed internal temporary staffing departments to reduce the handling costs of external temporary agency use for temporary employees.

Some healthcare organizations employ **independent contractors** to perform specific services on a contract basis, such as information technology workers helping to prepare for a major new software conversion. However, those contractors must be truly independent, as determined by the U.S. Internal Revenue Service and the U.S. Department of Labor. (See Chapter 12 for details.)

Float Pools

Nursing departments typically use RN **resource pools,** where RNs are specifically hired to be available to "float" to various units when patient census or acuity needs are higher than core staffing needs can meet. Resource pools (or *float pools*) are an especially good way to allow new nurses the opportunity to work in a variety of settings before deciding which unit, department, or even type of nursing is the most desirable. However, due to the ever-increasing specialization within nursing, such as oncology or cardiac care, float nurses cannot be expected to safely work in all areas of a hospital, clinic, or treatment center.

Employee Leasing

In physician practices and clinics, **employee leasing** is a concept that has grown rapidly in recent years. An example of an employee leasing process is a clinic that signs an agreement with an employee leasing company, after which the existing staff is hired by the leasing firm. For a fee, the clinic "leases" its employees from the leasing company, which then writes the paychecks, pays the taxes, provides benefits, prepares and implements HR policies, and keeps all the required personnel records.

INTERNAL RECRUITING

Internal recruiting means focusing on current employees and others with previous contact with an employing organization. Promotions, demotions, and transfers also can provide additional people for an organizational unit, if not for the entire organization. Friends of current employees, former employees, and previous applicants may also be sources. One advantage of internal recruiting sources over external sources is that management can observe the candidate for promotion (or transfer) over a period of time and can evaluate that person's potential and specific job performance. Healthcare organizations have also found that another advantage of promoting from within to fill job openings is that it gives current employees added motivation to stay with their organization and prepare for advancement through additional education and training.[6]

Job Posting and Bidding

The major means for recruiting employees for other jobs internally within healthcare organizations is through **job posting and bidding,** whereby the employer provides notices of job openings, and employees respond by applying for specific openings. The organization can notify employees of job vacancies by posting notices in cafeterias, break rooms, and on an organizational intranet Web site.

Internal Recruiting Database

Computerized internal talent banks, or applicant tracking systems, can be used to identify the inventory of employees' KSAs. Employers that must deal with a large number of applications and job openings have found it beneficial to use such software as part of a human resource information system. With the growth of e-mail and intranets, more healthcare organizations are using this approach to internally post their positions.

Job posting and bidding systems can be ineffective if handled improperly. Jobs generally are posted before any external recruiting is done. The organization must allow a reasonable period of time for current employees to check on available jobs before it considers external applicants. A sample of a hospital job posting policy is available at: *http://flynn.swlearning.com*

Promotion and Transfer

Many healthcare organizations choose to fill vacancies through promotions or transfers from within whenever possible. Although most often successful, promotions from within have some drawbacks as well. The person's performance on one job might not be a good predictor of performance on another, because different skills may be required on the new job. For instance, healthcare organizations have certainly promoted the best nurse or the best respiratory therapist to supervisory positions based on their technical competence. Because of the different capabilities required for supervisory success, these promotion decisions may not be the most effective for the organization. Also, if an organization does not have a diverse workforce, promotions may not be an effective way to speed up the movement of protected-class individuals through the organization.

Current Employee Referrals

One of the most reliable sources of people to fill vacancies is composed of personal acquaintances or professional associates of current employees. To potential applicants, employees can describe the advantages of a job with the organization, furnish letters of introduction, and encourage them to apply. These are external applicants recruited using an internal information source. Many healthcare employers pay employees incentives for referring individuals with specialized skills that are difficult to recruit through normal means. As an example, in a large west coast radiology practice, employees are encouraged to refer qualified applicants for open positions. There is the enticement of a $500 bonus for the referral if it leads to a hire.

Former employees and former applicants are also good internal sources for recruitment. In both cases, there is a timesaving advantage, because more information already exists about the potential employee.[7] For instance, Baptist Health South Florida has implemented a "Bridgement of Service" policy. This policy allows former employees who have left in good standing to return within five years of their previous employment with full restoration of their previous seniority and benefits.[8]

EXTERNAL RECRUITING

If internal sources do not produce enough acceptable candidates for jobs, many external sources are available. These sources include schools, colleges and universities, media sources, trade and competitive sources, employment agencies, executive search firms, and the Internet.

Employment "Branding"

To become an "employer of choice" for excellent job candidates, healthcare organizations find that it is advantageous to have a recognized "brand," or identity. Healthcare organizations seen as desirable employers are better able to attract more qualified applicants than organizations with poor reputations.

For example, the Cleveland Clinic is known for its sophisticated diagnostic capabilities combined with a caring approach towards patients. Its reputation does not require mass marketing, because patients, referring doctors, and the press tell the clinic's story. As a result, the clinic has a consistent supply of highly qualified applicants for many of its jobs.

This melding between marketing, public relations, and HR is not always easy, or may not be possible in some healthcare organizations. But when it has occurred, indicators that branding has been effective include:[9]

- The employer experiences positive name recognition because both individuals inside and outside the organization discuss it favorably.

- The employer is a top choice for high performers because they see the organization as a prestigious place that invests in their future.

- If individuals quit, they are more likely to return once they discover that another employer is not as desirable a place to work.

Schools, Colleges, and Universities

High schools or vocational/technical schools may be a good source of new employees for many healthcare organizations. These include such positions as medical assistants, emergency medical technicians, and lab aides. A successful recruiting program with these institutions is the result of careful analysis and continual contact with individual schools. There are a number of positions within healthcare organizations where a high school degree or GED is an appropriate educational requirement; these jobs include a wide variety of service worker, clerical, and clinical support positions.

At the college or university level, the recruitment of graduating students is a large-scale operation for many healthcare organizations. Most colleges and universities maintain placement offices in which employers and applicants can meet.

Media Sources

Media sources such as newspapers, magazines, television, radio, and billboards are widely used. Whatever one is used, it should be tied to the relevant labor market and provide sufficient information on the company and the job. When using recruitment advertisements in the media, employers should ask five key questions:

1. What is the ad supposed to accomplish?
2. How should the message be presented?
3. Who are the people we want to reach?
4. Where should it be placed?
5. What should the advertising message convey?

Professional Associations

Many healthcare professional societies and associations publish newsletters or magazines containing job ads. Such publications may be a good source of applicants for specialized professionals. In addition many professional associations maintain recruitment links on their Web sites, such as the site for the American Society of Healthcare Human Resources Administration (*http://www.ashhra.org*).

Employment Agencies

Every state in the United States has its own state-sponsored employment agency. These agencies operate branch offices in many cities throughout the state and do not charge fees to applicants or employers. Private employment agencies are also found in most cities. For a fee collected from the employee or the employer (usually the employer), these agencies do some preliminary screening and refer applicants for open positions.

Executive Search Firms

Some employment agencies focus their efforts on executive, managerial, and professional positions. These executive search firms are split into two groups: (1) contingency firms that charge a fee only after a candidate has been hired by a client company, and (2) retainer firms that charge a client a set fee whether or not the contracted search is successful. Both types of firms are widely used by healthcare organizations to staff specialized clinical, management, and executive positions. Figure 6-3 lists the five top executive search firms ranked according to their revenues, all of which work extensively in the healthcare industry.[10]

FIGURE 6-3   Five Top Executive Search Firms (Ranked according to revenues)

1. Korn/Ferry International—*http://www.kornferry.com*
2. Heidrick & Struggles—*http://www.heidrick.com*
3. Spencer Stuart—*http://www.spencerstuart.com*
4. Egon Zehnder International—*http://www.egonzehnder.com*
5. Russell Reynolds Associates—*http://www.russellreynolds.com*

INTERNET RECRUITING

Healthcare organizations first started using computers as a recruiting tool by advertising jobs on a *bulletin board service* from which prospective applicants would contact the employer. Then some organizations began to take e-mail applications. Today, the Internet has become a primary means for many healthcare employers to search for job candidates and for applicants to look for jobs. The explosive growth in the Internet is a key reason; it is estimated that 12.2 percent of Internet users in the United States visited a Web site for recruitment purposes.[11] Internet users often tap the Internet to search for jobs more frequently by reading newspaper classified ads online. Also, resumes are submitted or posted on the Internet by many of these Internet users.

HR professionals and recruiters are using the Internet regularly, as well. Various surveys found that a significant percentage of healthcare employers use the Internet for recruiting. Estimates are that there are more than 100,000 recruiting Web sites on which to post jobs and review resumes of various types that employer and job candidates can access. But the explosive growth of Internet recruiting also means that HR professionals can be overwhelmed by the breadth and scope of Internet recruiting.

E-Recruiting Methods

There are several different methods used for Internet recruiting. The most common are job boards, professional/career Web sites, and employer Web sites.

Job Boards Numerous job boards exist on which employers can post jobs or search for candidates. Some of the most commonly used by healthcare organizations include:[12]

- Monster.com
- CareerBuilder.com
- Yahoo!HotJobs.com

- CareerSite.com
- Dice.com
- Craigslist.com

Although job boards provide access to numerous candidates, many individuals accessing the sites are *job browsers*. These people may not be serious about changing jobs, but are checking out compensation levels and the job availability in their areas of interest. Despite these concerns, HR recruiters find the general job boards useful for generating applicant responses.

Professional/Career Web Sites Many professional associations have employment sections on their Web sites. As illustration, for HR jobs see *http://www.shrm.org* or *http://www.astd.org*. Also, a number of private corporations have set up specialized health career Web sites in order to focus on such areas as nurse anestheticists, physician assistants, or other areas. Using these more targeted Web sites limits somewhat the recruiters' search time and efforts. Also, posting jobs on such Web sites is likely to target applicants specifically interested in the job field and may reduce the number of less-qualified applicants who actually apply.

Employer Web Sites While job boards and other job sites are very popular, many recruiters have found employer Web sites to be effective and efficient when recruiting candidates. Numerous employers have included employment and career information as part of their organizational Web sites. On many of these sites, jobseekers are encouraged to e-mail resumes or complete online applications.

An example of an employer Web site which includes a job board can be seen on the Mayo Clinics' Web site at *http://www.mayoclinic.org/jobs.*

Effective Online Job Postings

The rapid growth of the Internet for recruiting has changed the way many organizations find applicants. Instead of newspaper ads as a primary source for recruiting, online job posting is an integral part of most recruiting efforts. However, developing effective online job announcements is not simply putting a newspaper ad into an electronic form. Some of the suggestions for preparing effective online job postings include:

- *Make the Posting Appealing*—It must grab people's interest, so it is useful to have some graphics, company logo, and other simple artwork to make the posting stand out.

- *Make it Readable*—Use easy-to-read language, including avoidance of too many abbreviations and jargon not easily recognizable by applicants. Also, do not use all capital or bold letters, as it looks too dense.

- *Shorter is Better*—Too many employers start online ads with fifty- to sixty-word paragraphs on the company and general descriptive words that are overused, such as *challenging, progressive,* and so on.

- *Start with Clear Job Title and Overview*—The job title and the brief description of the job responsibilities determine if anything else is read. These items are like the headline and first paragraph of a news article. If they are not interesting, the rest of the details do not get read.

- *Describe the Employer Concisely*—A brief description of the employer, especially the division and location of the job, should provide information and create interest in the organization.

- *State Necessary Qualifications Clearly*—Care should be taken that the level of qualifications are reflected accurately, so that exceptional candidates see that the qualifications are not too low, thus discouraging them from applying. Alternatively, "puffing up" qualifications may eliminate candidates who see the job as above their capabilities.

- *Provide Compensation and Benefits Information*—A job posting should provide a salary range and emphasize competitive benefits, especially by noting any special benefits available. However, care should be taken to avoid a "laundry-list" look to the benefits.

- *Indicate How to Apply*—It is important to build in automatic links to e-mail or to an employment application so that an applicant can *click to apply.* As back up, fax number and mailing address information should be provided, along with a contact name or code number. Generally, it is recommended that phone numbers only be included if the employer wishes to field telephone inquiries, which may be too numerous in some cases but desirable in others.

It is important that the recruiting and employment portions of an employer's Web site are seen as part of coordinated marketing efforts. Also, the Web site should market the employer by providing information on the organization, organizational growth potential, and organizational operations, so that potential applicants can learn general information about the employer. Unfortunately, many employers' Web sites do not effectively incorporate career and employment information.

Advantages of Internet Recruiting

There are a number of advantages that employers have found using Internet recruiting. A primary advantage is that many employers have experienced *cost-savings* using Internet recruiting compared to other sources such as newspaper advertising, employment agencies and search firms, and other external sources.

Internet recruiting also can save considerable time. Applicants can respond quickly to job postings by sending e-mails, rather than using regular mail. Recruiters can respond to qualified candidates more quickly and establish times for interviews or request additional candidate information.

An *expanded pool of applicants* can be generated using Internet recruiting. Depending on the Internet sources used, job openings can be made available to a large number of candidates: jobs are literally posted globally, so potential applicants in other geographic areas and countries can view job openings posted on the Web.

Disadvantages of Internet Recruiting

The positives associated with Internet recruiting also come with some disadvantages. By getting broader exposure, employers also may get *more unqualified applicants.* More resumes must be reviewed, more e-mails dealt with, and specialized applicant tracking software may be needed to handle the increase in applicants caused by Internet recruiting efforts.

Another issue with Internet recruiting is that some applicants may have *limited Internet access.* This is especially true of individuals from lower socioeconomic groups and certain racial/ethnic minority groups. Consequently, employers might not be getting as diverse a recruitment pool as might be desired through Internet recruiting. Despite these disadvantages, Internet recruiting will continue to grow in usage. Healthcare employers and job seekers alike are seeing e-recruiting as a major part of external recruiting.

OTHER SOURCES FOR HEALTHCARE RECRUITMENT

Thanks in part to the unique aspects of the educational preparation, as depicted in Figure 6-4 for most clinical degrees and some administrative degrees, many healthcare employers have a ready-made source of applicant flow. Clinical rotations, preceptorships, and internships are part of the education and clinical

FIGURE 6-4   **Unique Sources of Healthcare Applicants**

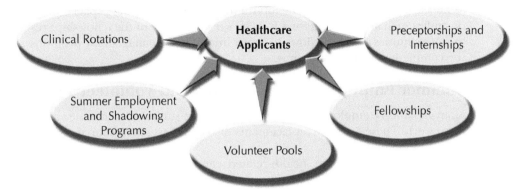

development for such fields as nursing, pharmacy, medical technology, and other therapies. Fellowships are a part of the education development for Healthcare Administration degrees. The individuals in these educational areas pursue their "clinicals" in hospitals, clinics, nursing homes, and other healthcare provider environments, so they are easily accessed to discuss current or future openings and career opportunities.

Clinical Rotations

In clinical-preparation degree programs, a clinical rotation is required to facilitate the students' learning of the "hands-on" nature of their professions. These rotations are typically hosted by clinics, hospitals, nursing homes, or other care provision facilities. Many organizations that host clinical rotations take full advantage of the opportunity to recruit the students while they are on-site.[13]

Preceptorships and Internships

Similar to clinical rotations, preceptorships and internships may be part of the educational experience, but usually occur at the later stages or end of a health professional's training. Many healthcare organizations have incorporated the preceptorships and internships into their normal recruitment cycle—in some instances, exclusively relying on the individuals who complete their preceptorships or internships at their facilities to fill open positions. Advanced practice healthcare professionals, such as nurse practitioners and pharmacists, are especially recruited in this manner. In some cases there is educational assistance, tuition loan, or forgiveness programs tied to employment offers.[14]

Fellowships

Many undergraduate and graduate degree programs in Healthcare Administration, Public Health, and Health Planning include post-graduation fellowship programs. These fellowships place the new graduates in high-level support positions to administrators, CEOs, or other healthcare executives. The *"fellows,"* as they are called, receive on-the-job training, typically by doing special projects or studies such as preparing for a JCAHO site visit. Some of the fellowships result in opportunities for the fellows to move into middle-management positions at the completion of their programs.

Summer Employment, Shadowing, and Volunteer Pools

Many healthcare employers have relied on college students for summer replacement work. These summer replacements may be an excellent source of recruits once they graduate.

In order to encourage health-related careers, healthcare employers have established *shadowing programs*. These programs provide an individual who is considering a healthcare occupation or educational program the opportunity to accompany a healthcare professional during a typical workday. The shadowing experience allows the potential employee or student to gain a unique, up-close glimpse of the healthcare environment and position responsibilities.

Volunteer pools have also been used to attract applicants. Hospitals and extended care facilities have historically used volunteers to perform a wide array of hospitality, reception, delivery, or other services. Many healthcare facilities have well-developed programs with hundreds of volunteers that augment the paid staff. In addition to providing labor cost savings, the volunteers are an excellent source of applicants for positions if paid employment is desired.

RECRUITING EVALUATION AND METRICS

Evaluating the success of recruiting efforts is important. General areas for evaluating recruiting include the following:

- *Quantity of Applicants*—Because the goal of a good recruiting program is to generate a large pool of applicants from which to choose, quantity must be sufficient to provide choices and fill job vacancies.

- *EEO Goals Met*—The recruiting program is the key activity used to meet goals for hiring protected-class individuals. This is especially relevant when a company is engaged in affirmative action to meet such goals.

- *Quality of Applicants*—There is the issue of whether the qualifications of the applicant pool are sufficient to fill the job openings, whereby the applicants meet job specifications and perform the jobs.

- *Cost per Applicant Hired*—Cost varies, depending on the position being filled, but knowing how much it costs to fill an empty position puts turnover and salary levels in perspective.

- *Time Required to Fill Openings*—The length of time it takes to fill openings is another means of evaluating recruiting efforts. If openings are filled quickly with qualified candidates, the work and productivity of the organization are not delayed by vacancies.

In summary, the effectiveness of recruiting sources will vary, depending on the nature of the job being filled and the time available to fill it. But unless calculated, the effectiveness may not be recognized.[15]

NATURE OF SELECTION

Selection is the process of choosing qualified individuals from an applicant pool to fill jobs in an organization. Without qualified competent employees, a healthcare organization will not be able to meet its mission.

Selection is much more than just choosing the best available person. Selecting the appropriate set of KSAs—which come packaged in a human being—is an attempt to get a "fit" between what the applicant can and wants to do, and what the organization needs. Fit between the applicant and the organization affects both the employer's willingness to make a job offer and an applicant's willingness to accept a job. Fitting a person to the right job is called **placement.** More than anything else, placement of human resources should be seen as a *matching process.* Whether an employer uses specific KSAs or a more general approach, effective selection of employees involves understanding *criteria* and *predictors* of job performance.

Criteria, Predictors, and Job Performance

At the heart of an effective selection system is knowledge of what constitutes appropriate job performance and what characteristics in employees are associated with that performance. Once the definition of employee success (performance) is known, the employee specifications required to achieve that success can be determined. A **selection criterion** is a characteristic that a person must have to do the job successfully. Figure 6-5 shows that ability, motivation, intelligence, conscientiousness, appropriate risk, and permanence might be good selection criteria for many jobs. To predict whether a selection criterion (such as motivation or ability) is present, employers need to identify **predictors** as visible indicators of the selection criteria.

Legal Concerns

Sophisticated healthcare employers use a variety of pre-employment steps and predictors to ensure that applicants will fit available jobs. Selection is subject to all EEO requirements.

It is increasingly important for employers to define carefully and exactly who is an applicant, given the legal issues involved. If there is no written policy defining conditions that make a person an applicant, anyone who sends unsolicited resumes might later claim that he or she was not hired because of

FIGURE 6-5 Job Performance, Selection Criteria, and Predictors

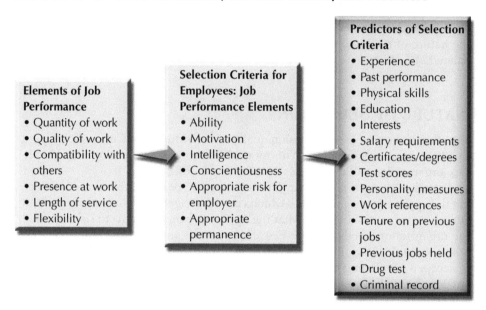

Elements of Job Performance
- Quantity of work
- Quality of work
- Compatibility with others
- Presence at work
- Length of service
- Flexibility

Selection Criteria for Employees: Job Performance Elements
- Ability
- Motivation
- Intelligence
- Conscientiousness
- Appropriate risk for employer
- Appropriate permanence

Predictors of Selection Criteria
- Experience
- Past performance
- Physical skills
- Education
- Interests
- Salary requirements
- Certificates/degrees
- Test scores
- Personality measures
- Work references
- Tenure on previous jobs
- Previous jobs held
- Drug test
- Criminal record

illegal discrimination. A policy-defining *applicant* might include the following aspects:

- Applications are accepted only when there is an opening.
- Only individuals filling out application blanks are considered applicants.
- A person's application ceases to be effective after a designated date.
- Only a certain number of applications will be accepted.
- People must apply for specific jobs, not "any job."

Immigration Forms The Immigration Reform and Control Act of 1986, as revised in 1990, requires that within 72 hours of hiring, an employer must determine whether a job applicant is a U.S. citizen, registered alien, or illegal alien. Applicants who are not eligible to work in this country must not be hired. Employers use the I-9 form to identify the status of potential employees. Employers are responsible for ensuring the legitimacy of documents submitted by new employees, such as U.S. passports, birth certificates, original Social Security cards, and driver's licenses. Also, employers who hire employees on special visas must maintain appropriate documentation and records.[16]

Selection Responsibilities

Healthcare organizations vary in how they allocate selection responsibilities between HR specialists and managers. Selection activities may be centralized into a specialized organizational unit that is part of an HR department. In smaller organizations, such as clinics (especially those with fewer than 100 employees), a full-time employment specialist or unit might be impractical.

Most organizations take certain common steps to process applicants for jobs. Variations on this basic process depend on organizational size, nature of jobs to be filled, number of people to be selected, and pressure of outside forces. The selection process shown in Figure 6-6 is typical in a large healthcare organization. However, all or some of the components of the process are easily utilized in smaller organizations, such as physician or dental practices.

Reception and Job Preview/Interest Screening

In addition to matching qualified people to jobs, the selection process has an important public relations dimension. This is especially true for healthcare employees. Discriminatory hiring practices, impolite interviewers, unnecessarily long waits, inappropriate testing procedures, and lack of follow-up letters can produce unfavorable impressions of an employer.

In some cases, it is appropriate to have a brief interview, called an *initial screening* or a *job preview/interest screen*, to see if the applicant is likely to match any jobs available in the organization after allowing the individual to fill out an application form. As noted in Figure 6-6, in many cases healthcare organizations conduct the preview/interest screen interview by phone.

Increasingly, the job preview/interest screen is done effectively over the Internet. Computerized processing of applicants can occur on several different levels. Computers can search resumes or application blanks for key words. Many large healthcare organizations use types of artificial-intelligence (AI) or *text-searching* software to scan, score, and track resumes of applicants. Another means of computerizing screening is conducting initial screening interviews electronically. Computer-assisted interviewing techniques can use tools such as videotaped scenarios to which applicants react.

The purpose of a **realistic job preview (RJP)** is to inform job candidates of the "organizational realities" of a job so that they can more accurately evaluate their own job expectations. By presenting applicants with a clear picture of the jobs, the organization hopes to reduce unrealistic expectations, thereby reducing employee disenchantment, dissatisfaction, and turnover.[17]

Application Forms

Application forms are widely used. A sample application is available on this book's Web site: *http://flynn.swlearning.com*. Properly prepared, an application form serves four purposes:

1. It is a record of the applicant's desire to obtain a position.
2. It provides the interviewer with a profile of the applicant that can be used in the interview.
3. It is a basic employee record for applicants who are hired.
4. It can be used for research on the effectiveness of the selection process.

FIGURE 6-6 **Selection Process**

Selection Process

Retirement, resignation, or termination initiates process.

1. Requisition received from Department Director:
A. Department Director & HR determine accuracy of job description.
B. Budgetary approval is received.

2. Posting/advertisement initiated:
A. HR posts position internally
B. HR determines appropriate external sources:
Internet sites, Newsprint, Associations, Journals, etc.

3. Applications and resumes received:
A. HR screens applications & resumes relative to position qualifications and requirements.
B. HR determines qualified applicants; forwards applications & resumes for department
directors review; records on applicant flow log.

4. Department Director reviews applications & resumes provided by HR:
A. Director determines interest in interviewing candidates, & advises HR

5. HR conducts phone interview with applicants identified by Department Director, &
schedules in person interviews.

6. Interviews conducted by HR, Department Director, other supervisory personnel:
A. Interviewers are determined by level of position & reporting relationship
B. Structured interview format utilized
C. Applicant assessment form completed by all interviewers

7. Selection decision made by Department Director:
A. References checked by HR
B. Interviewer assessment forms evaluated by Department Director
C. "Authorization To Hire" communicated to HR by Department Director

8. HR extends employment offer and coordinates orientation activities.

Application Disclaimers and Notices   Application forms need disclaimers and notices so that employers state appropriate legal protections. Recommended disclosures and notices appearing on applications include:

- *Employment-at-Will*—Indicates the right of the employer or applicant to terminate the employment relationship at any time with or without notice or cause (where applicable by state law).

- *Employment Testing*—Notifies applicants of required drug tests, physical exams, or other tests.

- *Reference Contacts*—Requests permission to contact references listed by applicants.

- *Application Time Limit*—Indicates how long applications are active (typically six months) and that individuals must reactivate applications after that period.

- *Information Falsification*—Conveys to an applicant signing the form that falsification of application information is grounds for termination.

Resumes   One of the most common methods applicants use to provide background information is the resume. Technically, a resume used in place of an application form must be treated by an employer as an application for EEO purposes. However, substituting a resume for an application form is discouraged. The application form, if properly designed, should require the applicant's signature attesting to the accuracy and truthfulness of the information provided by the applicant. When organizations rely exclusively on resumes they do not have those assurances to legally act if the applicants have misrepresented or falsified their information.

SELECTION TESTING

Many kinds of tests may be used to help select good employees. Literacy tests, skills tests, psychological measurement tests, and honesty tests are the major categories. Carefully developed and properly administered employment tests allow healthcare employers to predict which applicants have the abilities to do specific jobs, who may learn better in training, and who may be more likely to stay. Tests are even available to screen out candidates who may create behavioral or other risks to the employer.[18]

A recent survey found that 41 percent of the employers polled use basic skills tests (essentially testing ability to read and do math), and 68 percent use some kind of job skills test (focusing on skills necessary to do a specific job). In addition, 29 percent use some kind of psychological measurement test (including cognitive ability, personality, and honesty).[19] A look at the most common types of tests follows.

- **Ability Test**—This test assesses the skills that individuals have already learned.

- **Aptitude Test**—This test measures general ability to learn or acquire a skill.

- **Mental Ability Test**—This test measures reasoning capabilities.

- **Assessment Center**—An assessment center is not necessarily a place, but a series of evaluative exercises and tests used for selection and development. The assessment uses multiple exercises and multiple raters.

- **Psychological/Personality Test**—This evaluates a unique blend of individual characteristics that affect interaction with the environment and help define a person. Historically, predictive validity has tended to be low for personality tests used as predictors of performance on the job. However, some studies have shown that carefully chosen personality tests that logically connect to work requirements can help predict the interpersonal aspects of job success.

- **Physical Ability Test**—This evaluation measures individual abilities such as the applicant's strength, endurance, and muscular movement. Care should be taken to limit physical ability testing until after a conditional job offer is made in order to avoid violating the provisions of the ADA.

- **Psychomotor Test**—This measures a person's dexterity, hand–eye coordination, arm–hand steadiness, and other factors.

SELECTION INTERVIEWING

A selection interview is designed to identify information on a candidate and clarify information from other sources. This in-depth interview is designed to integrate all the information from application forms, tests, and reference checks, so that a decision can be made. Because of the integration required and the desirability of face-to-face contact, the interview is the most important phase of the selection process in many situations. Conflicting information may have emerged from tests, application forms, and references. As a result, the interviewer must obtain as much pertinent information about the applicant as possible during the limited interview time and evaluate this information against job standards. Figure 6-7 details the "do's" and "don'ts" of employment interviewing. Finally, a selection decision must be made, based on all of the information obtained in the preceding steps.

Types of Interviews

The interview is not an especially valid predictor of job performance, but it has high "face validity"—that is, it seems valid to employers, and they like it. Virtually all employers are likely to hire individuals using interviews of different types. Generally the following types of interviews can improve the validity of the selection process.

Structured Interview The structured interview uses a set of standardized questions that are asked of all applicants. Every applicant is asked the same basic questions, so that comparisons among applicants can more easily be made. This type of interview allows an interviewer to prepare job-related questions in advance and then complete a standardized interviewee evaluation form. Completion of such a form provides documentation if anyone, including an EEO enforcement body, should question why one applicant was selected over another.

FIGURE 6-7   Employment Interviewing Do's and Don'ts

DO:

Use reminders to get back to the original line of inquiry.

Ask open-ended questions (How do you like . . .?).

Use one and two-step probes (What? Why?).

Ask for laundry lists (What are the satisfactions that you look for in a job?).

Use echoes (. . . .boring work?).

Use summaries (Looking back, how did you like the place?).

Pause (15 seconds is a *long* time!).

Ask self-evaluation questions.

Present hypothetical situations.

DON'T:

Ask "yes" or "no" questions.

Ask leading questions.

Ask questions which reveal <u>your</u> perspective.

Ask redundant questions.

Rudely interrupt.

Talk down to an applicant.

Behavioral Event Interview   When responding to a **behavioral event interview,** applicants are asked to give specific examples of how they have performed a certain procedure or handled a problem in the past. Consistent with information detailed earlier, behavioral event interviews provide insight on how the applicant will perform in the future based on how they have performed in the past. For example, a behavioral event interview question for a clinic manager applicant might be: "Describe how you have handled difficult employee relations situations in your past supervisory positions, include examples and outcomes." Applicants' responses to this question could provide important insight regarding how they would handle future employee relations situations they were confronted with, and whether their approach is compatible with the approach the organization typically would want. Like other structured selection methods, behavioral event interviews generally provide better validity than unstructured interviews.

Panel Interview

Usually, applicants are interviewed by one interviewer at a time. But when an interviewee must see several people, many of the interviews are redundant and therefore unnecessarily time-consuming. In a **panel interview,** several interviewers interview the candidate at the same time. All the interviewers hear the same responses. On the negative side, applicants are frequently uncomfortable with the group interview format.

BACKGROUND CHECKING

Due to the very nature of providing patient care and the close personal and physical contact many healthcare workers have with patients, residents, and clients, healthcare organizations have a special duty to conduct background checks. This duty is to ensure that the patient caregivers have no previous conviction record involving crimes of violence, sexual misconduct, or criminal behavior.

Background checking may take place either before or after the in-depth interview. It costs the organization some time and money, but it is generally well worth the effort. Unfortunately, some applicants misrepresent their qualifications and backgrounds.

Legal Constraints

Various federal and state laws have been passed to protect the rights of individuals whose backgrounds may be investigated during pre-employment screening. States vary in what they allow employers to investigate. In some states, healthcare employers can request information directly from law enforcement agencies on applicants. In Ohio, for example, healthcare organizations and daycare centers must submit the fingerprints of applicants to determine if the applicants have disqualifying criminal histories.

Fair Credit Reporting Act   Some healthcare employers check applicants' credit histories. The logic is that individuals with poor credit histories may be irresponsible managers of money. However, this assumption may be questioned, and firms that check applicants' credit records must comply with both the Federal Fair Credit Reporting Act (FCRA) and EEO guidelines or selection. FCRA basically requires disclosing that a credit check is being made, obtaining written consent from the person being checked, and furnishing the applicant a copy of the report. Some state laws also prohibit employers from getting certain credit information.

Credit history checking should be done on applicants for jobs in which use, access, or management of money is an essential job function. Commonly, healthcare organizations check credit histories on employees who handle money or are responsible for sensitive financial information, such as accountants or business office personnel, or financial executives.

Giving References on Former Employees   In a number of court cases, individuals have sued their former employers for slander, libel, or defamation of character as a result of what the employers said to other potential employers that prevented the individuals from obtaining jobs. Because of such problems, many organizations have adopted policies restricting the release of reference information. Lawyers advise organizations who are asked about former employees to give out only name, employment date, and title.

Under the Federal Privacy Act of 1974, a governmental employer must have a signed release from a person before it can give information about that person to someone else. The recommendation is that all employers obtain a signed release

ETHICAL PRACTICES AND COMPLIANCE

Given the recruitment issues most healthcare organizations face, it is a constant challenge to balance the need to quickly fill a vacant position versus the need to carefully evaluate a candidate's background and competency to determine if they can effectively and safely perform the duties of the position for which they are being considered. Many healthcare organizations have dramatically streamlined their selection processes in order to quickly identify, respond, evaluate and make employment offers, in some cases as quickly as 24 hours from the time of first contact with the applicant. However, ultra-responsive and streamlined selection processes can result in negligent hiring. When important evaluative aspects of the selection process are skipped or ignored, bad hiring decisions may result.

Under the legal doctrine of *Respondeat Superior*, patients can hold a healthcare organization responsible for the acts of its employees. In addition, the courts can find the organization liable for improperly hiring its employees.[20] There have been numerous incidences of healthcare organizations that have failed to conduct the appropriate background checks, including criminal checks, and it was later learned that the individual had abused a patient. Had checks been performed the employee would never have been employed. Many of these cases have resulted in significant monetary damage awards to the injured patients and their families and to significant loss of credibility on the part of the healthcare organization that made the bad hire.

Healthcare HR professionals are often challenged by operating and departmental managers and supervisors to speed up their processes or "cut corners" in order to fill positions. This occurs because of the pressure on supervisors to maintain appropriate staffing ratios or to keep patient/resident rooms open or a clinic staffed. Sometimes HR professionals are even viewed as obstructive if they don't comply with the manager's wishes of "just get the person started; we can do the silly paperwork later." Yet the right approach is to avoid sacrificing some part of the selection process to expediency. Consistently and conscientiously following an effective selection process will result in better hires and reduce the likelihood of organizational liability due to improper hiring.[21]

from individuals during exit interviews authorizing employers to provide reference information in the future.

Clearly, employers are in a difficult position. Because of threats of lawsuits, they must obtain information on potential employees but are unwilling to give out information in return. To address these concerns, more and more states have laws that protect employers from civil liability when giving reference information in good faith that is objective and factual in nature.

Risks of Negligent Hiring The costs of failing to check references may be high. Some organizations have become targets of lawsuits that charge them with negligence in hiring workers who have committed violent acts on the job. Lawyers say that an employer's liability hinges on how well it investigates an applicant's background. Prior convictions and frequent moves or gaps in employment should be cues for further inquiry. Details provided on the application form by the applicant should be investigated to the greatest extent possible, so the employer can show that due diligence was exercised. Also, employers should document their efforts to check background information by noting who was contacted, when, and what information was or was not provided. This documentation can aid in countering negligent hiring claims.

Medical Examinations and Inquiries

Medical information on applicants may be used to determine the individual's physical and mental capability for performing jobs. Physical standards for jobs should be realistic, justifiable, and geared to the job requirements. Workers with disabilities can perform satisfactorily in many jobs. However, in many places they are rejected because of their disabilities, rather than being screened and placed in appropriate jobs.

ADA and Medical Inquiries The ADA prohibits the use of pre-employment medical exams, except for drug tests, until a job has been conditionally offered. Also, the ADA prohibits a company from rejecting an individual because of a disability and from asking job applicants any questions relative to current or past medical history until a conditional job offer is made. Assuming a conditional offer of employment is made, some organizations ask applicants to complete a pre-employment health checklist or ask for a physical examination paid for by the employer.

Drug Testing Drug testing may be a part of a medical exam, or it may be done separately. Using drug testing as a part of the selection process has increased in the past few years, although some employers facing tight labor markets have discontinued drug testing. Employers should remember that the accuracy of drug tests varies according to the type of test used, the items tested, and the quality of the laboratory where the test samples are sent. Whether urine, blood, saliva, or hair samples are used, the process of obtaining, labeling, and transferring the samples to the testing lab should be outlined clearly, and definite policies and procedures should be established. Because of the potential impact of prescription drugs on test results, applicants should complete a detailed questionnaire on this matter before the testing. If an individual tests positive for drug use, then an independent medical laboratory should administer a second, more detailed analysis.

Genetic Testing   Another controversial area of medical testing is genetic testing. Employers that use genetic screening tests do so for several reasons. First, the tests may link workplace health hazards and individuals with certain genetic characteristics. Second, genetic testing may be used to make workers aware of genetic problems that could occur in certain work situations. The third use is the most controversial: to exclude individuals from certain jobs if they have genetic conditions that increase their health risks. Because people cannot change their genetic makeup, the potential for illegal discrimination based on genetic predisposition to future health issues is a concern that should be evaluated.

MAKING THE JOB OFFER

The final step of the selection process is making a job offer. Often extended over the phone, many job offers are then formalized in letters sent to applicants. It is important that the offer document be reviewed by legal counsel and that the terms and conditions of employment be clearly identified. Care should be taken to avoid vague, general statements and promises about bonuses, work schedules, or other matters that might change later. These documents also should provide for the individuals to sign an acceptance of the offer and return it to the employer, who should place it in the individual's personnel file.

Relocation Assistance

Once selected, new employees may require relocation assistance. Healthcare employers may provide relocation assistance for individuals selected who live away from the new job site. Relocation assistance enables new employees to become more productive more quickly in their new locations. Such relocation assistance often includes sales of existing homes, moving expenses, house-hunting trip costs, automobile transportation, and new home mortgage assistance. Regardless of the type of relocation assistance, the nature and extent of relocation assistance may set the tone for how new employees view their new jobs. Such assistance also aids in the adjustment of the employees' family members.

CASE

PrimeHealth Nursing and Care Centers (PrimeHealth) is a 65-bed geriatric, skilled nursing facility. Like many nursing and extended care facilities, PrimeHealth has been struggling to attract applicants for many of its open positions. Its current vacancy rated for key positions includes the following: a) LPNs 20 percent, b) Nursing 40 percent, and c) Housekeeping assistants 20 percent.

In the past its external recruitment efforts have been to utilize the traditional methods of newspaper ads and notifying the local high schools and trade schools of openings. Internally, PrimeHealth posts all open positions and encourages employees to monitor the postings and refer their friends and relatives for consideration. However, the lack of applicants for open positions is reaching a critical point, resulting in a moratorium for any new patient admissions. In addition, PrimeHealth has been forced to utilize temporary staffing agencies for LPNs to cover open night and weekend shifts.

To deal with this crisis, a task force composed of department heads has been established. The role of the task force is to evaluate the recruitment situation and make recommendations.

Questions

1. Identify a strategic HR approach that the task force should consider for dealing with PrimeHealth's recruitment issues.
2. What other methods of recruitment should the task force consider?

END NOTES

1. Peter D. Buerhaus, Douglas O. Staiger, and David Averback, "New Signs Of a Strengthening U.S. Nurse Labor Market?" *Health Affairs* (November 17, 2004), 526–533.
2. Melanie Evans, "Reaping Rewards, Increase Recruitment, Better Wages Start to Pay Off," *Modern Healthcare* (November 22, 2004), 1, 12.
3. "Nursing a Shortage," *Fedgazett* (January 2005), 5.
4. Elizabeth A. Robb, Amy Determan, Lucy Lampat, and Mary Scherbring, "Self-Scheduling: Satisfaction Guaranteed?" *Nursing Management* (July 2003), 16.
5. Julie Schmit, "Nursing Shortage Drums Up Demand for Happy Nomads," *USA Today* (June 9, 2005), 3B.
6. Linda Hollinger-Smith, "It Takes a Village to Retain Quality Nursing Staff," *Nursing Homes Magazine* (May 2003), 52, 54.
7. Ella-May Seth, "Competing for Talent," *Healthcare Executive* (May/June 2003), 86–87.
8. Joe Mullich, "New Ideas Draw Older Workers," *Workforce Management* (March 2004), 44, 46.
9. Gene C. George, et al., "Building the Brand Through People," *World at Work Journal* (First Quarter 2004), 39–45; Eilene Zimmer-

man, "Hospital President Sparks Groundbreaking Recruitment Campaign," *Workforce Online* (May 2003), http://www.workforce.com.
10. Adapted from "The Hot List—Top Executive Search Firms," *Workforce Management* (July 2004), Outfront.
11. Anne Freedman "The Web World-Wide," *Human Resource Executive* (March 6, 2002), 44–46.
12. "Advertising 2005 Outlook: Online Recruitment Advertising," Borrell Associates, http://www.borrellassociates.com.
13. Kathy Cullen, "Recruiting and Retaining Nurses and Health Care Employees," *Cullen Recruitment Consulting* (2002), 40–41.
14. Tracy A. Cox, "Meeting the Nursing Shortage Head On: A Roundtable Discussion," *Healthcare Financial Management* (March 2003), 52–60.
15. Charlotte Garvey, "The Next Generation of Hiring Metrics," *HR Magazine* (April 2005), 71–76.
16. W. J. Manning and Joyce R. Lopez, "New Concerns About Immigration Procedures Merit Review of I-9 Requirements," Jackson/Lewis, http://www.jacksonlewis.com/legalupdates/articles.cfm?aid=77.

17. Betty R. Kupperschmidt, "Unlicensed Assistive Personnel Retention and Realistic Job Previews," *Nursing Economics* (November/December 2002), 279–283.

18. David Aarnold and John Jones, "Who the Devil's Applying Now? Companies Can Use Tests to Screen Out Dangerous Job Candidates," *Security Management* (March 2002), 85.

19. "2001 AMA Survey on Workplace Testing," AMA Research, *http://www.amanet.org/research.*

20. Melinda S. Monson, "Should You Hire That Nurse?" *Nursing Magazine* (October 2001), 21.

21. Caroll Lachnit, "Why Ethics is HR's Issue," *Workforce* (March 2002), 10.

ORGANIZATIONAL RELATIONS AND EMPLOYEE RETENTION IN HEALTHCARE

Learning Objectives

After you have read this chapter, you should be able to:

- Explain the factors affecting the relationship between employees and healthcare organizations.

- Discuss the importance of employee retention for healthcare organizations.

- Identify the common reasons employees voluntarily leave organizations.

- Define the various organizational retention determinants.

- Describe how to compute the cost of organizational turnover.

Healthcare HR Insights

The unit supervisor of a residential treatment facility, upon the birth of her second child, debated with herself whether it would hurt or possibly end her career as a supervisor if she requested to go part-time or job share with another half-time supervisor. Her organization had not been especially receptive to non-traditional work schedules. Yet she knew that working full-time while trying to meet the needs of her growing family would definitely be in conflict and could negatively impact her ability to balance both demands well.

Whether the healthcare organization is a suburban family practice, a rural long-term care facility or a residential treatment facility, it takes dedicated employees in a wide variety of positions and roles to provide and support the provision of patient care. But individuals who work in healthcare also have personal lives which exert demands on their time, energy, and focus. Most successful healthcare organizations understand the importance of establishing policies for work-life balance. In fact, those healthcare organizations, such as the Mayo clinic, that have been acclaimed as one of the "Best 100 Organizations to Work For" according to *Fortune Magazine,* focus extensively on finding solutions for their employees' work-life balance challenges.[1] They do this by effectively weaving work-life balance into their cultures and by implementing HR policies that support and sustain that culture.

Healthcare organizations are recognizing the challenge of sustaining their recruitment and retention successes; the key is that they must create and support environments and cultures where employees don't want to leave. Otherwise, the recruitment accomplishments that many healthcare employers have experienced will be wasted.

The Healthcare HR Insight demonstrates is that to stimulate culture changes that support work-life balance, policies need to be backed up with changes in organizational staffing practices and in the attitudes of key people in the organization. The organization needs to examine its:

- *Processes for work*—How it delegates duties and responsibilities;
- *Technology*—Support work from home and/or other technologies that reduce unnecessary time spent at work; and
- *HR systems*—Recruitment, appraisal, succession planning, and access to training, making sure they support work-life balance objectives.

Most importantly, organizations need to assess their training of top management, individual employees, and operating managers, so that these three groups are aligned in their understanding of the issues, the priorities, and how to achieve the changes necessary to truly achieve a work-life balance culture.[2]

Many healthcare employers are starting to make significant strides in their retention efforts. Examples would include:

- Saint Francis Medical Center in Grand Island, Nebraska reported a surge in applicants and a significantly reduced turnover rate for a recent reporting period.[3]
- Children's National Medical Center in Washington, D.C., recently reported a 4 percent vacancy rate for RNs, down from a vacancy rate of 26 percent.[4]
- Summit Orthopedics in St. Paul, Minnesota, a large specialty practice with its own diagnostic facilities, recently reported zero vacancies for the once nearly impossible-to-fill position of radiologic technician.[5]

These are just a few of the many success stories of healthcare organizations that have worked hard to deal successfully with critical staffing shortages. However, as their recruitment targets are being met, their focus is now turning to retention.

Retaining competent employees of all types is a critical requirement for all healthcare providers. Given the difficulty of recruiting healthcare professionals from an aging workforce and declining new graduate pool, it is imperative that healthcare providers focus attention on retaining their current healthcare professionals.[6]

INDIVIDUAL/ORGANIZATIONAL RELATIONSHIPS

The long-term economic success of healthcare organizations depends on the efforts of employees with the appropriate capabilities and motivation to perform their jobs well. Organizations that are successful over time have understood that individual relationships do matter and should be managed.

At one time, loyalty and long service with one healthcare organization was considered an appropriate individual/organizational relationship. Recently, changes have been noted in both loyalty and length of service, with employees leaving more frequently. It has been estimated that one out of six employees may be ready to leave their current jobs.[7] One Society for Human Resource Management (SHRM) study found that 75 percent of all employees are interested in looking for new opportunities. The top three reasons cited were their desire for better compensation, better career opportunities, and dissatisfaction with current jobs.[8]

The Psychological Contract

One concept that has been useful in discussing employees' relationships with organizations is that of a **psychological contract,** which refers to the unwritten expectations that employees and employers have about the nature of their work relationships. Because the psychological contract is individual and subjective in nature, it focuses on expectations about "fairness" that may not be defined clearly by employees.

Both tangible items (such as wages, benefits, employee productivity, and attendance) and some intangible items (such as loyalty, fair treatment, and job security) are encompassed by psychological contracts between employers and employees in healthcare organizations of all types.

Changing Psychological Contract   The psychological contract has changed over the years. In the "good old days," employees exchanged their efforts and capabilities for a secure job that offered rising pay, comprehensive benefits, and career progression within the organization. But as healthcare organizations have restructured and cut workers who have given long and loyal service, a growing number of employees are questioning whether they should be loyal to their employers. Closely related to the psychological contract is the concept of *psychological ownership*.[9] When individuals feel that they have some control and perceived rights in the organization, they are more likely to be committed to the organization.

The transformation in the psychological contract mirrors an evolution in which organizations have moved from employing individuals just to perform tasks, to employing individuals expected to produce results. Rather than just paying them to follow orders and put in time, increasingly employers are expecting employees to utilize their skills and capabilities to accomplish organizational results. As Figure 7-1 depicts, both employers and employees are affected by the new psychological contract.

FIGURE 7-1   The New Psychological Contract

EMPLOYERS PROVIDE:	EMPLOYEES CONTRIBUTE:
• Competitive compensation and benefits	• Continuous skill improvement
• Career development opportunities	• Reasonable time with organization
• Flexibility to balance work and home life	• Extra effort when needed

Factors Affecting the Individual/ Organizational Relationship

The relationship between individuals and healthcare organizations is influenced by outside forces. Four of the biggest influences are economic changes, the expectations of different generations of individuals, loyalty, and changing career expectations for women. These factors affect the psychological contracts in a number of ways.

Economic Changes   One major factor affecting employee expectations is the ebb and flow of the economy. Some individuals have chosen technology, sales, or real estate careers, where they can expect higher starting salaries, flexible scheduling, relaxed and casual workplaces, and frequent career promotions or changes. As many of these individuals made their career decisions, the healthcare work place did not look as appealing. Healthcare careers, in contrast to many sales and technology jobs, demand 24/7 coverage, some high-tech, but more high-touch care, combined with stressful work environments.

Generational Differences Much has been written about the differing expectations of individuals in different generations. It should be recognized that many of these observations are anecdotal and give generalizations about individuals in the various age groups. Some of the common generational labels are

- The Matures (born before 1945)
- Baby Boomers (born 1945–1965)
- Generation X (born 1966–1980)
- Generation Y (born 1980–1990)

Rather than identifying the characteristics cited for each of these groups, it is most important here to emphasize that people's expectations differ between generations, as well as within these generation labels. For healthcare employers, the differing expectations present challenges. For instance, many of the Baby Boomers and Matures are concerned about security and experience, whereas the younger Generation Ys often are seen as the "why?" generation who expect to be rewarded quickly, are very adaptable, and tend to be more questioning about why managers and organizations make the decisions they do.[10]

Also, consider the dynamics of a Mature manager directing Generation X and Y individuals, or Generation X managers supervising older, more experienced Baby Boomers. These generational differences are likely to continue to create challenges and conflicts in organizations because of the differing expectations that various individuals have. One of the most common areas of difference is seen in loyalty to organizations.

Loyalty Employees *do* believe in psychological contracts, and hope their employers will keep their sides of the "agreement." Most employees want security and stability, interesting work, supervisors they respect, and competitive pay and benefits. When they are not provided these items, employees may feel a diminished need to contribute to organizational performance. When organizations merge, lay off large numbers of employees, outsource work, and use large numbers of temporary and part-time workers, employees see fewer reasons to give their loyalty to employers in return for this loss of job security. Healthcare employers are finding that in any type of labor market, especially tight labor markets, turnover of key people occurs more frequently when employee loyalty is low. Thus, retaining a loyal and committed workforce is important.

One important organizational value that affects employee loyalty is *trust.* Employees who believe that they can trust their managers, coworkers, and the organizational justice systems are much less willing to leave their current employers. According to a survey conducted by a nursing magazine, one of the top reasons given for RNs leaving their previous employers was a lack of trust and confidence in management.[11]

Career Expectations for Women Closely aligned with the generational differences are changing career expectations for women. Many women have more career opportunities than in past generations. The design and the nature of work, as well as the characteristics of employers, can affect the willingness of women to seek employment in healthcare organizations. Often, hospitals and nursing homes are not viewed as attractive places to work, because the hours are unpredictable, the work can be dangerous and physically taxing, and workers fail to garner respect from physicians and administrators.[12]

JOB SATISFACTION AND ORGANIZATIONAL COMMITMENT

In its most basic sense, **job satisfaction** is a positive emotional state resulting from evaluating one's job experiences. Job *dissatisfaction* occurs when these expectations are not met. For example, if a laboratory technician expects clean and safe working conditions, then the tech is likely to be dissatisfied if the lab is dirty and dangerously unsafe.

Dimensions of job satisfaction frequently mentioned include work, pay, promotion opportunities, supervision, and coworkers. Job satisfaction appears to have declined somewhat in recent years, and elements of the employee/employer relationship were cited among the major reasons for this decline in a 10-year study of 10,000 people.[13] More demanding work, fewer traditional hierarchical relationships with management, shorter relationships, and less confidence in long-term rewards were the reasons cited most frequently.

There is no simple formula for predicting an individual employee's job satisfaction. Furthermore, the relationship between productivity and job satisfaction is not entirely clear. The critical factor is what employees expect from their jobs and what they are receiving as rewards from their jobs. Although job satisfaction itself is interesting and important, perhaps the "bottom line" is the impact that job satisfaction has on organizational commitment, which affects employee turnover and organizational performance.

As Figure 7-2 depicts, the individual's ability, motivation, and support are brought to the job. Based on how the interaction of the individual and the job varies, levels of job satisfaction or dissatisfaction and organizational commitment result. Those two factors provide influences that can impact the performance of the individual and the organization.

Organizational Commitment

If employees are committed to an organization, they are more likely to be productive. **Organizational commitment** is the degree to which employees believe in and accept organizational goals and desire to remain with the organization. People who are relatively satisfied with their jobs will be somewhat more committed to the organization. Also, people who are relatively committed to the organization are more likely to have greater job satisfaction.

A logical extension of organizational commitment focuses specifically on *continuance commitment* factors, which suggests that decisions to remain with or leave an organization are ultimately reflected in employee absenteeism and turnover statistics. Individuals who are not as satisfied with their jobs or who are not as committed to the organization are more likely to withdraw from the organization, either occasionally through absenteeism or permanently through turnover.

FIGURE 7-2 Individual and Organizational Characteristics That Influence Performance

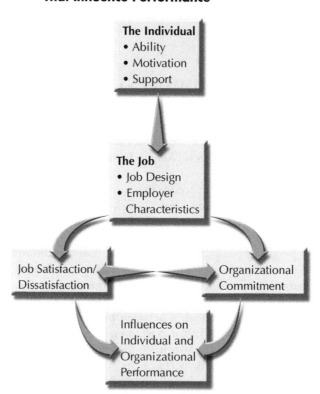

RETENTION OF HUMAN RESOURCES

Retention of employees has become a primary concern in healthcare organizations for several reasons. Every healthcare worker who is retained means one less worker to have to recruit, select, and train. Also, organizational and individual performance is enhanced when there is continuity with employees who know their jobs, coworkers, organizational service, and patients or clients. Continuity of employees provides a better employee image for attracting and retaining other individuals. There is also a link between patient satisfaction and employee retention. Employee satisfaction probably affects the level of patient/customer satisfaction.[14]

Healthcare providers who understand the relationship between patient satisfaction and employee satisfaction are counted among the nation's 100 Best Companies. Annually, *Fortune* magazine develops a list of the "100 Best Companies to Work For," and a number of hospitals recently made the list. Honorees included Baptist Health South in Coral Gables, Florida, at number six on the list in the large company category and Griffin Hospital located in Derby, Connecticut, at number three on the list of small companies. These organizations were cited for their ability to retain their employees and were recognized for their outstanding patient care and customer service.[15]

Retention as a Continuing Concern   Healthcare managers face a growing crisis in how to take care of more patients with fewer employees, with high turnover and a tight labor market in the healthcare industry. Further, consumers are becoming more informed about their healthcare choices and are increasingly advocating more for themselves when receiving services. Their knowledge leads to greater demands on healthcare workers, especially nurses, who have the most interaction with patients. These increased demands cause significant stress, increasing the likelihood that healthcare employees will seek less stressful work environments. Therefore, it is imperative that healthcare organizations and managers recognize that retention must be a continuing HR emphasis.

Retention as a Supervisory and Management Measure   Another sign of the importance of employee retention is that a growing number of healthcare employers have identified retention as a significant responsibility for their supervisors and managers. Even more directly, healthcare organizations are evaluating managers and supervisors on how effective they are at recruiting and retaining workers, not just budgeting, safety compliance, and operations functions.

ETHICAL PRACTICES AND COMPLIANCE

Ethical practices and a strong organizational commitment to corporate compliance can contribute to the retention of healthcare employees. Employees are very aware of an employer's approach to ethics and compliance. If it is generally perceived by employees that their organization is willing to cut ethical corners or ignore its compliance responsibilities, their commitment to the organization may be impacted.

Healthcare professionals such as pharmacists or physicians have their own ethical standards to adhere to due to their profession and as required by their licensure or certifications. These individuals wish to associate with organizations that will support and ensure mutual adherence to their professional standards of practice. Employees who find the practices of a hospital, clinic, or nursing home unethical or inappropriate also will be concerned about how those practices will reflect on them and their professional standing. These concerns could easily lead to employee turnover.

The Joint Commission on Accreditation of Healthcare Organizations (JCAHO) and Retention

A number of JCAHO's HR standards underscore the importance of the retention of a competent staff. JCAHO recognizes that the ability of a healthcare organization to fulfill its mission and provide for patients' needs is directly related to its ability to provide qualified, competent staff. Each provider must ensure an adequate number and mix of staff to fulfill its staffing plan.[16]

In large healthcare organizations there is often an individual in the HR department who is assigned the responsibility of focusing on retention to ensure that it receives high priority and on the efforts needed to increase employee retention. In some healthcare organizations with a high priority on retaining its staff, an HR professional may focus exclusively on retention programming.

Retention Determinants

Reviewing a wide range of studies and situations faced by healthcare employers and employees, it appears that there are some common areas that affect employee retention. As Figure 7-3 depicts, there are some broad organizational retention components that are important. Assuming those organizational components are being delivered appropriately to individuals, then there are other factors that also affect retention. Surveys of employees consistently show that career opportunities and compensation are the two most important determinants of retention. Finally, the job design/work factors and fair and supportive employee relationships with others inside the organization contribute to retention as well. If all of these components are present to meet individual employee

FIGURE 7-3   Retention Determinants

Career Opportunities
• Training continuity
• Development and mentoring
• Career planning

Rewards
• Competitive pay and benefits
• Performance reward differentiation
• Recognition
• Special benefits and perks

Organizational Components
• Values and culture
• Strategies and opportunities
• Well-managed and results-oriented
• Job continuity and security

Job Design and Work
• Job responsibilities and autonomy
• Work flexibility
• Working conditions
• Work/Life balancing

Employee Relationships
• Fair/Nondiscriminatory treatment
• Supervisory/Management support
• Coworker relations

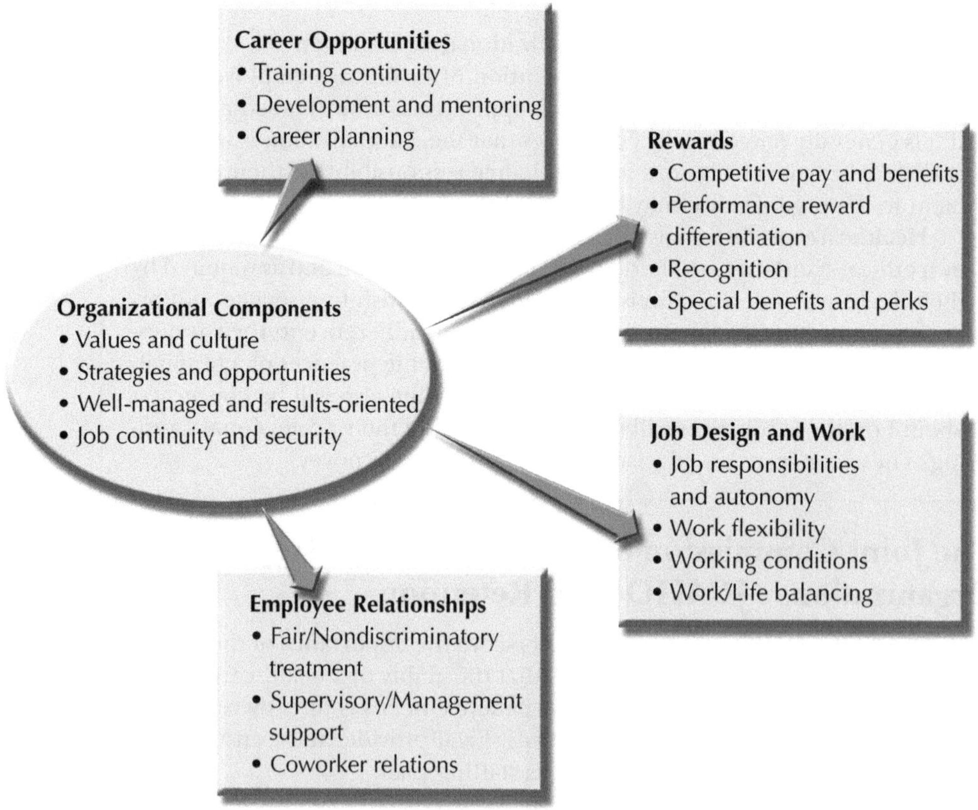

expectations, then there is a greater likelihood that voluntary and controllable turnover will be lower, thus increasing employee retention.

Organizational Components

There are a number of organizational factors that impact decisions by individuals to stay or leave their employers. Generally, organizations that have positive, distinctive cultures and values have fewer turnovers.

Organizational Culture and Values Organizational culture is a pattern of shared values and beliefs giving members of an organization meaning and providing them with rules for behavior. These values are inherent in the ways organizations and their members view themselves, define opportunities, and plan strategies. Much as personality shapes an individual, organizational culture shapes its members' responses and defines what an organization can or is willing to do.[17]

One health system well-known for its culture and values is the Mayo Clinic. Mayo focuses considerable effort on instilling its values of high-quality patient care and employee excellence in customer service and employee involvement through its HR efforts. These efforts have paid off in Mayo's performance in retaining employees and being widely seen as an "employer of choice" in the healthcare industry.

Job Continuity and Security Many healthcare employees have seen a decline in job security over the past decade. Downsizings, layoffs, mergers and acquisitions, and organizational restructuring have affected employee loyalty and retention. Also, as coworkers have been affected by layoffs and job reductions, the anxiety levels of the employees that are still employed rises. Consequently, employees start thinking about leaving before they, too, get cut. However, employees who work in organizations where job continuity and security is high tend to have higher retention rates.

Organizational Career Opportunities

Workers in all types of jobs consistently seek career opportunities and development efforts as affecting employee retention. This is even more true for technical professionals and those workers under age 30, where opportunities to develop skills and promotions rank above compensation as a retention concern.

Career Development Career opportunities and development are dealt with by organizations in a number of ways. Tuition aid programs, typically offered as benefits by many healthcare employers, allow employees to pursue additional educational and training opportunities. Employees who participate in tuition assistance programs have been found to have higher retention rates than individuals who do not do so. However, just offering such a program is not sufficient. Organizations must also identify ways to use the employees' new knowledge and capabilities inside the organization. Otherwise, employees are more likely to take their new capabilities to another employer because they feel their increased "value" is not being recognized. Overall, the thrust of organizational career development efforts is designed to meet many employees' expectations that their employer is committed to keeping their knowledge, skills, and abilities current.

An example of an effective career development program is seen at the Rehabilitation Hospital of the Pacific in Hawaii, where clinical level achievement and salary growth have been connected. Their program rewards employees for advancements in clinical certifications. The program is open to both therapists and nurses. The hospital reports that the program has resulted in increased leadership roles by their nurses and therapists in their respective professions and the community.[18]

Career Planning Healthcare organizations also increase employee retention by having formal career planning efforts. Employees and their managers mutually discuss career opportunities within the organization and what career development activities will enhance employees' future growth. Job posting programs have proven to be an especially effective HR program for healthcare organizations for facilitating both inter- and intra-departmental transfers and promotions. These programs encourage employees to pursue new opportunities without leaving their current organizations.

Rewards and Retention

The tangible rewards that people receive for working come in the form of pay, incentives, and benefits. This compensation is what provides the economic means for individuals to meet their financial obligations. Numerous surveys and experiences of HR professionals reveal that one of the most important keys to retention is to have *competitive compensation practices*. Many managers believe that money is the prime retention factor, and many employees cite better pay or higher compensation as reasons when they leave an employer.[19] However, the reality is a bit more complex.

Pay and benefits must be competitive, which means they must be "close" to what other employers are providing and what individuals believe to be consistent with their capabilities, experience, and performance. If compensation is not close (often defined as within 10 percent of the market) then turnover is likely to be higher.

This is especially true for individuals making lower rates of pay, such as those making less than $15.00 per hour. Simply put, their living costs and financial requirements make how much they are paid crucial. Therefore, if these lower-paid workers can get $1 per hour more, or get greater employer-paid family health benefit coverage elsewhere, they are more likely to leave. However, for more highly paid individuals, especially those paid salaries of $60,000 and higher, their retention is affected by having compensation relatively competitive. Then other considerations are more likely to enter into decisions to stay or leave. In fact, money might be why some people leave a job, but other factors might be the reason many stay.

Competitive Benefits Another compensation issue affecting employee retention is having competitive benefits programs. Offering health insurance, retirement, tuition assistance, and many other benefits commonly offered by competing employers is vital. Employers also are learning that having some *benefits flexibility* aids retention. When employees choose how much and what benefits they will have from a "cafeteria" of choices, given a set sum of money available from the employer, the employees can tailor the benefits to what they want. For instance, a married worker who has health insurance coverage under a spouse's health plan at another organization may instead prefer to contribute more to a 401(k) or 403(b) plan or purchase additional life insurance.

Special Benefits and Perks   A number of healthcare employers have used a wide range of special benefits and perks to attract and retain employees. The more creative perks include providing access to a day care center, hair salon, post office, and dry cleaners to make their lives easier. By offering these special benefits and perks, healthcare employers hope to reduce the time employees spend after work on personal chores and to thus be seen as more desirable employers where individuals will remain for longer stays. Flextime, signing bonuses, and relocation cost reimbursement are frequently offered to employees in areas of critical shortage, especially RNs, therapists, and pharmacists.[20]

Differentiation of Compensation   Based on performance, many individuals expect their rewards to be differentiated from others based on performance. For instance, if an employee receives about the same pay increase and overall pay as others who have lower productivity, more absenteeism, and work fewer hours, then the lack of differences in compensation may create a feeling of "unfairness." This inequity may lead to the individual deciding to look for another job that pays more money and where differences lead to differential compensation amounts.

When healthcare organizations have surveyed their employees, many have found that individuals are more satisfied with the levels of their pay than the processes used to determine pay. That is why the performance management system and performance appraisal processes in healthcare organizations must be linked to compensation increases. If some individuals receive high performance ratings, but compensation only changes the same as to others, then their desire to stay with the organization may diminish.

To achieve greater links between individual performance and compensation, a growing number of healthcare organizations are using variable pay and incentive programs. These programs provide bonuses or lump sum payments to reward extra performance.

The introduction of variable pay programs has been viewed in a controversial light for nonprofit healthcare organizations. Critics argue that extreme levels of variable pay for executives or employed physicians are inappropriate and contribute to the rising cost of healthcare. However, healthcare organizations frequently compete for the same talent with private-sector firms who can offer a wide range of variable pay options, including stock options.

Recognition   As depicted in Figure 7-4, employee recognition as a form of reward can be both tangible and intangible. The tangible recognition comes in many forms, such as employee of the month, perfect attendance, or other special awards. Recognition also can be intangible and psychological in nature. Feedback from managers and supervisors that acknowledges extra effort and performance of individuals provides recognition, even though monetary rewards are not given. For instance, many nursing homes use both tangible and intangible recognition as part of employee retention efforts. Employees who receive a

FIGURE 7-4 **Employee Recognition**

Tangible Recognition	Intangible Recognition

• Movie Tickets
• Extra Days Off
• Bonuses
• Gift Certificates
• Special Merit Awards
	• Thank You Notes
	• Public Acknowledgement
	• Personal Compliments About a
	  Job Well Done by Managers
	• Certificates of Recognition For:
	  - Perfect Attendance
	  - Perfect Safety Record
	  - Special Patent Care

recognition card from either residents or from their coworkers are recognized in newsletters or banquets held in their honor.[21]

Retention and Selection

Retention is affected by the *selection process* that tries to achieve a *person/job match* whereby individuals' knowledge, skills, and abilities are matched to the demands of the jobs they could be hired to perform. A number of organizations have found that high employee turnover rates in employees' first few months of employment often are linked to inadequate selection screening efforts. Once individuals have been placed into jobs, several job/work factors affect retention. Because individuals spend significant time at work, they expect *working conditions* to be good, given the nature of what is being done. Such factors as space, lighting, temperature, noise, layout, and other physical and environmental factors affect retention of employees. Also, employees expect to work with modern equipment and technology.

Additionally, there should be a *safe work environment,* whereby risks of accidents and injuries have been addressed. This is especially true for healthcare employers where safety risks can include exposure to disease, harmful chemicals, and radiation.

WORK/LIFE BALANCE

The changing demographics of the U.S. workforce have led to many individuals having to balance work responsibilities, family needs, and personal life demands. With more single parent families, dual-career couples with children, and workers' responsibilities for aging elderly relatives, balancing work and family roles may sometimes be very difficult. Such factors as work and family time demands and resources all must be considered.

Work/life programs offered by employers can include a wide range of items. Some include work/job options, such as flexible work scheduling, job sharing, or telecommuting. Others include benefits program components, such as flexible benefits, on-site fitness centers, childcare or elder-care assistance, veterinarian care for pets, flexible time off, and sick leave policies. Perhaps the greatest benefit of work flexibility is that it meshes well with work/family efforts by employers. The purpose of all these offerings is to communicate to individuals that the employer cares about the employees and recognizes the challenges of balancing work/life demands.

Balancing Patient Care Needs with Work Schedule Flexibility   The ability to have flexibility in work schedules and in how work is done has grown in importance for retention. Nearly two-thirds of the respondents of a recent Work & Family Connection's survey said work flexibility would most influence them to stay in their current jobs.[22] Healthcare professionals frequently cite this issue as the reason for leaving the healthcare workplace, especially hospitals, and finding positions in workplaces with less scheduling variability.

Healthcare managers are very aware of the need to balance patient care delivery, staffing requirements, and work schedule flexibility. Patient care must come first, but the lack of predictability of patient census in environments such as in-patient nursing units or emergency rooms requires scheduling that can frustrate even the most flexible workers.

One way hospitals, clinics, physician and dental offices, and nursing homes have creatively provided work flexibility is through the use of a variety of *work scheduling alternatives*. Examples of these alternatives include:

- *Staffing with Part-Time and Casual Workers*—replacing one or two full-time employees with multiple part-time and casual employees who can be scheduled for up to 16 or more hours per week, but with the opportunity to pick up additional hours if patient care needs require additional staff.

- *Developing Patient Census Prediction and Staffing Models*—although it is difficult to predict with 100 percent accuracy, some healthcare providers have become proficient at predicting the *core* staffing needs of their units, clinics, or departments. Based on such variables as the time of year, surgery demands, or seasonal infectious disease patterns, higher levels of *variable* staffing can be used. Based on good historical data, these staffing models can be surprisingly accurate.

- *Weekend Shifts*—many healthcare organizations rely on employees that only work week-end shifts. As an example, Saint Luke's Hospital of Kansas City uses a core of staff nurses for the week and a different core of staff nurses for the weekend.

- *Parent Shifts*—in an effort to provide shifts that allow employees to achieve work-life balance, some healthcare organizations have established parent shifts. These shifts are designed to provide employees with the time availability to be with their children during critical childcare times during the workday. The Cleveland Clinic offers flexible schedules for RNs who have trouble committing to 8- or 12-hour schedules because of childcare and related parenting obligations. Nurses can choose shorter shifts of 2 to 6 hours that work more effectively around their parenting needs.

- *Internal Staffing Pools*—Many healthcare organizations have developed internal staffing or float pools in lieu of utilizing external temporary employment agencies. These pools allow the organization to tap into the necessary staffing as patient care needs require and also offer a significant amount of flexibility for the staff on the pool.[23]

Employee Relationships with Supervisors and Co-workers

A final set of factors found to affect retention is based on the relationships that employees have in organizations. Healthcare organizations have long been aware of how poor supervisory skills and attitudes have affected employee retention. A poor supervisor can outweigh all the other positive efforts extended by the organization. Figure 7-5 depicts what the supervisor can do to contribute to employee retention.

One expectation that employees have is that they will be treated fairly at work. Such areas as the reasonableness of HR policies, the fairness of disciplinary actions, and the means used to decide work assignments and opportunities all affect employee retention. If individuals feel that policies are unreasonably restrictive or applied inconsistently, then they might be more likely to look at jobs offered by other employers.

Particularly important with the increasing demographic diversity of U.S. workplaces is that all employees, regardless of their gender, age, and other factors, have *nondiscriminatory treatment*. Organizational commitment and job satisfaction of ethnically diverse individuals may be affected by perceived discriminatory treatment.

Other concerns that affect employee retention are supervisory/management support and coworker relations. Many individuals build close relationships with those with whom they work. Coupled with coworker relationships is having supportive supervisory and management relationships. A supervisor builds positive relationships and aids retention by providing clear performance expectations, providing a safe, clean work environment, valuing the employee's contribution,

FIGURE 7-5 Supervisory Retention Efforts

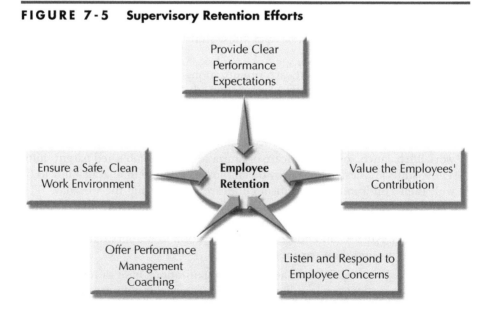

and providing coaching. As defined by individual employees, having a "good" boss means that communication is likely to be more open and the supervisor listens and responds to the employees' concerns.

RETENTION MANAGEMENT PROCESS

Given the above identified determinants of retention, it is important that HR professionals and their organizations have processes in place to manage retention of employees. Left to chance or infrequent attention, retention of employees is not as likely to be as successful. As indicated in Figure 7-6, the retention management process contains three primary phases, each of which is discussed next.

Retention Measurement and Assessment

To ensure that appropriate actions are taken to enhance retention and reduce turnover, it is important that management decisions be made using data and analyses, rather than subjective impressions, anecdotes of selected individual situations, or panic reactions to the loss of a few key people. That is why having several different types of measures and analyses is important.

Measures of Turnover   The turnover rate for an organization can be computed in different ways. The following formula from the U.S. Department of Labor is widely used where *separation* means leaving the organization.

$$\frac{\text{Number of employee separations during the month}}{\text{Total number of employees at mid-month}} \times 100$$

FIGURE 7-6   The Retention Management Process

I. Measurement and Assessment
- Employee surveys
- Exit interviews
- Data analysis

II. Managing Retention
- Recruiting and selection
- Orientation and training
- Compensation and benefits
- Career development and planning
- Employee relations

III. Evaluation and Follow-Up
- Regular review of turnover data
- Tracking of intervention results
- Adjustment of intervention efforts

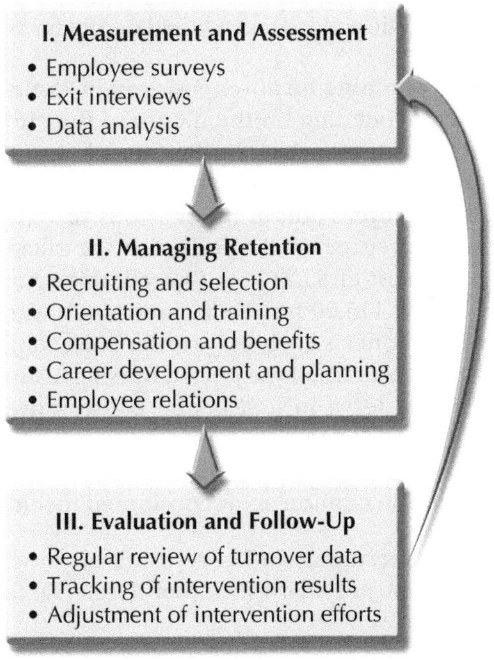

Turnover figures can range from almost 0 to over 100 percent per year, and normal turnover rates vary among industries and by positions. As an example, in a recent study[24] the national turnover rate for RNs is calculated to be 17 percent. Organizations that require entry-level employees to have few skills are likely to have higher turnover rates among those employees than among managerial personnel. Often a part of human resource information systems, turnover data can be gathered and analyzed in a number of ways, including the following:

- Jobs and job level
- Departments, units, and location
- Reason for leaving
- Length of service

- Demographic characteristics
- Education and training
- Skills and abilities
- Performance ratings/levels

Several examples illustrate why detailed analyses of turnover are important.[25] One long-term care organization had an organization-wide turnover rate that was not severe—but 80 percent of the turnover occurred in one unit. This imbalance indicated that some action was needed to resolve problems in that unit. At a family practice clinic there was 20 percent annual turnover, with 60 percent of that turnover occurring in the first 60 days of employment. By analyzing turnover rates by length of service, the HR manager of the clinic learned that the recruiting, selection, and training processes needed to be changed. By reducing the number of individuals hired who could not successfully complete training and perform satisfactorily after training, the clinic reduced turnover significantly.

Likewise, a medical center found that its greatest turnover in RNs occurred 24 to 36 months after hire, so the organization instituted a two-year employee recognition program and expanded the career development and training activities for employees with at least two years of service. In all of these examples, the turnover rates declined as a result of the actions taken based on the turnover analyses done.

Costs of Turnover   Determining turnover costs can be done in a relatively simple or complex manner, depending on the nature of the efforts and data used. Figure 7-7 is a simplified costing model. In that model, if a job pays $25,000 (A) and benefits cost 30 percent (B), then the total annual cost for one employee is $32,500. Assuming 10 employees quit in the previous year (D) and that it takes three months for the employee to be fully productive, the calculation in (F) results in a per person turnover cost of $3,217.50. Overall, this means that the annual turnover cost would be $32,175.00 for the 10 individuals who left. It should be noted that this simplified model is likely very conservative, but it makes the point that turnover is costly. For instance, if the job is a nursing assistant in a large nursing home and 150 people leave in a year, the conservative model results in turnover costs of more than $500,000 per year.

More detailed and sophisticated turnover costing models consider a number of factors. Some of the most common areas considered include the following:

- *Hiring Costs*—includes recruiting and advertising expenses, search fees, HR interviewer and staff time and salaries, employee referral fees, relocation and

FIGURE 7-7   Simplified Turnover Costing Model

JOB TITLE _____

A. Typical annual pay for job   _____
B. Percentage of pay for benefits times (×) annual pay   _____
C. Total employee annual cost (add A + B)   _____
D. How many employees voluntarily quit in this job in the past 12 months?   _____
E. How long does it take for one employee to become fully productive (in months)?   _____
F. Per person turnover cost:
   (Multiply E ÷ 12 × C × 30%*)   _____
G. Annual turnover cost for this job:
   (Multiply F × D)   _____

*Assumes 30% productivity throughout the learning period (E).

moving costs, supervisor and managerial time and salaries, employment testing costs, reference checking time, preemployment medical expenses, etc.

- *Training Costs*—Includes paid orientation time, training staff time and salaries, costs of training materials, supervisors' and managers' time and salaries, coworker "coaching" time and salaries, etc.

- *Productivity Costs*—Includes lost productivity due to "break-in" time of new employees, loss of customer knowledge and contacts, unfamiliarity with organizational products and services, more time to use organizational resources and systems, etc.

- *Separation Costs*—Includes HR staff and supervisor time and salaries to prevent separations, exit interview time, unemployment expenses, legal fees for separations challenged, etc.

Employee Surveys   The use of employee surveys is helpful to diagnose specific problem areas, identify employee needs or preferences, and reveal areas in which HR activities are well-received or are viewed negatively. For example, questionnaires may be sent to employees to collect ideas for revising a performance appraisal system or to determine if employees are satisfied with their benefits programs. Regardless of the topic of the survey, obtaining employee input provides managers and HR professionals with data on the "retention climate" in an organization.[26]

One specific type of survey used by many organizations is an **attitude survey** that focuses on employees' feelings and beliefs about their jobs and the organization. By serving as a means to obtain data on how employees view their jobs, their supervisors, their coworkers, and organizational policies and practices, these surveys can be starting points for reducing turnover and increasing employee retention for longer periods of time. Some employers conduct attitude surveys on a regularly scheduled basis (such as every year), while others do so intermittently. As the use of the Internet has spread, more organizations have begun conducting attitude surveys electronically.[27]

Often a "research" survey developed in-house is poorly structured, asks questions in a confusing manner, or leads employees to respond in ways that will give "favorable" results.[28] By asking employees to respond candidly to an attitude survey, management is building up employees' expectations that action will be taken on the concerns identified. Therefore, a crucial part of conducting an attitude survey is to provide feedback to those who participated in it. It is especially important that even negative survey results be communicated to avoid fostering the appearance of hiding the results or placing blame. Generally, it is recommended that employee feedback be done through meetings with managers, supervisors, and employees; often, this is done in small groups to encourage interaction and discussion.

Exit Interviews A widely used data source on turnover is the **exit interview,** in which those who are leaving the organization are asked to identify the reasons for their departure. Exit interviews are widely used among healthcare employers to gather information needed to make changes to aid retention. A wide range of issues can be examined in exit interviews.

HR specialists, rather than department managers or supervisors, usually conduct these interviews because a skilled HR interviewer may be able to gain useful information that departing employees may not share with managers and supervisors, particularly if it pertains to problems and issues with those managers and supervisors. Departing employees may be reluctant to divulge their real reasons for leaving because they may wish to return to the organization someday. Also, they may fear that candid responses will hinder their chances of receiving favorable references. The following suggestions may be useful when conducting exit interviews:[29]

- Decide when the discussions will occur. Usually, they are done on the last day of a departing individual's employment. Emphasize that the information provided by departing employees will be treated confidentially.
- Develop a checklist or a set of standard questions so that the information can be summarized. Typical areas covered include reasons for leaving, supervision, pay, training, best- and least-liked aspects of the job, and organization to which the employee is moving.
- Emphasize that the information provided by the departing employee will be treated confidentially, and will be summarized to use for making future improvements and changes in the organization.
- Recognize that former employees may be more willing to provide information on questionnaires mailed to their homes or in telephone conversations conducted some time after they have left the organization.

Retention Interventions

Based on what the measurement and assessment data reveal, a variety of HR interventions can be undertaken to improve retention. Turnover can be controlled and reduced in several ways. During the *recruiting process,* the job should be outlined and a realistic preview presented, so that the reality of the job matches the expectations of the new employee. By ensuring that the expectations of potential employees match what the organization is likely to offer, this may reduce voluntary turnover.

Another way to eliminate turnover is to improve the *selection process* in order to better match applicants to jobs. By fine-tuning the selection process and hiring people who will not have disciplinary or performance problems or whose work histories suggest higher turnover potential, employers can reduce turnover. Once selected, individuals who receive effective orientation and training are less likely to leave.

Other HR factors are important as well. *Compensation* is important because a competitive, fair, and equitable pay system can help reduce turnover. Inadequate benefits also may lead to voluntary turnover, especially if other employers are offering significantly higher compensation levels for similar jobs. *Career development* and *planning* can help an organization keep employees. If individuals believe they have few opportunities for career development and advancement, they are more likely to leave the organization. *Employee relations,* including fair/nondiscriminatory treatment and enforcement of HR policies, can enhance retention, also.

Healthcare organizations can adopt programs to enhance their retention efforts. One example of successful retention interventions for nurses is the "Magnet Hospital" designation awarded by the American Nurses Credentialing Council (ANCC), an affiliate of the American Nurses Association. The magnet program is the result of research conducted by the American Academy of Nursing that analyzed how to attract and retain qualified nurses. The research suggests that hospitals that pursue retention initiatives that include more collaborative effort between staff and management, flatter organizational structures that allow nurses more say in their job design and patient care delivery, and supportive top nursing management have more job satisfaction and better patient outcomes.[30]

Healthcare HR professionals should use the information on retention determinants and the assessment information to identify what changes are needed to improve retention. Usually, a multifaceted approach is needed, rather than just focusing on one area. For example, just changing benefits without considering the recruitment and selection processes may not result in attracting and hiring individuals more likely to stay longer. That is why it is important to evaluate and follow up to see if retention intervention efforts have produced lower turnover rates and extended the stays of existing employees.

Evaluation and Follow-Up

Once retention intervention efforts have been implemented, it is important that they be evaluated and that appropriate follow-up and adjustments be made. Regular *review of turnover data* can identify when turnover increases or decreases among different employees classified by length of service, education, department, gender, or other factors.

Tracking intervention results also should be part of evaluation efforts. Some healthcare organizations may use pilot programs to see how turnover is affected before extending the changes to the entire organization. For instance, to test the effect of flextime scheduling on employee turnover, a clinic might allow flexible scheduling in one department on a pilot basis. If the turnover rate of the employees in that department drops in comparison with the turnover in other departments still working set schedules, then the experimental pilot project may indicate that flexible scheduling can reduce turnover. Next, the clinic might extend the use of flexible scheduling to other departments.

Retention of employees can be increased through use of a coordinated process. Numerous examples of healthcare organizations that have focused on retention management illustrate that attracting and retaining human resources can contribute significantly to organizational success.

CASE

A nonprofit health system is composed of seven hospitals with about 2,000 beds, more than 200 clinic and outpatient locations, 1,200 physicians, and over 7,500 other employees who work throughout the organization. Management saw that HR issues needed "acute care treatment." Turnover rates of 24 percent, coupled with over 500 unfilled positions, were costing the firm over $15 million annually.

Four years later, the turnover rates have declined to 12 percent and open positions have dropped to fewer than 100. Because of their improvements, and especially its retention successes, the healthcare system's HR practices won several local and national awards.

To specifically focus on retention efforts, the system created an Employee Retention Task Force whose focus was to decrease turnover and increase employee satisfaction. The task force identified several strategies to be used. One program illustrates how they approached retention of nurses. The Nursing Residence Program has caught national attention. Each resident (or new nurse) is paired with an experienced nurse or "preceptor" based on interests, personality, and so on. Also, a mentor outside the nursing department adds support and encouragement to indi-

viduals. Nursing staff meet monthly for training. In addition, they can visit various other departments (pediatrics, cardiology, etc.) in which they may have career interests. Nurses interested in management can shadow the department director to see how the department is managed. Returning nurses who have been out of the field five or more years are enrolled, retrained, and paired with recently finished residents.

The system is the exception to the turnover levels in nursing. Compared to the U.S. health care industry rate of 20 percent, its turnover rate of 7.6 percent is exceptional. Another key to aiding nursing recruitment and retention is an extensive training and development program. Many different short courses and classes are provided to employees at no cost. As part of this program, the organization pays up to $20,000 for employees selected for a career advancement program to obtain nursing degrees.

Questions

1. Describe how the system's practices match with the recommended retention practices covered in the chapter.
2. Why was a broad-based approach to nursing retention important?

END NOTES

1. Robert Levering and Milton Moskowitz, "The 100 Best Companies to Work For," *Fortune* (January 24, 2005), 61–72.

2. David Clutterbuck, "How to Get the Payback From Investment in Work-Life Balance,"

Journal for Quality & Participation (Fall 2004), 17–19.

3. Charlotte Huff, "Hospital Aims for Culture Where Employees Never Want to Leave," *Workforce Management* (February 2005), accessed at *http://www.workforce.com*.

4. Nellie C. Robinson and Sue Ellen Pinkerton, "The Children's National Medical Center Story: Nursing Shortage to Employer of Choice," *Nursing Economics* (March/April 2004), 91–93.

5. Used with permission, Summit Orthopedics, St. Paul, Minnesota.

6. Adapted from Melanie Evans, "Reaping Rewards," *Modern Healthcare* (November 22, 2004), 12.

7. Louis Lavelle, "Coming Next: A War for Talent," *Business Week Online* (September 29, 2003), 1, accessed at *http://www.businessweek.com*.

8. "The 2004 U.S. Job Recovery and Retention Poll Findings," The Society of Human Resources Management (SHRM), accessed at *http://www.shrm.org*.

9. Denis Rousseau and Zipi Sherling, "Piece of the Action: Owners and the Changing Employment Relationship," *Academy of Management Review*, 28 (2003), 553–570.

10. Virgil Larson, "Age Differences Key to Motivation," *Omaha World Herald* (March 17, 2003), D1.

11. "What Nurses Want," *Marketing Health Services* (Fall 2003), 3.

12. Edward H. O'Neil, "The Workforce Challenge and Opportunity," *Futurescan Healthcare Trends and Implications* (Health Administration Press 2005), 32–35.

13. "As Job Satisfaction Declines Further, Demands on Workers Rise, Survey Says," Bulletin to Management (October 2, 2003), 314.

14. James Peltier, John A. Schebrowsky, and Alexander Nil, "Crossing Cultures," *Marketing Health Services* (Spring 2004), 26–34.

15. Levering and Moskowitz, "The 100 Best Companies to Work For," *Fortune* (January 24, 2005), 61–72.

16. Joint Commission Resources, "The Role of Human Resources Professionals in Providing Competent Staff," *Issues in Human Resources for Hospitals* (2004), 19.

17. "Organizational Climate Helps Predict Performance," *TD* (June 2005), 16.

18. "Workforce Ideas in Action 3," *American Hospital Association* (January 2004), 13. Also, for more information contact Thomas Au, M.D., *Thomasaumd@hawaii.rr.com*.

19. Cindy Marano, "Beating the Nursing Home Staffing Blues," *Nursing Homes Long-Term Care Management* (2003), 48–49.

20. Sandy Morgan and Patricia Tobin, "Managing the Nursing Workforce," *Nursing Management* (October 2004), 4–5.

21. Adapted from Golden Bethume, Dennis Sherrod, and Linda Youngblood, "Tips to Retain a Happy, Healthy Staff," *Nursing Management* (April 2005), 25–29; and Roger Schenkel and Cathy Gardner, "5 Ways to Retain Good Staff," *Family Practice Management* (November/December 2004), 57–58.

22. "Flexibility, Raise Would Convince Workers to Stay," *IOMAS Human Resources Management Report* (September 2004), 9.

23. "Short-Term Fixes with Long-Lasting Implications," *Healthcare Financial Management* (January 2005), Special Section, 6.

24. The Advisory Board Company, Washington, DC. 2003–2004 Registered nurse recruitment and turnover range averages. *http://www.theadvisoryboardcompany.com*.

25. Brenda Campbell, "The High Cost of Turnover," *Black Enterprise* (December 2002), 61.

26. For more information on surveys used in healthcare organizations visit *http://stanard.com*.

27. Marcie Levine and Peter Tobias, "Take Stock Then Take Action," *HR.com* (January 2004), 1–5, accessed at *http://www.hr.com*.

28. Charlotte Garvey, "Getting Feedback You Can Depend On," *HR Magazine*, 48 (March 2003), 1–2.

29. Fay Hansen, "Weighing the Truth of Exit Interviews," *Workforce* (December 2002), 37; and Theresa Sweeney, "Exit Interviews," *Credit Union Management* (November 2002), 38–39.

30. Jan Greene, "Attracting Nurses—Why Magnet Hospitals Succeed," *Trustee* (April 2003), 20–23.

Training and Development in Healthcare Organizations

Learning Objectives

After you read this chapter, you should be able to:

- Discuss how job performance and training can be integrated.

- Identify how organizational and training strategies are linked.

- Define various learning styles.

- Describe the orientation, training, and staff development requirements of the Joint Commission.

- Explain the unique aspects of healthcare employee development.

Healthcare HR Insights

Because of the current staffing shortage in the healthcare industry, many healthcare organizations have developed "grow your own" strategies in order to fill their vacant positions. This approach means taking individuals with little or no previous healthcare experience or education and providing them with the training and experiences to help them develop the necessary knowledge, skills, and ability (KSAs) to successfully perform a healthcare job.

In some cases healthcare organizations have partnered with governmental or not-for-profit agencies in developing special work programs designed to help individuals who are often referred to as the chronically unemployed or underemployed. These efforts are allowing healthcare organizations to access a human resource that may not have otherwise been considered.

- The Hospital of Saint Raphael in New Haven, Connecticut, has partnered with a State Agency to develop a program referred to as HOPE (Having an Opportunity to Prepare for Employment). This 16-week program addresses Connecticut's Welfare-to-Work legislation, offering job skills training at the hospital for 30 hours per week. The hospital has hired nearly 50 percent of the 200 participants who have graduated from the program.[1]

- Achieve, a job retention program based in Cuyahoga County, Ohio, is serving the staffing needs of the long-term care employers in the county. The goal is to increase entry-level employee retention, promote skill building for employee success, and reduce employee absenteeism and turnover. This very unique program pairs social workers and job coaches with long-term care employers to help recently hired, low-wage, entry-level workers keep their jobs. Achieve is reporting an 82 percent retention rate for employees in the program after 90 days of employment.[2]

These examples illustrate the importance for healthcare HR professionals to think creatively. Utilizing untapped human resource sources, combined with effective training and development programs, will be increasingly needed.

Both training and development are critical in healthcare organizations to ensure the ongoing delivery of safe, competent care. **Training** is a process whereby people acquire capabilities to aid in the achievement of organizational goals. Because this process is tied to a variety of organizational purposes, training can be viewed either narrowly or broadly. In a limited sense, training provides employees with specific, identifiable knowledge and skills for use on their current jobs. **Employee development** is broader in scope and focuses on individuals gaining new capabilities useful for both current and future jobs.

NATURE OF TRAINING IN HEALTHCARE ORGANIZATIONS

Contemporary training in healthcare organizations has evolved significantly over the past decade. Overall, more employers are recognizing that training their human resources is vital. Currently, U.S. employers spend at least $60 billion annually on training. For the average employer, training expenditures average at least 1.5 percent to 2 percent of payroll expenses, and run $677 per eligible employee, according to a study by the American Society for Training and Development (ASTD). Organizations that see training as especially crucial to business competitiveness average $1,665 in training expenditures per eligible employee.[3] Historically, healthcare organizations have lagged behind in training expenditures in comparison to organizations in other industries.

As part of strategic competitiveness, employees whose capabilities stay current and who receive regular training are better able to cope with the challenges and changes occurring in healthcare. Compare the healthcare environment of today—with all of the new technologies, the explosion of Web technology, and the increasing cost pressures—to five years ago. Without continual training, healthcare organizations may not have staff members with the KSAs needed to provide care and manage organizations. Training in healthcare organizations is offered in many different areas and different ways, as noted in Figure 8-1.

Training also assists organizational competitiveness by aiding in the retention of employees. A primary reason why many individuals stay or leave organizations is career training and development opportunities. Healthcare employers that invest in training and developing their employees do so in part to enhance their retention efforts.

Something else is changing as well. An old axiom in HR management traditionally has been, "When times get tough, training is the first expenditure to be cut." But a growing number of healthcare employers have recognized that training is not just a cost; it is an investment in the human capital of the organization that benefits the entire organization longer-term. Although training expenditures may decline some as organizational cost-cutting occurs, more progressive healthcare organizations seldom reduce training efforts significantly. In fact, some healthcare organizations have invested in training as a way to increase revenues. As an example, Sarasota Memorial Hospital, located on the west coast of Florida, has developed a customer service initiative that focuses extensively on

---

FIGURE 8-1   Common Types of Nonclinical Healthcare Training

- Sexual harassment prevention
- Fire safety
- Personal computer courses
- Team building skills
- JCAHO (Joint Commission on Acreditation of Healthcare Organizations) standards
- Patient safety
- Quality improvement techniques
- Customer service skills
- Diversity awareness
- Interpersonal communications skills

employee training to improve previously low customer service ratings. Training as a key part of the initiative has had a measurable impact on the hospital's customer service scores and has also helped to improve its bottom line.[4]

Chief Learning Officers

To emphasize the importance of training, some healthcare organizations have created a position titled *Chief Learning Officer (CLO)* or *Chief Knowledge Officer (CKO)*. The CLO is not just a training director with an inflated new title. Instead, the CLO is a leader who contributes clinical, administrative, and regulatory knowledge through training for individual employees and for the organization. CLOs must demonstrate a high level of comfort in working with boards of directors and the top management team, as well as with physicians and other clinical professionals.

Integration of Job Performance, Training, and Learning

Job performance, training, and employee learning must be integrated to be effective. First, because training interventions are best when moved closer to the job in order to achieve real-time learning, the linkage between training and job performance is vital. Consider the following example. As a new respiratory therapist receives orientation to the Intensive Care Unit (ICU), the trainee works closely with an experienced respiratory therapist. The experienced therapist serves in the role of preceptor, providing the new therapist with guidance and hands-on training. Trainees can watch the trainer (preceptor) perform procedures in the proper manner, attempt to safely replicate the actions, and receive real-time feedback in the actual work setting.

Second, organizations prefer more authentic (and hence more effective) training experiences for their trainees, using real organizational problems to advance employee learning. Rather than separating the training experience from actual job performance context, trainers who incorporate everyday operations as learning examples increase the realism of training exercises and scenarios. Many healthcare organizations, such as Cincinnati's Children's Hospital, have initiated diversity awareness and skills training. The objective of Cincinnati's Children's Hospital's diversity training is to present actual employee, patient/parent, and visitor situations that include diversity-related issues to the trainees and to teach them how to react and respond appropriately. During the training, real incidents of diversity conflict are discussed, along with what actions were effective and ineffective in dealing with the various situations.[5] Effective responses are presented as best practice approaches to dealing with various diversity issues. This is an example of another way that training, learning, and job performance have become more integrated. As a result, training becomes more performance-focused.

Training as Performance Consulting

Performance consulting is a process by which a training facilitator (either internal or external to the organization) and the organizational client work together to

---

FIGURE 8-2 **Performance Consulting**

boost workplace performance. As depicted in Figure 8-2, performance consulting is based on desired and actual organizational results being compared to desired and actual employee performance. Once these comparisons are made, then performance consulting considers all the factors in dealing with performance issues:[6]

- Focusing on identifying and addressing *root causes* of performance problems
- Recognizing the *interaction of individual and organizational factors* that work together to influence employee performance
- Comparing the *actions and accomplishments of high performers* with actions of more typical performers.

Regardless of whether the trainer is internal to the organization or is an outside training consultant, training cannot automatically solve every employee performance problem. Instead, training must be viewed as one piece of a larger *bundled* solution. For instance, some employee performance issues might be resolved by creating a training program for employees, while other situations might call for compensation or job design changes.

The following example illustrates the performance consulting approach. Assume you are the HR training specialist in a large medical center and the Director of Patient Care contacts you about creating a training program for the nurses on the patient care units. Over the last six months, the Director has received various complaints about the nurses' interactions and communications with staff from other medical center departments that support the units. The Director asks you to develop a customized training program on effective communications and collaborative working relationships.

Instead of just developing a training program, users of performance consulting gather more information in order to identify: (1) the root causes of the communication problems; (2) the various individual RNs and organizational factors that are contributing to this issue; and (3) the primary reasons for the gap between effective RNs and lower performance RNs on the units. Obtaining all of this information helps in determining whether *any* form of training will play a role in an integrated performance improvement solution. Perhaps recent changes in patient volumes have resulted in higher work demands on the RNs and have contributed to their need to demand more responsiveness from support department personnel. Whatever the causes, a tailored and comprehensive approach is needed to address the communications and interaction issues.

Integrating Training Responsibilities

One of the most important implications resulting from the performance consulting approach is that HR staff members and trainers work as partners with operating managers to integrate training that bolsters both individual, employee, and organizational performance. A typical division of training responsibilities is shown in Figure 8-3. HR can serve as a source of expert training assistance and coordination. HR often has a more long-range view of employee careers and the development of the entire organization than do individual operating managers. The difference is especially true at lower levels in the organization. However, managers are likely to be the best source of technical information used in skills training. They also are in a better position to decide when employees need

FIGURE 8 - 3   Typical Division of HR Responsibilities: Training

HR UNIT

- Prepares skill-training materials
- Conducts the organizational new employee orientation
- Coordinates training efforts
- Conducts or arranges for off-the-job training
- Coordinates career plans and employee development efforts
- Provides input and expertise for organizational development
- Maintains organizational training records (Safety and Joint Commission)

HEALTHCARE MANAGERS

- Conduct departmental new employee orientation
- Provide technical information
- Monitor training needs
- Conduct on-the-job training
- Continually discuss employees' growth and future potential
- Participate in organizational change efforts
- Determine on-going training needs for their areas of responsibility

training or retraining. Because of the close and continual interaction they have with their employees, it is appropriate that managers determine and discuss employee career possibilities and plans with individual employees. Therefore, a training partnership between the HR staff members and operating managers is very important.

Legal Issues and Training

There are a number of legal issues that must be considered when designing training. The primary one is to ensure that the criteria and practices used to select individuals for inclusion in training programs are job-related and must not unfairly restrict the participation of protected-class members. Another concern is differences in pay based on training to which protected-class members have not had equal access. A third is the use of training as a basis for selecting individuals for promotions, particularly if protected-group individuals have not had adequate opportunities for the training needed. Failure to accommodate individuals with disabilities to participate in training has led to equal employment opportunity (EEO) lawsuits against a number of employers.

Another contemporary legal issue is the use of *training contracts* whereby employers require employees participating in expensive training to sign training contracts in order to protect the costs and time invested in specialized employee training. For instance, a clinic that has paid $15,000 to have a therapist certified may use a training contract whereby one-fourth of the cost is forgiven for each year the therapist stays with the organization following the training. If the therapist leaves sooner, then the clinic can use the contract to collect the unpaid balance.

Strategic Training

Training adds value to an organization by linking training strategy to organizational objectives, goals, and business strategies. **Strategic training** focuses on efforts that develop individual worker competencies and can produce ongoing value and competitive advantages for the organization. This basically means that training must be based on organizational plans and HR planning efforts.[7] Strategic training also implies that HR and training professionals must help the organization create competitive advantage. Ultimately, to the extent that organizational training efforts are inherently difficult for competitors to imitate or copy, training can be considered a strategic asset.

A strategic training mindset also reduces the idea that training can solve most employee or organizational problems. As in the earlier situation where the Director of Patient Care was convinced that her employees needed communications skills training, it is not uncommon for operating managers, HR professionals, and trainers to react to problems by saying, "I need a training program on X." With a strategic training focus, it is more likely that there will be an assessment of such requests to determine what training or nontraining solutions should be used to address the performance issues. Such a focus also encourages performance and training expectations to be set so that results of the training are measurable.

ETHICAL PRACTICES AND COMPLIANCE

As part of new employee orientation programs, many healthcare organizations include requirements for new employees to sign off on various components of the organizational compliance program. Typical elements include:

- *Patient Data Privacy and Health Insurance Portability and Accountability Act (HIPAA) requirements*—require healthcare workers to protect the confidentiality of patients' protected health information
- *Internet and Computer Usage*—requires workers to utilize the Internet and access their work computer in a professional manner, not accessing pornographic, gambling, or other sites inappropriate to the workplace
- *Conflict of Interest*—ensures that employees are acting in the best interest of the organization, not making purchasing decisions or developing vendor relations based on bribes or other forms of personal gain
- *Vulnerable Adult (Patient) Standards*—depending on the type of healthcare organization or facility and in accordance with various state statutes, organizations require employees to be protective of patients, clients, or residents with mental or judgment impairment due to illness or age. These standards also require sensitivity to these individuals' vulnerability to physical and sexual abuse, financial fraud, and other forms of mistreatment.

It is important that healthcare organizations maintain high standards in ensuring the delivery and documentation of this information. If issues arise and organizations have failed to provide orientation or to document its efforts, the penalties and liabilities to the organizations are typically greater.

THE TRAINING PROCESS

Effective training requires the use of a systematic training process. Figure 8-4 depicts the training process as having four phases: *assessment, design, delivery,* and *evaluation.* Using such a process reduces the likelihood of unplanned, uncoordinated, and haphazard training efforts that may significantly reduce the learning that should happen from occurring. A discussion of each phase of the training process follows.

Assessment of Training Needs

Because training should be designed to help the organization accomplish its objectives, assessing organizational training needs is the diagnostic phase of setting training objectives. **Assessment** considers employee and organizational performance issues to determine if training can help. Using the performance

FIGURE 8-4   Training Process

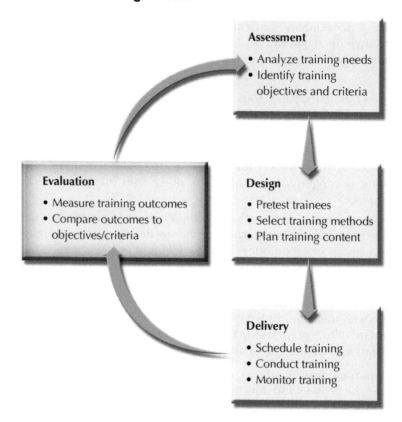

consulting approach mentioned earlier, managers must consider nontraining factors as well, such as compensation, organization structure, job design, physical work settings, and others. But if training is necessary, then the assessment efforts lead to analyzing the need for training and specifying the objectives of the training effort.[8] For example, looking at the performance of clerks in a patient accounting department, a manager might believe that their data-entry and keyboard abilities are weak and that they would profit by having instruction in these areas. As part of assessment, the clerks might be given a keyboard data-entry test to measure their current skills. An objective of increasing the clerks' keyboard entry speed to 60 words per minute without errors might be established. The number of words per minute without errors is the criterion against which training success can be measured, and it represents the way in which the objective is made specific.

Establishing Training Objectives and Priorities   Once the training needs have been identified using the various analyses, then training objectives and priorities should be established. All of the gathered data is used to compile a **gap analysis,** which identifies the distance between where an organization is with its employee capabilities and where it needs to be. Training objectives and priorities are set to close the gap. Three types of training objectives can be set:

Knowledge: Impart cognitive information and details to trainees.

Skill: Develop behavior changes in how jobs and various task requirements are performed.

Attitude: Create interest in and awareness of the importance of training.

The success of training should be measured in terms of the objectives set. Useful objectives are measurable. For example, an objective for a new Medicare biller might be to "demonstrate the ability to explain the various billing processes in the department within two weeks." This objective serves as a check on internalization, or whether the person really learned and is able to use the training.

Because training seldom is an unlimited budget item and there are multiple training needs in an organization, it is necessary to prioritize needs. Ideally, training needs are ranked in importance on the basis of organizational objectives. The training most needed to improve the performance of the organization should be done first in order to produce visible results more quickly.

Training Design

Once training objectives have been determined, **training design** can be established. Regardless of whether the training is job specific or broader in nature, designing the training determines how the assessed needs are to be addressed. Effective training design considers learning concepts, legal issues, and different types of training.

Learning: The Focus of Training   Working in organizations should be a continual learning process, and learning is at the heart of all training activities. Different learning approaches are possible, but learning is a complex psychological process that is not fully understood even by practitioners or research psychologists. There are three primary considerations when designing training: (1) determining learner readiness, (2) understanding different learning styles, and (3) designing training for transfer. Each of these elements must be considered in order for the training design to mesh together.[9]

Adult Learning   Malcolm Knowles' classic work on adult learning and subsequent work suggest these five principles for designing training for adults:[10]

1. Have the need to know why they are learning something
2. Have a need to be self-directed
3. Bring more work-related experiences into the learning process
4. Enter into a learning experience with a problem-centered approach to learning
5. Are motivated to learn by both extrinsic and intrinsic factors

Because adults compose most learners in healthcare organizations, there are many implications for training design from Knowles' principles. For instance, trainers cannot expect to do a brain dump of material (i.e., the *fire-hose approach*) without giving trainees the context or bigger picture of why the participants need to know the training information. This concept is referred to as **whole learning** or **Gestalt learning.** As applied to job training, this means that instructions should be divided into small elements, but only *after* employees have had the opportunity to see how all the elements fit together.

Reinforcement and Immediate Confirmation   The concept of **reinforcement** is based on the **law of effect,** which states that people tend to repeat responses that give them some type of positive reward and avoid actions associated with negative consequences. Closely related is another learning concept called **immediate confirmation:** people learn best if reinforcement and feedback are given as soon as possible after training.

Transfer of Training   Finally, training interventions should be designed for the highest positive transfer of training. Transfer occurs when trainees actually use on the job what they learned in training. Estimates of how much training effectively gets transferred in corporate training are fairly dismal.[11]

Effective transfer of training meets two conditions. First, the trainees can take the material learned in training and apply it to the job context in which they work. Second, employees maintain their use of the learned material over time. A number of approaches can increase the transfer of training.[12] Offering trainees an overview of the training content and process before the actual training seems to help with both short-term and longer-term training transfer. Another specific way to aid transfer of training to job situations is to ensure that the training mirrors the job context as much as possible. For example, training nursing managers to be better selection interviewers should include role-playing with "applicants" who respond in the same way that real applicants would.

TYPES OF TRAINING

Training can be designed to meet a number of different objectives. Consequently, several types of training must be designed. One useful classification tool is to view training as being of several types:

- *Required and Regular Training*—Done to comply with various mandated or legal requirements (e.g., JCAHO, Equal Employment Opportunity or EEO), and as training for all employees (new employee orientation)

- *Job/Technical Training*—Done so that employees can perform their jobs, tasks, and responsibilities well (e.g., customer service, computer and machine operations)

- *Interpersonal and Problem-Solving Training*—Conducted to address both operational and interpersonal problems and improving organizational working relationships (e.g., team building, conflict resolution)

* *Developmental and Innovative Training*—Focused to enhance individual and organizational capabilities for the long-term future (e.g., organizational change, creative thinking)

Orientation: Training for New Employees

As required by the Occupational Safety and Health Administration (OSHA) and for those healthcare organizations that subscribe to JCAHO, all newly employed healthcare employees must attend orientation. All employees who routinely rotate to different areas of the health facility should also receive orientations to each of the areas. Examples of employees who rotate include RNs, respiratory therapists, agency nurses, and other contingency staff employees. Additionally, orientation is required for employees who have been reemployed, transferred, or promoted to new duties and for employees who have been impacted by departmental or organizational redesigns.

There are several key purposes of orientation. The most important ones are to:

* Establish a favorable employee impression of the organization and the job.
* Provide organization and job information.
* Enhance interpersonal acceptance by coworkers.
* Accelerate new employees' socialization and integration into the organization.
* Ensure quicker employee performance, productivity, and safety.

Effective orientation efforts contribute to both short-term and longer-term employment success.[13] One way that orientations are being made more effective is through the use of electronic orientation. Employers place general employee orientation information on organizational intranets or on corporate Web sites. New employees can log on and go through much of the general material on organizational history, structure, products and services, mission statements, and other background information instead of having to sit in a classroom where the information is delivered in person or by videotape. The more specific questions and areas can be addressed by HR staff and others after the Web-based information has been reviewed by the new employees. Figure 8-5 shows the typical components of organizational and departmental orientations. As noted, many of the topics would lend themselves to Web-based presentation complemented by group meetings.

Unfortunately, many new employee orientation sessions are seen as boring, irrelevant, and a waste of time by both new employees and by their department supervisors and managers. Many healthcare organizations are reconsidering their approach to new employee orientations in an effort to make the event more interesting and relevant. As an example, a large home health agency conducts its new employee orientation at a breakfast meeting, with extensive use of videos and presenters that incorporate humor and real-situation information in the presentations.

FIGURE 8-5 **Typical Components of Healthcare Orientations**

ORGANIZATIONAL ORIENTATION	DEPARTMENTAL ORIENTATION
• Mission vision and values	• Departmental structure
• Organizational ethics	• Patient/work flow
• Organizational structure	• Tour of area
• Customer service requirements	• Job responsibilities
• Patient safety	• Performance standards
• OSHA and general safety	• Departmental relationships
• Maintaining confidentiality	• Unit/Department-specific safety information
• Infection control practices	• Department policies
• Patient rights	
• Benefits, compensation, and HR policies	
• Security and fire safety	

Encourage Self-Development

Not all of the training and education needs of healthcare employees can be met through organizational, departmental, or supervisory-guided training. Employee training needs are often individualized and require employees to take the initiative to meet their own needs. However, the organization must encourage and provide employees with the resources and encouragement to pursue self-development.[14] Encouraging and facilitating self-development can take many forms, including the following:

- Resource libraries or learning labs where employees can research information or develop procedural skills in a self-paced manner
- Computer-based training (CBT) that employees can access either at the health facility or from their home computers
- Opportunities to attend professional society meetings that offer a variety of workshops and educational forums
- Tuition reimbursement or stipends to pursue technical or college-level course work

Beyond the importance of encouraging self-development for purposes of ensuring staff competency, a healthcare organization's investment in the self-development efforts described above can contribute to staff retention. Retention of competent staff further contributes to safe, high-quality patient care.

On-going Training and Development

Training and development take many forms in the healthcare setting. These include, among others, on-the-job preceptorship by the supervisor or another proficient employee; in-service education on new procedures, policies, or processes; continuing education classes; and professional development workshops or seminars. The general objectives of these training and development efforts are to continually ensure employee competence and to enhance employees' overall knowledge of their job duties, department, and organization. The specific objectives include the following:

- Correct performance or competence deficiencies
- Provide training on new technology, techniques, or processes
- Meet safety or regulatory compliance requirements in such areas as blood-borne pathogens or fire safety standards
- Prepare employees for new job duties or promotional opportunities

Ensuring on-going training and development of healthcare employees is typically the responsibility of the employees' supervisors or department heads. However, HR plays a significant role in helping supervisors monitor attendance at organizational-level training such as safety training and providing processes for documenting attendance at these programs.

Delivery of Training

The amount of each type of training done varies by organization, depending on the strategic plans, resources, and needs identified in various organizations. Once training has been designed, the actual delivery of training can begin. It is generally recommended that the training be piloted or conducted on a trial basis in order to ensure that the training meets the needs identified and that the design is appropriate. However, regardless of the type of training done, there are a number of different approaches and methods of training that can be used. The growth of training technology has expanded the choices available.

Regardless of the approaches used, there are a variety of considerations that must be balanced when selecting training approaches and methods. The common variables considered are:

- Nature of training
- Subject matter
- Number of trainees
- Individual versus team
- Self-paced versus guided

- Training resources
- Costs
- Geographic locations
- Time allotted
- Completion timeline

To illustrate, supervisory training for a large clinic with three locations in different, nearby geographic areas may bring supervisors together for a two-day workshop, once every quarter. However, a large, multistate nursing home system may use Web-based courses to reach supervisors throughout the country.

Internal Training

Training internally tends to be viewed as being very applicable to the job. It is also popular because it saves the cost of sending employees away for training, and it often avoids the cost of outside trainers. Often, skills-based technical training is conducted inside organizations. Technical training is usually skills-based (e.g., training to run laboratory equipment). Due to rapid changes in healthcare technology, the building and updating of technical skills have become crucial training needs. Basic technical skills training is also being mandated by federal regulations in areas where OSHA, the Environmental Protection Agency (EPA), and other agencies have regulations. Web-based training and intranets also are growing as internal means of training.

- *Informal Training*—One internal source of training is **informal training,** which occurs through interactions and feedback among employees. Much of what employees know about their jobs is learned informally from asking questions and getting advice from other employees and their supervisors, not from formal training programs.

- *On-the-Job Training*—The most common type of training at all levels in an organization is **on-the-job training (OJT).** Different from informal training that often occurs spontaneously, OJT should be planned. The supervisor or manager doing the training must be able to teach, as well as to show, the employee what to do. On-the-job training is by far the most commonly used form of training in healthcare organizations because it is flexible and relevant to what the employee is doing.

External Training

External training is also used extensively by organizations of all sizes. In large organizations, external training may be used because of the absence of needed internal training capabilities or the need to train many people quickly. External training may be the best option for training in smaller healthcare employers due to limitations in the size of their HR staffs and in the number of employees who may need various types of specialized training.

Training Outsourcing   The **outsourcing** of training to external training firms, consultants, and other entities is used by many employers of all sizes. According to data from the American Society of Training and Development (ASTD), approximately 28 percent of training expenditures go to outside training sources. Interestingly, over a three-year period outsourcing of training has been declining, especially in firms with fewer than 500 employees.[15] The reasons for the decline may be budgetary concerns, greater emphasis on internal linking of training to organizational strategies, or general cost reduction initiatives.

One external source that is popular is to use vendors and suppliers to train employees. Several different computer software vendors offer employees technical certifications on their software. For example, being Microsoft Certified Product Specialists gives employees credentials that show their level of technical expertise. The certifications also provide employees items to put on their resumes should they decide to change jobs. These certifications also benefit employers, who can use the certifications as job specifications for hiring and promotion purposes.

E-Learning: Training Online

E-learning is defined as the use of the Internet or an organizational intranet to conduct training online. Many people are quite familiar with the Internet, given that it has so dramatically altered the way people do business, locate information, and communicate. An *intranet* is similar to the Internet, but it is a private organizational network behind "firewall" software that restricts access to authorized users, which includes employees participating in e-learning. According to one recent survey, training managers viewed e-learning as one of the most effective ways to control training costs.[16]

There are a number of training methods which take advantage of technology:

- *Instructor-Led Classroom and Conference Training*—Instructor-led training is still the most prevalent method of training. Particularly important in classroom training is to recognize that adults in classroom training have different expectations and learning styles than do younger students. Accordingly, many professional healthcare trainers augment classroom and conference training with technology, such as noted below.

- *Distance Training/Learning*—The e-learning presence in training departments is similar to what has happened in distance training and learning. A growing number of college and university classes use some form of Internet-based course support. Blackboard and WebCT are two of the more popular support packages that thousands of college professors are using to make their course content available to students. These packages enable virtual chat and electronic file exchange among course participants, and facilitate enhanced instructor–student contact. Also, many colleges and universities are using interactive two-way television to present classes. The medium allows an instructor in one place to see and respond to a "class" in any number of other locations. If a system is fully configured, employees can take courses from anywhere in the world.[17]

- *Technology and Training*—The use of technology in the training arena has escalated substantially in the past few years and involves a wide array of *multimedia technologies,* including *video streaming* and *interactive video training.*

Computer-supported *simulations* also are being used in organizational training to replicate the psychological and behavioral requirements of a task, often in addition to providing some amount of physical resemblance to the trainee's work environment. From highly complicated surgical simulations replicating difficult surgical scenarios, to training that helps phlebotomists draw blood, the main advantages of simulations are that they allow for safe training when the risks associated with failure are high.[18] Computer-based simulators also incorporate sound learning principles, such as immediate feedback reinforcement, self-directed learning, and work-relevant problems.

New technologies are being incorporated into training delivery, design, administration, and support of training. For example, healthcare organizations are investing in electronic registration and record-keeping systems that allow trainers to register participants, record exam results, and monitor learning progress. To support training, there are computer applications providing requested information, advice, and skills training, known as *electronic performance support systems* (EPSS). These computer-based systems allow continuous learning on the job and aid in training transfer. For example, a hospital uses an electronic system to provide additional support to clinical engineers when using a diagnostic system to identify and repair equipment troubles.

Generally speaking, what is occurring is a movement from technology taking center stage in training to "technology in the background," whereby technology becomes embedded in learning and training. In the future as learning and work merge even closer, technology likely will become seamlessly integrated into more employees' work environments, so that employees will spend less time learning how to use technology, and more time on the desired learning content.

Evaluation of Training

Evaluation of training compares the post-training results to the objectives expected by managers, trainers, and trainees. Too often, training is done without any thought of measuring and evaluating it later to see how well it worked. Because training is both time-consuming and costly, evaluation should be done.

Cost–Benefit Analyses One way to evaluate training results is to examine the costs associated with the training and the benefits received through a cost–benefit analysis. Figure 8-6 shows some costs and benefits that may result from training. Although some benefits (such as attitude changes) are hard to quantify, comparison of costs and benefits associated with training remains a way to determine if training is cost effective. For example, one nursing home evaluated a traditional safety training program and found that the program did not lead to a reduction in

FIGURE 8-6   Balancing Costs and Benefits of Training

Typical Costs
- Trainer's salary and time
- Trainees' salaries and time
- Materials for training
- Expenses for trainer and trainees
- Cost of facilities and equipment
- Lost productivity (opportunity cost)

Typical Benefits
- Increase in production
- Reduction in errors and accidents
- Reduction in turnover
- Less necessary supervision
- Ability to use new capabilities
- Attitude changes

accidents. Therefore, the training was redesigned so that better safety practices resulted.

Return on Investment   In organizations today, training is expected to produce a return on investment (ROI) on the training costs. Like other parts of organizations, HR and training must be justified on the value-added for the training investments made. At Baptist Healthcare in Pensacola, Florida, one of *Fortune Magazine*'s "100 Best Places to Work" and *Training Magazine's* "100 Best Training Organizations", managers have rigorously measured training ROI. They have shaved $2.3 million from operations, market share has risen every year for the past five years, and patient satisfaction and employee morale have also improved.[19]

Benchmarking Training   Rather than doing training evaluation internally, some organizations are using benchmark measures of training that are compared from one organization to others. To do benchmarking, HR professionals in an organization gather data on training and compare it to data at other organizations of similar size in the industry. Comparison data are available through the American Society of Training and Development (ASTD) and its Benchmarking Service. This service has training-related data from more than 1,000 participating employers who complete detailed questionnaires annually. Training also can be benchmarked against data from the American Productivity and Quality Center and the Saratoga Institute. In addition, there are a number of private healthcare benchmarking services that provide benchmark studies for individual hospitals, clinics, and other providers.[20]

Evaluation Designs   If evaluation is done internally because benchmarking data are not available, there are many ways to design the evaluation of training programs to measure improvements. Depending on the nature of the program or material presented, post-measure and pre-/post-measures may be effective approaches to consider.

- *Post-Measure*—The most obvious way to evaluate training effectiveness is to determine after the training whether the individuals can perform in a more effective manner or their knowledge has increased. This may not always be obvious, however. As an example, assume that a nursing manager has 20 health unit coordinators (HUCs) who need to improve their data entry speeds. The HUCs are given a one-day training session and then given a test to measure their speeds. If the HUCs can all type at the required speed after training, was the training beneficial? It may be difficult to know whether the typing speed is a result of the training or could have been achieved without training.

- *Pre-/Post-Measure*—Had the data entry evaluation been designed differently, the issue of pre-test skill levels could have been considered. If the nursing manager had measured the data entry speed before and after training, she could have known whether the training made any difference. However, a question still remains. If there was a change in speed, was the training responsible for the change? Or did these people simply work faster because they knew they were being tested, because individuals often perform better when they know they are being tested on the results.

FIGURE 8-7 **Ensuring Staff Competence**

Joint Commission Standards and Orientation, Training, and Development

JCAHO standards have a significant focus on staff orientation, training, and development. As depicted in Figure 8-7, the standards require a process for the ongoing and continuous effort of assuring staff competency through orientation, training, and development, and through encouraging self-development. In addition, the standards require that data on competence patterns be monitored to identify trends and respond to employees' learning needs. These factors work together to ensure staff competency.

Competence Trends and Employees' Learning Needs   In addition to the training described above, the Joint Commission also requires organizations to monitor patient care and safety incidents to determine employee-learning needs. As an example, a medical center evaluates the number of incidents of inadvertent needle sticks on each of the patient care units. This evaluation determines if any special training would be required on a particular unit based on an exceptionally high number of sticks in comparison to other units. Training focusing on remedying competence issues is extremely important in meeting Joint Commission HR standards. Monitoring trends and initiating training efforts designed to deal with issues should be well-documented and "showcased" during a Joint Commission review.

DEVELOPING HUMAN RESOURCES

Development represents efforts to improve employees' abilities to handle various assignments and to cultivate capabilities beyond those required by the current

FIGURE 8-8   Development vs. Training

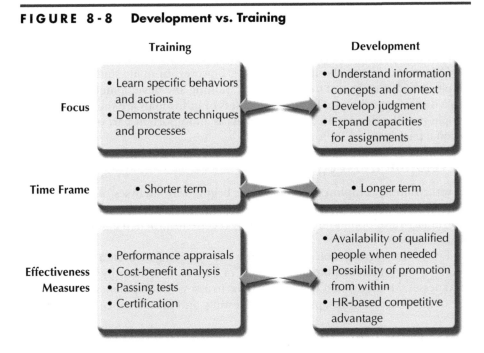

	Training	Development
Focus	• Learn specific behaviors and actions • Demonstrate techniques and processes	• Understand information concepts and context • Develop judgment • Expand capacities for assignments
Time Frame	• Shorter term	• Longer term
Effectiveness Measures	• Performance appraisals • Cost-benefit analysis • Passing tests • Certification	• Availability of qualified people when needed • Possibility of promotion from within • HR-based competitive advantage

job. Development benefits both organizations and individuals. The employees and managers with their experiences and abilities may enhance organizational competitiveness and the ability to adapt to a changing environment. In the development process, individuals' careers also may evolve and gain new or different focus.[21]

Development starts with the HR plans of an organization because these plans analyze, forecast, and identify current and future organizational needs for human resources. HR planning anticipates the movement of people in the organization due to retirements, promotions, and transfers. Further, it helps identify the capabilities needed by the organization in the future and the development necessary for people to be available to meet those needs.

As depicted in Figure 8-8, development differs from training. It is possible to train most people to run a copy machine, answer customer service questions, or operate a computer. However, development in areas such as judgment, responsibility, decision making, and communications presents a bigger challenge. These areas may or may not develop through life experiences by individuals. A planned system of development experiences for all employees, not just managers, can help expand the overall level of capabilities in a healthcare organization.

Developing Specific Capabilities

Exactly what kind of development individuals might need to expand their capabilities depends on both the person and the capabilities needed. However, some important and common management capabilities often include action orientation, quality decision making, ethical values, and technical skills. Team building, developing subordinates, directing others, and dealing with uncertainty are equally important, but much less commonly developed capabilities for successful managers.

One point is clear about development, however. In many studies that asked employees what they want from their jobs, training and development consistently ranked at or near the top. Because the assets of individuals are their KSAs, many people view the development of their KSAs as an important part of their organizational package.

Development Needs Analyses

As with training, employee development begins with analyses of the needs of both the organization and individuals. Evidence indicates that these analyses of individuals' development needs frequently receive insufficient attention in many organizations.

Either the organization or the individual can analyze what a given person needs by way of development. The goal, of course, is to identify strengths and weaknesses. Methods used by organizations to assess development needs include use of assessment centers, psychological testing, and performance appraisals.

Succession Planning

Succession planning is an important part of HR development. **Succession planning** is a process of identifying a longer-term plan for orderly replacement of key employees.[22] The need to replace key employees results from promotions, transfers, retirements, deaths, disability, departures, or other reasons. Succession planning often focuses on top management, such as ensuring a CEO successor.[23] However, succession planning should not be limited to top executive positions. For example, a large clinic whose director of nursing is planning retirement must consider the implications for maintaining continuity in delivering competent patient care and nursing leadership. The need to plan for and eventually replace this key manager is a *strategic HR issue.*

Two coordinated activities begin the actual succession planning process. First, the development of preliminary replacement charts ensures that the right individuals with sufficient capabilities and experience to perform the targeted jobs are available at the right time. These charts both show the backup "players" for each position and identify positions without a current qualified backup. The charts identify who could take over key jobs if someone leaves, retires, dies unexpectedly, or otherwise creates a vacancy, and the development necessary to ready some of the others to do so.

CHOOSING A DEVELOPMENT APPROACH

Common development approaches can be categorized under two major headings—**job-site development** and **off-site development.** Both are appropriate in developing managers and other employees. Investing in human intellectual capital, whether at work or off the job, becomes imperative for organizations as "knowledge work" aspects increase for almost all employers.

Development Approaches: Job-Site Methods

A number of job-site development methods are available. However, all too often unplanned and perhaps useless activities pass as development on the job. To ensure that the desired development actually occurs, managers must plan and coordinate development efforts, and several means can be used.[24]

Coaching   The oldest on-the-job development technique is **coaching,** which is the observation and feedback given to employees by immediate supervisors. Coaching involves a continual process of learning by doing. For effective coaching, a healthy and open relationship must exist between employees and their supervisors or managers. Many firms conduct formal training courses to improve the coaching skills of their managers and supervisors.

Committee Assignments/Meetings   Assigning promising employees to important committees may broaden their experiences and can help them understand the personalities, issues, and processes guiding the organization. For instance, employees on a safety committee can gain a greater understanding of safety management, which would aid them to become supervisors. They may also experience the problems involved in maintaining employee safety awareness. However, managers need to guard against committee assignments that turn into time-wasting activities.

Job Rotation   The process of shifting an employee from job to job is **job rotation.** In some organizations, job rotation is unplanned. However, other organizations follow elaborate charts and schedules, precisely planning a rotation program for each employee's development. When opportunities for promotion are scarce, job rotation through use of lateral transfers may be beneficial in rekindling enthusiasm and developing employees' talents.

"Assistant-To" Positions   Some firms create "assistant-to" positions, which are staff positions immediately under a manager. Through such jobs, trainees can work with outstanding managers they might not otherwise have met. Some organizations set up "junior boards of trustees" or "management cabinets" to which trainees may be appointed. These assignments provide useful experiences if they present challenging or interesting assignments to trainees.

Development Approaches: Off-Site Methods

Off-the-job development techniques give individuals opportunities to get away from the job and concentrate solely on what is to be learned. Moreover, contact with others who are concerned with somewhat different problems and come from different organizations may provide employees with new and different perspectives. Various off-site methods are used.

Classroom Courses and Degrees   Most off-the-job development programs include some classroom instruction. Most people are familiar with classroom training, which gives it the advantage of being widely accepted. But the lecture system sometimes used in classroom instruction encourages passive listening and reduced learner participation, which is a distinct disadvantage. Often trainees have little opportunity to question, clarify, and discuss the lecture material. The effectiveness of classroom instruction depends on multiple factors: group size, trainees' abilities, instructors' capabilities and styles, and subject matter.

Healthcare organizations often send employees to externally sponsored seminars or professional courses, such as those offered by the Medical Group Management Association or American Hospital Association. Many healthcare organizations also encourage continuing education by reimbursing employees for the college tuition costs of courses. Such programs provide incentive for employees to study for advanced degrees, such as Masters of Health Administration, through evening and weekend classes, outside of their regular workdays.

Human Relations Training   This type of training attempts to prepare supervisors to deal with "people problems" brought to them by their employees. The training focuses on the development of the human relations skills a person needs to work well with others. Most human relations training programs typically are aimed at new or relatively inexperienced first-line supervisors and middle managers. Content areas covered include motivation, leadership, employee communication, and other behavioral topics.

The most common reason managers fail after being promoted to management is poor teamwork with subordinates and peers. Other common reasons for management failure include not understanding expectations, failure to meet goals, difficulty in adjusting to management responsibilities, and inability to balance work and home life.

Sabbaticals and Leaves of Absence   A **sabbatical leave** is paid time off to develop and rejuvenate oneself. These have been popular for many years in academic environments but sabbaticals have also been adopted in other areas of healthcare as well. About 19 percent of U.S. corporations offer sabbaticals.[25] Some organizations give employees three to six months off to work on socially desirable projects. Such projects have included leading training programs in underserved neighborhoods or participating in corporate volunteer programs to aid nonprofit organizations. As an example, United Way and Community Chest organizations have "Executive-on-Loan" programs that are excellent opportunities for both healthcare executives and the healthcare organization. The executive gets to learn and do new and different activities, and the organization gets to contribute in a high value and unique way to the community.

Organizations that offer sabbaticals speak well of the results. They say sabbaticals help prevent employee burnout, offer advantages in recruiting and retention, and boost individual employee morale. One obvious disadvantage of paid sabbaticals is the cost. Also, the nature of the learning experience generally falls outside the control of the organization, leaving it somewhat to chance.

Leaves of absence for educational purposes may or may not be provided with pay. Some healthcare organizations allow employees the opportunity to access vacation time or continue benefits while on leaves of this nature. An educational leave of absence is typically granted to allow employees the time to commit full attention and effort to their education in order to enhance their job performance when they return.

Management Development

Although development is important for all employees, it is essential for managers. Effective management development imparts the knowledge and judgment needed by managers. Without appropriate development, managers may lack the capabilities to best deploy and manage resources (including employees) throughout the organization. Necessary capabilities are often a focus of management development and include leadership, dealing with change, coaching and advising subordinates, controlling operations, and providing performance feedback.

Experience plays a central role in management development. Indeed, experience often contributes more to the development of senior managers than classroom training does, because much of their experience occurs in varying circumstances on the job over time. Yet, despite a need for effective managers, finding such managers for middle-level jobs is often difficult. At the middle-management level, some individuals refuse to take management jobs. Many very talented healthcare professionals such as RNs, respiratory therapists, or pharmacists who could potentially make excellent managers refuse to do so because it would remove them from day-to-day patient care responsibilities. Sometimes the increase in pay is not enough to compensate for the increased workload and responsibilities. Many are also disenchanted with the "thanklessness" of the job, commenting that they would be caught between unhappy employees and nonsupportive senior management.

Managerial Modeling   A common adage in management development says that managers tend to manage as they were managed. In other words, managers learn behavior by modeling or copying someone else's behavior. This tendency is not surprising, because a great deal of human behavior is learned by modeling. Children learn by modeling the behaviors of their parents and older children. Management development efforts can take advantage of natural human behavior by matching young or developing managers with appropriate models and then reinforcing the desirable behaviors exhibited. Note that the modeling process involves more than straightforward imitation or copying; it is considerably more complex. For example, one can learn what not to do by observing a model who does something wrong. Thus, exposure to both positive and negative models can benefit a new manager.

Management Coaching   Coaching combines observation with suggestions. In the context of healthcare management development, coaching involves a relationship between two managers for a period of time as they perform their jobs. Effective coaching requires patience and good communication skills. Like modeling, it complements the natural way humans learn. Effective coaching often includes the following:

- Explaining appropriate behavior
- Making clear why actions were taken

- Accurately stating observations
- Providing possible alternatives/suggestions
- Following up/reinforcing

Mentoring

Mentoring is a relationship in which experienced managers aid individuals in the earlier stages of their careers. Such a relationship provides an environment for conveying technical, interpersonal, and organizational skills from the more-experienced to the less-experienced person. Not only does the inexperienced employee benefit, but also the mentor may enjoy the challenge of sharing his or her wisdom.[26] According to a national study conducted by Witt/Kiefer on fostering and developing future leaders in health care, having a mentor also enhances career growth.[27]

However, mentoring is not without its problems. Young minority managers frequently report difficulty finding mentors. Also, men generally show less willingness than women to be mentors. Further, mentors who are dissatisfied with their jobs and those who teach a narrow or distorted view of events may not help in the development of new managers. Fortunately, many managers have a series of advisors or mentors during their careers and may find advantages in learning from the different mentors.

SPECIAL ISSUES IN HEALTHCARE EMPLOYEE DEVELOPMENT

The healthcare industry is a diverse collection of various types and sizes of organizations. From an employment perspective, the jobs and careers within the industry are even more diverse. From physician to medical assistant, CEO to line supervisor, architect to repair technician, many types of positions and professions are represented in the healthcare industry. There are a number of important considerations in healthcare employee development, including the size and sophistication of the organization, academic and credential requirements, and organizational strategies.

Depending on the type of facility or entity within the healthcare industry, employee development can be nonexistent or unplanned and haphazard, or be very well-developed and thoroughly planned. In small facilities, such as clinics or rural nursing homes, the organizational structures are often flat with minimal opportunities for promotion or even lateral transfers; consequently, employee development is typically not a priority. Conversely, large, integrated health systems carefully craft employee development plans aimed at identifying and developing the best and the brightest for future clinical management and executive positives within their organizations.

FIGURE 8-9   **Samples of Healthcare Positions and Academic Preparation/Credentials**

POSITION	ACADEMIC PREPARATION/CREDENTIAL
Clinical	
Director of Pharmacy	Pharm D.
Director of Nursing	RN, MSN
Director or Respiratory Care	BS Respiratory Care, Registered Respiratory Therapist (RRT)
Administrative	
Nursing Home Administration	Certification in Nursing Home Administration
Facilities Director	Professional Engineer (PE)
Director of Finance	Certified Public Accountant (CPA)
Director of Health Information	Registered Health Information Administrator (RHIA)

Academic and Credential Requirements

For many healthcare environments advancement is entirely dependent on academic attainment and credentials. As an example, medical laboratory technicians cannot be promoted to physicians because they lack the appropriate educational background. Although this example seems obvious, this reality and others like it are important considerations in healthcare employee development. Although physicians are rarely provided with management or leadership skills development, they often find themselves in positions of leadership. Because they provide medical direction and leadership and own the practice, clinic, or hospital, it follows that they would also provide leadership in non-medical areas.

The key criterion for their leadership role is their academic preparation as an MD, without which they could not be in their position.[28] In many of the clinical and administrative management roles, similar situations occur. Figure 8-9 provides examples of other healthcare management positions that normally require specific academic preparation or credentials.

HR Development and Organizational Restructuring

When healthcare organizational strategies involve restructurings and downsizing, it is difficult to know what a career is, much less how to develop one. Further, some employers wonder why they should worry about career "development" for employees when the future likely holds fewer internal promotion opportunities and more movement in and out of organizations by individuals. Even though these views may seem extreme, employee development has changed recently in three significant ways:

• The middle management "ladder" in healthcare organizations now includes more horizontal than upward moves.

• Many organizations target their efforts to ensure that their focus is on core competencies.

- The growth of project-based work makes careers a series of projects, not just steps upward in a given organization.

Traditionally, career development efforts targeted managerial personnel to look beyond their current jobs and to prepare them for a variety of future jobs in the organization. But development for all employees, not just managers, is necessary for organizations to have the needed human resource capabilities for future growth and change.[29]

Mergers, acquisitions, restructurings, and layoffs all have influenced the way healthcare employees and organizations look at careers and development. In the "new career world," individuals—not the organization—manage their own development. Such self-development consists of personal educational experiences, training, organizational experiences, projects, and even changes in occupational fields. Under this system, the individual defines career success, which may or may not coincide with the organizational view of success.

CASE

Associated Community Health Center (ACHC), a family practice with 250 employees and nine locations servicing the suburbs of a large city, is facing a variety of HR issues. The HR manager conducted an HR audit in order to evaluate the problems and make recommendations for improvement. Her findings fell into four categories:

- *Retention Issues*—Focusing specifically on RN staffing, one of the most critical positions for ACHC, the current RN turnover rate is 26 percent. The RN vacancy rate or the percentage of open positions for RNs is 20 percent.
- *Staff Complaints*—The HR manager, through staff interviews, learned that ACHC's employees were concerned about a variety of issues, including late performance reviews, a lack of promotional opportunities, and poor communications between supervisors and staff.
- *Patient Concerns*—The HR manager evaluated patient feedback forms to gain insight into the HR issues. From the patients' feedback a number of related HR issues were identified. These included: rude behavior on the part of patient schedulers, inattentiveness to patients

by reception staff, and long patient waits without explanation.
- *Clinical Incidents*—In order to evaluate the effect of the HR issues on the quality of patient care being provided by the ACHC, the HR manger reviewed data on clinical incidents. Two important categories of clinical incidents were noted:
  - 20 percent of X-rays taken had to be retaken due to poor quality.
  - 15 percent of laboratory test results were lost or misfiled, requiring either retests or a delay in reporting.

The HR manager was very concerned about the findings. However, she was confident that with effective HR programming, the issues detailed above could be addressed.

Questions

1. Which of ACHC's issues could be improved through orientation, training, or staff development programming?
2. Based on your answer to Question 1, detail the types of activities that could be effective in dealing with the issues you identified.

END NOTES

1. American Hospital Association "Diversity Strategies," *Workforce Ideas in Action 3, Case Examples* (January 2004), 18.
2. Linda Zinn, "Tackling Staff Turnover: A Novel Approach," *Nursing Homes/Long-Term Care* (March 2004), 50–57.
3. ASTO, Press Release (March 26, 2001), accessed at *http://www.astd.org.*
4. Linda Heuring, "Patients First," *HR Magazine* (July 2003), 65–69.
5. Contact Emory Livers, Director of Diversity at Cincinnati Children's Hospital, for more information.
6. "Action Learning as a Strategy for Enhancing Market Competitiveness," *Global Competitiveness* (January 2002), 1–7.
7. Kristina L. Guo, "An Assessment Tool for Developing Healthcare Managerial Skills and Roles," *Journal of Healthcare Management* (November 2003), 367–376.
8. Kathryn Walker Zavaleta, "A Pragmatic Approach to Quality Training," *Journal of Healthcare Management* (November/December 2003), 409–415.
9. Ed Welsch, "Cautious Steps Ahead: A Slow Economy Means Readiness Assessments Are Back," *Online Learning* (January 2002), 20–24.
10. Shawn B. Merriam and Rosemary Caffarella, *Learning in Adulthood: A Comprehensive Guide,* 2nd ed. (San Francisco: Jossey-Bass, 1999).
11. Jathon W. Janove, "Use It or Lose It," *HR Magazine* (April 2002), 1–3.
12. Chrysanthos Dellarocas, "Learning Negotiation Skills: Four Models of Knowledge Creation and Transfer," *Management Science* (April 2003), 1–13.
13. Charlotte Garvey, "The Whirlwind of a New Job," *HR Magazine* (June 2001), 1–5.
14. "Developing Leaders Among Your Employees," *The Receivables Report* (March 2005), 3–4.
15. Mark E. Van Buren, *ASTD State of the Industry Report, 2003* (Alexandria, VA: American Society of Training and Development, 2001), 1–12.
16. "Training Management and Cost Control Survey," *HR Focus* (May 2005), 9; Also see *http://www.ioma.com* for more information on the survey.
17. Delbert L. Hall and Dan Brown, "Using the Internet for Training," *Hospital Material Management Quarterly* (August 2000), 71–75.
18. Holly Dolezolek, "Pretending to Learn," *Training* (July/August 2003), 20–26; and Wendy Webb, "Who Moved My Training?" *Training* (January 2003), 1–4.
19. Susan Karlin, "Training's Lasting Effect at Baptist Health Care," *Workforce Management* (February 2003), accessed from *http://www.workforce.com.*
20. For more information visit *http://www.nachri.org,* *http://www.ashhra.org,* and *http://www.astd.org.*
21. Mike Broscio, "Creating and Implementing a Reality-Based Career Plan," *Journal of Healthcare Management* (March 2003), 76–82.
22. Joan Pyns, "The Implementation of Workforce and Succession Planning in the Public Sector," *Public Personnel Mangement* (Winter 2004), 389–405.
23. Errol L. Biggs, "CEO Succession Planning: An Emerging Challenge for Boards of Directors," *Academy of Management Review,* 28 (2003), 657–666.
24. Phyllis Cowling, "Create Your Future," *Healthcare Financial Management* (July 2002), 12.
25. Toddi Garner, "The Pause That Refreshes," *Business Week* (November 19, 2001), 138.
26. "A Mentor is a Key to Career Success," *Healthcare Financial Management* (February 2003), 92–94.
27. Witt/Keifer, "Preparing Future Leaders in Health Care," *Leaders@wittkieffer.com.*
28. Michael Romano, "Ready. Or Not," *Modern Healthcare,* Special Report (April 26, 2004).
29. Monica E. Oss, "The Workforce Countdown," *Behavioral Health Management* (May/June 2005), 6.

PERFORMANCE MANAGEMENT IN HEALTHCARE ORGANIZATIONS

Learning Objectives

After you read this chapter, you should be able to:

- Discuss the importance of performance management.

- Compare and contrast the administrative and development uses of performance appraisals.

- Review the informal versus systematic appraisal processes.

- Describe the various methods of appraising performance.

- Identify the various rater errors that occur during the appraisal process.

Healthcare HR Insights

Evaluating employee performance is a critical part of HR management in smaller physician groups, which rarely have HR professionals on their staff. It is not unusual for a physician group to either adapt performance evaluation tools they have purchased from the Internet or use a tool their administrator may have received at a professional conference.

One clinic administrator of a 200-employee specialty physician practice and clinic decided that his organization needed a comprehensive approach to management and employee performance evaluation. The evaluation tools the group had been using were an assortment of miscellaneous grading scales combined with supervisory comments. This system was not very effective for the organization, the managers, or the employees. To develop a new appraisal program, the following steps were taken:

- A thorough review of the existing process to identify gaps and deficiencies
- Extensive discussions with the clinic administrator to determine what organizational objectives should be met by the process
- Interviews with managers and focus group meetings with employees to discuss improving the evaluation process

The new performance management system includes three separate evaluation tools: one for managers, one for administrative staff, and one for clinical staff. Each tool has a unique set of behavioral-based skills, knowledge, and performance criteria pertaining to the type of work performed by each category of employee. Included in all of the tools was a pay-for-performance link that allows the evaluator to award a pay increase based on the total score of the evaluation.

Since this system's inception, the administrator has reported a high level of satisfaction with the process, acknowledging that the employees are finding more value in the feedback they are receiving from their managers through the process.[1]

PERFORMANCE MANAGEMENT

Regardless of size or type of the organization it is important to utilize an evaluation process that is designed to meet both the organizational objectives and the performance evaluation needs of its managers and employees. Healthcare organizations develop performance management systems to define expectations for employees and to manage their performance. These systems identify job expectations; measure, evaluate, and reward performance; and provide for improvement where needed.[2]

As depicted in Figure 9-1, performance management is a vital link between organizational strategy and its outcomes. For example, if a nurse manager at a rehabilitation hospital has the ability to perform her duties but the organization does not support her with the appropriate equipment and staff, she will not succeed in her position. In many cases, some performance factors are present,

FIGURE 9-1   Performance Management Linkage

but if any of the factors are missing, individuals will not be able to perform according to their job standards.

Based on organizational goals, healthcare managers organize their employees' jobs to provide care and services that patients, residents, or clients value. Employee performance is monitored to ensure that each job is performed successfully in a manner that supports the accomplishment of organizational objectives. Employee performance is then measured by job standards defined by job criteria.

Job Criteria

Job criteria identify factors employees must meet for satisfactory job performance. Criteria in most jobs are weighted for importance. As an example, a laboratory technician's job may have several criteria, but those that require the technician to do quality-control checks on lab results may receive greater weight.

Criteria may be classified as trait-based, behavior-based, or results-based. **Trait-based criteria** identify subjective personal traits, such as having a positive attitude, that may contribute to job success. **Behavior-based criteria** identify behaviors, such as persuasion skills, that may lead to successful completion of job expectations. In some cases, both trait-based and behavior-based qualities are difficult to identify and evaluate objectively. **Results-based criteria,** such as completing projects on time, are easier to identify and evaluate.

Criteria Relevance   When developing systems to measure performance, managers should include criteria that are relevant to the job. Job criteria relevance is determined by job description accuracy and its translation into performance standards. For example, measuring the performance of a nurse anesthetist for presentation skills would not be relevant, but measuring his or her anesthesia management abilities would be relevant because they are tied to a primary job responsibility. Reviewing the job description and the criteria before doing a performance appraisal helps to eliminate criteria that are not vital for use.

Potential for Criteria Problems   All jobs are a compilation of duties and tasks. Most healthcare organizations formally or informally develop job descriptions and performance appraisals. When the measurement process omits significant criteria, the measures are **deficient.** For example, if an appointment scheduler was not measured for the ability to meet patient, physician, and staff needs when scheduling appointments, the criteria for evaluation would be considered deficient. If irrelevant criteria are included in the measurement process, it is **contaminated.** The same scheduler should be measured for scheduling accuracy, but measuring the scheduler's ability to program a computer would be an illustration of contaminated criteria. It is advisable for HR professionals and line managers to review job descriptions and performance appraisals regularly to prevent using deficient or contaminated criteria.

Performance Standards

Each job is assigned a set of standards with which to compare employees' performance levels. Managers, with the assistance of HR professionals, determine performance standards for each job before employees begin work. Employees should be given performance standards when they are first employed because they will be evaluated during performance appraisals on how they meet those standards.

PERFORMANCE APPRAISAL

One of the most important managerial duties in healthcare organizations is to evaluate employees' performance.[3] During performance reviews, managers should discuss how well employees are meeting their job standards. The process of evaluating an employee's performance is called the **performance**

appraisal. For healthcare organizations that subscribe to the Joint Commission on Accreditation of Healthcare Organizations (JCAHO) process, an important consideration in the development and implementation of a healthcare organizational performance appraisal process is compliance with JCAHO standards.

Joint Commission Standards and Performance Appraisal

Acknowledging the linkage between the provision of safe patient care and effective performance evaluation, a number of the JCAHO's human resources, leadership, and organizational performance improvement standards affect performance appraisals. The components of a JCAHO-acceptable performance appraisal system include the following characteristics:

- Job descriptions identifying duties and required competencies
- A performance evaluation process and supporting documents
- Competency assessment checklists

Performance evaluation and competency assessment are two different, but much related, processes. Some healthcare organizations conduct performance evaluations and competency assessments simultaneously, and others treat them as separate processes. Performance evaluations are used to determine how well employees are performing the duties and responsibilities of their positions as described in the job descriptions. Competency assessments are used to determine whether the employees have the knowledge, skills, ability, training, education, and licensure to meet the requirements of their position.[4]

CONFLICTING ROLES OF PERFORMANCE APPRAISAL

Performance appraisals have two major, sometimes conflicting, uses in healthcare organizations. Figure 9-2 illustrates the two potentially conflicting roles for performance appraisal.

FIGURE 9-2   Conflicting Roles of Performance Appraisal

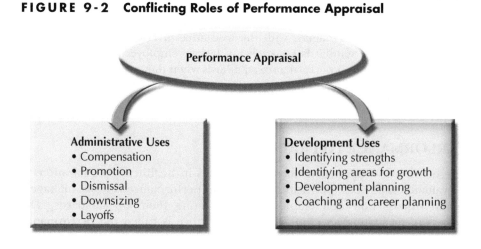

Administrative Uses

There are several administrative uses of performance appraisal, with compensation management being the most common. Pay increases awarded as a result of performance are referred to as merit-based or performance-based increases. When performance is tied to compensation, employees should expect that performance appraisals are being conducted in an equitable, unbiased manner.[5]

The performance appraisal process is also used administratively for promotions, terminations, and layoffs. Performance appraisals are useful to supplement other documentation regarding performance deficiencies that may lead to termination. Some organizations use performance appraisals to determine who is laid off when downsizing is necessary. It is advisable that accurate and objective performance appraisals be used to support decisions of managers that differentiate employees for promotions, dismissals, and layoffs.

Legal Issues and Performance Appraisals   Performance appraisals have increased in importance to organizations as employees have increasingly pursued their legal rights through Federal and State compliance agencies and courts. When performance appraisals are utilized to make important employment decisions, the appraisal process must be objective, fair, and defensible to withstand legal scrutiny. The major legal challenges are usually regarding allegations of discriminatory practices in the use of performance appraisals.

Healthcare managers and HR professionals must adhere to legal requirements that affect the rights of employees and employers. Topics to consider before a significant performance management intervention such as serious discipline or demotion include discrimination, public-policy issues, contractual issues, and tort-liability issues. These legal issues typically provide the basis for employee claims made against employers.[6]

Development Uses

Performance appraisals are also used to help identify development opportunities for employees. Effective performance appraisals typically contain information that describes where employees need development to meet job expectations or to enhance their career development. When employees do not meet job expectations, managers are responsible for providing feedback about unsatisfactory work. Similarly, when employees are performing well and show the ability to advance, managers should provide feedback and suggestions on how employees can develop to the next level. Regardless of employees' circumstances, the appraisal feedback interview should be constructive and supportive for the employee by suggesting a development plan and resources to improve or enhance performance.[7]

Because managers are ultimately the judges of employees' performance, they must play a key role in designing and assessing the development-plan components and provide advice and support to help employees. When a development plan has been established, managers and their employees should regularly review employees' progress toward improving performance or career development.

Informal Versus Systematic Appraisal

Healthcare managers can conduct performance appraisals formally or informally. The **informal appraisal process** is typically conducted at the manager's discretion, and is triggered by an event or situation requiring appraisal feedback. The informal appraisals can be used to praise good work or motivate an employee to improve behavior. As an example, a supervisor for a home healthcare agency may find it necessary to provide an informal appraisal for a homecare aide if she receives numerous complaints about how the aide is communicating with patients. The informal feedback should be documented and retained for further review and consideration at the employee's annual review.

A **formal appraisal process** systematically defines the organizational policies and procedures on performance appraisal. This type of system involves using an official form that documents the important aspects of the job and formally evaluates employees' performance. The formal appraisal process begins with the development of an appraisal form that documents the current responsibilities for the job. The manager uses the job criteria to guide the collection of information and to summarize the performance. Behavior and attendance-related data provide the context for appraisal discussion.

Appraisal Responsibilities The responsibility for completing the appraisal process usually rests with a supervisor or manager, but the HR staff plays a vital role in assisting the managers. Both managers and HR professionals monitor completed performance appraisals in order to improve the process by revising it when necessary.

Some healthcare organizations have developed performance-appraisal systems that require a lengthy review every other year and a shortened checklist review for the off year. Other healthcare organizations have developed performance reviews, called *exception-based reviews*. This type of review shortens the process and may be viewed more positively because it recognizes behaviors that exceed the job standards or identifies behaviors that can be improved.

When to Conduct Appraisals Many healthcare organizations have policies that require formal appraisals once a year. Some healthcare organizations schedule reviews on employees' anniversary dates in their jobs. Another popular method is to conduct all evaluations at the same time, such as January 1, or June 1. As healthcare organizations have become flatter, with manager to staff ratios of 1 to 20 or more, this approach to performance appraisal can be extremely burdensome for individual managers. Whichever timing is used, appraisals are often coupled with a pay increase for employees and the evaluation is used to set the specific amount or percentage an individual employee will receive.

Employees may also receive a *probationary* or *introductory performance review* in their first few months on the job. This type of evaluation helps managers decide how well employees are learning their new job responsibilities and whether or not employees should continue employment.

Appraisals and Pay Coupling the performance appraisal process with pay increases is typically referred to as *pay-for-performance*. This approach to performance

FIGURE 9-3   Who Conducts Performance Appraisals

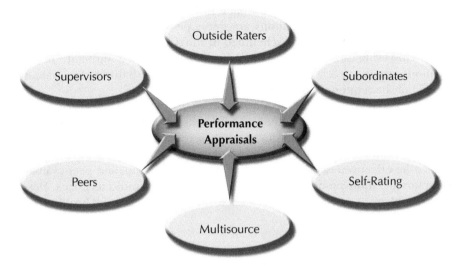

appraisal and compensation administration is an important HR strategic decision that requires extensive training of managers to administer. Many healthcare HR professionals believe that linking pay to performance is the best way to influence performance.

WHO CONDUCTS APPRAISALS

It is important to determine who is involved in appraisals in an organization. As indicated in Figure 9-3, there are a variety of means used to conduct appraisals.

Supervisory Rating of Subordinates

In most healthcare organizations, the immediate supervisor conducts the performance review for the employee. The most common way to conduct this review is a face-to-face meeting between the supervisor and the employee. In order to maximize the effectiveness of the performance appraisal event, the supervisor and employee should meet privately and discuss the employee's performance in a conversational mode. In an effort to encourage employee development and performance improvement, the supervisor may develop performance objectives and goals with planned check-ins.

Employee Rating of Managers

In some healthcare organizations, the performance-appraisal philosophy has been expanded to include the performance rating of supervisors and managers by their employees. This method of appraising performance takes advantage of the fact that employees frequently have first-hand knowledge of their supervisor's or manager's performance.

Team/Peer Ratings

A common performance-rating approach in healthcare is **team** or **peer rating.** However, Healthcare organizations are generally organized into large departments and the workers may be scheduled in shifts around a 24/7 operation that makes observing an individual employee's performance difficult. In these situations, teams or peers that employees have worked with during the evaluation period may be requested to provide evaluation feedback.

The team or peer ratings are advantageous because they offer the benefit of direct feedback about performance. The downside includes potential disagreements among employees or, in the absence of training or instruction on how to complete team appraisals fairly, other rater errors may occur that will negatively impact the effectiveness of the appraisal. Most of the team- and peer-evaluation programs are anonymous in order to encourage more candid feedback. Despite these problems, team/peer performance ratings, especially in healthcare settings, are probably necessary.[8]

Self-Rating

Another way to gather information about employees' performance is to ask employees to conduct a **self-rating.** The self-rating method is helpful for employees because it requires them to examine their own strengths and weaknesses. This kind of evaluation may involve employees in constructing their own development plans, as a result of their identification of performance deficiencies or in pursuit of career advancement. Self-rating is helpful, but it usually is supplemental to other forms of information gathering.

Outside Raters

In some situations, an organization may employ **outside raters** to evaluate employee performance. As an example, outside raters are typically utilized at academic research hospitals to evaluate the performance of researchers. One of the advantages of using an outside rater to evaluate performance is that the rater offers a different perspective. The outsider will likely bring an objective view to the process that might not be possible with internal staff members.

Another use of outside raters is by Boards of Directors to rate top executives' performance. Board members who participate on executive committees also evaluate executives. For example, the members of an assisted living facility's board's HR committee may be involved in appraising the performance of the director of HR.

Multisource/360-Degree Ratings

In order to do an effective job of reviewing employees' performance, supervisors or managers must collect information about the employee's performance. Prior to the development of the evaluation, supervisors and managers may circulate evaluation questionnaires for completion to individuals who have worked with or observed the performance of employees that are being evaluated. Collecting information from coworkers, other supervisors, and even patients, residents, or clients are common ways to receive information. Information from all of these sources may result in a performance appraisal that is referred to as a 360-degree evaluation.[9] The popularity of 360-degree feedback systems has led to the results being used for making compensation, promotion, termination, and other administrative decisions. When using 360-degree feedback for administrative purposes, managers must anticipate potential problems.[10]

Evaluating Multisource Feedback Research on multisource/360-degree feedback has revealed both positives and negatives. Studies have found that there can be more variability than expected in the ratings given by the different sources. Thus, supervisor ratings must carry more weight than peer or subordinate input to resolve the differences.[11] Other studies have found differences between employee self-ratings and multisource ratings. One concern is that those peers who rate poor-performing coworkers tend to inflate the ratings of those people so that the peers themselves can get higher overall evaluation results.[12]

One concern is whether 360-degree appraisals improve the process or simply multiply the number of problems by the total number of raters. Also, some wonder whether multisource appraisals really create better decisions that offset the additional time and investment required. These issues appear to be less threatening when the 360-degree feedback is used *only for development*. But they may effectively reduce the use of multisource appraisals as an administrative tool in many situations.

METHODS OF APPRAISING PERFORMANCE

Many healthcare organizations use one of the methods as depicted in Figure 9-4 to conduct appraisals: category methods, comparative methods, behavioral and objective methods, or narrative methods. An example of a performance appraisal form can be found at the Web site for the book, *http://flynn.swlearning.com*.

Category Methods

Performance appraisals apply rating methods such as rating scales and checklists. The appraiser rates an employee on a **graphic-rating scale,** or a continuum, of scores from unacceptable to acceptable to exemplary. This type of appraisal is easy to use but may have limitations, such as, combined job criteria, descriptive words that require interpretation, and loosely defined rating-scale descriptors, such as outstanding, average, and poor.

The **checklist method** of appraising performance offers a list of words or statements that describe employees' performance. The managers evaluate these statements and check those that describe the employees' behavior. Some examples of these statements are, "On time for work," "Completes assignments on time," "Works well with other employees," "Has pursued self development," and "Has effective conflict-management skills." The checklist method, while easy to

FIGURE 9-4 Performance Appraisal Methods

use, limits both the manager and employee because the performance rating information can be interpreted in a variety of ways.

Comparative Methods

This method of performance appraisal requires managers to compare the performance of one employee against another. Comparative appraisal methods include **ranking** all employees, paired comparison of employees from a full list, and ranking employees in a **forced distribution** along a bell curve.

Narrative Methods

The **narrative** performance-appraisal method provides comments using essays, documentation of critical incidents, or field reviews. The *essay* describes employees' performance during the evaluation period. This appraisal usually contains a few general performance areas for which managers document their comments. This method allows managers significant flexibility in describing employees' work performance. In the **critical-incident narrative,** managers document incidents that are highly favorable or unfavorable representations of employees' work performance. The incidents are documented throughout the year and are summarized at the time of the appraisal. The **field-review** may be conducted by an outside professional. This person reviews the manager's comments about each employee's performance. Based on these comments, the outside reviewer rates each employee.

ETHICAL PRACTICES AND COMPLIANCE

Healthcare organizations have recognized the importance of including the evaluation of employees' general conduct in the appraisal process. In order to provide clear behavioral expectations against which the employees will be evaluated, a number of organizations have an "employee code of conduct." These codes of conduct are presented to new employees during orientation, are contained in employee handbooks, and are included on evaluation forms.

The code of conduct presented here covers a number of important areas. When employees receive feedback concerning these areas along with an evaluation of their performance and attendance, the appraisal can be very comprehensive and meaningful.

Employee "Code of Conduct"

The following are examples of the conduct required of every employee:

1. *Performance*—Perform all job duties and fulfill all responsibilities in a careful manner, following prescribed procedures, policies, and good judgment.
2. *Supervision*—Willingly accept and follow the directions of your supervisor.
3. *Attendance and Punctuality*—Be punctual and regular in attendance including being ready to work at your scheduled start time and continuing to work until your scheduled quit time.
4. *Drugs and Alcohol*—Do not use, have in your possession, or work under the influence of alcohol or undocumented drugs.
5. *Confidentiality*—Maintain the confidentiality of information regarding patients and other employees.
6. *Respect*—In all relationships, abide by standards of common sense and courtesy as they apply to people working together to satisfy the needs of patients and each other.
7. *Professional Responsibilities*—Obtain and maintain license(s) and/or certification required by professional, industry, or regulatory standards.
8. *Ethical Practices*—In all dealings with patients, fellow employees, and vendors, conduct yourself in a manner which demonstrates your responsibility, honesty, and regard for the privileges, rights, and property of others.

Behavioral/Objectives Methods

Several performance approaches measure behaviors rather than job characteristics. This approach is most commonly associated with *behaviorally-anchored rating scales (BARS)*, which provide behavioral descriptions of employee actions on the job. This method compares standardized behavioral descriptions to the employee's actual performance. The behavioral standards are measured against a scale of performance levels.

Management by objectives (MBO) develops performance goals that an employee and the manager agree to complete within a defined period. The goals are usually tied to organizational objectives. The basic assumption underlying MBO is that planning and mutual goal setting will result in higher performance. MBO clearly defines goals and objectives, which makes it more measurable than other appraisal methods.

Combination of Methods

Combining methods of appraisal is very common in healthcare organizations. Some strengths of each method may be advantageous to incorporate into the performance-appraisal system. Combined methods may include a checklist, a narrative method for development, and an MBO approach.

For healthcare organizations that subscribe to the JCAHO, performance appraisals must meet JCAHO standards. These standards encourage the organization to link job descriptions to performance appraisals. The job descriptions must be specific and accurate descriptions of the duties, rather than simply general observations about all jobs.

RATER ERRORS

For employees to benefit from feedback during the appraisal process, managers should be trained to avoid evaluation errors. Figure 9-5 illustrates some of the common types of errors that occur in appraisals. A discussion of each follows.

Recency

One of the most common errors managers make when conducting appraisals is to use only recent events to judge employees' performance. To avoid this error, managers need to keep information about employees' performance throughout the year and use that information during the annual review. Reviewers should keep both negative and positive information from the entire evaluation period.

Central Tendency, Leniency, and Strictness Errors

Managers who tend to rate all of their employees within a narrow range are referred to as **central-tendency raters.** In this error, managers would not distinguish among poor, average, and above average performers.

FIGURE 9-5   Common Rater Errors

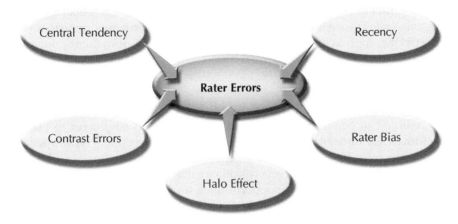

Managers who give all of their employees high ratings are described as **lenient raters.** Conversely, managers who give their employees low ratings make the mistake of being overly **strict raters.** In all of these situations, managers undermine the performance appraisal process, leaving employees without ideas about where they really stand. Also, not evaluating each employee objectively against performance standards is more likely to result in frustration on the part of the evaluated employee.

Rater Bias

Rater bias occurs when a manager reflects a bias against a certain employee or employee group based on the manager's own values or prejudices. Biased appraisals may be associated with age, gender, or religion, among others. In these cases, the manager's supervisor should also be involved in the process before the manager meets with the employee.

Halo Effect

The **halo effect** occurs when a manager rates an employee high or low on all job standards based on one characteristic. For example, if a hospital housekeeping employee is always willing to assume extra shifts, the manager may rate that employee highly on all aspects of his or her performance, based entirely on that one characteristic. Another example of the halo effect would be if an employee who admits patients provides excellent customer service but is consistently disagreeable with coworkers. The manager, in this example of the halo effect, would give a favorable overall rating based only on the employee's excellent customer skills, ignoring the divisive behaviors that lead to departmental problems.

Contrast Errors

Contrast errors in the performance-review process occur when a manager compares employees to each other rather than to job performance standards. The more effective approach is to rate employees against job requirements, not other employees.

APPRAISAL FEEDBACK

It is important to communicate appraisal information to employees to provide them with a clear understanding about how they are performing.[13] At an appraisal meeting, any misunderstanding about an employee's performance can be clarified. Effective healthcare managers typically coach employees about their performance and provide development opportunities, which can also enhance employee retention efforts. The performance feedback meeting is most effective when it is interactive and mutually beneficial to managers and employees. While the formal performance appraisal process provides information in longer-term time intervals, generally annually, the use of informal appraisal feedback is effective when used more frequently and summarized at the formal feedback session.

Feedback Systems

Feedback systems have three components: collecting data, evaluating the data, and taking action based on the data.[14] As shown in Figure 9-6, collecting data is how a manager gathers information about an employee's performance. Evaluating the data is the critical second step, which includes objectively determining how the employee performed relative to job standards. For example, if a ward clerk in a hospital can process significantly higher numbers of doctors' orders for lab tests, that data might lead the manager to give high marks for performance. But if the employee accomplishes this task at the expense of not responding to questions from other staff members or from patients and their families, the performance rating might be different.

The final step in the feedback system is taking action based on the results of the appraisal. In some cases, the action is processing a pay increase. In other cases, the action is a development plan. For many employees, the action is recognition of performance and encouragement to continue to perform well.

Appraisal Interview

The appraisal interview, where the employee and the manager meet to discuss the employee's performance, is a critical event for both parties. Employees are concerned about their evaluation, while managers understand that they need to

---

FIGURE 9-6 Feedback Process

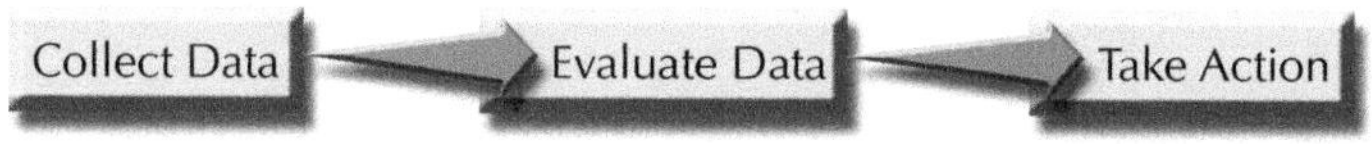

Collect Data → Evaluate Data → Take Action

communicate information about performance and maintain an effective working relationship with their employees. The key to an effective appraisal interview is preparation. Having accurate, objective information about employees' performance, job-related behaviors, and attendance is important, and then communicating it to the employees effectively is critical to the value of the appraisal.

Reactions of Managers

Many managers do not like to do performance appraisals.[15] The preparation and delivery time of performance appraisals requires a significant commitment, and managers may not like to be ultimate decision makers. Judging performance and supporting the employee who needs development and mentoring are difficult and contradictory responsibilities for managers. Many healthcare organizations have recognized that managers who have difficulty with the appraisal process should be supported with supervisory training.

Reactions of Employees

Employees who are being evaluated demonstrate a variety of reactions to the appraisal process. Some employees become defensive as they imagine how the manager will appraise their performance. If the review is positive, defensiveness often dissipates.[16] When the discussion is about making improvements, the employee may challenge the reviewer about the data collected and the evaluation.

To be effective at delivering performance appraisals, supervisors can use a variety of appraisal methods; emphasizing self-development and performance improvement is viewed by employees as the most effective. In this case, the manager's role as a supportive coach and mentor may have a positive impact on the employee.

EFFECTIVE PERFORMANCE MANAGEMENT

Managing employees' performance is an especially crucial issue for healthcare organizations that must rely on employees to achieve organizational goals and objectives. With the labor shortage in the healthcare industry projected for the next two decades, managers must dedicate significant organizational resources to programs that manage and improve employees' performance.[17]

Managers use tools such as job descriptions, performance appraisals, and progressive discipline processes to improve employees' performance. The program should follow a sequence when dealing with performance management issues including identifying the problem, meeting with the employee to review the issue, and developing a performance improvement plan.[18] Figure 9-7 shows the steps in dealing with performance problems.

Developing a Performance Improvement Plan

A **performance improvement plan** is implemented when the manager and the employee meet to discuss job expectations and construct the

FIGURE 9-7 Dealing with Performance Problems

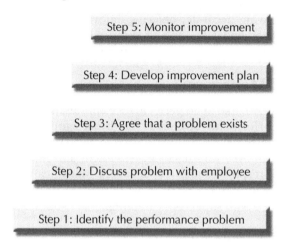

Step 5: Monitor improvement

Step 4: Develop improvement plan

Step 3: Agree that a problem exists

Step 2: Discuss problem with employee

Step 1: Identify the performance problem

improvement plan. The typical components of an improvement plan include the following:[19]

- Clear job expectations
- Plan that improves performance
- Resources available to the employee
- Process to evaluate performance
- Timeline for improvement
- Consequences if performance does not improve

If a formal improvement plan is developed and documented, the employee should receive a copy and another copy should be placed in the employee's personnel file. In the event the documented issues lead to more severe actions, such as suspension or discharge, the plan is signed by the employee and the manager. But many employees won't sign this type of document, especially when they dispute the evaluation. In this case, managers should document the employee's refusal to the sign the plan. The employee's refusal to sign does not change the requirement for the employee to follow the improvement plan.

CASE

Queen City Clinic is an established multispecialty clinic with 300 employees. The clinic is owned by 35 physicians whose Board of Directors includes the administrator and the president of the medical group. Queen City Clinic has never utilized a formal performance-appraisal process.

The clinic administrator, who is new to the clinic, has decided to implement a performance appraisal system. The management staff, consisting of 15 department directors, has resisted a performance-appraisal system, because they do not recognize the value of doing employee appraisals, nor are they interested in taking the time required to complete appraisals of their employees. Consequently, they are concerned about the administrator's enthusiasm for such a system.

In addition, some of the clinic's employees, who have not been interested in a performance appraisal system, have approached the physicians to lobby against establishing it. The clinic administrator has led meetings and information sessions for both employees and managers about the benefits of a performance appraisal system. For the employees, he noted the value of regular feedback on their performance and the opportunity to increase their productivity, which could result in developmental opportunities. For the directors, he described the value a performance appraisal system would provide in helping them manage their employees more effectively.

Questions

1. Why would the employees object to the implementation of an appraisal system?
2. Given the concerns of the directors and employees, what would be the most effective performance appraisal system to implement?

END NOTES

1. Human Resource Consultation conducted by Langan and Flynn, LLC for a Minneapolis-based Radiology Practice.
2. Jonathan Tompkins, "Strategic Human Resources Management in Government: Unresolved Issues," *Public Personnel Management* (Spring 2002), 95–110.
3. Erin Wilkins, "Healthcare @ Work 2003," *HR Pulse* (Winter 2003), 8–16.
4. Joint Commission Resources, "Issues in Human Resources for Hospitals" (2004), 17–55.
5. Steve Bates, "Top Pay for Best Performance," *HR Magazine* (January 2003), 31–38.
6. Robert Grossman, "Are You Ignoring Older Workers?" *HR Magazine* (August 2003), 40–46.
7. Jay M. Jackman and Myra H. Stober, "Fear of Feedback," *Harvard Business Review* (April 2003), 101–107.
8. Susanne G. Scott and Walter O. Einstein, "Strategic Performance Appraisal in Team-Based Organizations: One Size Does Not Fit All," *Academy of Management Executive* (May 2001), 107–116.
9. Andrew N. Garmon, Larry Tyler, and Jodi S. Darnall, "Development and Validation of a 360-degree-feedback Instrument for Healthcare Administrators," *Journal of Healthcare Management* (September/October 2004), 307–322.
10. Ginka Toegel and Jay A. Conger, "360-Degree Assessment: Time for Reinvention," *Academy of Management Learning and Education,* 2 (2003), 297–311.
11. Gary J. Greguras, John M. Ford, and Stephan Brutus, "Manager Attention to Multisource Feedback," *Journal of Management Development,* 22 (2003), 345.
12. Paul Atkins and Robert E. Wood, "Self Versus Others' Ratings as Predictors of Assessment Center Ratings: Validation Evidence for 360-Degree Feedback Programs," *Personnel Psychology,* 55 (2002) 871–904.
13. Gardiner Morse, "Feedback Backlash," *Harvard Business Review* (October 2004), 28.
14. Kathy Williams, "New Developments in Performance Management," *Strategic Finance* (April 2002), 19, 22.
15. Jonathan R. Anderson, "Measuring Human Capital: Performance Appraisal Effectiveness," Presentation, Indianapolis, IN, Midwest Academy Of Management (October 2002).
16. "A Manager Asks: Dealing with the Troublesome Employee," *The Health Care Manager* (June 2002), 78–86.
17. Annette Simmons, "When Performance Reviews Fail," *T&D* (September 2003), 47–52.
18. Melissa Fitzpatrick, "Let's Bring Balance to Healthcare," *Nursing Management* (March 2002), 35–38.
19. Paula Robinson, "Master the Steps to Performance Improvement" *Nursing Management* (May 2004), 45–49.

EMPLOYEE RELATIONS IN THE HEALTHCARE INDUSTRY

Learning Objectives

After you have read this chapter you should be able to:

- Review the common components of an employment agreement.

- Define *employment-at-will* and identify exceptions to this concept.

- Describe *due process* and explain alternative dispute resolution processes.

- Discuss issues associated with drug testing for healthcare employees.

- Identify elements common to employee handbooks.

- Outline the progressive discipline process.

Healthcare HR Insights

A medical assistant employed by a suburban nursing home and skilled nursing facility had recently returned from a maternity leave. Prior to her leave she worked full-time on the day shift in the nursing home. Upon her return, she was placed in a full-time aide position, at the same rate of pay, but on the evening shift in the skilled nursing facility.

The medical assistant decided to contest her placement in a different position than the one she left prior to the initiation of her leave. She cited the medical leave of absence policy contained in the employee handbook, which was in compliance with the Federal Family Leave Act (FMLA). According to the policy, she was guarnteed to return to the same or comparable position to the one she left, without loss of pay, benefits, or working conditions.

The facility's HR director met with the employee to hear her grievance. The HR director subsequently met with the administrator of the facility and the medical assistant's manager to discuss the issue and consider the leave of absence policy. In addition, they also reviewed their responsibilities under the FMLA. They concluded, that although the employee had not incurred any loss of wages or benfits, she in fact was not returned to the same or a comparable position. Consequently, they decided to immediately reinstate her to the position she was in prior to the initiation of her leave. In addition, the HR director was instructed by the administrator to conduct an in-service for all supervisors and managers on FMLA complinace.

Healthcare organizations typically manage their relationships with employees through HR policies, procedures, and practices. Employers also base their relationships with employees upon a series of rights that are defined and mandated by various federal, state, and local laws and statutes and through important court decisions, referred to as case law. In addition, employers and employees may define their rights and obligations with contractual agreements. Regardless, organizations either purposefully or by inference develop philosophies and practices that define the nature of their employment relationships with employees.

NATURE OF EMPLOYER EMPLOYEE RELATIONS

An **employee relations philosophy** includes all aspects of how an organization guides, responds to, and communicates with its employees. How this philosophy is used strategically serves as an important differentiation that may cause an employee to select one organization over another. As noted in Chapter 7, employee satisfaction has become a retention issue as well. Managers, employees, and candidates for employment might consider the following questions as they evaluate whether to remain employed or take a job at an organization:

- Is the work environment governed by too many policies and procedures?
- Is the organization willing to manage the relationship with realistic and appropriate rules and requirements?

An organization may elect to develop an employee relations philosophy statement that outlines the employment relationship. In healthcare organizations, HR can provide strategic leadership when it encourages and facilitates the development of an employee relations statement and the policies and procedures that support the organizational philosophy. In today's healthcare work place, employee relations philosophies are more important than ever because of the shortage of healthcare personnel. It is important for healthcare organizational leadership to carefully articulate its philosophy and adopt policies that provide a positive work environment, which can contribute to higher levels of employee satisfaction and productivity.[1]

RIGHTS AND RESPONSIBILITIES

There are two types of employee rights: those guaranteed by law and those governed by contracts. Figure 10-1 depicts the key laws, regulations, and agreements that affect the rights and responsibilities of both employees and employers.

Statutory Rights

Existing laws, legislation, and evolving case law identify and protect healthcare employees' rights. In addition to general **statutory rights,** other regulations apply specifically to healthcare workers. An example of a law specific to healthcare employees is the Health Insurance Portability and Accountability Act of 1996

FIGURE 10-1   Rights and Responsibility of Employees and Employers

STATUTORY RIGHTS	CONTRACTUAL RIGHTS
• Federal and state regulations	• Employment contracts/agreements
• Equal employment opportunity (EEO)	• Separation agreements
• Health and safety regulations (OSHA)	• Retention agreements
• Employee benefits laws (ERISA)	• Training contracts
• Wage and hour law (FLSA)	• Drug testing permissions
• Professional association guidelines	
• Workers' compensation	
• Unemployment compensation	

(HIPAA). Certain aspects of this act require healthcare organizations and healthcare workers to protect the access to and confidentiality of healthcare consumers', including employees', medical information as revealed through medical records, employee benefits information, or processes that facilitate the payment of medical bills. Failure to do so can result in significant liability and penalties for organizations and individual workers, especially if they willfully violate the law.[2] Although aspects of HIPAA are healthcare-specific, most statutory rights apply to workers in all industries.

Many of the general rights guaranteed for employees in all industries have been created to allow employees to assert their rights and be heard by external agencies, such as the Equal Employment Opportunity Commission, the National Labor Relations Board, and OSHA (Occupational Safety and Health Administration). These rights are a matter of law and employers must recognize them, but employers and employees sometimes disagree with the intent of regulations and negotiate clarifications as they resolve their differences.

In addition, professional regulatory bodies for healthcare workers generate regulations that define and govern the conduct of their members. In some professions, such as physician assistants, states have implemented practice standards and professional behavior requirements. These standards usually define clinical competency and professional behavior. In addition, as an obligation of a practice standard, healthcare professionals, in a given state, may be required to report unsafe staffing issues that could lead to unsafe patient care.

Contractual Rights

Rights of employees may be extended by a contract based on terms and conditions agreed to by employers and employees. These contracts specifically define and formalize working relationships.

A formal agreement between an employer and an employee about their working relationship is called an **employment contract.** The contract, in most cases, is a written document prepared by an attorney who represents the organization.[3] In most organizations, employment contracts are reserved for executives and key managers. Employment contract provisions for executives may include compensation, general benefits, performance-based incentive and bonus provisions, executive benefits such as additional retirement benefits, severance pay, benefit continuation, outplacement services, and others. However, in the healthcare industry, employment agreements have also been used to attract and retain employees for hard-to-fill positions such as physical therapists or ICU nurses.

Employment agreements often include provisions identifying job expectations, length of employment, termination rights, and protection from claims based on federal and state laws. In some contracts, provisions prohibit the employees from competing with the organization when they leave voluntarily. These **non-compete provisions** are usually offered in exchange for substantial benefits and economic security for the employees agreeing to be bound by the non-compete restrictions.[4] Figure 10-2 describes common elements in an employment contract.

FIGURE 10-2 **Employment Contract Contents**

Employment Contract Contents

- Terms of the contract—Duration
- Provisions for renewing the contract—Automatic or mutually agreed
- Duties and responsibilities—Job description
- Compensation—Salary and variable pay
- Benefits—Group and individual
- Severance benefit—Continuation of salary and benefits after job ends
- Noncompete clauses—Restriction on choice of future employers
- Nonsolicitation clauses—Raiding clients and staff after job ends
- Dispute-resolution clauses—Settling contract disputes
- Change-in-control clauses—Change of ownership, board, management
- Termination and resignation clauses—Immunity from state and federal laws

Retention Agreements Another type of agreement is a **retention agreement,** designed to retain key employees during mergers, consolidations, or changes in organizational leadership. In healthcare organizations, retention agreements help to provide stable leadership and management during times of change. Retention agreements usually provide for cash bonuses and special benefits to the recipients for staying with the employer for a specified period during times of change or instability.

Contract Clauses that Protect Employees In most agreements, an employee has certain rights and responsibilities, generally known as **review and rescission rights.** These rights allow the employee time to review the agreement and rescind it even after agreeing to it. Federal and state laws define the time periods; a minimum review period is 7 days and may be extended to 21 days in some legal jurisdictions. After the contract is signed, the rescission period is usually 7 to 14 days.

Implied Contracts

Employees without agreements are subject to the employer's policies and procedures, including employee handbooks, which have been held to be implied contracts defining the employment relationship. Unwritten agreements between employers and employees are called **implied contracts.** These contracts are often the focus of disputes between employers and employees. For instance, if an employer hires an employee for an undefined period or promises job security and no document is written and signed, a court may decide whether an implied contract exists. If an employee believes that the terms of the employment agreement were implied in conversations or through an oral job offer, the employee may sue to achieve the implied terms that were denied.[5]

Employment Practices Liability Insurance

A new type of liability insurance protects organizations against costly lawsuits initiated by their employees. This insurance is known as **employment practices liability insurance** (EPLI). The key goal of EPLI is to offer legal and risk-management advice to organizations to minimize their legal exposure and negotiate settlements to employee claims. In organizations, general liability insurance policies do not include coverage for suits filed by employees based on employment-related claims.[6] The types of claims typically filed include discrimination, sexual harassment, wrongful termination, and breach of contract. To obtain EPLI coverage, the insurance company usually requires an organization to undergo an audit of its HR policies and practices, including policy manuals, employee handbooks, employment forms, and other HR practices and processes.[7]

EMPLOYEE RELATIONS AND RIGHTS OF EMPLOYEES

Employees' rights and organizational employee relations philosophies may clash when employees think their contractual or implied-contractual rights have been violated. Several doctrines—employment-at-will, just cause, and due process—affect both employees and employers when settling disputes.

Employment-At-Will

Hiring and firing employees has historically been the employer's right. However, several employment law cases have challenged that right, and employers and their attorneys have responded by establishing and communicating **employment-at-will provisions.** The employment-at-will statements are usually contained in the employee handbook or in HR policy and procedure manuals. The statement says that employers have the right to hire, fire, and promote whomever they choose. In exchange for the employer's right to employment-at-will, employees receive the right to terminate their employment at any time for any reason.[8] Typical employment-at-will verbiage is shown in Figure 10-3.

Exceptions to the At-Will Doctrine   The legal system has identified three exceptions to the at-will doctrine: *public-policy decisions, implied contractual disputes,* and *good faith and fair dealing.* These arguments are raised to assert employees' rights when they believe their rights have been violated, and many legal jurisdictions have recognized these exceptions to the employment-at-will doctrine.

FIGURE 10-3 Employment-At-Will Language

Employment-At-Will Language

I understand that my employment is at-will with no specific duration, which means that no contractual agreement limits my right to terminate my employment. I also understand that my company retains the right to terminate my employment or change any term or condition of employment at any time, with or without cause or proper notice.

I understand that the employee handbook I received from my company is not a contract or legal document and nothing in the handbook should be construed to be a contract whether expressed or implied. I also understand that only the CEO and the vice president of human resources have the ability to promise or agree to any substantive terms or conditions of employment.

I have been informed of my at-will status and have been given an opportunity to ask questions of my supervisor.

Signed _____

Dated _____

Witnessed _____

- A **public-policy violation** occurs when an employee is fired for reporting illegal activities by the employer as required by federal or state law.
- An **implied contract** might promise that an employee will be employed indefinitely or might seem to suggest continued employment as long as an employee performs the job satisfactorily.
- A **good faith** and **fair dealing** exception provides that the employer and the employee have entered into a relationship whose objective is treating each other fairly. If the employer is treating the employee unfairly by being unreasonable, such as assigning difficult work or inconvenient shifts, the employee can assert that the employer is not acting in good faith.

Wrongful Discharge and the Importance of Documentation

One of the most prevalent claims against employers by disgruntled former employees is that of *wrongful discharge*. Wrongful discharge occurs when employers discharge their employees for reasons that are illegal, improper, or are inconsistent with organizational policies, procedures, or rules. To avoid wrongful discharge claims, organizations must ensure that discharged employees are dealt with properly by following applicable policies and procedures that relate to discharge. For example, if a clinic has a process for discipline, the employee should be discharged only after that process has been followed. If the process is not followed, the clinic could be accused of not providing the employee with due process.[9]

Wrongful discharge suits have become a major issue for many healthcare organizations. The items listed in Figure 10-4 are commonly used to defend healthcare organizations against wrongful-discharge lawsuits, including some of the key preventions discussed next.

FIGURE 10-4 Documentation for Defense in Wrongful Discharge Lawsuits

New employee orientation materials	Discharge letter with reason for termination
Employee handbook	Performance appraisals
At-will employment statement—Signed	Job description
Departmental orientation documents	Discipline process documentation
Documentation of employee meetings	Performance management activities (counseling statements, warnings, and suspensions)

New Employee Orientation Materials Employees receive a wide variety of orientation information as they begin their employment. Included in that information should be a thorough review of key policies, such as: sexual harassment prevention policies, appropriate use of the Internet and e-mail policies, employee code of conduct, and related policies that provide new employees with clear expectations for their behavior while on the job. Many healthcare employers also include a review of their employee handbook, requiring employees to sign a form acknowledging that the employee has a responsibility to read the handbook and agree to follow the employer's policies and procedures, contained therein.

In the healthcare industry a review of *patient confidentiality policies* is part of the orientation materials. Confidentiality of patient information is a highly held value by healthcare organizations, and as noted earlier, a compliance issue due to HIPAA. Many healthcare employers have included a special sign-off for employees attesting to their understanding and commitment to protecting patient confidentiality. This type of documentation can be used in discharge decisions by the employer and used to defend against wrongful discharge claims.

Employee Handbooks   The employee handbook in most organizations acts as a guideline for employees about the policies and work rules that need to be followed. Job expectations and behaviors are also explained in the handbook, and employees are required to acknowledge that they will, as a condition of employment, follow the handbook. An example of a typical table of contents for an employee handbook for a clinic is depicted on the book's web site at *http://flynn.swlearning.com.*

Discharge Letters   Discharge letters document the reason and conditions of the discharges. Some states require the disclosure of the reasons for discharges to employees within a set time period.[10]

Discipline Processes and Performance Appraisals   The majority of information that is used to defend an employer against wrongful discharge suits is generated through discipline and performance management policies and programs. Documentation of discipline decisions and the performance management process helps employers explain the reasons for discharge decisions.

Job Descriptions   Job descriptions contain vital information about the job duties and responsibilities for employees. In many cases, employees are given their job descriptions and sign a document acknowledging that they have received a copy.

Just Cause

Just cause is typically defined by whether the organization acted reasonably, fairly, and impartially in administering discipline, including discharge. The facts and circumstances of each case usually determine whether there was just cause for the action taken by the organization. Figure 10-5 contains points that determine just cause.

FIGURE 10-5   Just Cause Determinants

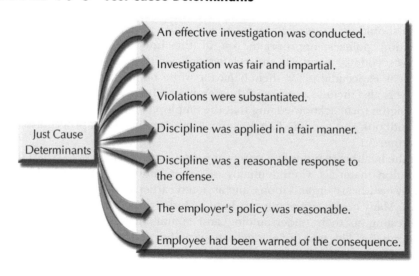

Just Cause Determinants

- An effective investigation was conducted.
- Investigation was fair and impartial.
- Violations were substantiated.
- Discipline was applied in a fair manner.
- Discipline was a reasonable response to the offense.
- The employer's policy was reasonable.
- Employee had been warned of the consequence.

Constructive Discharge

When an employer creates adverse working conditions that force an employee to resign, **constructive discharge** has occurred. Sometimes a supervisor or manager will wage a purposeful campaign against an employee to get the employee to quit. Work schedules are changed or work assignments are unfavorable or supervisors just make the job difficult. When courts have ruled that constructive discharge has occurred, an employee may be awarded compensation, including back pay and punitive damages.[11] Constructive discharge claims are becoming more frequent, and healthcare employers should be aware of this issue when "encouraging" employees to resign.

Due Process

Healthcare employees may contest disciplinary actions if they feel they are not afforded **due process,** which is the opportunity to explain and defend their actions against charges of misconduct or other reasons relating to the disciplinary process. Due process is a way in which employees can question discipline against them. Prior to initiating serious discipline such as a suspension or termination, it is good practice for an employer to conduct an investigation to determine whether the employee was provided the recourse allowed by the employer's policies. The investigation should also determine how the employee was informed of his or her rights and if valid documentation exists to support the employer's position.

   Managers need to be certain that employees' due-process rights are maintained to avoid negative decisions by state and federal regulatrory agencies and courts. The following are key questions:

- Is an employee complaint process available to employees?
- Did the employee use the process?
- Did the employee voice any concerns about potential retaliation?
- Were there any policies or precedents that impacted the outcome of the complaint?
- If the complaint had been reviewed by EEOC or a human rights agency, how would the case have been decided?
- Was the decision based on the facts of the case?

Resolving Employee Complaints

As part of ensuring due process, many employers have established problem resolution policies that define the employee complaint process. Having an internal problem or conflict resolution process in place is advantageous when outside agencies such as EEOC or OSHA review employees' complaints. In a unionized setting, a union contract includes a grievance procedure that must be followed.

Resolving differences between employees and their employers is an everyday occurrence in the workplace. When issues cannot be resolved, one effective option is to utilize **alternative dispute resolution** (ADR). ADR methods include arbitration, peer-review panels, and company ombudsmen.[12]

Arbitration Using a third party to resolve disputes has gained popularity as both employees and employers try to avoid time-consuming and expensive legal proceedings. Some organizations have elected to use **arbitration,** which requires an employer and employee to present their cases to a neutral third party for a binding decision.

Peer Review Panels Some healthcare organizations utilize a **peer review panel,** which is an internal committee of employees who review employee complaints and make recommendations regarding a resolution. Panel members receive training in peer review techniques. HR managers typically facilitate the peer review process. In some healthcare organizations, the committee is limited to making recommendations to management; in other healthcare organizations, the panel may make actual decisions about complaint resolution. A sample conflict resolution policy is available at the website for the book: *http://flynn. swlearning.com.*

Federal and state agencies and courts frequently view peer review panels positively when employees file claims against their healthcare employers. Such panels are often considered as enhancing due process. However, existence of such panels does not guarantee that employers will automatically prevail if the employees pursue claims or suits.

Employee Ombudsman Some healthcare organizations use an ombudsman to help resolve employees' problems. Ombudsmen are usually staff employees who are not part of the formal management hierarchy. They receive special training to administer their roles in a way that is fair to both the employer and employees.

BALANCING EMPLOYER SECURITY AND EMPLOYEE RIGHTS

Many employees have exercised their rights to privacy in the workplace, and employers have been forced to agree that some employee information is private and confidential and cannot be used for or against employees. Balancing employer security with employee rights requires managers to review HR policies and practices regularly.

Employee Records

The **Privacy Act of 1974** issued regulations that affect HR record-keeping systems, policies, and procedures for governmental employers. In some states, laws have been passed regarding employee records issues.

FIGURE 10-6   Personnel File Contents

INCLUDE:

- Application for employment
- New employee orientation information—Checklist
- Letter offering the job
- Employee group insurance benefit forms
- Compensation records
- Performance appraisals
- Performance management documentation

DO NOT INCLUDE:

- Employee health files
- Performance comments by co-workers

Many healthcare organizations have responded to federal and state laws by developing policies regarding access to personnel records. The purpose of these policies is to protect employee information. Often, such policy statements include who has access to the employee record and how employees can dispute information in their personnel file. Figure 10-6 lists the documents that should and should not be included in personnel files.

Other policies that govern personnel files deal with information available through a Human Resource Information System (HRIS). An HRIS is an electronic record system. Access to an HRIS should be restricted and protected by confidential passwords and access codes.

Employees' Right to Free Speech

Employees have challenged employers' right to enforce policies that limit free speech. Several areas of conflict between employers and employees are discussed next.

Whistleblowing   An employee's free speech is protected when reporting employer public-policy violations. Employees who report such activity are called *whistleblowers,* and statutes that allow employees to report illegal activities by their employers protect them. A common area for healthcare whistleblowers is Medicare fraud and abuse. Legislation has been developed to protect whistleblowing healthcare workers from retaliation, such as discipline and termination. Under current federal legislation, employees may receive payment for reporting fraud and abuse that is verified by federal agencies. The award to the employee can be up to 10 percent of the penalty assessed against the organization.[13]

Most large healthcare organizations provide some process, such as a confidential telephone hotline number to call, to bring the alleged impropriety forward within the organization before the whistleblower identifies potential issues to federal or state agencies. Employees in healthcare organizations that have internal processes are not required to use them, but they are encouraged by their employers to do so.

Monitoring E-mail and Voicemail Growth in technological capabilities has caused healthcare organizations to further define employer rights and employee privacy rights.[14] Monitoring employees' e-mail and voicemail is a privacy issue that organizations must keep in mind as they write policies to protect business interests. Policy statements include limiting technology use for business purposes only, restricting personal e-mail and voicemail use, prohibiting shared passwords, and retaining a right to monitor or search all e-mail and voicemail.

Healthcare organizations also want to prevent using e-mail and voicemail to transmit information that would violate HR policies. These policies would prohibit transmitting jokes and cartoons that may be discriminatory based on sex, religion, or race. HR staff and operational managers must address these issues with policies and consistent enforcement.

To protect themselves, healthcare organizations must establish policies, train employees frequently, and enforce the policies consistently. Many healthcare organizations have even developed statements on computer screen savers to remind employees about appropriate and inappropriate computer use. Many healthcare organizations require employees to sign an acknowledgement at the end of orientation or training that indicates that the employee understands the computer use policies and the consequences of failing to comply with them.

Tracking Internet Use Healthcare employers may encourage Internet use for business purposes, but most are concerned about reduced productivity when employees spend work time "surfing the net."[15] In addition, some employers are concerned that employees might view inappropriate Web sites that may tarnish the organization's image. Employers are especially concerned about Web sites with pornographic content. Many healthcare organizations have installed software that tracks Internet use and prevents access to certain Web sites.

Honesty in the Workplace

One of the most significant problems facing employers is theft by employees. All theft is serious, but in healthcare organizations drug theft is particularly disconcerting. Drug theft can occur when drugs are taken from the drug inventory; however, a more serious violation occurs when staff divert drugs from patients for their own use.

Most healthcare employers use background checks to screen new employees and deny employment to individuals convicted of drug-related crimes. In addition, managers, security personnel, and pharmacy staff should cooperatively develop a plan to prevent the theft of drugs, especially narcotics. Elaborate systems, including inventory checks after each shift, have reduced theft of drugs from supply cabinets, but diverting patients' medications is more difficult to discover.

Performance Surveillance An employer is allowed to search an employee's work area if a manager has legitimate business reasons for doing so, such as suspicion of theft or illegal activities. Employees are not protected from monitoring and searches if there is reason to believe they are engaged in activities that violate the employer's work rules.

Employer Investigations Healthcare employers have typically conducted investigations when employees were suspected of theft; however, healthcare employers are now concerned about a variety of issues including illegal drug use, workplace violence, and workers' compensation fraud. Investigations are conducted by security personnel when the organization is large enough to have a security department. In other cases, managers or HR professionals investigate employees' activities. It is important to conduct thorough inquiries to avoid concerns about improper or incomplete investigations which could result in misleading information about a particular incident or issue.

An organization can develop rules that facilitate investigations. Some examples of these rules follow: Have at least one witness present when confronting an employee. Don't touch or restrain the employee. Inform the employee that he or she is free to leave the meeting at any time. Have at least one witness of the same gender present to avoid harassment claims. If the employee refuses to respond or participate, make clear that such behavior is insubordination and that disciplinary action will be taken if the incident warrants it. Figure 10-7 illustrates techniques for investigations.

Because some of the more common reasons for investigations in healthcare settings include the illegal use of or theft of drugs, patient mistreatment, or other behavior that reflects on professional competency, some of the issues investigated by healthcare managers need to be reported to the agencies that license healthcare professionals.

Honesty/Integrity Testing Testing prospective employees using an honesty or integrity test is one method used by employers. Healthcare organizations should review state court cases before administering these tests because various courts have held that the tests are not reliable or valid for job-related purposes.

FIGURE 10-7 Methods of Workplace Investigations

Off-the-Job Behavior

Employers are reluctant to monitor employees' off-the-job behaviors unless the activities have definite job-related consequences. For example, a healthcare employer would want to know if an employee will miss work because he or she is incarcerated, particularly if the employee is in the final stages of progressive discipline for attendance problems. However, the situation becomes more complex if the employee is jailed for public intoxication during chemical dependency rehabilitation.

Healthcare employers are typically not concerned about their employees off-the-job behaviors unless the behaviors disrupt the work environment and jeopardize patient care. Then the employer must take action. Some organizations establish employee assistance programs to help employees with on- and off-the-job behaviors that threaten their jobs. Employee assistance programs provide counseling and other help to employees who have emotional, physical, or personal problems.

Employee Substance Abuse and Employer Drug Testing Policies

Healthcare organizations have shown leadership in designing policies and practices to provide a drug-free workplace. These policies are consistent with the **Drug-Free Workplace Act of 1988** whose purpose is to make workplaces safe, healthy, and efficient for employees, patients, and visitors. Policy violations in healthcare organizations may include unlawful possession, use, distribution, or

---

ETHICAL PRACTICES AND COMPLIANCE

Each day healthcare workers are confronted with situations and dilemmas that can and do place them in positions requiring ethical and legal compliance decision making. These include protecting the confidentiality of:

- medical information
- financial data and proprietary business information
- medical treatment decisions and related issues

The effectiveness of ethics and compliance practices in healthcare organizations is highly correlated with how consistently applied and well-communicated the employee relations' standards and policies are.[16] Healthcare organizations must guide and direct the decisions, behavior, and practices of their employees through clear and concise standards and policies, effectively supported through thorough orientation and training on these standards and policies.

manufacture of a controlled substance at the facility or on facility grounds. Policy statements prohibit employees from arriving at work under the influence of drugs, including alcohol. Many healthcare organizations have adopted drug-testing policies that help to ensure that the workplace is free from drug use. Many healthcare employers test for drugs during preemployment screening. Most healthcare organizations will withdraw conditional job offers to candidates who fail the test. Other drug testing may occur "for cause," randomly, or after an injury or incident.

HR Policies, Procedures, and Rules

All organizations have policies, procedures, and rules that govern their employee relationships program. In many organizations these documents are recorded and organized into an employee handbook or HR policy and procedure manual. The employee handbook could be a stand-alone source of policies and procedures, for smaller healthcare organizations, or a condensed version of the HR policy and procedure manual for larger employers. There are differences between policies, procedures, and rules, which can be described as follows:

- Policies are general statements about the organization's position on an issue and are used to guide management decision making.
- Procedures define the customary way an organization deals with the policy issue.
- Rules define expected behaviors of employees at work.

Coordinating Policies and Procedures

Coordinating, implementing, and using policies in healthcare organizations is an important HR responsibility. Effective policies, when interpreted consistently and applied uniformly, may protect organizations from lawsuits and complaints. Agencies that monitor and periodically review policies in the healthcare industry include State Departments of Health, Federal Health Care Finance Administration, and the Joint Commission on Accreditation of Healthcare Organizations (JCAHO).

Several steps assure successful development and implementation of policies and procedures. The process includes identifying the need for a policy, developing a draft, formally reviewing the draft with the organizational leadership team, outside legal counsel review, distributing the policy, training the management group to use the policy for its intended purpose, and implementing the policy.

Policies are usually drafted in a standard format and contain a policy statement with procedures and definitions. Cross-referencing policies helps managers who want additional or related information. HR practitioners usually provide consultative resources to managers regarding interpretation and implementation.

Communicating HR Information

Keeping the lines of communication open between management and employees is very important, especially when the organization has made important decisions, such as adding new services or building new facilities.[17] Communicating HR information is equally important to employees. Healthcare employers want workers to know about HR changes, such as training and development opportunities, benefit enrollment information, and new rules, among many others.

HR communication focuses on the receipt and dissemination of HR data and information throughout the organization. *Downward communication* flows from senior management to the rest of the organization, informing employees about what is and will be happening in the organization and what are the expectations and goals of top management. *Upward communication* enables managers to know about the ideas, concerns, and information needs of employees. Various methods are used to facilitate both types of communication.

Organizations communicate with employees through internal publications and media, including company newspapers and magazines, organizational newsletters, videotapes, Internet and Intranet postings, and e-mail announcements. Whatever the means used, managers should continually make efforts to communicate information employees need to know. The spread of electronic communications allows for more timely and widespread dissemination of HR information.

One form of upward communication is a *suggestion system*. This program encourages employees to offer ideas that might improve the organization and its operations. Suggestion systems often include recognition and financial rewards to employees who provide cost-saving or process-improvement ideas.

EMPLOYEE DISCIPLINE

Following established HR policies, procedures, and regulations, and maintaining high-quality job performance are required for organizations to deliver excellent products and services. Healthcare organizations develop discipline systems to help employees meet their job responsibilities, improve their performance, and establish successful employee–employer working relationships.

Although they usually represent a small number, problem employees can be disruptive to the work environment, and their performance must be dealt with in a timely manner.[18] In these cases, management provides training and feedback to employees, with the expectation that their behaviors and performance will improve. Typical discipline issues include absenteeism, tardiness, interpersonal issues, insubordination, inability to meet job standards, and low productivity.

Reasons for Not Using Discipline

Managers may be reluctant to use discipline for a variety of reasons. The most common reasons for not using discipline include fear of lawsuits, lack of support from the organization, fear of retaliation from employees, fear of not being liked by employees, guilt, loss of friendship, and the loss of time and energy to manage the discipline process. To counter these reasons, healthcare organizations should train supervisors and managers about the effective and fair use of discipline.

Training Managers

Management training programs should be designed to include the importance of discipline, including treating employees with respect and dignity. Building supervisory skills to facilitate discussions and to counsel employees is especially important. Performance discussions should provide positive assistance so that employees can improve their job performance.

To determine when to use the discipline process, managers must evaluate each issue on a case-by-case basis to determine which type of discipline to administer. When the issue is easily resolved, no disciplinary action may be necessary.

A common employee discipline process is called **progressive discipline,** which utilizes a series of identifiable steps to communicate concerns to employees. Each step is separate and distinct and is designed to warn the employee to change his or her work performance or behavior or further discipline will occur. Figure 10-8 depicts a typical progressive discipline system.

FIGURE 10-8   Progressive Discipline Process

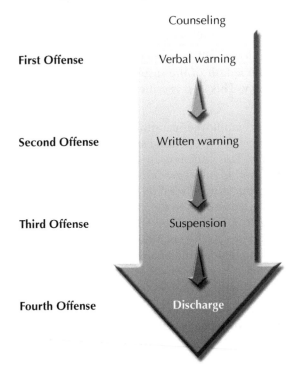

	Counseling
First Offense	Verbal warning
Second Offense	Written warning
Third Offense	Suspension
Fourth Offense	Discharge

Counseling The goal of this step is to tell the employee what job expectations are not being met and talk about how to make improvements in performance. The employee may be unaware of a problem; therefore, counseling by the manager should be positive and encouraging. As an example, if a laboratory technician fails to follow appropriate safety guidelines in the laboratory, counseling from the manager may be needed.

Verbal Caution The second step is a verbal caution, which represents an escalation in the process. If the employee has not improved work performance, the manager then issues a verbal warning. The goal of this step is to point out behavior or performance deficiencies and explain the importance of improvement in these areas. In this step, the manager decides whether to require any additional training to help the employee meet expectations. In the laboratory technician example, the manager might initiate a verbal caution and require the technician to review and dsicuss the safety guidelines for the laboratory.

Written Reprimand If the employee does not improve performance or behavior, the manager can conduct another conference in which job expectations are outlined and documented in writing. Additional resources including training may be offered to help the employee achieve the expected performance results. This step is a warning that performance or behavior needs to improve to avoid the next step in the disciplinary process. If, as noted in the previous example, the technician continues to disregard safety guidelines, the manager would give a written warning, clearly stating the reason for discipline, the steps that must be taken to improve, and the consequences if disregard for safety procedures continues. Specifically, if disregard for safety procedure continues, the technician could be suspended and then ultimately discharged.

Suspension An employee will be suspended if performance or behavior still has not improved. The length of the suspension depends on the severity of the performance deficiency. This step is critical for the employee because the next step is final—discharge.

Discharge When an employee cannot or will not perform satisfactorily, termination may be necessary. The final stage in the discipline process must be managed very carefully. This stage is used when an employee's performance is so below standard or behavior is so egregious that termination is appropriate and consistent with the progressive discipline process. Except in serious situations, employees have received warnings so the discharge should not be a surprise. The manager should clearly define why the employee is being discharged. The discharge meeting should be carefully planned and is often attended by an HR representative. All wage and benefit information should be communicated in writing in the event the employee doesn't remember all of the discussion. It is important to end the meeting and help the employee exit the workplace in a dignified way.

Separation Agreements In some termination situations, formal contracts may be used. One type is a **separation agreement,** in which an employee who is being terminated agrees not to sue the employer in exchange for specified benefits, such as additional severance pay or other "considerations."

For such agreements to be legally enforceable, the financial considerations should usually be additional items not part of normal termination benefits. When using separation agreements, care must be taken to avoid the appearance of constructive discharge of employees. Use of such agreements should be reviewed by a legal counsel.

EMPLOYEE RELATIONS PROGRAMS

In addition to all of the policies, procedures, rights and responsibilities, and discipline procedures, most organizations strive to affect their employees positively by using innovative strategies. Some of the more common strategies follow.

Employee Attitude Surveys

When an organization makes a commitment to perform employee attitude surveys, they may be scheduled as frequently as once per year. However, most healthcare organizations conduct surveys every two to three years. Conducting an attitude survey encourages feedback from employees about their work environment and measures their morale. Surveys help organizations gather information from their employees about potential problems that may be developing. For example, a hospital might wish to conduct an attitude survey when the administrator determines that employee issues may lead to difficulties in recruiting new staff members. Healthcare administrators might want survey information analyzed by departments or shifts. Information from the survey is interpreted and translated into an action plan to make improvements.

Employee Assistance Programs

Organizations provide employee assistance programs (EAPs) to help their employees cope with personal life management issues that affect their work. Initially, the most common use of EAPs was to deal with drug and alcohol abuse but EAPs have been extended to include legal, financial, marital, and interpersonal issues. The services may be offered two ways: through internal programs staffed by company employees, or by an outside sevice. EAP programs, whether offered internally or externally, are designed to help employees with problems that may affect their productivity. EAP counselors must be qualified to treat a wide variety of employee issues and problems.

Employer of Choice Programs

Organizations interested in becoming an "employer of choice" (EOC) must redefine their HR practices to clearly demonstrate their commitment to their employees. A successful employer of choice philosophy requires a plan with the following components:[19]

- Long-term top management commitment to becoming an EOC
- Defined organizational purpose

- Innovative and competitive compensation and benefit programs
- Staff-development opportunities
- Rewards for innovation and creativity
- Rewards aligned with performance
- Culture that respects diversity, encourages staff participation, and rewards employee and organizational success

Standards of Behavior

Another popular method to improve organization–employee relationships is to develop a series of expectations the organization has for all employees. Standards of behavior, especially revolving around patient satisfaction initiatives, have become popular as a means to clearly identify behavioral expectations. The standards may include the following expectations:

- Respect
- Excellence
- Cooperation
- Compassion

- Communication
- Fairness and Equity
- Self Care
- Personal Accountability

Standards are usually developed and aligned to organizational values which are communicated continuously. The standards should define how the expectations affect employees on a daily basis.

CASE

Carol County Hospital (CCH) is a private, not-for-profit acute care hospital located in a medium size market. It is a 75-year-old corporation, offering full-service care, including general medical, emergency, and general surgical, with special emphasis on oncology, cardiac, obstetrical, and rehabilitation treatment and care.

	2004	2005	2006	COMPARATIVE DATA
EMPLOYEE RELATIONS INDICATORS				
Turnover rate	14%	22%	26%	12%
Absence rate	5%	7%	12%	10%
Vacancy rate	8%	18%	20%	10%
Discrimination charges	2	8	12	n/a
OSHA complaints	2	12	14	n/a
EMPLOYEE ASSISTANCE REFERRALS				
• drug/alcohol	60	75	100	70
• career stress	30	35	50	30
• other	20	30	20	50
Totals	110	140	170	150

Questions

1. Assess CCH's employee relations program. What statistics have you considered in your assessment?

2. What HR metrics are important to consider in assessing any (potential) employee relations issues?

END NOTES

1. Dave Carpenter, "Can We Talk?" *H&HN: Hospitals and Health Networks* (December 2003), 20.
2. For details on HIPAA, see *http://www.hhs.gov/ocr/hipaa*.
3. Yale D. Tauber and Carol S. Silverman, "Employment Contacts Get the Employers in the Game," *Workspan* (August 2002), 38–42.
4. Michael J. Garrison and Charles D. Stevens, "Sign This Agreement Not to Compete or You're Fired," *Employee Responsibilities and Rights Journal* (September 2003), 103.
5. Debbie Harrison, "Is a Long-Term Business Relationship an Implied Contract," *Journal of Management Studies*, 41 (2004), 107.
6. Dave Lenckus, "EPLI Policy Pays Off for Verizon," *Business Insurance* (April 4, 2003), 28.
7. Jon G. Miller, "Analyzing Employment Practices Liability Insurance," *Compensation and Benefits Review* (November/December 2003), 38.
8. Alan Rupe, "Discovering the Laws of Gravity," *Workforce Management* (September 2003), 16–18.
9. "Answers to this Month's Legal Checkpoints," *Nursing Management* (May 2004), 53.
10. As an example, the State of Minnesota requires employers to provide a letter disclosing the reason for discharge within five days of the written request of a terminated employee, "Notice of Termination Statute," M.S.A. 181.932.
11. Robert J. Paul and Kathryn Seeberger, "Constructive Discharge: When Quitting Constitutes Illegal Termination," *Review of Business* (Spring 2002), 23–30.
12. Richard Nimark, "Getting Dispute-Wise," *Dispute Resolution Journal* (February/April 2004), 56–57.
13. For more information see *http://www.medicare.gov/fraudabuse/howtoreport.asp*.
14. Joan T. A. Gabel and Nancy Mansfield, "The Information Revolution and Its Impact on the Employment Relationship," *American Business Law Journal*, 40 (2003), 301–353.
15. Carl J. Case and Kimberly S. Young, "Employee Internet Management: Current Business Practices and Outcomes," *Cyber Psychology and Behavior*, 5, No. 4, (2002), 355–361.
16. Curtis C. Verschoor, "Organizational DNA Should Contain Ethics Component," *Strategic Finance* (February 2005), 19–21.
17. Dave Carpenter, "Can We Talk?"
18. Ben Wilmott, "How to Manage Difficult Staff," *Community Care* (June 23, 2005), 51.
19. Adapted from Gary Mecklenberg, "Helping Hospitals be 'Employers of Choice,'" *AHA News* (December 10, 2001), 7–8; and Nellie C. Robinson and Sue Ellen Pinkerton, "The Children's National Medical Center Story: Nursing Shortage to Employer of Choice," *Nursing Economics* (March/April 2004), 91–94.

LABOR RELATIONS AND HEALTHCARE ORGANIZATIONS

Learning Objectives

After you have read this chapter, you should be able to:

- Explain the labor relations challenges facing the healthcare industry.
- Describe the National Labor Relations Act, including the unique healthcare provisions.
- Outline the stages of the unionization process.
- Discuss the collective bargaining process.
- Identify the contract negotiations process in the healthcare industry.

Healthcare HR Insights

The union organizer from the local affiliate of a national union representing service and technical workers stood before a small group of medical laboratory and central sterilization technicians from a local hospital. The hospital workers had been invited to a meeting in one of their coworker's homes to discuss the possibility of a union for the hospital. The audience, although small, was made up of primarily long-term employees, many of whom would never have thought they would be actually considering union representation. But staffing shortages, low wages and demanding supervisors have motivated them to seek out help, potentially through union representation.

The union organizer explained the process of signing cards, receiving approval to go forward with a compaign from the National Labor Relations Board, and conducting the election. She also discussed the advantages of being a union member, promising better pay and benefits, better staffing, and better treatment by hospital administration and supervisors, and how those covered by the contract would pay union dues by monthly check-off.[1] The union organizer's words got her audience's attention and definitely held their interest. These types of meetings are very common throughout the healthcare industry today. Unions as widely diverse as the Teamsters and the United Food and Commercial Workers are aggressively pursuing what they see as a significant opportunity to unionize healthcare workers, due to the healthcare industry'staffing and pay issues.[2]

A union is a formal association of workers that promotes its members' interests through collective bargaining. It is the official employee representative, and it executes its responsibilities by negotiating labor contracts and administering the contracts until they expire.

Today unions in the United States represent about 14 percent of all civilian workers but only 9.5 percent of the private-sector workforce. Additionally, the actual number of members has declined in most years even though more people are employed than previously. Of the approximately 120 million U.S. workers, only about 16 million belong to a union.[3]

UNIONS IN THE HEALTHCARE INDUSTRY

To offset the decline in union membership, unions are targeting the service sector for their membership drives.[4] Healthcare is a major employer in the service sector, so HR practitioners in the industry are and should be increasingly concerned about unionizing attempts. Additionally, unions are winning a higher percentage of elections in healthcare ballots when compared with all U.S. industries. In one recent study, healthcare labor victories were at 67 percent, compared to all other industries at 58 percent.[5]

Union activity in healthcare has been heavily concentrated in metropolitan areas and on the east and west coasts of the United States. Also, unions tend to be more successful in northern U.S. states—in part, because these areas have a long history of unionism.

Increased unionism in the future of healthcare seems likely. Service workers in healthcare organizations are seeking union protection and local nurses' unions are merging with larger national unions to enhance their protection. Unions that typically have not represented healthcare workers are making organizing attempts as they see opportunities in healthcare. Even physicians are forming unions to negotiate their compensation through contractual agreements.

Why Employees Unionize

Generally, healthcare employees seek union assistance because they believe that their employers have not treated them respectfully, and they believe a union can negotiate better financial benefits, job security, and working conditions. Financial concerns may cause employers to find ways to deliver care more cost effectively, but some of the new systems result in lower staffing ratios that may affect quality of patient care. Employees involved in patient-care professions have worried about changes in staff-to-patient ratios and have asked unions to represent them and to negotiate staffing ratios with their employers.[6]

The process of unionizing a healthcare employee group can be initiated either by employees or union organizers. The union assesses the potential for success before it commits union resources to a costly organizing campaign. Once the union decides there is potential interest by a group of employees, representatives begin the campaign.

A survey by the American Organization of Nurse Executives found that RNs were satisfied with their employment and employers for the following reasons: peer relationships, performance recognition, independent decision making, interdepartmental and intradepartmental communications, contributions to the decision making process, and support from management. In the same study, nurses indicated other specific reasons for satisfaction in the workplace, including competitive compensation, flexible work schedules, continuing education, and respect from management.[7] Figure 11-1 shows the reasons for nurse job satisfaction and dissatisfaction.

Healthcare administrators must understand their workers' reasons for job satisfaction and dissatisfaction when they develop HR policies, if their goal is to avoid unionization.[8] The risk of unionization decreases significantly when an organization adopts positive policies and supportive HR practices for employees. Healthcare workers want to be informed, respected, and included in decision making. Also, they want to participate in care decisions for patients.

FIGURE 11-1   Registered Nurses' Job Satisfiers and Dissatisfiers

JOB SATISFIERS	JOB DISSATISFIERS
• Peer relationships	• Poor working conditions
• Performance recognition	• Lack of recognition
• Effective communication	• Job stress
• Input into decisions	• Lack of career opportunities
• Competitive compensation	• Competing personal family commitments
• Support from management	
• Flexible work schedules	
• Continuing education opportunities	
• Management respect	
• Independent decision making	

LABOR-RELATIONS PHILOSOPHY

In healthcare organizations that have unions, union and management representatives adopt strategic positions about the types of relationships they will have with each other. As a product of these positions, the union-management relationship is developed and a philosophy emerges that mirrors past relationships. Union–management relationships exist somewhere on a philosophical continuum between **adversarial** and **collaborative.**

A healthcare organization's philosophy of labor relations reflects a strategic decision whether to have a relationship that is adversarial, collaborative, or somewhere between the two. Upper management must support the philosophy, middle management must agree to implement the intent of the philosophy, and supervisors should be trained to deal effectively with employees and unions, whether the philosophy is adversarial, collaborative, or somewhere in between.

Adversarial Relationships

Traditionally, the relationships between healthcare organizations and unions have been adversarial, an atmosphere in which both parties try to control the process and relationship by winning beneficial contracts for the organization or the workers. Decisions made in adversarial relationships are usually not favorable for long-term relationships, especially when one party perceives that it is continually compromising to maintain the relationship. Both parties are suspicious and may use information and communication selectively to gain a negotiating advantage. The organization controls the economics, while the union has the power to call a strike when a satisfactory agreement is not reached.

Collaborative Relationships

In some unionized healthcare organizations, a philosophy emerges that supports collaborative relationships. The goal of these nonadversarial relationships of shared responsibility is to address the mutual interests and issues of both sides. They openly share information and make decisions in a collaborative manner. A fundamental belief is that decisions made by consensus are more durable than decisions resulting from compromise.[9]

LEGAL FRAMEWORK FOR UNION–MANAGEMENT RELATIONS

Three acts, passed over a period of years, constitute what has been labeled the "National Labor Code": (1) the Wagner Act, (2) the Taft-Hartley Act, and (3) the Landrum-Griffin Act. Each act was passed to focus on some facet of the relations between unions and management. Figure 11-2 indicates the primary focus of each act.

National Labor Relations Act

In 1935, Congress passed the **National Labor Relations Act (NLRA),** also known as the **Wagner Act,** to provide more specific guidelines to govern the relationship between organizations and employees. Section 7 of the Act provides for the right to bargain collectively. Section 8a of the Act describes unfair labor practices by organizations. Section 8b, added later, covers unfair labor practices by unions.[10]

National Labor Relations Board The act also established the **National Labor Relations Board (NLRB),** whose purpose is to enforce the provisions of the act for both unions and organizations. The NLRB is a federal agency comprised of five members who interpret and enforce the NLRA. Two major functions of the board are to conduct representation elections and to investigate and resolve unfair labor practices by either organizations or the union.[11]

FIGURE 11-2 National Labor Code

Federal Mediation and Conciliation Services   A provision in the National Labor Relations Act created the **Federal Mediation and Conciliation Services (FMCS),** an agency charged with mediating labor negotiations when asked by negotiating parties or assigned by the FMCS Director. The director makes assignments when disputes substantially threaten to interrupt healthcare services. The FMCS trains managers and union representatives to negotiate collaboratively. The agency also mediates conflicts during adversarial negotiations.

Taft–Hartley Act

The **Taft–Hartley Act,** passed in 1947, equalized the effects of the NLRA by defining and prohibiting unfair labor practices by unions. Because unions had grown significantly with the passage of the NLRA, the U.S. Congress responded to pressure by employers to hold unions to the same fair labor practices that employers were required to follow.

Landrum–Griffin Act

The **Landrum–Griffin Act,** passed in 1959, was designed to curtail corrupt union practices, including officials using pension funds for their personal use and making threats and using physical force against members to retain their elected positions. The act, in essence, protects workers from the unions that represent them. It requires unions to develop bylaws, financial reports, and bills of rights for union members under the supervision of the U.S. Secretary of Labor.

NLRA and the Healthcare Industry

Prior to 1974, the healthcare industry was not covered by the NLRA. In Congress, lawmakers were concerned that if healthcare workers were allowed to organize, there could be a disruption in vital healthcare services.

During the 1960s and early 1970s, the healthcare industry was growing rapidly, and union leaders saw an opportunity to recruit a large number of members, many of whom believed their wage and benefits programs were not competitive. In 1974 Congress repealed the clause that had exempted the healthcare industry from employee unionization. However, lawmakers added several provisions to the NLRA that would protect communities in case of union strikes during contract negotiations. Important provisions in the law include a 10-day strike notice and a requirement to use federal and state mediation services.

Ten-Day Strike Notice   One of the provisions passed in 1974 required unions to give 10-days notice of their intent to strike. In most cases, the 10-day notice coincides with the contract expiration. If a union fails to give the 10-day notice to the employer, the NLRB is not required to protect striking workers, leaving healthcare employers the option of hiring permanent replacement workers and terminating the illegally striking employees.

Although this provision was created to provide healthcare organizations with some warning about an impending strike, most healthcare organizations begin planning well in advance. The 10-day notice is built into negotiation work plans and is usually coordinated with the contract ratification vote. If the members reject the contract and vote to strike, the 10-day notice is issued. However, the 10-day strike notice requirement is frequently a disputed issue as a strike looms for a healthcare organization. As an example, Alexandria Clinic in Minnesota terminated some striking nurses in the belief that the union, the Minnesota Licensed Practical Nurses Association (MLPNA), did not act in accordance with the 10-day strike notice requirement. However, the nurses were subsequently reinstated when the MLPNA appealed the decision.[12]

Negotiation Notification   The act also requires healthcare employers and unions to inform the FMCS of the parties' intent to begin negotiations 90 days before the contract expires. The notification process allows the mediation service to assign a mediator to the negotiations and offer any training the negotiating parties might need.

Impasse   Another provision in the act helps to expedite the negotiating process when an **impasse** occurs. If the negotiating parties have a dispute they cannot resolve, they must report the situation to FMCS. A mediator is assigned to facilitate a resolution. In healthcare organizations that use collaborative labor relations, a mediator is usually included in the negotiations from the initial meeting.

Strikes and the Board of Inquiry   When negotiations have failed and a strike is possible, the FMCS director may appoint a **board of inquiry** to investigate, report, and recommend to the director solutions to resolve the contractual disputes. In this case, the current labor contract must be extended for 30 days while the board of inquiry completes its work. The use of a board of inquiry is a last step in the process to settle a contract dispute.

THE UNIONIZATION PROCESS IN HEALTHCARE

The process of unionizing healthcare employees has been relatively unchanged since 1974, when healthcare employees gained the right to bargain collectively. Unions typically conduct campaigns in organizations if the relationship between employees and managers has been negative. The most common way to measure the potential of a union campaign is to assess those relationships. Unionizing is frequently a vote against management rather than a vote for the union. The role of the manager in creating a positive work environment is essential for the organization that is interested in a nonunion work environment. Managers interact with employees on a daily basis and have the opportunity to build positive working relationships that negate the need for union representation. If the organization and management fail to develop proactive policies and practices and fail to practice preventive labor relations, the employees may seek representation by the union.[13]

To unionize, it must be shown that a majority of employees who are eligible to vote want union representation. A number of steps comprise the unionization process, and they are shown in Figure 11-3.

FIGURE 11-3   Union Campaign Process

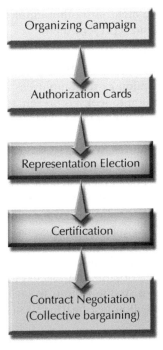

Organizing Campaign

The campaign to form a union usually begins when a group of employees who are dissatisfied with their employer approaches a union to seek its expertise in organizing workers into a union. Alternatively, a union may target an organization or a group of employees about their potential interest in being represented. Unions make an early determination of whether there is sufficient interest in representation before they agree to invest resources in an organizing campaign.

If a union decides interest is sufficient, it conducts informational meetings with the employees at an off-site location (as depicted in this chapter's HR Healthcare Insight) to share information about the union and its capabilities. The meetings, often unknown to managers, provide opportunities for employees to air concerns about their working conditions, which helps the union to assess the likelihood of a successful campaign. Union representatives also present data about wage and benefit contracts in the industry and other organizations to help convince workers that union representation will be financially beneficial for them. Typically, the union organizer will identify one to two informal leaders who are employees who have issues with or are generally unhappy with the organization to host the initial meetings. As an example, in a recent nursing home organizing attempt, the union organizer and a dietary aide who worked at the nursing home coincidentally met at their sons' little league game. The dietary aide was complaining about her job and the nursing home, and the organizer offered the assistance of the union. The dietary aide subsequently became the access point for the union to meet with other employees and discuss their concerns and how the union could represent them.

Authorization Cards   To prove that a sufficient number of employees are interested in union representation, the NLRB requires the union to get signatures from employees on **authorization cards.** Employees who sign the authorization cards have authorized the union to seek a representation election that could formalize the union's role in negotiating labor contracts on behalf of the employee group.

When the union has signatures from at least 30 percent of the employees, it can make a formal request to the NLRB to authorize a representation election. Some unions prefer at least a 50 percent signature rate or they will not file with the NLRB. Often times, an organization will challenge a number of the signed cards, arguing that they are not valid for a variety of reasons. If the union has more than the 30 percent of required signed cards, the invalidation of some of the cards won't halt the process from going forward. If the NLRB agrees that the union has met the 30 percent requirement, it orders an election.

Official notification to the organization occurs when the union requests an election. Management is given an opportunity to review and perhaps contest the union's request. The NLRB will hold a hearing, if necessary, to hear arguments from both sides.

Healthcare and Bargaining Units

Management often argues that the union is trying to organize a group that has not been determined to be an appropriate bargaining unit according rules developed by the NLRB in 1991. If the organization can prove that the union is not following the NLRB rules, the request for the representation election will be denied.

As the healthcare industry began to unionize, disputes occurred about the composition and number of unions. In response, Congress asked the NLRB to make recommendations about the appropriate number of and types of unions a healthcare facility could have. The NLRB determined that hospitals have eight distinct employee groups that could be considered bargaining units, as depicted in Figure 11-4.

Employees who constitute a bargaining unit generally have mutual interests in the following areas:

- Wages, hours, and working conditions
- Physical location and amount of interaction and working relationships between employee groups
- Supervision by similar levels of management

Usually, healthcare organizations prefer fewer groups with larger numbers of employees. Unions usually are interested in smaller groups, which often lead to more successful organizing campaigns.

FIGURE 11-4   Appropriate Bargaining Units in Healthcare

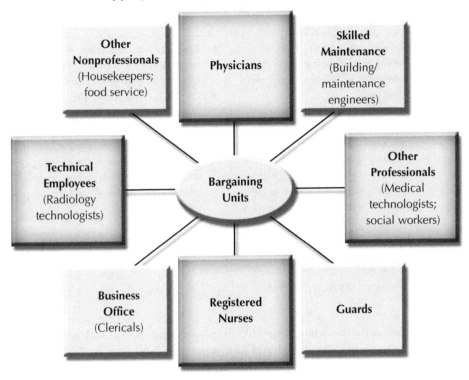

When management challenges a union's formation, the NLRB determines whether an employee group is part of the appropriate bargaining group. If management and the union do not agree on who is and who is not included in the unit, the regional office of the NLRB must make the determination. A major criterion in deciding the composition of a bargaining unit is what the NLRB calls a "community of interest." At a medical center where nursing assistants and orderlies work closely together and may even have interchangeable job duties, there would be every likelihood that the employees in those two jobs would be in the same bargaining unit, probably in a "other non-professionals" unit.

Supervisors and Bargaining Units   Provisions of the NLRA exclude supervisors from coverage when attempting to vote for or join unions. As a result, supervisors and managers in healthcare organizations cannot be included in bargaining units for unionization purposes.

But who qualifies as a supervisor is not always clear. The NLRB uses a detailed definition that identifies a supervisor as any individual with authority to hire, transfer, discharge, discipline, and use independent judgment with employees. Numerous NLRB and court decisions have been rendered on specific situations. A major case decided by the U.S. Supreme Court found that charge nurses with RN degrees were supervisors because they exercised independent judgment.[14]

FIGURE 11-5 Unfair Labor Practices

MANAGEMENT	UNIONS
• Interfering with, restraining, or coercing employees in the exercise of their right to organize or bargain collectively	• Interfering with, restraining, or coercing employees in the exercise of their right to organize or to bargain collectively
• Dominating or interfering with the formation or administration of any labor organization	• Causing an employer to discriminate or discourage union membership
• Encouraging or discouraging membership in any labor organization by discriminating with regard to hiring, tenure, or conditions of employment	• Refusal to bargain in good faith • Conducting secondary boycotts • Organization or recognition picketing by a union where the employer has recognized another union as the official bargaining agent
• Discharging or otherwise discriminating against an employee because he or she filed charges or gave testimony under the Act	
• Refusing to bargain in good faith	

This case and others have provided employers and unions with some guidance about who should be considered as a supervisor, and thus excluded from bargaining units.

Unfair Labor Practices   One of the major roles of the NLRB is resolving unfair labor practices. Figure 11-5 illustrates the unfair labor practices for both management and unions that are defined in Section 8a and 8b of the NLRA. Most charges of unfair labor practices are filed by unions. As an example, in one recent case the NLRB determined that a medical center committed an unfair labor practice when it eliminated its visiting nurse and hospice units and decided to move the unionized nurses associated with those progams to another location without recognizing their union contract. The union filed a complaint with the NLRB, which ruled in favor of the union nurses and required the medical center to recognize the contract.[15]

It is important for organizations to avoid unfair labor practices. Accordingly, managers should receive training about unfair labor practices. Most organizations provide a list of dos and don'ts, as described in the Ethical Practices and Compliance feature which follows, during unionization campaigns and when the contract is in place. A good general rule is to avoid making any promises or threats to employees during an organizing campaign.

Representation Elections

If the NLRB is satisfied that the union has received enough authorization cards and that the employees who seek representation are an appropriate bargaining unit, it orders an election, supervised by an NLRB official and representatives from both the union and management. A union election is determined by a **simple majority**—50 percent plus one—of the employees who voted on the election day.

Management and the union encourage employees to vote because the employees who vote on election day determine whether the union will be sanctioned as the official bargaining agent for all of the employees in that group. Generally, research and surveys have revealed that a higher turnout of voters usually is beneficial for management because employees with neutral feelings about the organization or the union are more likely to vote against the union.

If the union or management thinks the election was handled improperly or unfair labor practices occurred during the election, either entity may challenge the election results. If the NLRB determines no violations occurred, it rules on the election results. If the union does not win the election, it is prohibited from conducting another organizing campaign for 12 months.

ETHICAL PRACTICES AND COMPLIANCE

DO (LEGAL)	DON'T (ILLEGAL)
• Tell employees about current wages and benefits and how they compare with those in other firms • Tell employees that the employer opposes unionization • Tell employees the disadvantages of having a union (especially cost of dues, assessments, and requirements of membership) • Show employees articles about unions and relate negative experiences elsewhere • Explain the unionization process to employees accurately • Forbid distribution of union literature during work hours in work areas • Enforce disciplinary policies and rules consistently and appropriately	• Promise employees pay increases or promotions if they vote against the union • Threaten employees with termination or discriminate when disciplining employees • Threaten to close down or move the company if a union is voted in • Spy on or have someone spy on union meetings • Make a speech to employees or groups at work within 24 hours of the election (before that, it is allowed) • Ask employees how they plan to vote or if they have signed authorization cards • Encourage employees to persuade others to vote against the union (such a vote must be initiated solely by the employee)

Certification–Decertification

If the union receives the necessary votes and is **certified** by the NLRB, it then becomes the exclusive bargaining representative of the employee group, and the employer is required to negotiate in good faith with the union. As the certified employee representative, the union is then ready to negotiate the initial contract. Throughout union negotiations and contract administration, the union must be involved in discussions with employees about any items considered a subject of bargaining.

Decertification   When an employee group decides that the union no longer meets its needs, it can **decertify** the union. Only employees can initiate a decertification process, and management must stay out of the process altogether or risk an unfair labor charge. Decertification is rare in the healthcare industry because employees believe their unions will continue to protect them against employers who are unwilling to make significant workplace improvements.

The process for decertifying a current union is much like the certification process. Employees, without help from their employer, must obtain signatures from at least 30 percent of the employees who are union members. The NLRB conducts an election and decertifies the union when it determines that a **simple majority**—50 percent plus one—of employees want decertification. Six months must pass after certification before employees can decertify their union.

Collective Bargaining

Negotiating the initial contract can be difficult and time-consuming because both parties must start without any contract language about working conditions, wages, and benefits, among other issues. Developing an effective initial contract requires significant attention to detail because it will be the foundation for union–management relationships.

COLLECTIVE BARGAINING AND THE NEGOTIATING PROCESS

The collective bargaining process begins when the NLRB notifies the management and union that the union has the official right to represent the employees. Both sides are required to bargain in good faith; that is, they must meet and exchange information about contractual issues, including economic and workplace policies and procedures. Because the labor contract finally agreed to by both parties is a legal document, supervisors and managers, as agents of the organization, must follow the contract provisions to avoid grievances or unfair labor practice charges.

Contract Components

Most labor contracts contain common clauses that provide some degree of consistency among contracts. Common clauses appear in the following areas:

- Management rights
- Union security
- Wages and benefits
- Working conditions

Management Rights Clauses **Management rights clauses** contain language that gives management the exclusive right to manage, direct, and control its business, including any issues not covered in the contract. The management rights clause becomes more limited over time as each new contract identifies and documents some of the issues that the labor contract might not have covered previously. When management implements a practice that has not been covered by the clause and to which the union objects, the practice may become the subject of negotiations. The union might try to extend the contract or connect an issue to a related contract clause. For example, if the management of a hospital contends that instituting a smoke-free environment throughout its campus, including exterior areas, is a management right, the union might contend that smoking on the facility grounds is a contractual benefit and that any attempt to enforce a new no-smoking policy would need negotiation. In this case, because there was no language in the current contract about smoking, it is likely that the next contract negotiations will include proposals that clarify the issue before management implements the policy.

Union Security Clauses The **union security clause** recognizes the exclusive right of the union to bargain on behalf of the employees represented by the union. It also allows the union to contact current and new employees who would be union members. A **dues check-off process** to pay union dues automatically through payroll deductions is also part of the union security clause.

Wages and Benefits Union contract clauses about wages may include statements about base pay, premium pay, shift differential pay, and incentive pay for union members. Benefits clauses in contracts typically include health, dental, life, disability insurance, and retirement programs.

Working Conditions and Scheduling Healthcare contracts usually contain significant language about the employer's ability to schedule its employees' work. Staffing requirements for individual patient-care units are usually the subject of substantial discussion during negotiations. In addition to scheduling clauses, many contracts include language about workplace safety issues that are designed to protect union members from occupational hazards in the workplace.

Negotiation Process

The process for negotiating a labor contract varies from organization to organization, but certain steps must be followed to make the process successful. The four major steps in the negotiations process are listed in Figure 11-6.

Data Collection When the collective bargaining process begins, both parties collect data and develop competitive wage and benefit information that will support the positions they promote. Conflicts about data collection are common as the two parties compare other organizations' wage and benefits packages. Both

FIGURE 11-6   Negotiation Process

the union and management benefit from a contract that is competitive in the local job market. They collect the following information:

- *Base Pay*—Hourly pay for work performed
- *Premium Pay*—Additional pay for evening, night, and weekend work
- *Employee Benefits*—Health, dental, life, and disability insurance
- *Retirement and Pension Benefits*—Retirement income
- *Staffing and Scheduling Practices*—Staff-to-patient ratios and work times
- *Economic and Working Conditions*—Compared with other union and nonunion groups
- *Workplace Issues*—Health, safety, and security
- *Employee Grievances*—Evaluating trends that could be converted to demands

During data collection, management negotiators meet with managers and executives to collect data on issues that they want negotiated into the contract. Likewise, the union meets with employees to collect information to be converted into contract demands. Each party develops a formal presentation of contract demands and issues to begin the negotiations.

Negotiations   During the initial negotiating meeting, the two parties agree on how they will conduct negotiations. Developing a schedule and proposed agenda, while allotting sufficient time to resolve issues, can contribute to effective negotiations. The parties must determine how much time and how many meetings need to be scheduled to resolve the contract before the current one expires.

During the negotiations, the parties will review the current agreements, present new economic and noneconomic demands, provide data and information for each contract demand, discuss each issue, propose solutions, come to agreement, and document the agreement. When an agreement is reached on a demand, the proposed language is drafted and reviewed by both parties. They repeat this process for all issues that the parties raise.

Interest-Based Bargaining   A new technique that has been used effectively in the negotiating process is **interest-based bargaining,** which emphasizes problem solving and consensus building.[16] Employers and unions may receive training from the FMCS regarding how to discuss issues, interests, options, and solutions. Interest-based bargaining has been successful in some situations, but it requires both sides to be open to collaborative relations.

The typical steps in interest-based bargaining are as follows:

- Select an issue
- Clarify the issue
- Discuss each party's interests (not positions or demands)
- Generate options through brainstorming
- Evaluate options
- Select options that meet mutual needs
- Document agreed solutions

Tentative Agreement   A **tentative agreement** is reached when both parties agree to move forward with a recommended contract. Union representatives are required to take the proposal to their membership for a ratification vote. If the negotiation team for the employees believes that the contract offered by management is fair, the negotiating team will recommend contract passage.

During difficult discussions, the negotiating team may not recommend contract ratification but explain the contract as offered and let the members decide. If the members reject the contract, they can authorize sending the negotiating team back to the table for more discussions or they can authorize a strike.

Settlement or Impasse   To prove that they have bargained in good faith throughout the negotiation, each party demonstrates that it has met, exchanged proposals, and reviewed and considered the offers of the other party. In many cases, the parties agree on resolutions that are good for both sides.

However, in some cases, the parties bargain to impasse and a contract agreement is not reached. Bargaining to impasse does not necessarily mean that the parties have not negotiated in good faith, but rather that despite their best efforts, they could not reach an agreement. When they bargain to impasse, a strike is possible.

Planning for Strikes

Although it might seem contrary to the mission of contract negotiations, planning for a strike begins at about the same time negotiations start. Crucial concerns are listed in the Figure 11-7.

Unions prepare members for the economic and emotional realities of a work stoppage while managers prepare to care for patients during the strike. Managers and union officials have a variety of challenges and concerns to deal with when a strike is imminent. Managers are concerned about patient care, covering work schedules, diverting patients and services during the strike, the economic impact of the strike on the organization, the conflict between striking and nonstriking employees, and public image.

In the event of a strike, union officials are also faced with critical challenges that require time and thought. Common issues include: lost wages of striking members, solidarity of striking workers, emotional conflicts of care-giving union

FIGURE 11-7   **Strike Concerns**

MANAGEMENT	UNION
• Communicating to the community, physicians, and non-striking employees about the contingency plan • Training managers and supervisors to provide patient care • Determining how many patients the reduced staff can cover • Contacting temporary staffing agencies to provide temporary workers during the strike • Deciding where patients will be referred to other non-striking providers • Determining how to treat staff members who cross the picket line • Securing the facility and grounds to avoid disruptions • Arranging for supplies and equipment deliveries across the picket line • Contracting vendors with union contracts to assure no sympathy strike by other unions	• Communicating to NLRB and management of intent to strike • Communicating strike authorization to members • Planning logistics of maintaining the picket line • Scheduling pickets • Providing information hotline to update striking members • Planning public relations to influence public opinion

members, replacement workers, quality of patient care, relationships with non-striking employees, and public image.

Professional healthcare employees face several dilemmas in a strike situation. Among these is a reluctance about participating in a work stoppage when it means stopping patient care. But when a strike is called, each union member must decide whether to honor the strike or cross the picket line. Management's challenges include finding a balance in how managers treat striking workers, who will eventually return to work, and in negotiating a contract that is fair and equitable.

If the number of patients remains the same during the strike, other non-striking caregivers will likely have to fill in where striking staff members are absent. Assigning substitutes to care for patients is complex because managers must consider quality issues, including credentialed staff replacements, levels of authority for substitute caregivers, and appropriate staff-to-patient ratios. Conflict and resentment build in these situations. Long strikes cause even greater conflict. Because healthcare is labor intensive and specialized, the likelihood that managers and supervisors can continue to carry the workload alone is unrealistic during a long strike.

The emotional impact of a strike or difficult negotiations must not be minimized when an organization finally negotiates a contract. When the issues are resolved and the workforce returns to work, rebuilding relationships with the employees who were on strike will be vital to meeting organization objectives. In most cases, the objective of both parties is to come to a satisfactory settlement and return to work as soon as possible.

Formalizing the Agreement

When the negotiations are completed, the parties draft a contract agreement, and each reviews it for approval. The final contract is important because it governs the relationship between management and employees during the life of the contract, usually three years or more. Tentative agreements have been reached on individual issues throughout negotiations, and contract language has been documented.

The bargaining parties must present the tentative language to their constituents for review and a ratification vote. This is a crucial stage in the negotiation process, because if the members vote to reject the contract agreement, the parties will return to the table or the members will vote to strike. If the members ratify the tentative agreement, it will be converted into the final contract. The last stage in the negotiation process is writing an official version of the agreements. When the contract is in final form and approved, authorized representatives of the union and management formally sign the agreement.

CONTRACT ADMINISTRATION

Implementing the labor contract on a daily basis is the next critical issue that labor and management face. The contract is a legal agreement that must be followed during its term, and it must be implementable by managers who might not have been involved in the negotiations. During bargaining, negotiators must keep contract administration issues in mind and anticipate conflicts and contract interpretation issues to avoid administration problems.

Labor–Management Committees

Labor–management committees are comprised of management representatives, union members, and bargaining agents and they meet regularly. Union members are elected by their colleagues; management representatives are assigned by organization leaders. Managers and union members communicate issues to the committee as a result of their daily interactions.

Grievance Procedures

Because it is difficult to anticipate and clearly define all of the issues that may come up during the life of the contract, special clauses deal with disputes. A **grievance procedure** is a formal process used to resolve issues that arise out of daily interactions between managers and workers. The procedure, outlined in the contract, comprises several steps that allow employees to present their disputes to management. A typical grievance process is outlined in Figure 11-8.

FIGURE 11-8 Employee Grievance Process

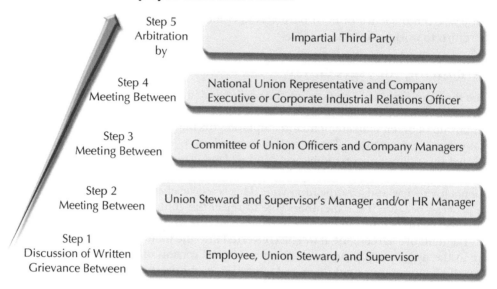

Step 5
Arbitration
by — Impartial Third Party

Step 4
Meeting Between — National Union Representative and Company Executive or Corporate Industrial Relations Officer

Step 3
Meeting Between — Committee of Union Officers and Company Managers

Step 2
Meeting Between — Union Steward and Supervisor's Manager and/or HR Manager

Step 1
Discussion of Written Grievance Between — Employee, Union Steward, and Supervisor

In most cases, the employee typically uses a union representative to help present the issues in each step of the grievance process. In some contracts, the process ends with binding arbitration. **Arbitration** requires the two parties to present their cases to a mutually selected arbitrator from a list provided by the American Arbitration Association. The arbitrator hears the grievance and makes a binding decision. **Mediation** is a process that involves a third party who facilitates discussions and proposes resolutions to the two parties. However, the mediator's suggestions are never binding.

CASE

A specialty clinic, with four unions representing 40 percent of the employees, has been notified that the Teamsters' Union has been contacted by an employee group to conduct a unionization campaign to represent some of the employees, including service workers, clerical workers, and all levels in the accounting department. The clinic's labor-relations philosophy would be characterized as traditional and non-collaborative. It has decided to resist the union's attempt to organize the employees.

The four groups of employees who are currently represented by unions include: technical employees, registered nurses, pharmacists, and maintenance workers. Some 70 employees are represented by the current contracts. The registered nurses constitute 40 percent of the 70 union members.

The group that has been proposed in the organizing attempt includes 45 employees, and the service workers (housekeeping, food service, and nursing assistants) constitute 75 percent of the proposed members.

Management is concerned about the organizing campaign. Relationships with the current unions have not been very productive, and further unionization will lead to more distrust between management and employees. Management is concerned about the union's ability to call strikes in the future, which may require the organization to severely limit services and could greatly affect its financial health.

Management must decide whether to mount a campaign to prevent the union from organizing. If it decides to mount a campaign, management must develop a strategy to present arguments to the employees for not having union representation.

Questions

1. What steps must the Teamsters' Union follow to cause an election to occur?
2. During the union campaign, how should the managers conduct themselves to avoid being accused of committing unfair labor practices?

END NOTES

1. For more information regarding Healthcare unions and labor issues, see *http://www.seiu.org/health/hosp/staffing_and_workloads/ index.cfm*.
2. Mary Jo Feldstein, "Many Striking Creve Coeur, Missouri, Nurses Turn to Temporary Work," *St. Louis Post-Dispatch* (December 18, 2004), A1.
3. "Union Rolls Hold Steady as Employment Declines," *Bulletin to Management* (February 21, 2002), 61.
4. "Some Workers Gain With New Union Tactics," *Wall Street Journal* (January 31, 2002), A2.
5. Melanie Zooms, "Labor's Success," *Modern Healthcare* (February 14, 2005), 24–26.
6. Melanie Evans, "Staffing Strife," *Modern Healthcare* (November 1, 2004), 12–14.
7. Bonnie Friedrick, "Staying Power," *Nursing Management* (July 2001), 26–28.
8. Stephen J. Cabot, "Keeping Labor Loyal," *Nursing Homes/Long-Term Care Management* (October 2003), 100–102.
9. Stephen J. Cabot, "Reducing the Threat of Labor Problems," *Nursing Homes/Long Term Care Management* (July 2004), 26–28.
10. For additional information on Unfair Labor Practices, see Holly J. McCammon, "Labor's Legal Mobilization," *Work and Occupations*, 28 (2001), 143–175.
11. For additional information see *http://www.nlrb.gov/nlrb/press/facts.asp*.
12. *Alexandria Clinic, P.A. and Minnesota Licensed Practical Nurses Association.* Case 18-CA-15371 (August 21, 2003).
13. *NLRB v. Kentucky River Community Care, Inc.* 121 S. Ct 1861 (2001).
14. Jennifer Gerarda Brown, "Creativity and Problem Solving," *Marquette Law Review* (April 2004), 697–709.
15. "The NLRB Rules in Favor of MNA In Unfair Labor Practices by Baystate Health, Franklin Medical Center," *Massachusetts Nurse* (October 2004), 5.
16. Jennifer Gerada Brown, "Creativity and Problem Solving."

Healthcare Compensation Practices

Learning Objectives

After you have read this chapter, you should be able to:

- Describe the differences between an entitlement compensation philosophy and a performance-focused compensation philosophy.

- Define the issues confronting the healthcare industry in complying with the Fair Labor Standards Act (FLSA).

- Identify the steps in the compensation administration process.

- Explain the issues associated with awarding pay increases.

- Discuss the five components of executive compensation.

The administrator of a long-term care facility located in the Southeast was confronted with a serious staffing delimma. Over the last six months she had lost eight nursing aides. She learned, through exit interviews, that all eight of the staff members had left for better pay and benefits, accepting positions with the local store of a national discount retailer. Due to the lost of these aides and the difficulty in replacing them, she was seriously thinking about closing residents rooms as vacancies ocurred, even though the facility had dozens of potential residents on the waiting list.

The administrator knew that the cost of replacing a front-line long-term care facility employee is approximately $3,500.00 when recruitment, orientation, and preceptor costs are all calculated.[1] Could she rationalize an adjustment to her organization's pay rates, based on the opportunity cost savings of not having to spend $3,500.00 in replacement costs?

Compensation costs represent significant expenditures in most healthcare organizations. Although actual compensation costs can be easily calculated, the value derived by employers proves more difficult to identify.

In developing compensation strategies, healthcare organizations are confronted with a number of challenges and issues. Consumer groups, insurance companies, HMOs, and federal and state governments are demanding higher-quality care at lower or contained costs.[2] Further, the demand for healthcare in this country is accelerating at an unprecedented rate as the baby-boom generation ages, yet fewer individuals are pursuing healthcare careers. In order to attract and retain competent and motivated workers, healthcare organizations must aggressively compete with each other and with other industries for skilled workers. The net effect is that healthcare HR compensation strategies must do the impossible: balance these competing factors and priorities and deliver compensation programs that meet the needs of their organizations and their employees.

HEALTHCARE COMPENSATION RESPONSIBILITIES

Healthcare HR professionals guide the development and administration of an organizational compensation system, including responsibilities for developing base pay programs, pay structures, and compensation administration policies. Healthcare HR professionals may or may not do actual payroll processing; payroll is often the responsibility of the accounting or finance departments. Although this labor-intensive responsibility has historically been outsourced, today many healthcare organizations are retaining in-house processing because of improvements in software and Internet processing. Operating managers evaluate the performance of employees and consider their performance when deciding compensation increases within the policies and guidelines established by the HR unit and upper management.

Compensation systems in healthcare organizations must be closely linked to organizational objectives and strategies. An effective compensation program addresses four objectives:

- Legal compliance with all appropriate laws and regulations
- Cost-effectiveness for the organization
- Internal, external, and individual equity for employees
- Performance enhancement for the organization

Healthcare employers must balance compensation costs at a level that both ensures organizational competitiveness and provides sufficient rewards to employees for their knowledge, skills, abilities, and performance accomplishments. In order to attract, retain, and reward employees, employers provide several types of compensation.

NATURE OF COMPENSATION

Compensation is an important factor affecting how and why people choose to work at one organization over others. Healthcare employers must be reasonably competitive with several types of compensation to attract and retain competent employees.

Rewards can be both intrinsic and extrinsic. **Intrinsic rewards** often include praise for completing a project or meeting performance objectives. Other psychological and social effects of compensation are reflected in the intrinsic rewards.[3] **Extrinsic rewards** are tangible and take both monetary and nonmonetary forms.

Compensation Components

Tangible components of a compensation program are of two general types (see Figure 12-1). With direct compensation, the employer exchanges monetary rewards for work done. Employers provide indirect compensation—like health insurance—to everyone simply based on membership in the organization. *Base pay* and *variable pay* are the most common forms of direct compensation. Indirect compensation commonly consists of employee *benefits*.

Base Pay The basic compensation that an employee receives, usually as a wage or salary, is called **base pay.** Many organizations use two base pay categories, *hourly* and *salaried,* which are identified according to the way pay is distributed and the nature of the jobs. Hourly pay is the most common means of payment based on time, and employees paid hourly receive **wages,** which are payments directly calculated on the amount of time worked. In contrast, people paid **salaries**

FIGURE 12-1   Components of a Compensation System

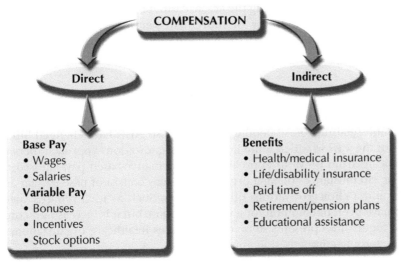

receive consistent payments each period regardless of the number of hours worked. Being salaried typically has carried higher status for employees than being paid wages. Figure 12-2 depicts examples of the the two pay types.

Variable Pay   Another type of direct pay is **variable pay,** which is compensation linked directly to individual, team, or organizational performance. The most common types of variable pay for employees take the form of bonuses and incentive program payments. Executives often receive longer-term rewards such as deferred compensation. Variable pay is discussed in greater detail in Chapter 13.

FIGURE 12-2   Examples of Salary and Hourly Pay

- The manager of radiology earns an annual salary of: $80,000.00 and is paid on a biweekly basis. Each pay day she would receive:

$$\$80,000.00 \div 26 = \$3,076.92 \text{ (every two-week pay period)}$$

- A health unit coordinator earns $12.50 per hour. In the first week of a biweekly pay period he worked 33 hours and in the second week he worked 38 hours. His pay would be computed as follows:

Week one: $12.50 × 33 hours = $412.50

+ Week two: $12.50 × 38 hours = $475.00

Total   = $887.50

The health unit coordinator would receive $887.50 for this particular pay period.

Benefits Many organizations provide numerous extrinsic rewards in an indirect manner. With indirect compensation, employees receive the tangible value of the rewards without receiving the actual cash. A **benefit** is an indirect reward—health insurance, vacation pay, or retirement pension—given to an employee or group of employees as a part of organizational membership, regardless of performance.

Healthcare Compensation Approaches

Healthcare organizations regard pay as an important tool for recruiting, motivating, and retaining good people. Indeed, those goals have changed little over time, but the ways in which some healthcare organizations approach them differ dramatically from previous approaches. Performance-based pay, tailored to the strategic circumstances of each organization, may consist of base pay, an annual bonus, and a choice of various other benefits. Such a "total rewards" package would have been uncommon for a worker in 1950, but it is increasingly common today.[4] Figure 12-3 presents some of the choices healthcare organizations must make regarding compensation approaches.

Traditional Compensation Approach For some healthcare organizations a traditional compensation approach makes sense and offers certain advantages in specific competitive situations. It may be more legally defensible, less complex, and viewed as more "fair" for average and below-average performing employees. However, the total rewards approach helps retain top performers, can be more flexible when the economy goes up or down, and is favored by top-performing organizations.[5] But it clearly will *not* work in every situation.

Traditional compensation systems have evolved over time to reflect a logical, rational approach to compensating employees. Job descriptions identify tasks and responsibilities and are then used to decide which jobs are more valuable. These systems calculate the value that each job contributes to the organization

FIGURE 12-3 Compensation Approaches: Traditional Versus Total Rewards

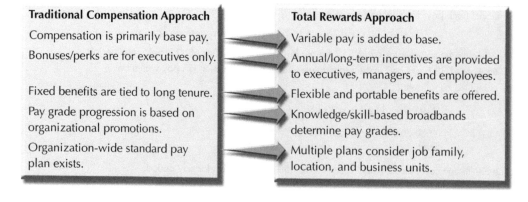

Traditional Compensation Approach	Total Rewards Approach
Compensation is primarily base pay.	Variable pay is added to base.
Bonuses/perks are for executives only.	Annual/long-term incentives are provided to executives, managers, and employees.
Fixed benefits are tied to long tenure.	Flexible and portable benefits are offered.
Pay grade progression is based on organizational promotions.	Knowledge/skill-based broadbands determine pay grades.
Organization-wide standard pay plan exists.	Multiple plans consider job family, location, and business units.

based on an evaluation of the job. That value is used to establish a pay range that reflects progression as employees grow and presumably improve their ability to perform the job.

Total Rewards Approach   The total rewards approach tries to place a value on individuals rather than just on jobs. When determining compensation, managers factor in elements such as how much an employee knows or how much competence an employee has. The need for such an approach becomes more evident in trying to pay healthcare workers with high demand clinical skills such as radiological technologists, pharmacists, and RNs.

Currently, some healthcare organizations incorporate variable pay programs as part of a total rewards approach for all levels of employees. Widespread use of various incentive plans, team bonuses, organizational gainsharing programs, and other creative pay programs are designed to link growth in compensation to results. Three main issues must be addressed when using variable pay:

- Should performance be measured and rewarded based on individual, group, or organizational performance?
- Should the length of time for measuring performance be short-term (less than one year) or longer-term (more than one year)?
- Are variable-pay programs compatible with the mission and values of the organization, especially when the organization operates as a not-for-profit?

The various types and facets of variable pay are discussed in the next chapter. But it is important to recognize the shift in all industries, including healthcare, toward compensation being allocated through such plans, rather than the organization relying solely on base pay to reward employees at all levels for attaining strategic organizational objectives.

Compensation Philosophies

The two basic compensation philosophies lie on opposite ends of a continuum. At one end of the continuum detailed in Figure 12-4 is the *entitlement* philosophy; at the other end is the *performance-oriented* philosophy. Most compensation systems fall somewhere in between.

FIGURE 12-4   Continuum of Compensation Philosophies

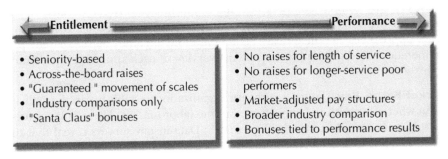

Entitlement ←————————————————————————→ Performance

- Seniority-based
- Across-the-board raises
- "Guaranteed " movement of scales
- Industry comparisons only
- "Santa Claus" bonuses

- No raises for length of service
- No raises for longer-service poor performers
- Market-adjusted pay structures
- Broader industry comparison
- Bonuses tied to performance results

Entitlement Orientation Many traditional organizations that give automatic increases to their employees every year practice the entitlement philosophy. Further, most of those employees receive the same or nearly the same percentage increase each year. Employees and managers who subscribe to the entitlement philosophy believe that individuals who have worked another year are *entitled* to a raise in base pay. They also believe all incentives and benefits programs should continue and be increased, regardless of changing industry or economic conditions. Commonly, in organizations following an entitlement philosophy, pay increases are referred to as *cost-of-living* raises, even if they are not tied specifically to economic cost-of-living indicators.

Following an entitlement philosophy ultimately means that as employees continue their employment employer's costs increase, regardless of employee performance or organizational competitive pressures. Market data will be monitored, but will not necessarily drive compensation strategy decisions unless significant recruitment or retention issues are identified for a particular job, group, or position (e.g., RNs or nurse anesthetists).

Hospitals and medical centers have especially struggled with the entitlement orientation of their long-term employees. Today's market pressures on healthcare organizations and the declining revenues described in earlier chapters would argue for a merit- or performance-based approach to paying annual increases. However, two factors have contributed to the entitlement orientation: 1) decades of paying automatic increases and 2) collective bargaining agreements that require automatic step increases.

Performance Orientation Where a performance-oriented philosophy is followed, organizations do not guarantee additional or increased compensation simply for completing another year of organizational service. Instead, pay and incentives reflect performance differences among employees. Employees who perform well receive larger compensation increases; those who do not perform satisfactorily see little or no increase in compensation. Thus, employees who perform satisfactorily maintain or advance in relation to market compensation levels, whereas poor or marginal performers may fall behind. Bonus compensation may be paid on the basis of individual, team, or organizational performance.

Decisions about Healthcare Compensation Levels

Even though healthcare organizations might wish to pay the top wages and salaries relative to their competition, that might not be possible because of the significant pressure healthcare organizations face to control their costs. Three basic approaches to healthcare compensation include market-based pay, competency-based pay, and team pay. An overview of each approach is presented in this section.

Market-Based Pay Some healthcare organizations establish specific policies about where they wish to be positioned in the labor market. These policies use a *quartile strategy*, as illustrated in Figure 12-5. Data in pay surveys reveal that the actual dollar difference between quartiles is generally 15 percent to 20 percent.

FIGURE 12-5 Market-Based Compensation Strategies

Third Quartile: Above-Market Strategy

(Employer positions pay scales so that 25% of firms pay above and 75% pay below)

Second Quartile: Middle-Market Strategy

(Employer positions pay scales so that 50% of firms pay above and 50% pay below)

First Quartile: Below-Market Strategy

(Employer positions pay scales so that 75% of firms pay above and 25% pay below)

Most employers choose to position themselves in the *second quartile,* in the middle of the market (median), based on pay survey data of other employers' compensation plans. Choosing this level attempts to balance employer cost pressures and the need to attract and retain employees by providing mid-level compensation levels.

An employer using a *first-quartile* approach might choose to pay below market compensation for several reasons. The employer might be experiencing a shortage of funds, and be unable to pay more and still meet objectives. Also, when an abundance of workers is available, particularly those with lower skills, a below-market approach can be used to attract sufficient workers at lesser cost. The downside of this strategy is that higher turnover of workers is more likely. If the labor market supply tightens, then attracting and retaining workers becomes more difficult.

A *third-quartile* approach uses an aggressive pay-above-market emphasis. This strategy generally enables an organization to attract and retain sufficient workers with the required capabilities and to be more selective when hiring. However, because it is a higher-cost approach, organizations often look for ways to increase the productivity of employees receiving above-market wages.

In many cases, depending on the availability of workers with certain skills (e.g., pharmacists or certified nurse anesthetists), organizations may adopt a strategy to utilize a third-quartile approach for those positions, yet pay at first- or second-quartile levels for less hard-to-fill positions. This approach entails a "market-driven" philosophy for the hard-to-fill positions.[6]

Competency-Based Pay The design of most compensation programs rewards employees for carrying out their tasks, duties, and responsibilities. The job requirements determine which employees have higher base rates. Employees receive more for doing jobs that require a greater variety of tasks, more knowledge and skills, greater physical effort, or more demanding working conditions.[7]

However, some healthcare organizations are emphasizing competencies rather than tasks, competencies such as the ability to perform a particular clinical procedure or the attainment of a clinical credential such as a certified emergency nurse. A number of organizations are paying employees for the competencies they demonstrate rather than just for the specific tasks performed. Paying for competencies rewards employees who exhibit more versatility and continue to develop their competencies.

In knowledge-based pay (KBP) or skill-based pay (SBP) systems, employees start at a base level of pay and receive increases as they learn to do other jobs or gain other skills and therefore become more valuable to the employer. For example, in an RN clinical ladder program, RNs will have the opportunity to move up two or more pay levels based on their ability to demonstrate higher levels of clinical competency.[8] Figure 12-6 depicts the pay structure of a clinical nursing ladder program. The success of competency plans requires managerial commitment to a philosophy different from those traditionally found in organizations.

This approach places far more emphasis on training employees and supervisors. Due to the extensive commitment to training and the need to monitor the competencies of employees that competency-based pay systems require, they are more likely to be implemented in larger healthcare organizations. Also, workflow must be adapted to allow workers to move from job to job as needed. Additionally, clinical ladder programs have been used effectively for other healthcare professions, such as medical technologists and pharmacists.

When a healthcare organization moves to a competency-based system, considerable time must be spent identifying the required competencies for various jobs. Progression of employees must be possible, and they must be paid appropriately for all of their competencies. Any *limitations* on the numbers of people who can acquire more competencies should be clearly identified. *Training* in the appropriate competencies is particularly critical. Also, a competency-based system needs to acknowledge or certify employees as they acquire certain competencies, and then to verify the maintenance of those *competencies*. In summary, use of a competency-based system requires significant investment of management time and commitment.

FIGURE 12-6 **Pay Structure of a Nursing Clinical Ladder Program**

POSITION	GRADE	RANGE (HOURLY)	
		MINIMUM	MAXIMUM
Clinical Nurse I	10	$28.00	$42.00
Clinical Nurse II	11	$31.00	$46.00
Clinical Nurse III	12	$34.00	$50.00

Individual Versus Team Rewards   As healthcare organizations have shifted to using work teams, they face the logical concern of how to develop compensation programs that build on the team concept. At issue is how to compensate the individual whose performance may also be evaluated on the basis of team achievement. Paying all members of a team the same amount, even though they demonstrate differing competencies and levels of performance, obviously creates equity concerns for many employees.[9]

Many organizations use team rewards as variable pay added to base pay. For base pay, individual compensation is based on competency- or skill-based approaches. Variable pay rewards for teams are most frequently distributed annually as a specified dollar amount, not as a percentage of base pay. Rather than substituting for base pay programs, team-based rewards appear to be useful in rewarding performance of a team beyond the satisfactory level. More discussion on team-based incentives is contained in the next chapter.

Compensation System Design Issues

Compensation decisions must be viewed strategically. Because so many organizational funds are spent on compensation-related activities, it is critical for top management and HR professionals to match compensation practices with what the organization is trying to accomplish. Consider the following examples. The compensation program for a new physician practice will probably be different from that of a mature, well-established clinic. If a new practice wishes to accelerate its capabilities to grow and expand, it may offer higher-than-market wages and recruitment bonuses in order to attract talented workers who can quickly contribute to the success of the practice. However, for a large, stable clinic with a well-established patient referral base, more structured pay and benefit programs will be more common.

Organizations must make a number of important decisions about the nature of a compensation system. Some decisions include the following:

- What philosophy and approach will be taken?
- How will the organization react to market pay levels?
- Is the job to be paid based on the person's level of competence?
- Will pay be individual or team-based?

Perceptions of Pay Fairness

Most people in healthcare organizations work in order to gain rewards for their efforts. Except in volunteer or charitable organizations, people expect to receive what they feel is fair tangible compensation for their efforts. Whether base pay, variable pay, or benefits, the extent to which employees perceive compensation to be fair often affects their performance and how they view their jobs and employers.[10]

Pay Secrecy Versus Openness   Another compensation issue concerns the degree of secrecy or openness that healthcare organizations have regarding their pay systems. Pay information kept secret in "closed" systems includes how much others make, what raises others have received, and even what pay grades and ranges exist in the organization. Some organizations have policies that prohibit employees from discussing their pay with other employees, and violations of these policies can lead to disciplinary action.[11] However, several court decisions have ruled that these policies violate the NLRA. If employees who violate these "secrecy" policies are disciplined, the employers can be liable for back pay, damages, and other consequences.[12]

Many healthcare organizations are opening up their pay systems by providing employees with more information on compensation policies, distributing a general description of the compensation system, and indicating where an individual's pay is within a salary range. Such information allows employees to make more accurate equity comparisons. For instance, an academic medical center in the Midwest posts all of its open positions with corresponding pay grades and ranges on its Web site and on various bulletin boards around its campus. This allows full access to pay information to both its own employees as well as potential applicants for its open positions. Having a more open pay system has been found to have positive effects on employee retention and organizational effectiveness.[13]

External Equity   **External equity** considers the rates paid by other organizations in determining a competitive position for an organization's compensation program. Maintaining external equity is extremely important for healthcare employers in order to effectively compete for workers, especially in consideration of the shortage of skilled healthcare workers today. If a healthcare employer does not provide compensation that employees view as equitable compared to other organizations, that employer is more likely to experience higher turnover.[14] Other drawbacks include greater difficulty in recruiting qualified and high-demand individuals. Also, by not being competitive, the employer is more likely to attract and retain individuals with less knowledge, skills, and abilities, resulting in lower overall organizational performance. Organizations track external equity by using pay surveys, which are discussed later in the chapter.

LEGAL REQUIREMENTS FOR PAY SYSTEMS

In managing compensation systems, healthcare organizations must comply with a myriad of federal, state, and local regulations and reporting requirements. Important areas addressed by the laws include minimum wage standards and hours of work. The following discussion examines the laws and regulations affecting base compensation; laws and regulations affecting incentives and benefits are examined in later chapters.

Fair Labor Standards Act (FLSA)

The major federal law affecting compensation is the Fair Labor Standards Act (FLSA), which was passed in 1938. Amended several times to raise minimum wage rates and expand employers covered, the FLSA affects both private- and public-sector employers.

Compliance with FLSA provisions is enforced by the Wage and Hour Division of the U.S. Department of Labor. To meet FLSA requirements healthcare employers must keep accurate time records and maintain these records for three years. Compliance investigations from the Wage and Hour Division investigate complaints filed by individuals who believe they have not received the overtime payments due them. Also, certain industries that historically have had a large number of wage and hour violations can be targeted, and firms in those industries can be investigated.

Penalties for wage and hour violations often include awards of back pay for affected current and former employees for up to two years. For example, a large medical center had allowed the nursing supervisors to arbitrarily pay overtime wages to some regularly scheduled charge nurses, who had been classified as exempt employees. This was done to encourage these charge nurses to pick up additional shifts. Some of the charge nurses who had not been recipients of the overtime pay complained to the Wage and Hour Division. Upon investigation, the division determined that the payment of indiscriminate overtime wages to otherwise exempt employees nullified their exempt status, and the Division subsequently negotiated a large back-pay award for the charge nurses.

Changes in FLSA Regulations   Many HR professionals had argued that the nearly 70-year-old law created great difficulties for employers trying to follow all the requirements of the law. For instance, it has been difficult to use the older regulations when examining jobs such as physician assistant, clinic office manager, or biomedical engineer that did not exist in 1938 or that have changed significantly since then.

The Department of Labor has revised various sections of the FLSA and its regulations governing who must be paid overtime. These changes took effect on August 23, 2004. For additional information on the key revisions, visit the book's Web site at *http://flynn.swlearning.com.*

The provisions of both the original act and subsequent revisions focus on the following major areas:

- Establish a minimum wage.
- Discourage inappropriate wage practices for child labor.
- Encourage limits on the number of hours employees work per week, through overtime provisions (exempt and nonexempt statuses).

Minimum Wage   The FLSA sets a minimum wage to be paid to the broad spectrum of covered employees. The actual minimum wage can be changed only by congressional action. A lower minimum wage is set for "tipped" employees, such as restaurant workers, but their compensation must equal or exceed the minimum wage when average tips are included. Minimum wage levels continue to spark significant political discussions and legislative maneuvering.

There also is a debate about the use of a living wage versus the minimum wage. A **living wage** is one that is supposed to meet the basic needs of a worker's family. In the United States, the living wage typically aligns with the amount needed for a family of four to be supported by one worker so that family income is above the officially identified "poverty" level. Currently in the United States, at about $8.20 an hour, the living-wage level is significantly higher than the minimum wage. Although many employees working in healthcare organizations earn significantly above the federal minimum wage and the liveable wage, many do not, especially front-line staff working in extended care facilities.

Without waiting for U.S. federal laws to change, over 80 cities have passed local living-wage laws. Those favoring living-wage laws stress that even the lowest-skilled workers need to earn wages above the poverty level.[15] Those opposed to living-wage laws point out that many of the lowest-paid workers are single, which makes the "family of four" test inappropriate. Obviously, there are ethical, economic, and employment implications on both sides of this issue.[16]

Child Labor Provisions   The child labor provisions of the FLSA set the minimum age for employment with unlimited hours at 16 years. For hazardous occupations the minimum is 18 years of age. Individuals 14–15 years old may work outside school hours with certain limitations. Many employers require age certificates for employees because the FLSA makes the employer responsible for determining an individual's age. A representative of a state labor department, a state education department, or a local school district generally issues such certificates.

Exempt and Non-exempt Statuses   Under the FLSA, employees are classified as exempt or non-exempt. **Exempt employees** hold positions classified as *executive, administrative, professional,* or *outside sales,* for which employers are not required to pay overtime. **Non-exempt employees** must be paid overtime under the Fair Labor Standards Act.

As noted, in 2004, the FLSA regulations changed the terminology used to identify whether or not a job qualifies for exempt status. The categories of exempt jobs are:

- Executive
- Administrative
- Professional (learned or creative)
- Computer employees
- Outside sales

The regulations identify factors related to salaried pay levels per week, discretionary authority, and other criteria that must exist for jobs to be categorized as exempt. In base pay programs, employers often categorize jobs into groupings that tie the FLSA status and the method of payment together. Employers are required to pay overtime for *hourly* jobs in order to comply with the FLSA. Employees in positions classified as *salaried nonexempt* are covered by the overtime provisions of the FLSA and therefore must be paid overtime. Salaried non-exempt positions sometimes include secretarial, clerical, and salaried blue-collar positions.

The FLSA does not require employers to pay overtime for *salaried exempt* jobs, although many healthcare organizations have implemented policies to pay a straight rate for extensive hours of overtime. For instance, hospitals may pay first-line supervisors extra using a special rate for hours worked over 50 a week during periods of high census or low staffing. A number of salaried exempt professionals in various information technology jobs also receive additional compensation for working extensive hours.

Overtime Provisions   The FLSA establishes overtime pay requirements. Its provisions set overtime pay at one and one-half times the regular pay rate for all hours over 40 a week, except for employees who are not covered by the FLSA. Overtime provisions do not apply to farm workers, who also have a lower minimum-wage schedule.

The workweek is defined as a consecutive period of 168 hours (24 hours × 7 days) and does not have to be a calendar week. If they wish to do so, hospitals and nursing homes are allowed to use a 14-day period instead of a 7-day week, as long as overtime is paid for hours worked beyond 8 in a day or 80 in a 14-day period.

The most difficult part of the act is distinguishing who is and is not exempt. Some recent costly settlements have prompted more white-collar workers to sue for overtime pay.

Compensatory Time Off   Often called *comp-time*, **compensatory time off** is hours given to an employee in lieu of payment for extra time worked. Unless it is given to nonexempt employees at the rate of one and one-half times the number of hours over 40 that are worked in a week, comp-time is illegal in the private sector. Also, comp-time cannot be carried over from one pay period to another. The only major exception to these provisions is for public-sector employees, such as fire and police employees, and a limited number of other workers. Additional information can be found at *http://www.dol.gov/esa/whd/*.

Independent Contractor Regulations

The growing use of contingent workers by many healthcare organizations has focused attention on another group of legal regulations—those identifying the criteria that independent contractors must meet. Figure 12-7 illustrates some of the key differences between an employee and an independent contractor.

Classifying someone as an independent contractor rather than an employee offers three advantages for the employer. First, the employer does not have to pay Social Security, unemployment, or workers' compensation costs. These additional payroll levies may add 10 percent or more to the costs of hiring the individual as an employee. Second, if the person is classified as an employee and is doing a job considered nonexempt under the federal FLSA, then the employer may be responsible for overtime pay at the rate of time-and-a-half for any week in which the person works more than 40 hours. Third, if the person is working enough hours to be eligible for organizational benefits, including pension eligibility, then the organization may be responsible for providing benefits consistent with its plan requirements.[17] With the escalating cost of employee benefits, this is a key reason many employers consider using independent contractors. Most

FIGURE 12-7 **Partial IRS Test for Employees and Independent Contractors**

An Employee	An Independent Contractor
• Must comply with instructions about when, where, and how to work • Renders services personally • Has a continuing relationship with the employer • Usually works on the premises of the employer • Normally is furnished tools, materials, and other equipment by the employer • Can be fired by the employer • Can quit at any time without incurring liability	• Can hire, supervise, and pay assistants • Generally can set own hours • Usually is paid by the job or on straight commission • Has made a significant investment in facilities or equipment • Can make a profit or suffer a loss • May provide services to two or more unrelated persons or firms at the same time • Makes services available to the public

Source: U.S. Internal Revenue Service, *http://www.irs.gov.*

other federal and state entities rely on the criteria for independent contractor status identified by the Internal Revenue Service (IRS).

Equal Pay and Pay Equity

Various legislative efforts address the issue of wage discrimination on the basis of gender. The Equal Pay Act of 1963 applies to both men and women and prohibits using different wage scales for men and women performing substantially the same jobs. Pay differences can be justified on the basis of merit (better performance), seniority (longer service), quantity or quality of work, or factors other than gender. Similar pay must be given for jobs requiring equal skills, equal effort, or equal responsibility or jobs done under similar working conditions.

Pay equity is an issue different from equal pay for equal work. Pay equity is the concept (similar to comparable worth) that the pay for all jobs requiring comparable knowledge, skills, and abilities should be the same even if job duties and market rates differ significantly. States with such laws for public-sector jobs include Hawaii, Iowa, Maine, Michigan, Minnesota, Montana, Ohio, Oregon, Washington, and Wisconsin. However, simply showing the existence of pay differences for jobs that are different has not been sufficient to prove discrimination in court in most cases.

State and Local Laws

Many states and municipalities have enacted modified versions of federal compensation laws. If a state has a higher minimum wage than that set under the Fair

Labor Standards Act, the higher figure becomes the required minimum wage. As an example, Alaska, Minnesota, California, and Florida have basic minimum wage requirements that are higher than the federal minimum wage.[18]

Garnishment Laws

Garnishment of an employee's wages occurs when a creditor obtains a court order that directs an employer to set aside a portion of one employee's wages to pay a debt owed a creditor. Regulations passed as part of the Consumer Credit Protection Act established limitations on the amount of wages that can be garnished and restricted the right of employers to discharge employees whose pay is subject to a single garnishment order. All 50 states have laws applying to wage garnishments.

DEVELOPMENT OF A BASE PAY SYSTEM

As Figure 12-8 shows, the development of a base wage and salary system begins with the assumption that accurate job descriptions and job specifications are

FIGURE 12-8   Compensation Administration Process

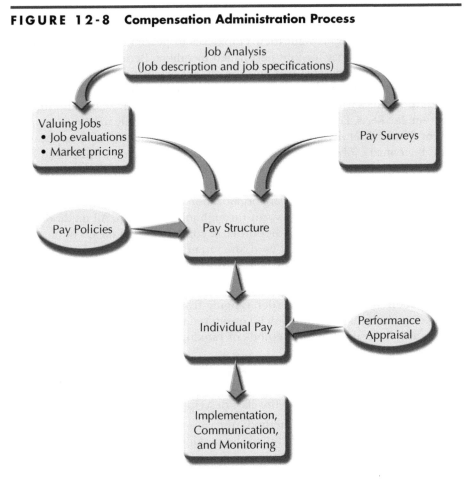

available. The job descriptions then are used for *job evaluation* and *pay surveys.* These activities are designed to ensure that the pay system is both internally equitable and externally competitive. The data compiled in these two activities are used to design *pay structures,* including *pay grades* and minimum-to-maximum *pay ranges.* After the development of pay structures, individual jobs must be placed in the appropriate pay grades and employees' pay adjusted based on length of service and performance. Finally, the pay system must be monitored and updated.

Job Evaluation

Job evaluation provides a systematic basis for determining the relative worth of jobs within an organization. It flows from the job analysis process and relies on job descriptions and job specifications. In a job evaluation, every job is examined and ultimately priced according to the following features:

- Relative importance of the job
- KSAs needed to perform the job
- Difficulty of the job

Healthcare employers want their employees to perceive their pay as appropriate in relation to pay for jobs performed by others. Because jobs vary widely in healthcare organizations, it is particularly important to identify **benchmark jobs**—jobs that are found in other healthcare organizations and performed by several individuals who have similar duties that are relatively stable and that require similar KSAs. For example, benchmark jobs commonly used in a hospital patient financial services department are biller, collector, and cash application clerk. Benchmark jobs are used with the job evaluation methods discussed here because they provide "anchors" against which unique jobs can be evaluated and then compared to benchmarked jobs.

Given the diversity of healthcare organizations, there are a variety of methods used to determine internal job worth through job evaluation. All methods have the same general objective, but they differ in complexity and means of measurement. Regardless of the method used, the intent is to develop a usable, measurable, and realistic system to determine compensation in an organization:

- *Ranking Method*—The ranking method is one of the simplest methods of job evaluation. It places jobs in order, ranging from highest to lowest in value to the organization. The entire job is considered rather than the individual components. Several different methods of ranking are available, but all present problems.
- *Classification Method*—In the classification method of job evaluation, descriptions of each class of jobs are written, and then each job in the organization is put into a grade according to the class description it best matches.
- *Point Method*—The point method, the most widely used job evaluation method, is more sophisticated than the ranking and classification methods. It

breaks down jobs into various compensable factors and places weights, or *points,* on them. A compensable factor identifies a job value commonly present throughout a group of jobs. Consequently, the compensable factors used and the weights assigned must reflect the nature of the jobs under study. A special type of point method used by a consulting firm, the Hay Group, has three major factors.[19] The three factors and their subfactors are identified as follows:

KNOW-HOW	PROBLEM SOLVING	ACCOUNTABILITY
• Functional expertise	• Environment	• Freedom to act
• Managerial skills	• Challenge	• Impact of end results
• Human relations	• Magnitude	

- *Factor Comparison*—The factor comparison method is a quantitative and complex combination of the ranking and point methods. It involves first determining the benchmark jobs in an organization, selecting compensable factors, and ranking all benchmark jobs factor by factor. Next, a comparison of jobs to market rates for benchmark jobs results in the assignment of monetary values for each factor. The final step is to evaluate all other jobs in the organization by comparing them with the benchmark jobs.

- *Integrated and Computerized Job Evaluation*—Increasingly, organizations are linking the components of wage and salary programs through computerized and statistical techniques.[20] Using a bank of compensable factors, employers can select those factors most relevant for the different job families in the organization. Because of the advanced expertise needed to develop and computerize the integrated systems, management consultants are the primary source for them. These systems really are less a separate method and more an application of information technology and advanced statistics to the process of developing a wage and salary program.

Legal Issues and Job Evaluation

Employers usually view evaluating jobs to determine rates of pay as a separate issue from selecting individuals for those jobs or taking disciplinary action against individuals. Because job evaluation affects the employment relationship, specifically the pay of individuals, it involves legal issues that must be addressed. Fairness, nondiscrimination, and objectivity are critical requirements of whatever job evaluation process is utilized.

Job Evaluation and the Americans with Disabilities Act (ADA)   The Americans with Disabilities Act requires employers to identify the essential functions of a job. It is important that all facets of jobs are examined during a job evaluation. For example, a materials management job in a community hospital requires a distribution clerk to stock and distribute stock carts to the patient units. Twice per day the clerk usually delivers a cart, which might weigh up to 100 pounds, to a unit. The movement of the cart probably is not an essential function. But if job evaluation considers the physical demands associated with pushing the cart, then the points assigned may be different from the points assigned if only the essential functions are considered.

Job Evaluation and Gender Issues   Critics have charged that traditional job evaluation programs place less weight on knowledge, skills, and working conditions for many female-dominated jobs in office and clerical areas than on the same factors for male-dominated jobs in craft and manufacturing areas. As discussed earlier, advocates of pay equity view the disparity in pay between men's jobs and women's jobs as evidence of gender discrimination. These advocates also have attacked typical job evaluations as being gender biased. Employers counter that because they base their pay rates heavily on external equity comparisons in the labor market, they are simply reflecting rates the market economy sets for jobs and workers, rather than engaging in discrimination. Most court decisions have supported the employers' opinion.

Wage Surveys

Another part of building a pay system is surveying the pay that other healthcare organizations provide for similar jobs. A **wage survey** is a collection of data on compensation rates for workers performing similar jobs in other organizations. An employer may use surveys conducted by other organizations, or it may decide to conduct its own survey.

Whether available electronically or in printed form, national surveys on many jobs and industries come from the U.S. Department of Labor, Bureau of Labor Statistics, and through national trade associations. Many healthcare employers participate in wage surveys sponsored by various healthcare trade associations, such as the Medical Group Management Association (MGMA), which surveys physician practices, clinics, and the ambulatory departments of hospitals and medical centers.

Properly using surveys from other sources requires that certain questions be addressed:

- *Participants*—Is the survey a realistic sample of those employers with whom the organization competes for employees?
- *Broad-based*—Is the survey balanced so that organizations of varying sizes, industries, and locales are included?
- *Timeliness*—How current are the data (determined by the date when the survey was conducted)?
- *Methodology*—How established is the survey, and how qualified are those who conducted it?
- *Job Matches*—Does it contain job summaries so that appropriate matches to job descriptions can be made?

The results of the pay survey usually are made available to those participating in the survey in order to gain their cooperation. Most surveys specify confidentiality, and data are summarized to assure anonymity. Different job levels often

FIGURE 1 2 - 9   **Sample Clinic Wage Survey**

REGION	NUMBER OF INCUMBENTS	NUMBER OF FTE'S	WEIGHTED AVERAGE HOURLY RATE	REPORTED PAY RANGES (AVERAGES)		
				MINIMUM HOURLY RATE	MIDPOINT HOURLY RATE	MAXIMUM HOURLY RATE
Administrative Secretary: Performs secretarial/receptionist duties, provides assistance to administration.						
Central	21	20.5	$14.06	$12.40	$15.05	$18.67
Metro	46	43.24	$18.33	$14.22	$16.92	$19.74
North	6	6	$12.05	$11.28	$12.95	$14.63
All	73	69.74	$14.81	$12.63	$14.97	$17.68
Medical Secretary: Assists physician with clerical and administrative duties						
Central	6	5.2	$12.60	$8.80	$11.48	$14.15
Metro	70	66.5	$16.33	$13.32	$15.38	$17.40
All	76	71.7	$14.47	$11.06	$13.43	$15.78
Medical Receptionist: Greets, registers, and rooms patients						
Central	5	3	$10.60	$10.03	$11.38	$13.07
Metro	91	78.28	$13.83	$11.70	$13.40	$15.17
North	5	4.25	$11.05	$10.00	$11.50	$15.00
South	27	23.71	$12.42	$13.05	$12.26	$14.55
All	128	109.24	$11.98	$11.20	$12.14	$14.45

Source: Used with permission, Langan and Flynn, LLC, St. Paul, MN, 2006.

are included, and the pay rates are presented both in overall terms and on a regional basis to reflect regional pay differences. Figure 12-9 depicts a section of a clinic wage survey.

Legal Issues and Pay Surveys

One reason for employers to use outside consultants to conduct pay surveys is to avoid charges that the employers are attempting "price-fixing" on wages. The federal government has filed suit in the past, alleging that by sharing wage data, employers may be attempting to hold wages down artificially, in violation of the Sherman Antitrust Act.

Different Pay Structures

In organizations that have a number of different job families, pay survey data may reveal different levels of pay resulting from market factors. These differences may lead to the establishment of several different pay structures, rather than just one structure. Examples of some common pay structures include: (1) hourly and salaried; (2) office, technical, professional, and managerial; (3) clinical allied health and support; and (4) clerical, information technology, professional, supervisory, management, and executive. The nature and culture of the organization are considerations for determining how many and which pay structures to have.

Establishing Pay Grades   In the process of establishing a pay structure, organizations use **pay grades** to group individual jobs having approximately the same job worth. Although no set rules govern establishing pay grades, some overall suggestions can be useful. Generally, from 11 to 17 grades are used in small and medium-sized healthcare organizations with fewer than 500 employees.

Broadbanding   **Broadbanding** is the practice of using fewer pay grades with much broader ranges than in traditional compensation systems. Combining many grades into these broadbands is designed to encourage horizontal movement and therefore more skill acquisition.[21]

The primary reasons for broadbanding are: (1) creating more flexible organizations, (2) encouraging competency development, and (3) emphasizing career development. However, broadbanding is not appropriate for every healthcare organization, many of which operate in a relatively structured manner, and the flexibility associated with broadbanding is not consistent with the traditional culture in many healthcare organizations.

Pay Ranges

The pay range for each pay grade also must be established. Using the market line as a starting point, the employer can determine minimum and maximum pay levels for each pay grade by making the market line the midpoint line of the new pay structure. For example, in a particular pay grade, the maximum value may be 20 percent above the midpoint located on the market line and the minimum value 20 percent below it.

As Figure 12-10 shows, a smaller minimum-to-maximum range should be used for lower-level jobs than for higher-level jobs, primarily because employees in lower-level jobs tend to stay in them for shorter periods of time and have greater promotion possibilities. For example, a clerk-typist might advance to the position of secretary or word-processing operator. In contrast, a pharmacist likely

FIGURE 12-10   Typical Pay Range Widths for Healthcare Positions

TYPES OF JOBS	RANGE ABOVE MINIMUM	% AROUND MIDPOINT
Executives	50%–70%	+ or −20–25%
Mid-Management/Professionals	40%–50%	+ or −16–20%
Technicians/Skilled Craft & Clerical	30%–40%	+ or −13–16%
General Clerical/Others	25%–35%	+ or −11–15%

would have fewer possibilities for upward movement in an organization. However, using the same percentage range at all levels can make administration of a pay system easier in small firms. If broadbanding is used, then much wider ranges, often exceeding 100 percent, may be used.

Compensation experts recommend having an overlap between grades. This structure means that an experienced employee in a lower grade can be paid more than a less-experienced employee in a job in the next pay grade. With pay grade overlap, an individual in the higher-grade job, for example grade 4, may be paid less than someone in a grade 3 job, but has more room for pay progression. Thus, over time the pay of a person in the grade 4 job may surpass the pay of a person in grade 3, who may "top out" because of the pay grade 3 maximum. Compensation experts have suggested that the same monetary amounts can appear in as many as four different pay grades.

Once pay grades and ranges have been computed, then the current pay of employees must be compared to the draft ranges. If the pay of a significant number of employees falls outside the ranges, then a revision of the pay grades and ranges may be needed. Also, once costing and budgeting scenarios are run in order to assess the financial impact of the new pay structures, then pay policy decisions about market positioning may have to be revised, by either lowering or raising the ranges.

Individual Pay

Once organizations have determined pay ranges, they can set the pay for specific individuals. Setting a range for each pay grade gives flexibility by allowing individuals to progress within a grade instead of having to be moved to a new grade each time they receive a raise. A pay range also allows managers to reward the better-performing employees while maintaining the integrity of the pay system.

Rates Out of Range

Regardless of how well-constructed a pay structure is, there usually are a few individuals whose pay is lower than the minimum or higher than the maximum. These situations occur most frequently when organizations that have had an informal pay system develop a new, more formalized one.

Red-Circled Employees   A **red-circled employee** is an incumbent who is paid above the range set for the job. For example, assume that an employee's current pay is $12.00 per hour but the pay range for that grade is $6.94 to $10.06. Over time, management would attempt to bring the employee's rate into grade.

Several approaches can be used to bring a red-circled employee's pay into line. Although the fastest way would be to cut the employee's pay, that approach is not recommended and is seldom used. Instead, the employee's pay may be frozen until the pay range can be adjusted upward to get the employee's pay rate back into the grade. Another approach is to give the employee a small lump-sum payment but not adjust the pay rate when others are given raises; this is referred to as a red-circled bonus.

Green-Circled Employees An individual whose pay is below the range is a **green-circled employee.** Promotion is a major cause of this situation. Generally, it is recommended that the green-circled employee receive pay increases to get him or her to the pay grade minimum fairly rapidly. Frequent increases should be considered if the increase to minimum would be substantial.

Pay Compression

One major problem many healthcare employers face is **pay compression,** which occurs when the pay differences among individuals with different levels of experience and performance becomes small. Pay compression occurs for a number of reasons, but the major one involves situations in which labor market pay levels increase more rapidly than current employees' pay adjustments. Such situations are prevalent in many healthcare occupational areas, such as registered nurses.[22]

In response to competitive market shortages of particular job skills, managers occasionally may have to deviate from the priced grades to hire people with skills that are scarce. For example, suppose the worth of a radiological special procedures technician's job is evaluated at $48,000 to $58,000 annual salary in a hospital, but qualified individuals are in short supply and other employers are paying annual salaries of $70,000. The hospital must pay the higher rate to attract new technicians. Suppose also that several technicians who have been with the hospital for several years started at $48,000 and have received 4 percent increases to their rates each year. These current employees will still be making less than salaries paid to attract new technicians from outside with less experience, causing a significant pay compression issue between the current employees and the new hires.

ISSUES INVOLVING PAY INCREASES

Decisions about pay increases often are critical ones in the relationships among employees, their managers, and the healthcare organization. Individuals express expectations about their pay and about how much increase is "fair," especially in comparison with the increases received by other employees. There are several ways to determine pay increases.

Pay Adjustment Matrix

Many healthcare employers profess to have a pay system based on performance. But relying on performance appraisal information for making a pay adjustment assumes that the appraisals are accurate and done well, which is not always the case. Consequently, a system for integrating appraisals and pay changes must be developed and applied equally. Often, this integration is done through the development of a **pay adjustment matrix,** or *salary guide chart.* Using pay adjustment matrices, adjustments are based in part on a person's **compa-ratio,** which is the pay level divided by the midpoint of the pay range, as shown in Figure 12-11.

Such charts can facilitate an employee's upward movement in an organization, which depends on the person's performance, as rated in an appraisal, and

FIGURE 12-11   Performance-Based Pay-Adjustment Matrix

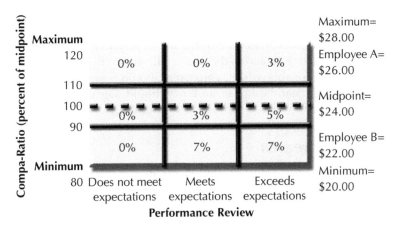

on the person's position in the pay range, which has some relation to experience as well. Notice that as employees move up the pay range, they must exhibit higher performance to obtain the same percentage raise as those lower in the range performing at the "meets performance expectations" level. This approach is taken because the firm is paying above the market midpoint but receiving only satisfactory performance rather than above expectations performance. Charts can be constructed to reflect the specific pay-for-performance policy and philosophy in an organization.

Seniority

Seniority, or time spent in the organization or on a particular job, can be used as the basis for pay increases. Many employers have policies that require a person to be employed for a certain length of time before being eligible for pay increases. Pay adjustments based on seniority often are set as automatic steps once a person has been employed the required length of time, although performance must be at least satisfactory in many nonunion systems.

Step systems, which use pay increases based solely on the attainment of a designated period of employment (typically 2,080 hours), continue to be a popular method of awarding pay increases in healthcare organizations, especially in states where there is significant unionization of healthcare employees. Each step represents the pay adjustment for employees as they attain one full-time equivalent year of employment (2,080 hours).

Cost-of-Living Adjustments (COLA)

A common pay-raise practice is the use of a *standard raise* or **cost-of-living adjustment (COLA).** Giving all employees a standard percentage increase enables them to maintain the same real wages in a period of economic inflation. Often, these adjustments are tied to changes in the consumer price index (CPI)[23] or some other general economic measure. However, numerous studies have revealed that the CPI overstates the actual cost of living.

Unfortunately, some healthcare employers give across-the-board raises and call them **merit raises,** which they are not. If all employees get the same increase, it is legitimately viewed as an across-the-board adjustment that has little to do with good performance. For this reason, employers should reserve the term *merit* for any amount above the standard raise, and they should state clearly which amount is for performance and which is the COLA adjustment.

Lump-Sum Increases

A compensation practice that has gained popularity among some healthcare organizations is to pay a lump-sum bonus in lieu of an incremental increase to an employee's base pay. As an example, employees who receive a pay increase, either for merit or seniority, may have their base pay adjusted and receive an increase in the amount of their regular monthly or weekly paycheck. For instance, an employee who makes $15.00 per hour and then receives a 3 percent increase will move to $15.45 per hour.

In contrast, a lump-sum increase (LSI) is a one-time payment of all or part of a yearly pay increase. The pure LSI approach does not increase the base pay. Therefore, in this example the person's base pay remains at $15.00 per hour. If an LSI of 3% is granted, then the person receives $936.00 (45¢ per hour for 2,080 working hours in the year.) However, the base rate remains at $15.00 per hour, which slows down the progression of the base wages. It also allows for the amount of the "lump" to be varied, without having to continually raise the base rate. Some organizations place a limit on how much of a merit increase can be taken as a lump-sum payment. Other organizations may split the lump sum into two checks, each representing one-half of the year's pay raise.

EXECUTIVE COMPENSATION

Executive compensation in healthcare organizations is typically treated much differently than nonexecutive pay. Executive compensation typically includes multiple components, whereas nonexecutive compensation may only include pay and benefits.

As Figure 12-12 shows, the common components of executive compensation are salaries, annual bonuses, long-term incentives, supplemental benefits, and perquisites.

Executive Salaries

Salaries of executives vary by type of job, size of organization, region of the country, and industry segment. On average, salaries make up about 40 percent to 60 percent of the typical top executive's annual compensation total.

FIGURE 12-12   Executive Compensation Components

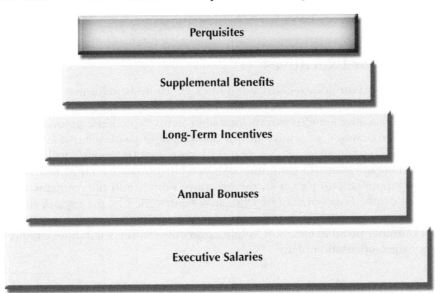

Executive Bonus and Incentive Plans

Executive performance may be difficult to evaluate, but incentive and bonus compensation must reflect some performance measures if they are to be meaningful. Bonuses for executives can be determined in several ways. A discretionary system whereby bonuses are awarded based on the judgments of the chief executive officer and the board of directors is one way. However, the absence of formal, measurable targets detracts significantly from this approach. Also, as noted, incentives can be tied to specific measures, such as effectively managing costs, improving patient satisfaction, or meeting revenue targets. More complex systems create incentive pools and thresholds above which payments are computed. Whatever method is used, it is important to describe it so that executives trying to earn incentives and bonuses understand the plan; otherwise, the incentive effect will be diminished.

As an example, a major medical center ties annual bonuses for senior managers to both operating cost reductions and employee retention. The bonuses have amounted to as much as 25 percent of each senior manager's base salary.

Performance Incentives: Long-Term Versus Short-Term

Performance-based incentives attempt to tie executive compensation to the long-term growth and success of the organization. However, whether the emphasis is really on the long term or merely represents a series of short-term rewards is controversial. Short-term rewards based on quarterly or annual performance may not result in the kind of long-run-oriented decisions necessary for the organization to continue to do well.

Benefits for Executives

As with benefits for nonexecutive employees, executive benefits may take several forms, including traditional retirement, health insurance, vacations, and others. However, executive benefits may include some items that other employees do not receive. For example, executive health plans without co-payments and without limitations on deductibles or physician choice are popular among small and middle-sized organizations. Organizational-owned life insurance on the life of the executive is popular and pays both the executive's estate and the company in the event of death. Trusts of various kinds may be designed by the organization to help the executive deal with estate tax planning issues. Deferred compensation offers another possible means of helping executives with tax liabilities caused by incentive compensation plans.

Executive Perquisites

In addition to the regular benefits received by all employees, executives often receive benefits called perquisites. **Perquisites (perks)** are special executive benefits—usually noncash items. Perks help tie executives to organizations and demonstrate their importance to their companies. Many executives value the status enhancement of perks because these visible symbols of status allow executives to be seen as very important persons (VIPs) both inside and outside their organizations.

Current Nature of Healthcare Executive Compensation

Healthcare executives—typically someone in the top two levels of an organization, such as CEO, administrator, president, or senior vice president—are paid very well.[24]

In most healthcare organizations, the Board of Directors sets policy.[25] For publicly traded companies covered by federal regulatory agencies, such as the Securities and Exchange Commission (SEC), the board must approve executive compensation packages. Even for many nonprofit organizations, IRS regulations require the board to review and approve the compensation for top-level executives.

The **compensation committee of the board of directors** usually is a subgroup of the board composed of directors who are not officers of the firm. Compensation committees generally make recommendations to the Board of Directors on overall pay policies, salaries for top officers, supplemental compensation such as bonuses, and additional perquisites for executives.

ETHICAL PRACTICES AND COMPLIANCE

Tax-exempt hospitals are becoming increasingly aware that they may be the focus of a broadening IRS enforcement initiative examining executive compensation practices. The IRS has announced that the initiative is aimed at organizations that pay excessive compensation and benefits to their officers and other insiders. The IRS has indicated that their efforts are designed to identify and halt abuses by tax-exempt organizations. Areas of critical concern may be paying executives more than $1 million per year and offering excessive benefit transactions, including such items as car leases, spousal travel, tickets to sporting events, and other similar perquisites.[26]

Most tax-exempt hospitals are very sensitive to their responsibilities with regard to paying reasonable executive salaries. In the event of an IRS executive compensation review, tax-exempt hospitals must be able to document the reasonableness of their executive compensation based on sound compensation practices, appropriate market analyses, and assessment of their executives' performance levels.

Determining "Reasonableness" of Executive Compensation

The reasonableness of executive compensation is often justified by comparison to compensation market surveys, but these surveys usually provide a range of compensation data that requires interpretation. Various questions have been suggested for determining if executive pay is "reasonable," including the following:

- Would another organization hire this person as an executive?
- How does the executive's compensation compare with that for executives in similar organizations in the industry?
- Are the executive's pay and benefits consistent with those for other employees in the organization?

Boards must address the need to continually link organizational performance with variable pay rewards for executives and other employees.[27] There is certainly more controversy about executive compensation in other industries, but healthcare boards of directors must also be mindful of the reasonableness of executive pay and benefits.

In the next chapter, the other key components of compensation (benefits and variable pay) are discussed. It is important that all compensation types are seen as interrelated components of a healthcare organization's total compensation program.

CASE

Gardenview Long-Term Care is a private, not-for-profit, retirement community located in a medium-size market. It is a 50-year-old facility offering three levels of care for its elderly residents: Independent Living, Assisted Living, and Skilled/Full Nursing Care. Gardenview's administration has recently identified a strategic initiative to aggressively pursue the area of dementia/Alzheimer's care. In order to pursue this new strategic initiative, Gardenview is attempting to recruit an executive director for the program.

The board of directors has contracted with an executive recruitment firm to conduct the search for the new executive director. The first step in the recruitment firm's process was to determine a market competitive compensation and benefits package for the position. Their market research determined the following:

- Starting Salary Range: $125,000.00 to 140,000.00
- Incentive Bonus potential: 10 percent to 15 percent of base salary
- Special Perks: travel allowance, conference funds, and expense account
- Benefits: fully paid health, dental, life, and disability insurance
- Pension: 10 percent contribution to a 403(b) plan

Questions

1. What proof or documentation should Gardenview's board request from the recruitment firm that the suggested compensation and benefits program is appropriate for the new executive director?
2. What should Gardenview's board do if the administrator is currently making $115,000.00?

END NOTES

1. Adapted from "Staffing Watch," *H&HN: Hospitals and Health Networks* (January 2005), 22.
2. Adapted from Frederick A. Hessler, "The Capital Crunch," *Futurescan, Healthcare Trends and Implications 2005–2010* (Health Administration Press, 2005), 11–15.
3. Lee Rasch, "Employee Performance Appraisal and the 95/5 Rule," *Community College Journal of Research & Practice* (June 2004), 407–414.
4. Frank H. Lyons and Dan Ben-Ora, "Total Rewards Strategy," *Compensations and Benefits Review* (March/April 2002), 34–40.
5. Bruce N. Pfau and Ira T. Kay, "The Five Key Elements of a Total Rewards and Accountability Orientation," *Benefits Quarterly* (Third Quarter 2002), 7–11.
6. "Demand Pushing Nurse Anesthetists' Salaries to All-time High," *Omaha World Herold* (June 2, 2002), CR1.
7. Carren Bersch, "Virtue Has Its Own Reward, But No Box Office," *MLO: Medical Laboratory Observer* (March 2003), 22–23.
8. Lee A. Schmidt, Deana Nelson, and Leah Godfrey, "A Clinical Ladder Program Based on Carper's Fundamental Patterns of Knowing in Nursing," *Journal of Nursing Administration* (March 2003), 146–152.
9. D. R. Ilgen and S. Merritt, "Individual and Team Rewards in Interdependent Teams: Managing the Tensions," *Australian Journal of Psychology* (2003 Supplement), 129.
10. Scoot Highhouse, Margaret E. Brooks-Laber, Lilly Lin, and Christians Spitzmueller, "What Makes a Salary Seem

Reasonable? Frequency Context Effects on Starting Salary Expectations," *Journal of Occupational and Organizational Psychology* (March 2004), 113–118.

11. Jonathan A. Segal, "Labor Pains for Union-Free Employers," *HR Magazine* (March 2004), 113–118.

12. Rafael Gely and Leonard Bierman, "Pay Secrecy/Confidentiality Rules and the National Labor Relations Act," *Journal of Labor and Employment Law* (Fall 2003).

13. Paul W. Mulvey et al., "Study Finds that Knowledge of Pay Processes Can Beat Out Amount of Pay in Employee Retention, Organizational Effectiveness," *Journal of Organizational Excellence* (Autumn 2002), 29; and Robert L. Heneman, Paul W. Mulvey, and Peter V. LeBlanc, "Improve Base Pay ROI by Increasing Employee Knowledge," *WorldWork Journal* (Fourth Quarter 2002), 21–27.

14. "Strategies for Retention," *Health Care Matters* (July 2005), 1–2.

15. David Neumark, "Detecting Effects of Living Wage Laws," *Industrial Relations*, 42 (2003), 531–565.

16. Julie Liedman, "Making a Living," *Human Resource Executive* (November 2002), 70–73.

17. See *http://www.dol.gov/dol/topic/retirement/erisa.htm* for more information on employee rights under the Employee Retirement Income Security Act (ERISA).

18. See *http://www.dol.gov/esa/minwage/america.htm* for a review of minimum wage laws in the United States (August 1, 2005).

19. Craig Skenes and Brian H. Kleiner, "The HAY System of Compensation," *Management Research News*, 26 (2003), 109–116.

20. Darin E. Hartley, "Job Analysis at the Speed of Reality," *T+D* (September 2004), 20–22.

21. Andrew S. Rosen and David Turetsky, "Broadbanding: The Construction of a Career Management Framework," *Worldatwork Journal* (Fourth Quarter 2002), 44–45.

22. Mary E. Greipp, "Salary Compression: Its Effect on Nurse Recruitment and Retention," *Journal of Nursing Administration* (June 2003), 321–323.

23. For more information on the CPI, visit *http://www.bls.gov/cpi/home.htm*.

24. Mark Taylor, "Tax-exempt Targets," *Modern Healthcare* (August 16, 2004), 10–11.

25. A. L. Spitzer, "Executive Compensation in Nonprofit Healthcare Organizations: Who's in Charge?" *Health Matrix*, 15:67 (2005), 67–82.

26. Melanie Evans, "Nonprofit CEO's Make Big Bucks," *Modern Healthcare* (October 4, 2004), 9.

27. Brent M. Longnecker and Christopher S. Crawford, "The IRS Tackles Excessive Executive Compensation," *USA Today Magazine* (May 2005), 18–19.

The Management of Benefits and Variable Pay in Healthcare

Learning Objectives

After you have read this chapter, you should be able to:

- Describe the challenges that confront healthcare employers in providing benefits and variable pay programs.

- Discuss why healthcare employers must offer competitive benefits programs to their employees.

- Identify various types of benefits.

- Explain the role that healthcare HR professionals must play in administering benefits.

- Compare and contrast individual and team-based incentives.

Healthcare HR Insights

A national home healthcare agency received the bad news from its broker that it once again had experienced a double digit increase in health insurance premiums. This was the third consecutive year that the agency was confronted with deciding how much of the premium increase would have to be passed along to the employees. Currently the agency paid 100 percent of the cost of single coverage for its employees and contributed a small percentage toward the cost of dependent or family coverages.

This time the agency decided to deal with the issue by implementing a new health insurance plan design that would give its employees more choices in how they could access health care and a different approach to managing the costs associated with their choices. The new program was rolled out with an extensive employee education program that included information on:

- How the health care system works
- The costs associated with their health care decisions
- How to use the new program and the potential savings that could occur with good health care choices
- How to evaluate the quality of the care they receive

Although costs would not initially be dramatically impacted, the organizational leadership was more confident in what they could explain to the current employees and "sell" to new recruits about rising health insurance costs.[1]

D eveloping and implementing compensation strategies for healthcare organizations is critically important for healthcare HR professionals. Whether considered as a part of a total compensation approach or viewed separately, developing and implementing employee benefits and variable pay programs for healthcare organizations is challenging.[2]

Healthcare employers provide employee benefits to their workers for being part of the organization. A **benefit** is a form of indirect compensation. Benefits for healthcare employers often include health, dental, life, and disability insurances, educational assistance, retirement plans, vacations with pay, and other programs.

Benefits clearly influence employees' decisions about which particular employer to work for, whether to stay or leave employment, and when to retire. However, the unique characteristics of benefits sometimes make them difficult to administer. For example, government involvement in benefits continues to expand. Federal and state governments *require* that certain benefits be offered (Social Security, workers' compensation, and unemployment insurance), and various governmental regulations apply to many of the nonrequired benefits as well (retirement, family leave, and flexible benefits).

Further, employees tend to take benefits for granted. For instance, so many organizations offer health insurance that employees expect it. However, because benefits are also complex, many employees do not understand them, or sometimes do not even know what benefits exist. Yet benefits are costly to employers, averaging up to 40 percent of employees' base pay.[3] These characteristics of benefits suggest that healthcare HR professionals should carefully consider the strategic role of benefits in their organizations.

STRATEGIC PERSPECTIVES ON BENEFITS

For many healthcare employers, providing employee benefits represents a double-edged sword. On one side, employers know that in order to attract and retain employees with the necessary training and competence, they must offer appropriate benefits that can have significant expense to the overall operation of the organization.[4] On the other side, they know the importance of controlling or even cutting costs. Too often, both managers and employees think of only wages and salaries as compensation and fail to consider the additional costs associated with benefits expenditures.

Healthcare employers find themselves on both sides of the healthcare insurance cost debate. Specifically, healthcare employers must negotiate for the most cost-effective coverage possible for their employees with their insurance carriers. As providers, they must defend the highest possible reimbursement for the health services they provide, often with the same carriers.

Because of their sizable proportion of organizational costs, the compensation components of base pay, variable pay, and benefits require serious and realistic assessment and planning. Figure 13-1 shows where each benefit dollar typically is spent based on various surveys conducted regularly.

Goals for Benefits

Benefits should be looked at as part of the overall compensation strategy of the organization. For example, healthcare organizations can choose to compete for employees by providing base compensation, benefits, or variable pay, or perhaps all three. Which approach is chosen depends on many factors, such as the competition, organizational life cycle, and corporate strategy. For example, a new clinic may choose to have lower base pay, and use high variable incentives to attract new employees, but keep the cost of benefits as low as possible. Or a hospital that hires predominately female employees might choose a family-friendly offering of benefits including on-site childcare and access to full-time benefits for part-time work to attract experienced employees.

Benefits Needs Analysis

Given the current challenges healthcare employers face in recruiting and retaining skilled workers, understanding what employees want in a benefit program is

FIGURE 13-1   How the Typical Benefits Dollar Is Spent

Insurance Payments
(medical premiums,
vision care, dental care,
life insurance, etc.)
About 25%

Payment for Time
Not Worked
(leaves, vacations,
holidays, etc.)
About 25%

Legally Required
Contributions
(Social Security,
unemployment, and
workers' compensation)
About 20%

Paid Rest Periods
(coffee breaks,
lunch period,
travel time)
About 10%

Miscellaneous Benefits
(educational assistance,
severance pay,
child care, etc.)
About 5%

Retirement Plans
(pensions, 401(k)
plans, etc.)
About 15%

Source: Based on information from the U.S. Department of Labor, Bureau of Labor Statistics, *National Compensation Survey: Employee Benefits in Private Industry in the United States,* 2003; and *Employee Benefits Study,* 2003 ed. (Washington, DC: U.S. Chamber of Commerce, 2004).

critical. A **benefits needs analysis** includes a comprehensive look at all aspects of benefits in an organization. Done periodically, such an analysis is more than simply deciding what benefits employees might want. In order to make certain that the mix of benefits is doing what it should, someone doing a benefits needs analysis might consider the following issues:

- How much total compensation, including benefits, should be provided?
- What part should benefits comprise of the total compensation of individuals?
- What expense levels are acceptable for each benefit offered?
- Why is each type of benefit offered?
- Which employees should be given or offered which benefits?
- What is being received by the organization in return for each benefit?
- How does having a comprehensive benefits package aid in minimizing turnover or maximizing recruiting and retention of employees?
- How flexible should the package of benefits be?

Funding Benefits

Total benefits costs can be funded both by contributions made by the employer and contributions made by the employee. If the employer fully subsidizes a benefit, the cost to the employee would be zero. But if an employer chooses to pay $650 per month toward an employee's health insurance premium while the employee pays $100, then the employee contributes to covering benefits costs.

Benefit plans also can be funded by purchasing insurance from an insurance provider. Premiums to be paid reflect the predicted claims and will be adjusted based on actual claims. Some large healthcare employers choose to "self-fund" and are their own insurers—they set aside money to cover benefits costs. Self-funding by larger employers often has been effective in containing the overall costs of providing this benefit.

TYPES OF BENEFITS

Employers offer some benefits to aid recruiting and retention, some because they are required to do so, and some because doing so reinforces the organization's HR philosophy. For example, life insurance can be purchased at a better rate if the purchaser is a large employer that qualifies for a group rate. Further, tax laws provide beneficial tax treatment of some employer-provided benefits for employees that they would not get if purchased by individuals. Figure 13-2 shows the many different benefits offered, classified by type.

Government-Mandated Benefits

There are many **mandated benefits** that employers in the United States must provide to employees by law. Social Security and unemployment insurance are funded through a tax paid by the employee and employer based on the employee's compensation.[5] Workers' compensation laws exist in all states. In addition, under the Family and Medical Leave Act (FMLA), employers must offer unpaid leaves to employees with certain medical or family difficulties. Other mandated benefits are available through Medicare, which provides healthcare for individuals who are age 65 and over. It is funded in part by an employer tax through Social Security. The Consolidated Omnibus Budget Reconciliation Act (COBRA) and the Health Insurance Portability and Accountability Act (HIPAA) mandate that an employer continue healthcare coverage paid for by the employees after they leave the organization, and that most employees be able to obtain coverage if they were previously covered in a health plan.

Voluntary Benefits

Employers voluntarily offer other types of benefits in order to compete for and retain employees. By offering additional benefits, organizations are recognizing the need to provide greater security and benefit support to workers with widely

FIGURE 13-2   Types of Benefits

Security	Health Care	Family Oriented
• Workers' compensation • Unemployment compensation	• COBRA and HIPAA provisions	• FMLA provisions
• Supplemental unemployment benefits (SUBs) • Severance pay	• Medical and dental • Prescription drugs • Vision • PPO, HMO, and CDH plans • Wellness programs • Flexible spending accounts	• Adoption benefits and dependent-care assistance • Domestic partner benefits
Retirement		**Time Off**
• Social Security • ADEA and OWBPA provisions	**Financial**	• Military reserve time off • Election and jury leaves
• Early retirement options • Health care for retirees • Pension plans • Individual retirement accounts (IRAs) • Keogh plans • 401 (k), 403 (b), and 457 plans	• Financial services (e.g., credit unions and counseling) • Relocation assistance • Life insurance • Disability insurance • Long-term care insurance • Legal insurance • Educational assistance	• Lunch and rest breaks • Holidays and vacations • Family leave • Medical and sick leave • Paid time off • Funeral and bereavement leaves
		Miscellaneous
		• Social and recreational programs and events • Unique programs

varied personal circumstances. The following sections describe the different types of benefits that are shown in Figure 13-2.

Part-Time Employee Benefits

Another key design issue is whether or not to provide benefits coverage to employees who are not regular full-time employees. Many healthcare employers provide benefits to part-time employees, which is different than the practices of many non-healthcare industry organizations. According to a study by the U.S. Bureau of Labor Statistics, only 24 percent of part-time workers are in company retirement plans, and only 17 percent are eligible for health care benefits.[6] Part-time employees who do receive benefits usually do so in proportion to the percentage of full-time work time they provide.

SECURITY BENEFITS

A number of benefits provide employee security. These benefits include some mandated by laws and others offered by employers voluntarily. The primary security benefits found in organizations include workers' compensation, unemployment compensation, and severance pay.

Workers' Compensation

Workers' compensation provides benefits to persons injured on the job. State laws require most employers to provide workers' compensation coverage by purchasing insurance from a private carrier or state insurance fund or self insuring the coverage.

The workers' compensation system requires employers to give cash benefits, medical care, and rehabilitation services to employees for injuries or illnesses occurring within the scope of their employment.[7] In exchange, employees give up the right of legal actions and awards. However, it is in the interests of both employers and employees to reduce workers' compensation costs through safety and health programs.[8]

Unemployment Compensation

Another benefit required by law is unemployment compensation, established as part of the Social Security Act of 1935. Because each U.S. state operates its own unemployment compensation system, provisions differ significantly from state to state. Employers finance this benefit by paying a tax on the first $7,000 (or more, in 37 states) of annual earnings for each employee. The tax is paid to state and federal unemployment compensation funds. The percentage paid by individual employers is based on *experience rates,* which reflect the number of claims filed by workers who leave.

Severance Pay

Severance pay is a security benefit voluntarily offered by employers to some employees who lose their jobs. Severed employees may receive lump-sum payments if the employer terminates their employment.

Some healthcare employers have offered reduced amounts of cash severance and replaced some of the severance value by offering continued health insurance and *outplacement* assistance. Through outplacement assistance, ex-employees receive resume writing instruction, interviewing skills workshops, and career counseling.

RETIREMENT SECURITY BENEFITS

Few people set aside sufficient financial reserves to use when they retire; instead, they count on retirement benefits for a large part of their income.[9] Many healthcare employers offer some kind of retirement plan. Generally, private pensions make up a critical portion of income for people after retirement. With the baby-boomer generation in the United States closing in on retirement, pressures on such funds are likely to grow.

Retirement Benefits and Age Discrimination

As a result of an amendment to the Age Discrimination in Employment Act (ADEA), generally employees cannot be required to retire at a specific age.

Employers have had to develop different policies to comply with this amendment. In many employer pension plans, "normal retirement" is the age at which employees can retire and collect full pension benefits. Employers must decide whether individuals who continue to work past normal retirement age (perhaps age 65) should receive the full benefits package, especially pension credits. Possible future changes to Social Security may increase the age for full benefits past 65, so modifications in policies are likely.

Early Retirement   Historically many healthcare organizations have included pension plan provisions for **early retirement** in order to give workers opportunities to retire early from their jobs. After spending 25 to 30 years working for the same employer, some individuals may wish to use their talents in other areas.

Some healthcare employers have used early-retirement buyout programs to cut back their workforces and reduce costs. Healthcare employers must take care to make these early retirement programs truly voluntary. Forcing workers to take advantage of an early retirement buyout program led to the passage of a federal law titled the Older Workers Benefit Protection Act (OWBPA).

Given the current state of healthcare staffing, some healthcare employers are rethinking incentives for early retirement. Some employers are moving to a concept referred to as **phased retirement,** defined as a program that helps employees retire in stages. These programs include options that allow employees to reduce the number of hours worked, take a different job, or be hired into a different job after retirement.

Social Security

The Social Security Act of 1935, with its later amendments, established a system providing *old age, survivors, disability,* and *retirement benefits.* Administered by the federal government through the Social Security Administration, this program provides benefits to previously employed individuals or their dependents. Employees and employers share in the cost of Social Security through a tax on employees' wages or salaries.

Since the system's inception, Social Security payroll taxes have risen to 15.3 percent currently, with employees and employers each paying 7.65 percent up to an established maximum. In addition, Medicare taxes have more than doubled, to 2.9 percent.

Pension Plans

Pension plans are retirement benefits established and funded by employers and employees. Organizations are not required to offer pension plans to employees, and they cover fewer than half of U.S. workers for all employers. Smaller organizations offer them less often than large organizations do.

Traditional Pension Plans   "Traditional" pension plans, where the employer makes the contributions and the employee gets a defined amount each month upon retirement, are no longer the norm. In these **defined-benefit plans** the employees' contributions are based on actuarial calculations that focus on the *benefits* to be received by employees after retirement and the *methods* used to determine such benefits. A defined-benefit plan gives the employee greater assurance of benefits and greater predictability in the amount of benefits that will be available for retirement.[10]

In a **defined-contribution plan,** the employer makes an annual payment to an employee's pension account. The key to this plan is the *contribution rate;* employee retirement benefits depend on fixed contributions and employee earnings levels. Because these plans hinge on the investment returns on the previous contributions, which can vary according to profitability or other factors, employees' retirement benefits are somewhat less secure and predictable.[11]

Cash Balance Plans Some healthcare employers changed from their traditional pension plans to **cash balance plans,** a hybrid based on ideas from both defined-benefit and defined-contribution plans. Cash balance plans define retirement benefits for each employee not on years of service and salary, but by reference to a hypothetical account balance. Cash balance plans were once viewed as an answer for employers who wanted to limit their financial liability and provide a more portable solution to employees. But a 2003 U.S. District Court ruling that said IBM's cash-balance plan violated age-discrimination laws changed all of that. In that decision, the judge sided with employees who claimed that the calculations the plan used to pay benefits discriminated against older workers. The case, which is on appeal, has caused many companies to freeze their cash balance plans and offer defined-contribution plans instead. Federal legislation is currently pending which may clarify the legal standing of such plans.[12]

Employee Retirement Income Security Act (ERISA) The widespread criticism of how pension plans were administered and how the pension funds were protected led to the passage of the Employee Retirement Income Security Act (ERISA) in 1974. The purpose of this law is to regulate private pension plans in order to assure that employees who put money into them or depend on a pension for retirement funds actually receive the money when they retire.

Pension Terms and Concepts

Pension plans can be either contributory or noncontributory. In a **contributory plan,** both the employee and the employer pay in money for pension benefits. In a **noncontributory plan,** the employer provides all the funds for pension benefits. As would be expected, employees and unions generally prefer the use of noncontributory plans.

Certain rights are attached to employee pension plans. Various laws and provisions have been passed to address the right of employees to receive benefits from their pension plans. **Vesting** assures employees of a certain pension, provided they work a minimum number of years. If employees resign or are terminated before they have been employed for the required time, no pension rights accrue to them except the funds that they have contributed. If employees stay the allotted time, they retain their pension rights and receive the funds contributed by both the employer and themselves.

Another feature of some employee pensions is **portability.** In a portable plan, employees can move their pension benefit from one employer to another. A growing number of organizations offer portable pension plans. Instead of requiring workers to wait until they retire to move their traditional pension plan benefits, the portable plan takes a different approach. Once workers have vested in a plan for a period of time, such as five years, they can transfer their fund balances to other retirement plans if they change jobs.

Individual Retirement Options

The availability of several retirement benefit options makes the pension area more complex. The most prominent options are individual retirement accounts (IRAs), 401(k) and 403(b) plans, and 457 plans. These plans may be available in addition to organizational pension plans.

Individual Retirement Accounts   An IRA is a special account in which an employee can set aside funds that will not be taxed until the employee retires. The major advantages of an IRA are the ability to accumulate extra retirement funds and the shifting of taxable income to later years, when total income—and therefore taxable income—is likely to be lower. Federal law changes in 1997 authorized a special type of IRA, called the *Roth IRA,* which likely will increase the usage of IRAs.

401(k), 403(b), and 457 Plans   The **403(b)** and **457 plans** are only available to employees of nonprofit employers, while **401(k) plans** are available to both nonprofit and for-profit organizations. These plans allow individual employees to elect to reduce their current pay by a certain percentage, which is then used to fund a retirement plan.

HEALTHCARE BENEFITS

Many healthcare employers provide a variety of healthcare and medical benefits, usually through insurance coverage. The most common plans cover medical, dental, prescription drug, and vision care expenses for employees and their dependents. Dental insurance is also important to many employees. Some dental plans include orthodontic coverage, which is a major expense for some families. Some employer medical insurance plans also cover psychiatric counseling, but many do not.

The costs of healthcare insurance have continued to escalate at a rate well in excess of inflation for several decades. Estimates are that the average healthcare cost per employee is more than $6,300.00 per year.[13] By the end of the 1990s, the rise in healthcare costs forced many employers to make concerted efforts to control medical premium increases and other healthcare costs. Although those cost-control efforts were successful for a while, the rate of increases in health-benefits costs has risen again. Currently many healthcare employers, especially small group practices and clinics, are reconsidering their ability to even offer health insurance for their employees.

Controlling Healthcare Benefits Costs

Healthcare employers offering healthcare benefits are taking a number of approaches to controlling their costs. The most prominent ones are changing co-payments and employee contributions, using managed care, and switching to consumer-driven health plans.

Changing Co-Payments and Employee Contributions As health insurance costs rise, employers have tried to shift some of those costs to employees. The **co-payment** strategy requires employees to pay a portion of the cost of insurance premiums, medical care, and prescription drugs.

In one survey, requiring new or higher employee contributions and co-payments is the most prevalent cost-control strategy identified by 400 employers.[14] Employers who have raised the per person deductible from $50 to $250 have realized significant savings in healthcare expenses due to decreased employee usage of healthcare services and prescription drugs. The administrative tracking mentioned in the figure is important because many employers have found that some of the healthcare provided by doctors and hospitals is unnecessary, incorrectly billed, or deliberately overcharged. Consequently, both employers and insurance firms often require that medical work and charges be audited through a **utilization review.** This process may require a second opinion, a review of the procedures done, or a review of the charges for the procedures done. This change is not easily accepted by healthcare workers, who have very strong opinions about where and by whom their care is delivered due to their personal experience with the healthcare delivery system.

Requiring higher co-pays and deductibles is also facing significant resistance from healthcare employees, especially those who have had *first-dollar coverage.* With this type of coverage, all expenses, beginning with the first dollar of

FIGURE 13-3 Cost-Control Strategies for Healthcare Benefits

healthcare costs, are paid by the employee's insurance. Experts claim that when first-dollar coverage is included in a basic health plan, many employees see a doctor for every slight illness, which results in an escalation of the benefits costs. Many union contracts have first-dollar coverage, and attempts by employers to negotiate co-payments or increases in co-payments have led to numerous strikes.

Using Managed Care   Several other types of programs attempt to reduce healthcare costs paid by employers. **Managed care** consists of approaches that monitor and reduce medical costs through restrictions and market system alternatives. Managed care plans emphasize primary and preventive care, the use of specific providers who charge lower prices, restrictions on certain kinds of treatment, and prices negotiated with hospitals and physicians.

One managed care approach is the **preferred provider organization (PPO),** a healthcare provider that contracts with an employer or an employer group to supply healthcare services to employees at a competitive rate. Employees have the freedom to go to other providers if they want to pay the differences in costs. *Point-of-service plans* are somewhat similar, offering financial incentives to encourage employees to use designated medical providers.

Another prominent managed care approach is a **health maintenance organization (HMO),** which provides services for a fixed period on a prepaid basis. The HMO emphasizes both prevention and correction. An employer contracts with an HMO and its staff of physicians and medical personnel to furnish complete medical care, except for hospitalization. The employer pays a flat rate per enrolled employee or per enrolled family. The covered individuals may then go to the HMO for healthcare as often as they need to. Supplemental policies for hospitalization are also provided. While HMOs remain widely used, a growing number of employers are focusing on other means to control the costs of healthcare benefits.

Consumer-Driven Health (CDH) Plans   Many employers are turning to employee-focused health benefits plans. The most prominent is a **consumer-driven health (CDH) plan,** which provides financial contributions to employees to cover their own health-related expenses. A significant number of companies have switched to CDH plans, and it appears that many more are actively considering switching to these plans.

In these plans, which are also called *defined-contribution health plans,* an employer places a set amount into each employee's "account" and identifies a number of healthcare alternatives that are available. Then, individual employees select from those healthcare alternatives and pay for them from their accounts. For instance, assume an employer sets aside $250 a month for each employee. One employee may choose an HMO costing $230 a month, and use her remaining $20 for purchasing additional life insurance. Another employee may choose a family plan costing $480 a month, and have the additional $230 deducted from his paycheck.

CDH plans can be coupled with *flexible health spending accounts* (discussed later), *health reimbursement arrangements, medical savings accounts,* and *health savings accounts.* Although slightly different in terms of tax regulations, these programs all allow individuals to make regular tax-free deposits into accounts.[15] Then, the money can be withdrawn to pay for qualified medical expenses, health insurance premiums, catastrophic health expenses, and other approved health-related costs not covered by employer contributions.[16]

There are two advantages to such plans for employers. One is that more of the increases in healthcare benefits are shifted to employees, because the employer contributions need not increase as fast as healthcare costs. Second, the focus of controlling healthcare usage falls on employees, who may have to choose when to use and not use healthcare benefits.

Many healthcare employers, regardless of their size, are offering programs to educate employees about healthcare costs and how to reduce them. Newsletters, Web sites, formal classes, and many other approaches are all designed to help employees understand why healthcare costs are increasing and what they can do to control them. Some employers even have *wellness programs* offering financial incentives to improve health habits. These programs, discussed more in Chapter 14, reward employees who stop smoking, lose weight, and participate in exercise programs, among other activities.

Healthcare Legislation

COBRA Provisions   Legal requirements in **COBRA** require that most employers (except churches and the federal government) with 20 or more employees offer extended healthcare coverage to the following groups:

- Employees who voluntarily quit, except those terminated for "gross misconduct"
- Widowed or divorced spouses and dependent children of former or current employees
- Retirees and their spouses whose healthcare coverage ends

Employers must notify eligible employees and/or their spouses and qualified dependents about COBRA within 60 days after the employees quit, die, get divorced, or otherwise change their status. The coverage must be offered for 18 to 36 months, depending on the qualifying circumstances. The individual no longer employed by the organization must pay the premiums, but the employer may charge this individual no more than 102 percent of the premium costs to insure a similarly covered employee.

For most healthcare employers, the COBRA requirements mean additional paperwork and related costs. For example, employers must not only track the former employees but also notify their qualified dependents. The 2 percent premium addition generally does not cover all relevant costs; the costs often run several percentage points more.

HIPAA Provisions   **HIPAA,** passed in 1996, allows employees to switch their health insurance plan from one employer to another to get new health coverage, regardless of preexisting health conditions. The legislation also prohibits group insurance plans from dropping coverage for a sick employee, and requires them to make individual coverage available to people who leave group plans. The HIPAA legislation also established very high standards and controls for healthcare providers, insurance companies, and other organizations that have access to or knowledge of an individual's medical information, referred to as Protected Health Information (PHI), to maintain and protect medical record confidentiality. These requirements also affect how employers deal with employees' PHI related to benefits information.

FINANCIAL, INSURANCE, AND OTHER BENEFITS

Healthcare employers may offer workers a wide range of special benefits: financial benefits, insurance benefits (in addition to health-related insurance), educational benefits, social benefits, and recreational benefits. These benefits can be useful in attracting and retaining employees. Workers like receiving special benefits, which often are not taxed as income.

Financial Benefits

Financial benefits include a wide variety of items. A *credit union* sponsored by the employer provides saving and lending services for employees. Employee *thrift savings plans* may be made available. To illustrate: in a savings plan the organization provides matching funds equal to the amount invested by the employee in the 401(k) plan. At a large family practice group, the employees receive a matched contribution of up to 6 percent of their contributions to the plan.

Insurance Benefits

In addition to health-related insurance, some employers provide other types of insurance. These benefits offer major advantages for employees because many employers pay some or all of the costs. Even when employers do not pay any of the costs, employees still benefit because of the lower rates available through group programs.

Life Insurance   It is common for employers to provide *life insurance* for employees. Life insurance is bought as a group policy, and the employer pays all or some of the premiums, but the level of coverage is usually low and is tied to the employee's base pay. A typical level of coverage is one or two times an employee's annual salary. Some executives may get higher coverage as part of executive compensation packages. Healthcare employers frequently provide their employees access to additional optional life insurance for which the employee pays the full premium for, but at discounted group rates.

Disability Insurance   Other insurance benefits frequently tied to employee pay levels are *short-term* and *long-term disability insurance.* This type of insurance provides continuing income protection for employees who become disabled and unable to work. Long-term disability insurance is much more common because many employers cover short-term disability situations by allowing employees to accrue sick leave granted annually. A growing number of health-care employers are integrating their disability insurance programs with efforts to reduce workers' compensation claims. There are a number of reasons to have **integrated disability management programs,** such as cost savings and better coordination.

Educational Benefits

Another benefit used by many healthcare employees is *educational assistance programs* to pay for some or all the costs associated with formal education courses and degree programs, including the costs of books and laboratory materials. Some employers pay for schooling on a proportional schedule, depending on the grades received; others simply require a passing grade of C or above. As an example, the employees of one family practice clinic receive an annual tuition benefit of $1,700.00. They can use these monies to attend classes that directly apply to their work or prepare them for advancement within the clinic. Unless the education paid for by the employer meets certain conditions, employees must count the cost of educational aid as taxable income.

Social and Recreational Benefits

Some benefits and services are social and recreational in nature, such as bowling leagues, picnics and parties, employer-sponsored athletic teams, organizationally-owned recreational lodges, and other sponsored activities and interest groups. As interest in employee wellness has increased, more firms are providing recreational facilities and activities. But employers should retain control of all events associated with their organizations because of possible legal responsibility.

Family-Oriented Benefits and the Family and Medical Leave Act

The composition of families in the United States has changed significantly in the past few decades. The number of traditional families—in which the man is the primary or exclusive "bread winner" and the woman stays home to raise children—has declined significantly, while the percentage of two-worker families has more than doubled. The growth in dual-career couples, single-parent households, and increasing work demands on many workers has increased the emphasis some employers are placing on family-oriented benefits. To provide assistance, employers have established a variety of family-oriented benefits, and the federal government passed the Family and Medical Leave Act in 1993.

The FMLA covers all employers with 50 or more employees who live within 75 miles of the workplace and includes federal, state, and private employers. Only employees who have worked at least 12 months and 1,250 hours in the previous year are eligible for leaves under FMLA.

FMLA Eligibility   The law requires that employers allow eligible employees to take a total of 12 weeks' leave during any 12-month period for one or more of the following situations:

- Birth, adoption, or foster-care placement of a child
- Caring for a spouse, child, or parent with a serious health condition
- Serious health condition of the employee

A **serious health condition** is one requiring inpatient, hospital, hospice, or residential medical care or continuing physician care. An employer may require an employee to provide a certificate from a doctor verifying such an illness as being covered. FMLA provides for the following guidelines regarding employee leaves:

- Employees taking family and medical leave must be able to return to the same job or a job of equivalent status or pay.
- Health benefits must be continued during the leave at the same level and conditions.
- The leave taken may be intermittent rather than in one block, subject to employee and employer agreements, when birth, adoption, or foster child-care is the cause. For serious health conditions, employer approval is not necessary.
- Employees can be required to use all paid-up vacation and personal leave before taking unpaid leave.
- Employees are required to give 30-day notice, where practical.

Family-Care Benefits

The growing emphasis on family issues is important in many healthcare organizations and for many workers. Many healthcare employers have a large female workforce, so adoption benefits, childcare programs, and elder programs are critical benefits for recruitment and retention purposes. Although studies indicate that males are becoming more involved in childcare responsibilities, a significant part of childcare responsibilities still rests on the shoulders of female employees. If healthcare employers wish to be competitive for skilled female employees, they must include these programs in their benefits offerings.

Adoption Benefits   As noted, healthcare employers provide maternity and paternity benefits to employees when they or their spouses give birth to children. In comparison to those giving birth, a relatively small number of employees adopt children, but in the interest of fairness, a growing number of organizations provide benefits for employees who adopt children.

ETHICAL PRACTICES AND COMPLIANCE

Since the passage of the FMLA, several factors have become apparent. First, a significant percentage of employees have been taking family and medical leave, and research indicates women and employees in the 25–34 age group take more family and medical leave, primarily related to childbirth.

Percentages of Employees Taking Family or Medical Leave

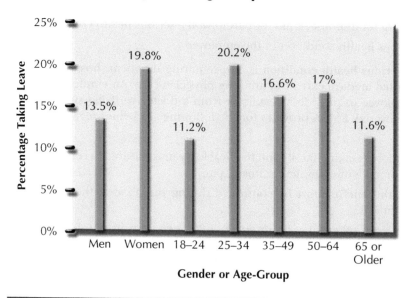

Source: Adapted from Jane Wald Fogel, "Family and Medical Leave," *Monthly Labor Review,* September 2001, 17–23; and U.S. Bureau of Labor Statistics, *http://www.bls.gov.*

Second, many employers have not paid enough attention to the law. Some employers are denying leaves or failing to reinstate workers after leaves are completed. Consequently, numerous lawsuits have resulted, many of which are lost by employers. Many employers' problems with the FMLA occur because of the variety of circumstances in which employees may request and use family leave. Often, employers have difficulty interpreting when and how the provisions are to be applied.[17] It took a U.S. Supreme Court decision in *Ragsdale v. Wolverine Worldwide* to clarify the communication requirements that employers have regarding granting FMLA leaves to employees.[18]

Third, employers are not required to pay employees for leave taken under the FMLA. However, some states have passed or are considering passing laws requiring employers to provide *paid family leave.* As an example, California law provides workers as much as 55 percent of their pay up to a weekly maximum, for leaves as long as six weeks. Finally, one especially difficult challenge for healthcare employers has been covering the workload for employees on family leave. This difficulty is compounded because the law requires that workers on these leaves must be offered similar jobs at similar levels of pay when they return to work. Balancing work demands for many different employees and their family and medical situations has placed significant demands on HR professionals to ensure compliance with FMLA provisions.

Child Care   Balancing work and family responsibilities is a major challenge for many healthcare workers. Whether single parents or dual-career couples, these employees often experience difficulty in obtaining high-quality, affordable child-care. Healthcare employers are addressing the child-care issue in several ways from providing on-site day-care facilities to having referral services to aid parents in locating competent, affordable child-care providers.

Elder Care   Another family-related issue of growing importance is caring for elderly relatives. Various organizations have surveyed their employees and found that as many as 30 percent of them have had to miss work to care for an aging relative. The responsibilities associated with caring for elderly family members have resulted in reduced work performance, increased absenteeism, and more personal stress for the affected employees.

Benefits for Domestic Partners and Spousal Equivalents

As lifestyles change in the United States, employees who are not married but have close personal relationships with others are confronting healthcare employers with requests for benefits. The terminology often used to refer to individuals with such living arrangements is *domestic partners* or *spousal equivalents.*

The argument made by these employees is that if an employer provides benefits for the spouses of married employees, then benefits should be provided for employees without spouses but with alternative lifestyles and relationships. This view is reinforced by: (1) data showing that a significant percentage of heterosexual couples live together before or instead of formally marrying; and (2) the fact that more gays and lesbians are being open about their lifestyles.

The proportion of couples fitting the "traditional" definition of a family, including husband, wife, and children, is only 25 percent today. The number of Americans living in unmarried-partner households is growing much more rapidly than those living in married households. Several studies have shown that employers who offer this coverage may experience an increase in enrollment in the 1 percent to 2 percent range. If coverage is offered to opposite-sex couples, enrollment rates will be closer to 2 percent. About 40 percent of Fortune 500 companies surveyed now offer such benefits, and two-thirds of the employers who offer the benefits cover both same- and opposite-sex couples who are not married.[19]

Decisions to extend benefits to domestic partners have come under attacks from certain religious leaders opposed to homosexual lifestyles. However, it must be noted that most employees using the domestic partner benefits are of the opposite sex and are involved in heterosexual relationships.

Time Off Benefits

Healthcare employers give employees paid time off under a variety of circumstances. Paid lunch breaks and rest periods, holidays, and vacations are common. But leaves are given for a number of other purposes as well. Time off benefits represent an estimated 5 percent to 13 percent of total compensation. Typical time off benefits include *holiday pay, vacation pay,* and *leaves of absence.*

Medical and Sick Leave   Employers grant **leaves of absence,** taken as time off with or without pay, for a variety of reasons. Medical and sick leave and paid time off programs are closely related. Many employers allow employees to miss a limited number of days because of illness without losing pay. Some employers allow employees to accumulate unused sick leave, which may be used in case of catastrophic illnesses. Others pay employees for unused sick leave. Some organizations have shifted emphasis to reward people who do not use sick leave by giving them **well pay**—extra pay for not taking sick leave.

Paid Time Off (PTO) and Extended Illness Banks (EIB)   Many healthcare employers have made use of the **paid time off (PTO) plan** and **extended illness banks (EIB).** PTO combines short-term sick/personal leave, vacations, and holidays, or some combination, into a total number of hours or days that employees can take off with pay.[20] EIB programs allow employees to accrue time to be used for longer-term illness or health-related care that does not result in a disability, such as maternity care. One healthcare organization discovered that when it stopped designating a specific number of sick-leave days and a PTO plan was implemented, absenteeism dropped, time off was scheduled better, and employee acceptance of the leave policy improved. An example of PTO and EIB accrual is depicted in Figure 13-4.

FIGURE 13-4   Paid Time-Off and Extended Illness Bank Accrual

	YEARS OF SERVICE	ANNUAL ACCRUAL FOR FULL-TIME EMPLOYEE # HOURS		
		PTO	EIB	TOTAL
Positions with 2 week (10 day) vacation allowances	1–5	176	56	232
Positions with 3 week (15 day) vacation allowances	5–12	216	56	272
Positions with 4 week (20 day) vacation allowances	20+	256	56	312

Other Leaves   Other types of leaves are given for a variety of purposes. Some, such as *military leave, election leave,* and *jury leave,* are required by various state and federal laws. Employers commonly pay the difference between the employee's regular pay and the military, election, or jury pay. Some firms grant employees military time off and give them regular pay while the employees also receive military pay. Federal law prohibits taking discriminatory action against military reservists by requiring them to take vacation time to attend summer camp or other training sessions. However, the leave request must be reasonable and truly required by the military.

   Funeral or bereavement leave is another common leave offered to healthcare employees. A leave of up to three days for the death of immediate family members is usually given, as specified in many employers' policy manuals and employee handbooks. Some policies also give unpaid time off for the death of more distant relatives or friends.

BENEFITS ADMINISTRATION

Employees generally do not know much about the values and costs associated with the benefits they receive from employers. Yet benefits communication and benefits satisfaction are linked.

Benefits Communication

Many employers have instituted special benefits communication systems to inform employees about the value of the benefits they provide. The use of organizational Web sites and intranets are excellent benefits communication methods.

Benefits Statements   Some healthcare employers also give each employee an annual *personal statement of benefits* that translates benefits into dollar amounts. Federal regulations under ERISA require that employees receive an annual pension-reporting statement, which also can be included in the personal statements. By having a personalized statement, each employee can see how much his or her own benefits are worth. Employers hope that by educating employees about benefit costs, they can manage expenditures better and can give employees a better appreciation for the employers' payments.

Human Resources Information System (HRIS) and Benefits Communication
The advent of HRIS options linked to intranets provides additional links to communicate benefits to employees. Employee self-service for benefit administration allows employees to obtain benefits information online. Utilizing their work or home computers and other information technology allows employees to change their benefits choices, track their benefits balances, and submit questions to HR staff members and external benefits providers.

Flexible Benefits

A **flexible benefits plan,** sometimes called a *flex* or *cafeteria* plan, allows employees to select the benefits they prefer from groups of benefits established by the employer. By making a variety of benefits selections available, the organization allows each employee to select an individual combination of benefits within some overall limits. As a result of the changing composition of the workforce, flexible benefits plans have grown in popularity.

Flexible Spending Accounts   Under current tax laws (Section 125 of the IRS Code), employees can divert some income before taxes into accounts to fund certain benefits. These **flexible spending accounts** allow employees to contribute pretax dollars to buy additional benefits.

The funds in the account can be used to pay for any of the following: (1) health care expenses, including offsetting deductibles, purchasing nonprescribed medications, such as aspirin, (2) life insurance, (3) disability insurance, and (4) dependent-care benefits. Flexible spending accounts have grown in popularity as more flexible benefits plans have been adopted by more healthcare employers.

Benefits in the Future

Employees' needs are changing. Those changes, along with the IRS code, have made benefits increasingly more complex. As a result, benefit functions are among the most outsourced in HR. Pension plans, health plan administration, or COBRA tracking are all targets for benefit outsourcing, as are benefits administration, service, financial reporting and accounting, and compliance and reporting.

Many employees also have access to Internet-based benefits support systems. For instance, use of the Internet allows employees in a growing number of organizations to check their retirement fund balances and move funds among various investment options.

VARIABLE PAY: INCENTIVES FOR PERFORMANCE

Pay and benefits make up two components of compensation. The third component for many healthcare workers is **variable pay,** which is compensation that is linked to individual, team, and organizational performance. Traditionally known as *incentives,* variable pay plans attempt to provide tangible rewards to employees for performance beyond normal expectations.[21] Several types of variable pay can be used for individuals, groups, and organizations.

Types of Variable Pay

Individual incentives are given to reward the effort and performance of individuals. The most common means of providing healthcare employees variable pay are bonuses. Others include special recognition rewards, time off, and gift certificates.

When an organization rewards an entire work group or ***team*** for its performance, cooperation among the members usually increases. However, competition among different teams for rewards can lead to decline in overall performance under certain circumstances. The most common team or group incentives are *gainsharing plans,* where employee teams that meet certain goals share in the gains measured against performance targets. Often, gainsharing programs focus on quality improvement, cost reduction, and other measurable results.

Organizational incentives reward employees based on the performance results of the entire organization. This approach assumes that all employees working together can generate greater organizational results that lead to better financial performance. These programs often share some of the organization's financial gains with employees through payments calculated as a percentage of each employee's base pay. Also, organizational incentives may be given as a lump-sum amount to all employees, or different amounts may be given to different levels of employees throughout the organization. For healthcare senior managers and executives, variable pay plans often are established to provide deferred compensation that minimizes the tax liabilities of the recipients. Figure 13-5 shows some of the programs under each type of incentive or variable pay plan.

Most healthcare employers adopt variable pay incentives in order to link individual performance to organizational goals and reward superior performance. Other goals might include improving productivity or increasing employee retention. Variable pay plans can be considered successful if they meet the goals the organization had for them when they were initiated.

The concept of rewarding healthcare workers on an incentive basis is relatively new. The great majority of the acute care hospitals in the United States are run as not-for-profits. The fact that they are a charity is an important component of their mission. One of the direct impacts of hospitals operating with a charitable mission is that paying employees incentive compensation was thought to be counter to that mission. In other segments of the healthcare industry, especially

FIGURE 13-5   Types of Variable Pay Plans in Healthcare

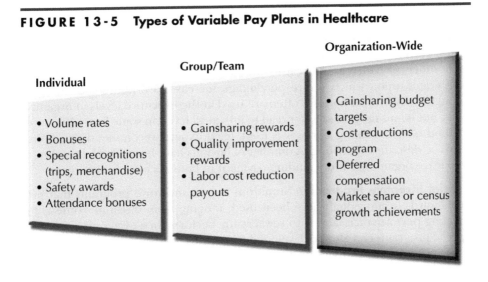

Individual
- Volume rates
- Bonuses
- Special recognitions (trips, merchandise)
- Safety awards
- Attendance bonuses

Group/Team
- Gainsharing rewards
- Quality improvement rewards
- Labor cost reduction payouts

Organization-Wide
- Gainsharing budget targets
- Cost reductions program
- Deferred compensation
- Market share or census growth achievements

those that operate as for-profit organizations such as physician and medical clinics, there has been a greater use of incentive compensation programs. With the current shortage of healthcare workers, healthcare organizations of all types must increase their ability to link rewards to performance, as well as utilize incentives to attract and retain competent employees.

Effective Variable Pay Plans

Variable pay systems should be tied to desired performance. Employees must see a direct relationship between their efforts and their financial rewards. Indeed, higher-performing organizations give out far more incentive pay to their top performers than do lower-performing companies.

Because people tend to produce what is measured and rewarded, healthcare organizations must make sure that what is being rewarded ties to meeting organizational objectives. Use of multiple measures helps assure that various performance dimensions are not omitted. For example, a hospital's patient scheduling department sets incentives for its employees to increase productivity by lowering their time spent per call. That reduction may occur, but customer service might drop as the schedulers rush callers to reduce talk time. Therefore, the department should consider both talk time and customer satisfaction survey results.

Indeed, linking pay to performance in a healthcare setting might not always be appropriate. For instance, if the output cannot be objectively measured, management may not be able to correctly reward the higher performers with more pay. Managers might not even be able to accurately identify the higher performers. Under those circumstances, individual variable pay is inappropriate.

Individual Incentives

As noted earlier, individual incentive systems try to relate individual effort to pay.

Bonuses   Individual employees may receive additional compensation payments in the form of a **bonus,** which is a one-time payment that does not become part of the employee's base pay. Generally, bonuses are less costly to the employer than other pay increases because they do not become part of employees' base wages, upon which future percentage increases are figured. Growing in popularity, individual bonuses often are used at the executive levels in organizations, but bonus usage also has spread to jobs at all levels in some firms. Whatever method of determining bonuses is used, legal experts recommend that bonus plans be described in writing. A number of lawsuits have been filed by employees who leave organizations demanding payment of bonuses promised to them.

Special Incentive Programs   Numerous special incentive programs that provide awards to individuals have been used, ranging from one-time contests for meeting performance targets to rewards for performance over time. Although special programs can also be developed for groups and for entire organizations, these programs often focus on rewarding specific high-performing individuals. Some hospitals and medical centers have awarded bonuses to all employees after successful JCAHO reviews. Special incentives include special awards, recognition awards, and service awards.

Group/Team-Based Variable Pay

A group of employees is not necessarily a "team," but either group or team work can be the basis for variable compensation. The use of work teams in organizations has implications for compensation of the teams and their members. Interestingly, although the use of teams has increased substantially in the past few years, the question of how to equitably compensate the individuals who compose the team remains a significant challenge. As Figure 13-6 notes, organizations establish group or team variable pay plans for a number of reasons.

Distributing Team Incentives   Several decisions about methods of distributing and allocating team rewards must be made. The two primary approaches for distributing team rewards are as follows:

1. *Same amounts of reward for each team member*—In this approach, all team members receive the same payout, regardless of job levels, current pay, or seniority.
2. *Different amounts of rewards for each team member*—Using this approach, employers vary individual rewards based on such factors as contribution to team results, current pay, years of experience, and skill levels of jobs performed.

Generally, more organizations use the first approach as an addition to different levels of individual pay. This method is used to reward team performance by making the team incentive equal, while still recognizing that individual pay differences exist and are important to many employees.

Problems with Team-Based Incentives   The difference between rewarding team members *equally* or *equitably* triggers many of the problems associated with team-based incentives. Rewards distributed equally in amount to all team

---

FIGURE 13-6   Why Organizations Establish Team Variable Pay Plans

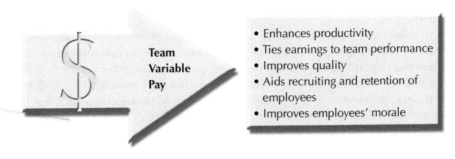

Team Variable Pay

- Enhances productivity
- Ties earnings to team performance
- Improves quality
- Aids recruiting and retention of employees
- Improves employees' morale

members may be perceived as "unfair" by employees who work harder, have more capabilities, or perform more difficult jobs. This problem is compounded when a poorly performing individual negatively influences the team results. Also, employees working in teams have shown a relatively low level of satisfaction with rewards that are the same for all, rather than having rewards based on performance, which often may be viewed more equitably.

Successful Team Incentives The unique nature of the team and its members figures prominently in the success of establishing team-based rewards. The employer must consider the history of the group and its past performance. Use of incentives generally has proven to be more successful where groups have been used in the past and where those groups have performed well.

Another consideration for the success of team-based incentives is the size of the team. If a team becomes too large, employees may feel their individual efforts will have little or no effect on the total performance of the group and the resulting rewards. Team-based incentive plans may encourage teamwork in small groups where interdependence is high. Therefore, in those groups the use of team-based performance measures is recommended.

Group/team-based reward systems use various ways of compensating individuals. The components include individual wages and salaries in addition to team-based rewards. Most team-based organizations continue to pay individuals based either on the jobs performed or their competencies and capabilities. The two most frequently used types of group/team incentives situations are work team results and gainsharing.

Organizational Incentives

An organizational incentive system compensates all employees in the organization based on how well the organization as a whole performs during the year. The basic concept behind organizational incentive plans is to produce better results by rewarding cooperation throughout the organization. To be effective, an organizational incentive program should include everyone from nonexempt employees to managers and executives. As an example, a large dental clinic developed an organizational incentive plan based on patient satisfaction. It used aggregated information from its patient surveys to determine a base level of acceptable patient satisfaction scores and then set goals to increase patient satisfaction. Upon attainment of the goals, the clinic awarded *all* employees a significant year-end cash bonus.

The results of variable pay plans, like those in other areas of HR, should be measured to determine the success of the programs. Different measures of success can be used, depending on the nature of the plan and the goals set for it.[22] Regardless of the plan, the critical decision is to gather and evaluate data to determine if the expenditures on it are justified by increased performance and results. If the measures show positive analyses, then the plan is truly pay-for-performance in nature.

Successes and Failures of Variable Pay Plans

Even though variable pay has grown in popularity, some attempts to implement it have succeeded and others have not. Incentives *do* work, but they are not a panacea because their success depends on the circumstances.

The positive view that many employers have for variable pay is not shared universally by all employees. If individuals see incentives as desirable, they are more likely to put forth the extra effort to attain the performance objectives that trigger the incentive payouts. As one indicator, a survey of employees found that only 29 percent believe that they are rewarded when doing a good job. Discouragingly for firms with incentive plans, approximately the same low percentage of employees indicated that they were motivated by their employers' incentive plans.[23] One problem is that many employees prefer that performance rewards increase their base pay, rather than be given as a one-time, lump-sum payment. Further, many employees prefer individual rewards to group/team or organizational incentives.

Providing variable pay plans that are successful can be complex and requires significant, continuing efforts. Some suggestions that appear to contribute to successful incentive plans are as follows:

- Develop clear, understandable plans that are continually communicated.
- Use realistic performance measures.
- Keep the plans current and linked to organizational objectives.
- Clearly link performance results to payouts that truly recognize performance differences.

CASE

Regional Hospital, a 400-bed community hospital, was struggling with recruitment and retention issues. These issues were occurring in spite of area labor statistics that indicated that there was a sufficient supply of skilled healthcare workers to meet their needs.

Regional's HR director undertook a comprehensive analysis of the recruitment and retention issues with the support of the board and senior management of the hospital. The HR director utilized information from a recent employee satisfaction survey and exit interviews. From those sources she learned the following:

- Current employees believed that Regional's benefit program was not com-

petitive in comparison to other hospitals and companies in the area.

- For the employees who voluntarily resigned from Regional in the last 12 months, benefit issues were critical. They reported receiving employment offers that included: lower healthcare insurance premiums; employer paid dental insurance; higher accruals on paid time off; and sign-on bonuses.

- Regional's healthcare competitors were aware of Regional's less-competitive benefits package and would aggressively recruit Regional employees, noting the differences when interviewing Regional employees.

Questions

1. Given the findings from the HR director, what additional benefits plans should be considered by Regional Hospital?

2. What would be the advantages and disadvantages to increasing the competitiveness of the benefits plan at Regional Hospital?

END NOTES

1. Adapted from Glen Huston, Duane Olson, and Pat Wiley, "Addressing Health Care Economics with Employees," *Employee Benefit News* (September 15, 2004), 18–21; and Randall K. Abbott and Arlene Weissman, "The Case for Consumerism in Health Care," *Journal of Compensation and Benefits* (March/April 2005), 30–34.

2. Joseph J. Martocchio, *Employee Benefits: A Primer for Human Resources Professionals* (New York: McGraw Hill/Irwin, 2003), Chapter 1.

3. "Employee costs for Employee Compensation" (December 2004), U.S. Department of Labor: Bureau of Labor Statistics: News (March 16, 2005), 1–26.

4. Fay Hansen, "The Cutting Edge of Benefit Cost Control," *Workforce* (March 2003), 36–42.

5. For more information regarding Social Security Taxes, also called payroll taxes, collected under the Federal Insurance Contributions Act, see *http://www.ssa.gov/mystatement/fica.htm.*

6. U.S. Bureau of Labor Statistics, *http://www.bls.gov.*

7. "Study: Workers' Comp Costs Rise Faster Than Payments," *Safety & Health* (September 2005), 12.

8 Peter Hoonakker, Todd Loushine, Pascale Carayon, James Kallman, Andrew Kapp, and Michael J. Smith, "The Effect of Safety Initiatives on Safety Performance: A Longitudinal Study," *Applied Ergonomics* (July 2005), 461–469.

9. Ruth Helman, Mathew Greenwald, Dallas Salisbury, Varinz Paladino, and Craig Copeland, "Encouraging Workers to Save: The 2005 Retirement Confidence Survey," *EBRI Issue Brief* (April 2005), 1–29.

10. George B. Kozol, "Defined-Benefit Plans Emerge as Better Choice for Held Businesses," *Journal of Financial Service Professionals* (March 2003), 41–48.

11. "Retirement Planning Back on Employee's Agenda, Following 3 Volatile Years," *Insurance Advocate* (November 10, 2003), 34, 40.

12. "Opinions Mixed on the Future of Cash-Balance Plans," *Workforce Management* (August 2005), 51–52.

13. See *http://www.uschamber.com* or *http://www.benefitstudy.com* for more information.

14. Bill Leonard, "Huge Increase Forecast for Consumer-Directed Health Plans," *HR News* (March 19, 2004).

15. A review of the provisions of each type is available by Haneefa T. Saleem, "Health spending Accounts," *Compensation and Working Conditions Online* (December 19, 2003), *http://www.bls.gov.*

16. Jay Greene, "Assessing the Health Savings Option," *HR Magazine* (April 2004), 103–108; and Jay Garriss, "Forging an Ideal HRA," *Workspan* (May 2004), 18–25.

17. Gregory M. Davis, "The Family and Medical Leave Act: 10 Years Later," *SHRM Legal Report* (July/August 2003), 1–8.

18. *Ragsdale v. Wolverine Worldwide*, 122 S. Ct. 1155 (2002).

19. Todd Henneman, "Benefits for Gay Partners More Common," *Workforce Management* (July 2005), 24; and Robin Wilson, "Pitts Bitter Battle Over Benefits," *Chronicle of Higher Education* (June 4, 2004), A8–A10.

20. Gretchen Weber, "Lost Time: Vacation Days Go Unused Despite More Liberal Time Off Policies," *Workforce Management* (December 2004), 66–67.

21. Jessica Smilko and Kathy Van Neck, "Rewarding Excellence Through Variable Pay," *Benefits Quarterly* (Third Quarter 2004), 21–25.

22. Ravin Jesuthasan, "Business Performance Management: Improving Return on Rewards Investments," *WorldatWork Journal* (Fourth Quarter 2003), 55–64.

23. Tom Wilson and Harold N. Altmansberg, "Taking Variable Pay to a New Level," *Workspan* (December 2003), 44–47.

Safety, Health, and Security in Healthcare Organizations

Learning Objectives

After you have read this chapter, you should be able to:

- Explain the nature of safety, health, and security in the healthcare workplace.
- Identify the various aspects of Occupational Safety & Health Administration (OSHA) compliance.
- Define the components of an effective ergonomics program.
- Discuss health issues in the healthcare workplace.
- Understand the importance of dealing with workplace violence.

Healthcare HR Insights

The importance of disaster planning and preparation for healthcare organizations was emphatically made clear when Hurricane Katrina struck the U.S. Gulf Coast in September of 2005. Dramatic events were widely depicted by the news media at the two largest health organizations in New Orleans, the 650-bed Charity Hospital and Tulane University Medical Center. When Katrina struck, Charity Hospital had 250 patients and Tulane University Medical Center had 122. Both organizations had taken steps to prepare for the crisis, most importantly by calling in healthcare providers, medical students, and technicians who had volunteered to staff the hospitals in order to save lives at significant personal risk.

Clearly, no one could have predicted the events immediately following Katrina's strike. The streets around the two hospitals were flooded, up to the first floors, cutting off vehicle access. This meant sick and injured patients couldn't get to the hospitals for care and that the hospitals' staffs and their patients were virtually stranded. The only way to leave was by relief helicopter flights off of Tulane's rooftop heliport. Unfortunately, Charity did not have a heliport on its roof. Additionally, communication systems, water lines, and power were cut off. Without access by street or air, Charity Hospital's food and water all but ran out. Ultimately, rescue did come for the survivors—both hospital employees and the remaining patients.[1] The toll that was exacted was enormous. Lives were lost, the damage to the two facilities will require millions of dollars to repair, and the organizations and their employees will be never be same.

Katrina's devastation has been determined to be one of the United States' worst natural disasters. For the healthcare system, many lessons were learned at a very high price. Healthcare organizational policies, protocols and systems involving patient evacuations, staffing for a crisis, and emergency systems for power, water, and food must be reevaluated and improved. The communications during a crisis between health providers and rescue responders from the local, state, and federal governments must be improved. Finally, healthcare organizations must plan and prepare for the worst-case scenarios. As Charity Hospital and Tulane University Medical Center experienced, major disasters can happen.[2]

Most healthcare workplaces offer a unique set of safety, health, and security challenges. Not only are there the usual workplace safety, health, and security issues to contend with, but there is also the issue of protecting the patients, residents, and clients that are cared for in the workplace. Protecting both healthcare workers and the individuals they provide care for is a critical responsibility for the leaders of healthcare organizations.[3] Addressing safety, health, and security issues is a critical part of effective HR management.

NATURE OF SAFETY, HEALTH, AND SECURITY

The terms *safety, health,* and *security* are closely related. Typically, **safety** refers to protecting the physical well-being of people. The main purpose of effective safety programs in organizations is to prevent work-related injuries and accidents. The broader and somewhat more nebulous term is **health,** which refers to a general state of physical, mental, and emotional well-being. A healthy person is one who is free of illness, injury, or mental and emotional problems that impair normal human activity. Health management practices in healthcare organizations strive to maintain the overall well-being of individuals.[4] The purpose of **security** is protecting employees, patients or residents, clients and visitors, and organizational facilities. With the growth of workplace violence, security at work has become an even greater concern for healthcare employers and employees alike.

Safety, Health, and Security Responsibilities

The general goal of providing a safe, secure, and healthy workplace is attained by operating managers and HR staff members working together. The primary safety, health, and security responsibilities in an organization usually fall on supervisors and managers. An HR manager or safety specialist can help coordinate health and safety programs, investigate accidents, produce safety program materials, and conduct formal safety training. However, department supervisors and managers play key roles in maintaining safe working conditions and a healthy workforce. For example, a dental clinic supervisor has several health and safety responsibilities: reminding employees to wear the appropriate protective equipment and clothing; checking on the cleanliness of the work area; observing employees for any alcohol, drug, or emotional problems that may affect their work behaviors; and conducting safety orientations and in-service training.

THE JOINT COMMISSION AND SAFETY, HEALTH, AND SECURITY

The Joint Commission on the Accreditation of Healthcare Organizations (JCAHO) has several topic areas that contain standards specifically relating to safety, health, and security. The primary topic areas are environment of care and surveillance, prevention, and control of infection.

Environment of Care (EC) Healthcare organizations must provide a safe, functional, and effective environment of care (EC) for patients, visitors, medical and nursing staffs, vendors, volunteers, students, and others. The standard requires the development of plans that address safety, security, hazardous materials and waste, emergency preparedness, life safety, medical equipment, and utility systems. These plans are designed to promote a safe, secure environment. With education and ongoing supervision, staff members implement each phase of the plans. Figure 14-1 shows the components of an environment of care plan.

FIGURE 14-1   Components of the Environment of Care Plan

Surveillance, Prevention, and Control of Infection (IC)

One significant element of concern not covered in the seven plan areas addressed in the EC standards is infection control. All staff in healthcare organizations have some infection control (IC) responsibilities and must competently perform their assigned roles. JCAHO has a set of standards that specifically addresses the protection of patients, staff, and visitors, and focuses on identifying organizational infection risks and taking the necessary risk-reduction steps. As an example, screening staff for tuberculosis, providing hepatitis B vaccinations, and implementing ongoing education regarding the importance of hand washing are risk-reduction activities.

The JCAHO and Emergency Preparedness

The EC standards for the JCAHO require member hospitals to conduct emergency preparedness drills regularly. The HR management implications of emergency preparedness are very significant. As proven by the events of September 11, 2001, and more recently the hurricane Katrina disaster, the importance of having competent, well-trained healthcare workers who have the ability and skills to provide care in times of disaster has increased in importance.

Healthcare HR professionals, along with healthcare managers and safety professionals, play key roles in preparing for disaster situations. Given the fact that healthcare organizations are both employers and care providers, disaster preparation is important for both the management of internal disasters, such as fires and hazardous chemical leaks or spills, and dealing with the patient care needs created by external disasters, such as a plane or train accidents. In both instances, healthcare workers are required to perform in extraordinary ways. Their personal safety maybe at risk or they may have to deal with the patient care needs of a high volume of critically injured or exposed patients. The American Hospital Association has recommended the following checklist in preparing for a disaster. Healthcare organizations should:

- Focus efforts on a general "all hazards" plan that provides an adaptable framework for any crisis situation.
- Upgrade their disaster plans to include components for mass casualty terrorism, including chemical or biological incidents.
- Be integrated with the emergency response agencies in the local community.
- Have a plan in place to support the families of staff members. In order for caregivers to remain at their jobs, they need assurance that their families and loved ones are being cared for.
- Ensure that clinical and medical staff report unexpected illness patterns to the public health department and, if appropriate, the Centers for Disease Control and Prevention.

Further, the American Medical Association has developed training courses for MDs and other healthcare professionals on emergency response for mass causality events. These courses are designed to standardize emergency response nationwide, regardless of the nature of the disaster. The curriculum includes information on recognizing environmental hazards, emergency management, medical decontamination, and mitigating stress on healthcare workers.[5]

LEGAL REQUIREMENTS FOR SAFETY AND HEALTH

Healthcare employers must comply with a variety of federal and state laws as part of their efforts when developing and maintaining healthy, safe, and secure workforces and working environments. A look at some major legal areas follows.

Workers' Compensation

Under state workers' compensation laws, employers contribute to an insurance fund to compensate employees for injuries received while on the job. Premiums paid reflect the accident rates at each employer; those employers with higher incident rates are assessed higher premiums. Also, these laws usually provide payments to injured workers for wage replacements, dependent on the amount of lost time and wage levels. Workers' compensation payments also cover costs for medical bills and for retraining if workers cannot go back to their current jobs.[6]

The Family and Medical Leave Act (FMLA) impacts workers' compensation as well. Injured employees may request additional leave time, even if it is unpaid. Some employers have policies that state that FMLA runs concurrently with any workers' compensation leave.[7]

Americans with Disabilities Act and Safety

The Americans with Disabilities Act (ADA) is another law affecting the health and safety policies and practices of healthcare employers. The ADA has created

HR challenges for some healthcare employers. For example, employers may try to return injured workers to "light-duty" work in order to reduce workers' compensation costs. Under the ADA, in making accommodations for injured employees through light-duty work, employers may be redefining what are really the essential functions of a job. Making such accommodations for injured employees for a period of time may also require an employer to make accommodations for job applicants with disabilities.

Safety and health record-keeping practices also have been affected by the following provision in the ADA:

> Information from all medical examinations and inquiries must be kept apart from general personnel files as a separate confidential medical record available only under limited conditions specified in the ADA.[8]

As interpreted by attorneys and HR practitioners, this provision requires that all medical-related information be maintained separately from all other confidential files. In healthcare environments where managers are also clinicians (MDs, RNs, etc.), the confidentiality of employee medical information is especially difficult to manage. Managers/clinicians are used to viewing and commenting on medical information and often find it difficult to draw the line for their employees, as required by ADA. Also, specific access restrictions and security procedures must be adopted for medical records of all types, including employee medical benefit claims and treatment records.

Occupational Safety and Health Act (OSHA)

The Occupational Safety and Health Act of 1970 was passed "to assure so far as possible every working man or woman in the Nation safe and healthful working conditions and to preserve our human resources." Every employer engaged in commerce who has one or more employees is covered by the act.[9] Employers in specific industries, such as coal mining, are covered under other health and safety acts. Federal, state, and local government employees also are covered by separate provisions or statutes.

The Occupational Health and Safety Act of 1970 established the Occupational Safety and Health Administration known as OSHA to administer its provisions. The act also established the National Institute of Occupational Safety and Health (NIOSH) as a supporting body to do research and develop standards. In addition, the Occupational Safety and Health Review Commission (OSHRC) has been established to review OSHA enforcement actions and address disputes between OSHA and employers who have been cited by OSHA inspectors.

OSHA Enforcement Standards

By making employers and employees more aware of safety and health considerations, OSHA has had a significant impact on organizations.[10] Figure 14-2 indicates the percentage of nonfatal workplace illnesses and injuries by industry. Note that healthcare and social assistance has a relatively high incidence of nonfatal injuries and illnesses.

FIGURE 14-2 **Nonfatal Workplace Total Recordable Injury and Illness Incidence Rates by Industry**

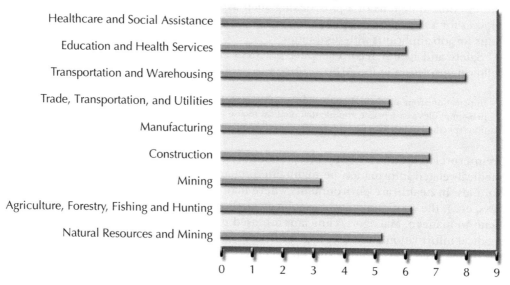

Incidence Rates per 100 Full-Time Workers

Source: Bureau of Labor Statistics, U.S. Department of Labor, December 2004.

OSHA has focused a great deal of attention on healthcare institutions with the establishment of the blood-borne pathogen standard, guidelines on the prevention of tuberculosis transmission, and training and consultation efforts in their targeting of the healthcare industry.[11]

A number of provisions have been recognized as key to OSHA compliance efforts by employers. Two of the most basic ones are important to all healthcare facilities:

1. *General duty*—The act requires that the employer has a "general duty" to provide safe and healthy working conditions, even in areas where OSHA standards have not been set. Healthcare employers who know or reasonably should know of unsafe or unhealthy conditions can be cited for violating the general duty clause. As an example, failing to remove snow or ice from an area that employees walk through could be a violation. The employer should know that the snow and ice could represent a slip hazard and should have the area rendered safe for employees.

2. *Notification and posters*—Employers are required to inform their employees of safety and health standards established by OSHA. Also, OSHA posters must be displayed in prominent locations in workplaces.

Personal Protective Equipment (PPE) One goal of OSHA has been to develop standards for personal protective equipment (PPE) and clothing. These

FIGURE 14-3 **Personal Protective Equipment Requirements**

POSITION	PPE
Dentist	Gowns, gloves, mask, protective eye wear
Operating Room Nurse	Gowns, gloves, mask, protective eye wear
Centrile Sterile Technician	Gowns, gloves, mask, protective eye wear
Autopsy Assistant	Mask, protective eye wear, impermeable (metal mesh) gloves and rubber aprons
Repair personnel	Safety glasses, hardhat, safety shoes
Cafeteria kitchen worker	Aprons, gloves, safety shoes

standards require healthcare employers to conduct an analysis of job hazards, provide adequate PPE to employees in those jobs, and train employees in the use of PPE items. If the work environment presents hazards or if employees might have work contact with hazardous chemicals and substances, then employers are required to provide PPE to employees.[12] Common PPE items required for various healthcare positions are indicated on Figure 14-3.

Hazard Communication OSHA has enforcement responsibilities for the federal Hazard Communication Standard, which requires users of hazardous chemicals to evaluate, classify, and label these substances. This is an especially important standard for healthcare facilities, where chemicals of all types represent significant potential hazards to employees. Healthcare employers also must make available information about hazardous substances to employees, their representatives, and health professionals. This information is contained in *material safety data sheets* (MSDS), which must be kept readily accessible to those who work with chemicals and other substances. The MSDS also indicate antidotes or actions to be taken should someone come in contact with the substances. The standard also requires organizations to have a written hazard communication plan that details how requirements for labels, MSDS, and employee training are met in the employer's facility. Unfortunately, many organizations fail to adequately comply with this part of this standard. This has resulted in the hazard communication standard being the most frequently violated standard across all industry sectors.

It should be noted that if there are numbers of workers for whom English is not their primary language, then the MSDS should be available in other languages. Workers must be trained annually on how to access, use, and read the MSDS information. Also, as new chemicals are introduced into the workplace, employees should receive MSDS guidelines and orientation prior to the use or application of the new chemicals.

As part of hazard communications, OSHA has established **lock-out/tag-out regulations.** To comply, locks and tags are provided to mechanics and trades persons for use when they make equipment inoperative for repair or adjustment, to prevent accidental start-up of defective machinery. These safety locks and tags must be removed only by the person whose name is printed on the tag or engraved on the lock.

FIGURE 14-4 **HIV Exposure by Occupation**

OCCUPATION	DOCUMENTED	POSSIBLE
Nurse	24 (42%)	35 (25%)
Laboratory worker, clinical	16 (28%)	17 (12%)
Physician, nonsurgical	6 (11%)	12 (9%)
Laboratory worker, nonclinical	3 (5%)	0
Housekeeping/maintenance	2 (4%)	13 (9%)
Technician, surgical	2 (4%)	2 (1%)
Embalmer/morgue technician	1 (2%)	2 (1%)
Health aide/attendant	1 (2%)	15 (11%)
Respiratory therapist	1 (2%)	2 (1%)
Technician, dialysis	1 (2%)	3 (2%)
Dental worker, dentist	0	6 (4%)
EMT paramedic	0	12 (9%)
Physician, surgical	0	6 (4%)
Technician/therapist, other	0	9 (7%)
Other HCW occupations	0	4 (3%)
Total	**57**	**138**

Source: U.S. Centers for Disease Control, *http://www.cdc.gov/*

Blood-Borne Pathogens The blood-borne pathogen standard resulted from a series of healthcare worker fatalities that were caused by workplace exposure to hepatitis B and HIV. The post-exposure assessment of the healthcare workplaces where the exposures occurred indicated that the workers were not provided with the necessary protective equipment or clothing, nor had they been given specific instruction on how to perform their jobs in a manner to protect them from exposure. As a result of these cases, OSHA issued a standard "to eliminate or minimize occupational exposure to hepatitis B virus (HBV), human immunodeficiency virus (HIV), and other bloodborne pathogens." This regulation is designed to protect employees who regularly are exposed to blood or body fluids. Physicians and other healthcare workers such as laboratory workers, nurses, and medical technicians are at greatest risk.[13] Figure 14-4 reviews details for the job categories of occupationally acquired HIV infection. Note that nurses are by far the most at-risk for exposure.

Ergonomics and OSHA

Ergonomics is the study and design of the work environment to address physiological and physical demands of individuals. In a work setting, ergonomic studies look at such factors as fatigue, lighting, tools, equipment layout, and placement of controls. Human factors engineering is a related field.

For a number of years, OSHA has been concerned about the large number of work-related injuries due to repetitive stress injuries, repetitive motion injuries, cumulative trauma disorders, carpal tunnel syndrome, and other ergonomic hazards in workplaces. **Cumulative trauma disorders (CTD)** occur when workers repetitively use the same muscles to perform tasks, resulting in muscular and skeletal injuries.

Carpal tunnel syndrome, one of the frequent cumulative trauma disorders, is an injury common to people who put their hands through repetitive motions. As an example, a pharmacist who must fill a significant number of liquid prescription medications may develop CTD from continually drawing back a syringe to measure out the appropriate volume for the prescription. The motion irritates the tendons in the "carpal tunnel" area of the wrist. As the tendons swell, they squeeze the medial nerve. The result is pain and numbness in the thumb, index finger, and middle finger. The hands of victims become clumsy and weak. Pain at night increases, and at advanced stages not even surgery can cure the problem. Sufferers of this trauma disorder eventually lose feeling in their hands if they do not receive timely treatment.

These problems are occurring in a variety of work settings. But healthcare office workers increasingly are experiencing CTD, primarily from extensive typing and data entry on computers and computer-related equipment.[14] Most recently, attention has focused on the application of ergonomic principles to the design of workstations where computer operators work with personal computers (PCs) and video display terminals (VDTs) for extended periods of time. OSHA has approached ergonomics concerns by adopting voluntary guidelines for specific problem industries and jobs, focusing on industries with serious ergonomic problems, and giving employers tools for identifying and controlling ergonomics hazards, including nursing homes.[15]

Successful Ergonomics Programs   There are several components of a successful ergonomics program. First, management must commit to reducing injuries caused by repetition and cumulative trauma, including providing financial and other resources to support the efforts. Involvement of employees is key to getting employee support. Other actions should include reviewing jobs where CTD problems could exist and ensuring that proper equipment, seating, lighting, and other engineering solutions are utilized. Also, supervisors and managers should be trained to observe signs of CTD and to know how to respond to employee complaints about musculoskeletal and repetitive motion problems. With the rising incidence of ergonomic issues in healthcare, it is important that healthcare employers establish an ergonomic program, no matter the size of the organization.

Work Assignments and OSHA

The rights of employees regarding certain work assignments have been addressed as part of OSHA regulations. Two prominent areas where work assignments and concerns about safety and health meet are described next.

Work Assignments and Reproductive Health   Related to unsafe work is the issue of assigning employees to work in areas where their ability to have children may be affected by exposure to chemical hazards, biomedical waste, or radiation.

Women who are able to bear children or who are pregnant have presented the primary concerns, but in some situations, the possibility that men might become sterile also has been a concern.

In a court case involving reproductive health, the Supreme Court held that an employer's policy of keeping women of childbearing capacity out of jobs that might involve lead exposure violated the Civil Rights Act and the Pregnancy Discrimination Act.[16] However, the duties of many healthcare occupations may pose a threat to a healthcare worker's ability to conceive, maintain pregnancy, or deliver a healthy baby.

Consistent with the Supreme Court ruling, healthcare organizations cannot bar workers from these occupations to protect the health of the fetus. However, healthcare employers need to protect themselves from liability from the effects of workplace exposure. Although there is no *absolute* protection from liability for employers, the following actions are suggested:

- Maintain a safe workplace for all by using the safest methods of working.
- Comply with all state and federal safety laws.
- Inform employees of any known risks.
- Document employee acceptance of any risks.

Refusing Unsafe Work Workers have refused to work when they considered the work unsafe. In many instances, that refusal has been found to be justified. Although such actions may be seen as insubordination by employers, in many cases regulatory bodies and court decisions have supported that insubordination. Based on several U.S. Supreme Court decisions, following are current legal conditions for refusing work because of safety concerns:

- The employee's fear is objectively reasonable.
- The employee has tried to have the dangerous condition corrected.
- Using normal procedures to solve the problem has not worked.

Record-Keeping Requirements

OSHA has established a standard national system for recording occupational injuries, accidents, and fatalities. Employers are generally required to maintain a detailed annual record of the various types of accidents for inspection by OSHA representatives and for submission to the agency. Employers that have had good safety records in previous years and that have fewer than 10 employees are not required to keep detailed records. However, many organizations must complete OSHA form 300, including the following:

- Firms having frequent hospitalizations, injuries, or illnesses
- Firms having work-related deaths
- Firms included in OSHA's annual labor statistics survey

No one knows how many workplace accidents go unreported. It may be many more than anyone suspects, despite the fact that OSHA has increased its surveillance of accident-reporting records. OSHA guidelines state that facilities whose accident record is below the national average rarely need inspecting.

Reporting Injuries and Illnesses   Four types of reportable injuries or illnesses have been defined by the Occupational Safety and Health Act of 1970:

1. *Injury- or Illness-Related Deaths*—These include death due to work-related injuries or illness.

2. *Lost-Time or Disability Injuries*—These include job-related injuries or disabling occurrences that cause an employee to miss his or her regularly scheduled work on the day following the accident.

3. *Medical-Care Injuries*—These injuries require treatment by a physician but do not cause an employee to miss a regularly scheduled work turn.

4. *Minor Injuries*—These injuries require first-aid treatment but do not cause an employee to miss the next regularly scheduled work turn.

OSHA Inspections

The Occupational Safety and Health Act provides for on-the-spot inspections by OSHA representatives, called compliance officers or inspectors. Under the original act, an employer could not refuse entry to an OSHA inspector, and the act prohibited a compliance officer from notifying an organization before an inspection. Instead of allowing an employer to "tidy up," this no-knock provision permitted inspection of normal operations. The U.S. Supreme Court ruled on the issue in the case of *Marshall v. Barlow's, Inc.* and rejected the government's arguments, holding that safety inspectors must produce a search warrant if an employer refuses to allow an inspector into the facility voluntarily. However, the Court ruled that an inspector does not have to show probable cause to obtain a search warrant. Thus, a warrant can easily be obtained if a search is part of a general enforcement plan.[17]

As a practical issue, most healthcare employers find that cooperating with a request for an OSHA inspection is appropriate. A senior-level manager, HR professional, or an internal health and safety specialist should accompany OSHA inspectors as they conduct an on-site review of the health facility or organizational health and safety policies, procedures, and records.

Citations and Violations   Although OSHA inspectors can issue citations for violations of the provisions of the act, whether a citation is issued depends on the severity and extent of the problems, and on the employer's knowledge of them. In addition, depending on the nature and number of violations, penalties can be assessed against employers. The nature and extent of the penalties depend on the type and severity of the violations as determined by OSHA officials.

There are five types of violations, ranging from severe to minimal, including a special category for repeated violations:

1. *Imminent Danger*—When there is reasonable certainty that the condition will cause death or serious physical harm if it is not corrected immediately, an

imminent-danger citation is issued and a notice posted by an inspector. Imminent danger situations are handled on the highest-priority basis. If the condition is serious enough and the employer does not cooperate, a representative of OSHA may go to a federal judge and obtain an injunction to close the company until the condition is corrected. The absence of guard railings to prevent maintenance employees from falling off a roof into heavy machinery is one example.

2. *Serious*—When a condition could probably cause death or serious physical harm, and the employer should know of the condition, a serious violation citation is issued. Examples are the absence of appropriate labeling on a container of hazardous chemical.

3. *Other Than Serious*—Other than serious violations could have an impact on employees' health or safety but probably would not cause death or serious harm. Having loose ropes in a work area might be classified as an other-than-serious violation.

4. *De Minimis*—A *de minimis* condition is one that is not directly and immediately related to employees' safety or health. No citation is issued, but the condition is mentioned to the employer. Lack of doors on toilet stalls is a common example of a *de minimis* violation.

5. *Willful and Repeated*—Citations for willful and repeated violations are issued to employers who have been previously cited for violations. If an employer knows about a safety violation or has been warned of a violation and does not correct the problem, a second citation is issued. The penalty for a willful and repeated violation can be very high. If death results from an accident that involves such a safety violation, a jail term of six months can be imposed on responsible executives or managers.

Critique of OSHA Inspection Efforts OSHA has been criticized on several fronts. Because the agency has so many work sites to inspect, healthcare employers have only a relatively small chance of being inspected. Some suggest that many employers pay little attention to OSHA enforcement efforts for this reason. Labor unions and others have criticized OSHA and Congress for not providing enough inspectors. For instance, it is common to find that many of the work sites at which workers suffered severe injuries or deaths had not been inspected in the previous five years. Employers, especially smaller ones, continue to complain about the complexity of complying with OSHA standards, the costs associated with penalties, and the changes required to remedy problem areas.

SAFETY MANAGEMENT

Effective safety management requires an organizational commitment to safe working conditions.[18] But well-designed and managed safety programs can reduce accidents and the associated costs, such as workers' compensation and possible fines. Further, accidents and other safety concerns do decline as a result of an effective safety management program with a number of components.[19]

ETHICAL PRACTICES AND COMPLIANCE

Healthcare organizations should perform regular internal reviews of their Safety and Health Programs to ensure that they are in compliance with OSHA standards, and as importantly, that they are providing a work environment that contributes to and demonstrates concern for employee safety, health, and well-being, and that produces the economic benefits derived from a safe work environment and a healthy workforce.

Detailed below are some key questions to consider and then evaluate to determine where gaps might exist between what is and is not done at a healthcare organization and best practices in the industry.

1. Does the organization have a policy stating its philosophy on employee safety, health, and wellness?
2. Does one position within the organization oversee and coordinate safety and health activities?
3. Are all aspects of OSHA regulations adhered to?
4. Does the organization have an Employee Assistance Program (EAP)?
5. Does the organization have a formal accident prevention program?
6. Does the organization measure the cost/benefit ratio of safety programs?
7. Does the organization engage in workplace evacuation drills?

The Organization and Safety

At the heart of safety management is an organizational commitment to a comprehensive safety effort. This effort should be coordinated from the top level of management to include all members of the organization.[20] It also should be reflected in managerial actions. There are three different approaches that employers such as these use in managing safety. Figure 14-5 shows the organizational, engineering, and individual approaches and their components. Successful programs may use all three in dealing with safety issues.

Safety and Engineering

Healthcare employers can prevent some accidents by designing processes, using equipment, and maintaining work areas so that workers who perform potentially dangerous jobs cannot injure themselves and others. Providing safety equipment, ensuring appropriate maintenance and repair, installing emergency switches and safety rails, keeping aisles clear, and maintaining adequate ventilation, lighting, heating, and air conditioning can all help make work environments safer.

FIGURE 14-5   Approaches to Effective Safety Management

Individual Considerations and Safety

Engineers approach safety from the perspective of redesigning the equipment, processes, or work area; industrial psychologists and human factors experts see safety differently. They are concerned with the proper match of individuals to jobs and emphasize employee training in safety methods, fatigue reduction, and health awareness. Experts have conducted numerous field studies with thousands of employees that looked at the "human factors" in accidents. The results show a definite relationship between emotional factors, such as stress, and accidents. Other studies point to the importance of individual differences, motivation, attitudes, and learning as key factors in controlling the human element in safety.

Attitudinal variables are among the individual factors that affect accident rates because more problems are caused by careless employees than by equipment or employer negligence. At one time, workers who were dissatisfied with their jobs were thought to have higher accident rates. However, this assumption has been questioned in recent years. Although employees' personalities, attitudes, and individual characteristics apparently have some influence on accidents, exact cause-and-effect relationships are difficult to establish.

Work schedules can be another cause for accidents. The relationship between work schedules and accidents can be explained as follows: Fatigue based on physical exertion sometimes exists in today's healthcare workplace. But boredom, which occurs when a person is required to do the same tasks for a long period of time, is rather common. As fatigue of this kind increases, motivation is reduced; along with decreased motivation, workers' attention wanders, and the likelihood of accidents increases. A particular area of concern in healthcare is *overtime* in work scheduling. Overtime work has been consistently related to accident or patient care incidents.[21] Further, the more overtime worked, the more severe accidents appeared to be. The healthcare industry has been especially concerned about the fatigue factor for employees who work 10 and 12 hour shifts, or who may be required to work double shifts. Consider the implications of an intensive care unit nurse that works a physically-demanding and emotionally-draining 10 hour shift being asked to stay on and work a double. The nurse's ability to render safe care could clearly be impacted.

Another area of concern is the relationship of accident rates to different shifts, particularly late-night shifts. Because there tend to be fewer supervisors and managers working the 11 P.M. to 7 A.M. shift, workers tend to receive less training and supervision. Both of these factors can lead to higher accident rates.

Safety Policies and Discipline

Designing safety policies and rules and disciplining violators are important components of safety efforts. Frequently reinforcing the need for safe behavior and supplying feedback on positive safety practices also are extremely effective in improving worker safety.[22] Such efforts must involve employees, supervisors, managers, safety specialists, and HR staff members.

HR and Safety Responsibilities

In a recent survey of HR generalists regarding their involvement in safety activities, most reported active involvement in safety activities. Workplace violence, workers' compensation, and accident investigations lead the list of areas of greatest involvement. The survey respondents also indicated that HR staffs in smaller organizations were more likely to be involved in safety activities than their counterparts in larger organizations. This difference was apparently due to the fact that larger organizations are more likely to have a separate safety department.[23]

Safety Committees

Employees frequently are involved in safety planning through safety committees, often composed of workers from a variety of levels and departments. A well-organized safety committee is a valuable tool to help organizations provide a safe workplace for employees and a broader base of support for safety initiatives.[24] A safety committee generally has regularly scheduled meetings, has specific responsibilities for conducting safety reviews, and makes recommendations for changes necessary to avoid future accidents. Usually, at least one member of the committee is from HR.

Care must be taken that managers do not compose a majority on a safety committee. Otherwise, the employer may be in violation of some provisions of the National Labor Relations Act (NLRA). That act prohibits employers from dominating a labor organization. Some safety committees have been ruled to be labor organizations because they deal with working conditions.

In 32 states, all but the smallest employers may be required to establish safety committees. From time to time, legislation has been introduced at the federal level to require joint management/employee safety committees. But as yet, no federal provisions have been enacted.

Safety Training and Communications

One way to encourage employee safety is to involve all employees at various times in safety training. It is frequently difficult to convince healthcare employees to focus on safety standards while performing their jobs. Often, employees think that safety measures are bothersome and unnecessary until an injury occurs. For example, it might be necessary for employees to wear safety glasses in a laboratory most of the time. But if the glasses are awkward, employees may resist using them, even when they know they should have eye protection. Also, some employees who may have worked without sustaining an injury without wearing the glasses might think this requirement is a nuisance. Because of such problems, safety training and communication efforts must address safety issues so that employees view safety as important, and they are motivated to follow safe work practices.

Employee Safety Motivation and Incentives

To encourage healthcare employees to work safely, many healthcare organizations have used safety contests and have given employees incentives for safe work behavior. As an example a community hospital in Wisconsin awards extra time off to the employees of departments that do not incur a loss-time injury during the calendar year. Unfortunately, there is a concern that in order to receive some incentives, employees and managers do not report accidents and injuries, so that they collect on the incentive rewards.[25] This concern about safety incentives was also raised by OSHA.

Inspections

It is not necessary to wait for an OSHA inspector to inspect the work area for safety hazards. Inspections may be done by a safety committee or by a safety coordinator. They should be done on a regular basis, because OSHA may inspect organizations with above-average lost workday rates more frequently. Additionally, given the parallel between JCAHO standards on the EC and OSHA standards, many healthcare organizations conduct mock surveys in advance of a JCAHO visit that are also useful for OSHA compliance. See this text's website: *http://flynn.swlearning.com* for an example of a healthcare workplace safety checklist.

Accident Investigation and Evaluation

Figure 14-6 depicts the steps in investigating an accident. When accidents occur, they should be investigated by the employer's safety committee or safety coordinator. In investigating the *scene* of an accident, it is important to determine the

FIGURE 14-6   Steps in Investigating an Accident

physical and environmental conditions that contributed to the accident. Poor lighting, poor ventilation, and wet floors are some possible contributors. Investigation at the scene should be done as soon as possible after an accident to ensure that the conditions under which the accident occurred have not changed significantly. One way to obtain an accurate view of the accident scene is with photographs or videotapes.

The second phase of the investigation is the *interview* of the injured employee, his or her supervisor, and any witnesses to the accident. The interviewer attempts to determine what happened and how the accident was caused. These interviews may also generate some suggestions on how to prevent similar accidents in the future. In the third phase, based on observations of the scene and interviews, investigators complete an *accident investigation report.* This report form provides the data required by OSHA.

Finally, *recommendations* should be made on how the accident could have been prevented, and what changes are needed to avoid similar accidents. Identifying why an accident occurred is useful, but taking steps to prevent similar accidents from occurring also is important.

Closely related to accident investigation is research to determine ways of preventing accidents. Employing safety professionals or having outside experts evaluate the safety of working conditions is useful. If many similar accidents seem to occur in an organizational unit, a safety education training program may be necessary to emphasize safe working practices. As an example, a nursing home reported a greater-than-average number of back injuries among employees who assisted the residents. Safety training on the proper way to lift was initiated to reduce the number of back injuries.

Organizations should *monitor* and *evaluate* their safety efforts. Just as organizational accounting records are audited, a firm's safety efforts should be audited periodically as well. Accident and injury statistics should be compared with previous accident patterns to identify any significant changes. This analysis should be designed to measure progress in safety management.

HEALTH

Employee health problems are varied—and somewhat inevitable. They can range from minor illnesses such as colds to serious illnesses related to the jobs performed. Some employees have emotional health problems; others have alcohol or drug problems. Some problems are chronic; others are transitory. But all can affect organizational operations and individual employee productivity.

Healthcare Workplace Health Issues

Healthcare employers face a variety of workplace issues. Previously in this chapter, cumulative trauma injuries, exposure to hazardous chemicals, and blood-borne pathogens have been discussed because OSHA has addressed these concerns through regulations or standards. But there are a number of other key health issues for healthcare workers, including substance abuse, emotional and mental problems, indoor air quality, latex allergies, inadvertent needle sticks, and slips and falls.

Substance Abuse   Substance abuse is defined as the use of illicit substances or the misuse of controlled substances, alcohol, or other drugs. There are millions of substance abusers in the general workforce, and they cost global employers billions of dollars annually. In the United States, chemical dependency affects an estimated 10 percent of the worker population. These workers are consistently late for work, are five times more likely to file a workers' compensation claim, are more likely to be absent for work, and have more on-the-job accidents.[26]

Healthcare workers are at an increased risk for developing chemical dependencies because they have easier access to controlled substances than does the general population. Also, healthcare workers experience unique stressors (e.g., regular exposure to death and individuals experiencing trauma or emotional suffering) that contribute to chemically-assisted coping. One study indicates that nurses are especially at risk, with 10 percent of nurses surveyed in the study indicating that they were addicted to at least one controlled substance. Figure 14-7 depicts the common signs of alcohol and drug abuse.

The Americans with Disabilities Act (ADA) affects how management can handle substance-abuse cases. Currently illegal drug users are specifically excluded from the definition of *disabled* under the act. However, those addicted to legal substances (alcohol, for example) and prescription drugs are considered disabled under the ADA. Also, recovering alcoholics are considered disabled under the ADA.

Pre-employment alcohol and drug testing is used by many healthcare employers. Testing is also done following an accident or for reasonable cause, or as part of a random testing program instituted by employers.

FIGURE 14-7   Common Signs of Substance Abuse

- Fatigue
- Slurred speech
- Flushed cheeks
- Difficulty walking
- Inconsistency
- Difficulty remembering details
- Argumentative behavior
- Missed deadlines

- Many unscheduled absenses (especially on Mondays and Fridays)
- Depression
- Irritability
- Emotionalism
- Overreacting
- Violence
- Frequently borrowing money

To encourage employees to seek help for their substance-abuse problems, a **firm-choice option** is usually recommended and has been endorsed legally. In this procedure, the employee is privately confronted by a supervisor or manager about unsatisfactory work-related behaviors. Then, in keeping with the disciplinary system, the employee is offered a choice between help and discipline. Treatment options and consequences of further unsatisfactory performance are clearly discussed, including what the employer will do. Confidentiality and follow-up are critical when employers use the firm-choice option.

As a profession, nursing has been very aggressive in managing workplace substance abuse issues. According to the American Nurses Associations (ANA) Code of Ethics, addicted nurses may have difficulty remaining accountable to themselves and others for their own actions or in assessing self-competence. It is the responsibility of management and coworkers to respond to questionable practices as an advocate for patients. The ANA suggests that an impaired nurse "receives assistance in regaining ability to function appropriately."[27]

Emotional/Mental Health Concerns   Many individuals today are facing work, family, and personal life pressures. These pressures are managed successfully by many people. But some individuals have difficulties handling these demands. Also, specific events, such as death of a spouse, divorce, or medical problems, can affect individuals who otherwise have been coping successfully with those pressures. As noted earlier, a variety of emotional/mental health issues arise at work that must be addressed by employers. It is important to note that emotional/ mental illnesses such as schizophrenia and depression are considered disabilities under the ADA. Therefore, employers should be cautious when using disciplinary policies if diagnosed employees have work-related problems.

Stress is one concern, when individuals cannot successfully handle the multiple demands they face. All people encounter stress, but it is when *stress overload* hits that work-related consequences can result. HR professionals, managers, and supervisors must be prepared to handle employee stress; otherwise, employees may burn out or exhibit various unhealthy behaviors, such as abusing alcohol, misusing prescription drugs, demonstrating outbursts of anger, or other symptoms. Healthcare employees are especially vulnerable to stress overload due to the nature and pace of their work. Beyond effects at communications and relieving some workload pressures, it is generally recommended that supervisors and managers contact the HR staff who may intervene and may refer the affected employees to outside resources through employee assistance programs.[28]

Depression is another common emotional/mental health concern. Estimates are that 20 percent of individuals in workplaces suffer from depression. One indicator of the extent of clinical depression is that the sales of prescription drugs such as Prozac and Zoloft covered by employee benefits plans have risen significantly in the past several years. The effects of depression are seen at all levels, from the nursing units and business offices to executive suites. Carried to the extreme, depression can result in employee suicide. That guilt and sorrow felt by those who worked with the dead individuals must be dealt with by HR staff, often aided by crisis counselors.[29] To deal with depression, it is recommended that HR professionals, managers, and supervisors be trained in recognizing the symptoms of depression and knowing what to do when symptoms are indicated in employees. Employees can be guided to employee assistance programs and aided with obtaining medical treatment.

Workplace Air Quality An increasing number of employees work in settings where air quality is a health issue.[30] One cause of poor air quality occurs in "sealed" buildings where windows cannot be opened when air flows are reduced to save energy and cut operating costs. Also, inadequate ventilation, as well as airborne contamination from carpets, molds, copy machines, adhesives, and fungi, can cause poor air quality and employee illnesses.

Latex Allergy For years, natural rubber latex allergies have been an employee concern. These rubber products, typically in the form of gloves, are used to protect employees from the spread of infection. Latex allergies were originally recognized in the 1970s but did not become a major concern until latex products began to gain wider use in response to the Center for Disease Control's 1987 recommendation that blood and body fluids should always be approached as if potentially infectious. In 1992, OSHA established the blood-borne pathogens standard requiring the use of barrier protection. Consequently, the use of latex gloves by healthcare workers increased dramatically.[31]

OSHA estimates that 6 percent to 17 percent of exposed healthcare workers are allergic to natural rubber latex. The allergic employee experiences a simple irritation reaction. Although uncomfortable, usually it is not a serious problem in itself. However, it can lead to more serious and detrimental allergic reactions, including serious health problems. Some argue that as more healthcare workers began to use latex gloves, the sheer increase in wearers statistically increased the number of people who might develop an allergy to latex.

Healthcare employers have attempted a number of actions to help allergic workers, including providing cotton glove liners for use with the latex glove, placing allergic workers in nonpatient-care positions, or by stocking latex-free carts on patient units.[32] As an example, a major health system uses vinyl gloves as the standard examination glove.

Inadvertent Needle Sticks Healthcare workers run the highest risk of disease transmission from injury by contaminated devises. Needles or syringes most frequently cause injury; about 20 percent of needle sticks fall into high-risk exposure to such blood-borne diseases as hepatitis B and C viruses and HIV. Estimates are that 500,000 needle stick injuries occur annually among healthcare workers in the United States. Nurses sustain the majority of these injuries, but other employees are also at risk, including physicians, nursing assistants, and environmental services personnel.

To address this concern, the Needle Stick Safety and Prevention Act (NSPA) was passed by Congress in November 2000. The NSPA mandated that OSHA revise the blood-borne pathogen standard to integrate the act's requirements. This act focuses attention on safer medical devises, such as needle-less medical devices for withdrawing fluids or administering medications and the incorporation of these devices in an organizational exposure control plan. The act also requires employers to solicit input from nonmanagerial healthcare workers regarding the identification, evaluation, and selection of safer medical devices.[33]

Slips and Falls   Slips and falls result in 15 percent of all accidental workplace deaths and 16 percent of accidents resulting in disability. Slips result in head or back injuries, lacerations, fractures, pulled muscles, and contusions, and cost employers billions of dollars annually.[34]

The healthcare workplace can offer its share of hazards, including wet floors, inclines, stairways, and cluttered passageways. Given the often-cluttered and busy nature of the healthcare workplace, protecting workers from slips and falls is a challenging task. Safety experts recommend the establishment of a comprehensive slip-prevention program focusing on risk assessment, good housekeeping, the use of slip-resistant flooring, and appropriate footwear. Employee awareness and safety training is also important.

Health Promotion

Healthcare employers who are concerned about maintaining a healthy workforce must move beyond simply providing healthy working conditions and emphasizes employee health and wellness in other ways. **Health promotion** is a supportive approach to facilitate, encourage, and help employees to enhance healthy actions and lifestyles. Going beyond just compliance with workplace safety and health regulations, organizations engage in health promotion by encouraging employees to make physiological, mental, and social choices that improve their health.

Health promotion efforts can range from providing information and enhancing employee awareness of health issues to creating an organizational culture supportive of employee health enhancements, as Figure 14-8 indicates. The first level is useful and may have some impact on individuals, but much is left to individual initiatives to follow through and make changes in actions and behaviors. Employers provide information on such topics as weight control, stress management, nutrition, exercise, and smoking cessation. Although such efforts may

FIGURE 14-8   Health Promotion Levels

LEVEL 1 Information and Awareness	LEVEL 2 Lifestyle Wellness	LEVEL 3 Health Emphasis
• Brochures and materials	• Wellness education program	• Benefits integrated with programs
• Health risk screenings	• Regular health classes	• Dedicated resources and facilities
• Health tests and measurements	• Employee assistance programs	• Continous health promotion
• Special events and classes	• Support groups	• Health education curriculum
	• Health incentives	

be beneficial for some employees, employers who wish to impact employees' health must offer second level efforts through more comprehensive programs and efforts that focus on the lifestyle "wellness" of employees.

Wellness Programs   Employers' desires to improve productivity, decrease absenteeism, and control health-care costs have come together in the wellness movement. **Wellness programs** are designed to maintain or improve employees' health before problems arise. Wellness programs encourage self-directed lifestyle changes.

There are a number of ways to assess the effectiveness of wellness programs. Participation rates by employees are one way. The participation rates vary by type of activity, but generally 20 percent to 40 percent of employees participate in the different activities in a wellness program. Although more participation would be beneficial, the programs have resulted in healthier lifestyles for more employees. Cost/benefit analyses tend to support the continuation of wellness programs as well.[35]

Employee Assistance Programs (EAPs)   One method that organizations are using as a broad-based response to health issues is the **employee assistance program (EAP),** which provides counseling and other help to employees having emotional, physical, or other personal problems. In such a program, an employer establishes a liaison with a social service counseling agency. Employees who have problems may then contact the agency, either voluntarily or by employer referral, for assistance with a broad range of problems. Counseling costs are paid for by the employer, either in total or up to a pre-established limit.

EAPs are attempts to help employees with a variety of problems. Generally, EAP counselors find that the most common employee issues dealt with are: (1) depression and anxiety, (2) marital and relationship problems, (3) legal difficulties, and (4) family and children concerns. Other areas that also are commonly addressed as part of an EAP include substance abuse, financial counseling, and career advice. Critical to employee usage of an EAP is preserving confidentiality. That is why employers outsource EAPs to trained professionals, who usually report only the numbers of employees and services provided, rather than details on individuals using the EAP.

The effectiveness of EAPs depends upon how well they are integrated and supported in the workplace. One study of EAPs found that such support results in five times more supervisory referrals of employees to EAPs, and three times the numbers of employees with substance abuse problems who receive assistance.[36]

Organizational Health Culture   A number of employers, both large and small, have recognized that an organizational culture that emphasizes and supports health efforts is beneficial. Common to these employers is an integrative, broad-based effort supported both financially and managerially. Development of policies and procedures supporting health efforts, establishing on-site exercise facilities, and consistently promoting health programs all contribute to creating a health promotion environment throughout the organization.

SECURITY

Traditionally, when healthcare employers have addressed worker health, safety, and security, they have been concerned about reducing workplace accidents, improving workers' safety practices, and reducing health hazards at work. However, over the past decade providing security for employees' patients, residents, or clients has grown in importance. Incidents of workplace violence occur regularly in hospitals, clinics, and nursing homes. The domestic problems of patients, residents, or clients and their family members can erupt in verbal or physical assaults. Healthcare workers can easily get caught in the middle of these issues or may be required to attempt to manage them.

Workplace Violence

Estimates by the National Institute for Occupational Safety and Health (NIOSH) are that 110 to 115 workplace homicides occur every week. Annually, NIOSH estimates that an additional million people are attacked at work.[37] About 70 percent of the workplace fatalities involved attacks against workers such as police officers, taxi drivers, and convenience store clerks. Often, these deaths occur during armed-robbery attempts. But what has shocked many employers in a variety of industries has been the number of disgruntled employees or former employees who have resorted to homicide in the workplace to deal with their anger and grievances. Research on individuals who have committed the most violent acts shows the relatively common profile that a profound humiliation or rejection, the end of a marriage, or the loss of a lawsuit or job may make a difficult employee take a distinct turn to violence.

Domestic Causes of Workplace Violence   Violence that begins at home with family or friends can spill over to the workplace. As noted, some healthcare employers are unaware of domestic violence and its effects on employees. The worst reaction by employers is to ignore the obvious signs of domestic violence. In fact, some employers have been sued and found liable for ignoring pleas for help from employees who later are victims of domestic violence in hospital parking lots or on an employer's premises.[38]

Management of Workplace Violence   The increase in workplace violence has led many employers to develop workplace violence prevention and response policies and practices. As recommended by the American Society of Safety Engineers (ASSE), it is important for employers to conduct a *risk assessment* of the organization and its employees. Once such a study has been done, it is recommended that HR policies identify how workplace violence is to be dealt with in conjunction with disciplinary actions and referrals to employee assistance programs. An example of a workplace violence policy is available on the book's website: *http://flynn.swlearning.com.*

Often one step is to establish a **violence response team.** Composed of security personnel, key managers, HR staff members, and selected employees, these individuals function much like a safety committee, but with a different focus. At medical centers such as Cincinnati's Children's Hospital, these teams conduct analyses, respond to and investigate employee threats, and might even aid in calming angry, volatile employees.

However, employers must be careful, because they may face legal action for discrimination if they discharge employees for behaviors that often precede violent acts. For example, in several cases, employees who were terminated or suspended for making threats or even engaging in physical actions against co-workers have sued their employers, claiming they had mental disabilities under the ADA.

Post-violence response is another part of managing workplace violence. Whether the violence results in physical injuries or deaths, or just intense interpersonal conflicts, it is important that employers have plans to respond afterwards. Commonly employees may be fearful of returning to work or experience anxiety and sleeplessness, among other reactions. Providing referrals to EAP resources, allowing employees time to meet with HR staff, and providing trained counselors on site are all part of post-violence response efforts.

Training on Workplace Violence Managers, HR staff members, supervisors, and employees should be trained on how to recognize the signs of a potentially violent employee and what to do when violence occurs. For instance, this training may be important for the first contact with an organization, the receptionist, who may need to recognize warning signs of a potentially violent employee, former employee, or outsider.

During training at many organizations, participants learn the typical profile of potentially violent employees and are trained to notify the HR department and to refer employees to outside counseling professionals. Those services often are covered by EAPs that are offered by employers.

Security Management

An overall approach to security management is needed to address a wide range of issues, including workplace violence. Often, HR managers have responsibility for security programs, or they work closely with security mangers to address employee security issues.

Security Audit Conducting a comprehensive review of organizational security is the purpose of a **security audit.** Sometimes called a *vulnerability analysis,* such an audit uses managers inside the organization—such as the HR manager and facilities manager—and outsiders, such as security consultants, police officers, fire officials, and computer security experts.

Typically, a security audit begins with a survey of the area around the facility. Such factors as lighting in parking lots, traffic flow, location of emergency response services, crime in the surrounding neighborhood, and the layout of the buildings and grounds are evaluated. Also included is an audit of the security available within the firm, including the capabilities of guards and others involved with security. Another part of the security audit is a review of disaster plans, which addresses how to deal with disasters such as earthquakes, floods, tornados, hurricanes, fires, and civil disturbances.

Access Control A key part of security is controlling access to the physical facilities of the organization. For instance, providing plexiglass partitions and requiring limited visitation have reduced violence in some emergency rooms.

Many healthcare organizations limit access to facilities and work areas by using electronic access or keycard systems. Although not foolproof, these systems can make it more difficult for an unauthorized person, such as an estranged husband or a gang member, to enter the premises. Access controls also can be used in elevators and stairwells to prevent unauthorized persons from entering certain areas within a facility. Many healthcare facilities that house patients or residents overnight do a complete lock-down overnight, with extremely tight controls on external access to the facility.

Computer Security Yet another part of security is controlling access to computer systems. With so many transactions and records being handled by computers, it is crucial that adequate security provisions be in place to prevent unauthorized access to computer systems, including human resource information systems (HRIS). The growth of the Internet and e-mail systems has made computer security issues an even greater concern. This is particularly evident when individuals are terminated or leave an organization. HR staff must coordinate with information technology staff to change passwords, delete access codes, and otherwise protect company information systems.

Employee Screening and Selection

A key facet of providing security is to screen job applicants. As discussed in Chapter 6, there are legal limits on what can be done, particularly regarding the use of psychological tests and checking of references. Healthcare employers must be careful when selecting employees to use only job-related screening means and to avoid violating federal EEO laws and the ADA.[39] However, firms that do not screen employees adequately may be subject to liability if an employee commits crimes later. For instance, an individual with a criminal record for assault was hired by a hospital to perform housekeeping duties. The employee assaulted and killed a pediatric patient, and the hospital was ruled liable.

Security Personnel

Having sufficient security personnel who are adequately trained is a critical part of security management. Many healthcare organizations contract for this service with firms specializing in security. If employees are to be used, they must be selected and trained to handle a variety of workplace security problems, ranging from dealing with violent behavior by an employee to taking charge in natural disasters.

CASE

Shining Smile Dental Services (SSDS) is staffed by 5 dentist and 14 staff employees. It is a general dental practice that is extremely busy and productive. SSDS's patients are very loyal, and many of them have used SSDS for years.

Marsha, one of SSDS's long-term dental assistants, has always been very popular with the patients and is frequently requested by the dentists to assist them with difficult procedures. Lately, Marsha has been late for work, and one of the dentists observed that she is regularly absent on Mondays. During procedures, she has had attention lapses, and in one instance she bruised a patient's tongue with a suction device. When asked what happened, she blamed the event on the dentist she was assisting and threatened to walk out if the "harassment" over the incident persisted.

SSDS's clinic manager was asked by the dentists to meet with them regarding Marsha's attendance, performance, and poor work attitude. During the meeting, drug and alcohol abuse was suggested, but the clinic manager quickly discarded that possibility as inconsistent with her knowledge of Marsha's history with SSDS. The dentists concluded the meeting by requesting that the clinic manager develop a plan as to how to address Marsha's work-related problems.

Questions

1. What approaches should be used to identify the causes of Marsha's problem behaviors?
2. If the clinic manager determines that drug or alcohol abuse is an issue, what steps should be taken to deal with Marsha's problem(s)?

END NOTES

1. Adapted from Steve Sternberg, "For City's Historic Hospital, Help is Needed 'in a Hurry,'" *USA Today* (September 2–5, 2005), 1A–2A.
2. Dan Hanfling, Klaus O. Schafer, and Carl W. Armstrong, "Making Healthcare Preparedness a Part of the Homeland Security Equation," *Topics in Emergency Medicine* (March 2003), 128–142.
3. Patrick J. Kiger, "Dealing with Disaster," *Workforce* (November 2004), 30–38.
4. Peter Hoonaker, Todd Loushine, Pascale Carayon, James Kallman, Andrew Kapp, and Michael Smith, "The Effect of Safety Initiatives on Safety Performance: A Longitudinal Study," *Applied Ergonomics* (July 2005), 461–469.
5. "New Emergency and Disaster Preparedness Course Work for Physicians and Other Healthcare Professionals," *Journal of Environmental Health* (October 2003), 46.
6. "Study: Workers' Comp Costs Rise Faster than Payments," *Safety & Health* (September 2005), 12.
7. Presley Reed and Alan M. Koral, "Keep FMLA Claims in Check," *Occupational Health and Safety* (2002/2003 Buyers guide), 70–75.
8. For more information visit: *http://www.eeoc.gov/facts/jobapplicant.html.*
9. Occupational Safety and Health Organization, U.S. Department of Labor.
10. "OSHA Alliance Develops Educational Information," *Professional Safety* (May 2005), 19–44.
11. Evelyn Bain, "OSHA Targeted Inspections Going on Right Now in Massachusetts Hospitals," *Massachusetts Nurse* (June 2004), 9; and "OSHA Plans Crackdown on Nursing-Home Safety Violations," *Wall Street Journal* (March 19, 2002), A1.
12. OSHA Standard 1910.132—Personal Protective Equipment.

13. Ronald T. Dobos, "Exposure to Bloodborne Pathogens in the Hospital," *Professional Safety* (February 2000), 29–31.

14. Lynn Grainer, "When it Comes to Keyboards, One Size Does Not Fit All," *Computing Canada* (January 14, 2005), 26.

15. "OSHA's New Ergo Plan: Guidelines Favored Over Rules," *Industrial Safety and Hygiene News* (June 2002), 14–15; and Bernie Knill, "Ergonomics Gets a Boost," *Material Handling Management* (August 2003), 54–56.

16. *United Autoworkers v. Johnson Controls, Inc.,* 111 S. Ct 1196 (1991).

17. *Marshall v. Barlow's Inc.,* 98 S. Ct 1816 (1978).

18. Don Nielsen and John Austin, "Behavior-Based Safety, Improvement Opportunities in Hospital Safety," *Professional Safety* (February 2005), 33–37.

19. "Creating a Safer Workplace: Simple Steps Bring Results," *Leadership for the Front Lines* (August 2002), 1–2.

20. "The Role of Leadership in Instilling a Culture of Safety: Lessons from the Literature," *Journal of Healthcare Management* (January/February 2004), 47–58.

21. Drew Dawson and Phyllis Zee, "Work Hours and Reducing Fatigue-Related Risk: Good Research vs. Good Policy," *Journal of the American Medical Association* (September 7, 2005) 1,104–1,106.

22. James J. Loud, "Corrective Action Programs, Fixing Safety Problems—And Keeping them Fixed," *Professional Safety* (December 2004), 32–36.

23. Laura H. Rhodes and David P. Rhodes, "Who is Performing the Safety Function? The Intersection of Safety and Human Resources," *Professional Safety* (April 2002), 48–54.

24. "OSHA: Laws Alone Don't Solve Problems: Safety Committees, an Essential Redundancy," *Chemical Health & Safety* (November 2002), 39.

25. Dennis R. Downing and Renae J. Norton, "Safety Incentives: Myths and Realities," *Occupational Health & Safety* (January 2004), 62–66.

26. Michael Prince, "Battling Workplace Drug Use," *Business Insurance* (January 29, 2001), 20.

27. Patricia Blair, "Report Impaired Practice—Stat," *Nursing Management* (January 2002), 24–25.

28. "Employers Taking Proactive Approach to EAPs," *Occupational Health* (January 2005 Supplement), 5.

29. Park Kyoung-Ok, Mark C. Wilson, and Sun Lee Myung, "Effects of Social Support at Work on Depression and Organizational Productivity," *American Journal of Health Behavior* (September/October 2004) 444–445.

30. William P. Bahnfleth and W. J. Kowalski, "Indoor-Air Quality: Issues and Resolutions," *Heating/Piping/Air Conditioning HPAC Engineering* (June 2005), 6–21.

31. Donna E. Corbin, "Latex Allergy and Dermatitis," *Occupational Health and Safety* (January 2002), 36–38.

32. Karleen Smith, Ann Wallace, and Betty Smith-Campbell, "What you Should Know About Latex Allergy," *Nurse/Practitioner* (December 2004), 24.

33. I. Hatcher, M. Sullivan, J. Hutchinson, S. Thurman, and F. Goffrey, "An Intravenous Medication Safety System: Preventing High-risk Medication Errors at the Point of Care," *Journal of Nursing* (2004), 437–439.

34. "Workplace Safety: Recognizing and Eliminating Hazards," *Manage Online* (February/March 2005), 1–2.

35. "Hot Topic Survey of HR and Benefits Managers," *Medical Benefits* (August 30, 2005).

36. Linda Sutton, "Setting a Two-Year Plan," *Journal of Employee Assistance* (April 2003), 16–19.

37. Marlene Piturro, "Workplace Violence," *Strategic Finance* (May 2001), 35–38.

38. Stacey Pastel Dougan, "Employers May Face Liability When Domestic Violence Comes to Work," *HR Focus* (February 2003), 11–14.

39. Teresa Butler Stivarius, John Skonberg, Rod Fuegel, Robert Blumberg, Russel Jones, and Kathleen Mones, "Background Checks: Four Steps to Basic Compliance In a Multistate Environment," *SHRM-Legal Report* (March/April 2003), 1–8.

GLOSSARY

A

Ability tests Tests that assess the skills that individuals have already learned.

Adversarial relationship Relationship between unions and management characterized by conflict and confrontation.

Alternative dispute resolutions Method of resolving differences between employees and their employers; these include arbitration, peer-review panels, and organizational ombudsmen.

Applicant pool All people who are actually evaluated for selection.

Applicant population A subset of the labor force population that is available for selection using a particular recruiting approach.

Aptitute tests Tests that measure general ability to learn or acquire a skill.

Arbitration Using a neutral third party to resolve a dispute.

Assessment center A series of evaluative exercises and tests used for selection and development.

B

Base pay Basic compensation that an employee receives, usually as a wage or salary.

Behavioral event interview An interview in which applicants are required to give specific examples of how they have handled a problem or situation in the past.

Behavior-based criteria Identification of behaviors that may lead to successful job performance.

Benchmark jobs Jobs that are found in other organizations and performed by several individuals who have similar duties that require similar KSAs.

Benefit An indirect reward given to an employee as a part of organizational membership, regardless of performance.

Benefits needs analysis A comprehensive look at all aspects of benefits in an organization.

Board of inquiry A board appointed by the FMCS Director to investigate, report, and recommend solutions to resolve contractual disputes.

Bona fide occupational qualification (BFOQ) A legitimate reason why an employer can exclude persons on otherwise illegal bases of consideration.

Broadbanding The practice of using fewer pay grades with much broader ranges than in traditional compensation systems.

C

Cash balance plans Pension plans that are a hybrid of defined-benefit and defined-contribution plans, based on a hypothetical account balance.

Central-tendency raters Managers who in the performance-review process, tend to rate all of their employees within a narrow range.

Certified Designation by the NLRB that a union has met the required conditions and received the necessary votes to become the bargaining representative of an employee group.

Chain-of-custody procedures Procedures that include keeping accurate records on how drug tests are conducted and tracked.

Checklist method Appraisal method that offers a list of words or statements that describes employees' performance.

Coaching Training and feedback given to employees by immediate supervisors.

Collaborative relationship The relationship between unions and management, characterized by an atmosphere in which there is shared responsibility to address the mutual interests and issues of both parties.

Compensation and benefits Rewards for performing organizational work, including wages or salary, incentive programs, and benefits.

Competencies Basic characteristics that can be linked to enhanced performance by individuals or teams.

Competency approach Method of job analysis that focuses on the competencies that individuals need in order to perform jobs, rather than on the tasks, duties, and responsibilities that compose a job.

Consolidated Omnibus Budget Reconciliation Act (COBRA) Law that requires that most employers offer extended healthcare coverage to designated groups of former employees or dependents of former employees.

Construct validity A method that shows a relationship between an abstract characteristic inferred from research and/or job performance.

Constructive discharge Situation when an employer creates impossible working conditions that force an employee to resign.

Contaminated criteria Measurement process that includes irrelevant criteria.

Content validity A logical non-statistical method used to identify the knowledge, skills, abilities, and other characteristics necessary to perform a job.

Contrast errors Situation in the performance-review process in which a manager compares employees to each other rather than to job-performance standards.

Contributory plan Pension plan in which the employee and employer both pay in money for benefits.

Co-payment Portion of a health insurance cost that employees are required to pay.

Core competency A unique capability in the organization that creates high value and differentiates the organization from its competition.

Cost-of-living adjustment (COLA) A standard raise based on an economic measure, such as the consumer price index.

Critical-incident narrative Appraisal method in which the manager documents incidents that are highly favorable or unfavorable representations of an employee's work performance.

Cumulative trauma disorders (CTD) Problems that occur when workers repetitively use the same muscles to perform tasks, resulting in muscular and skeletal injuries.

D

Decertified Designation by the NLRB that employees have met the required conditions to remove a union as their representative.

Deficient criteria Measurement process that omits significant criteria.

Defined-benefit plans Pension plans in which employees' contributions are based on actuarial calculations that focus on the benefits to be received by employees after retirement and the methods used to determine such benefits.

Defined-contribution plan Pension plan in which the employer makes an annual payment to an employee's account.

Delphi technique Forecasting method that uses input from a group of experts, whose opinions are sought through separate questionnaires on what forecasted situations will be.

Department A distinct grouping of organizational responsibilities.

Development An effort to improve employees' ability to handle a variety of assignments and to cultivate capabilities beyond those required by the current job.

Drug-Free Workplace Act of 1988 Law enacted to make workplaces free from the use of drugs or controlled substances.

Due process A method of questioning a disciplinary action.

Dues check-off process System in which union dues are automatically deducted from workers' paychecks.

Duty A work segment composed of several tasks that are performed by an individual.

E

Emotional intelligence Proficiencies in intra-personal and inter-personal skills in the areas of self-awareness, self-regulation, self-motivation, social awareness, and social skills.

Employee assistance program (EAP) A program which provides counseling and other help to employees having emotional, mental, or other personal problems.

Employee development A process that focuses on individuals gaining new capabilities useful for both current and future jobs.

Employee handbook A publication containing an organization's HR policies.

Employee-relations philosophy A philosophy that describes the relationship the employer wishes to have with its employees.

Employment contract Formal agreement between an employer and an employee contractually defining the working relationship.

Employment Practices Liability Insurance Insurance that protects employers against lawsuits initiated by their employees.

Employment-at-will provisions Provisions in employment agreements and handbooks that state that employees may be terminated at any time for any reason.

Environment of care standards Joint Commission standards that address the factors that go into making a safe and secure environment.

Environmental scanning The process of studying the environment of the organization to pinpoint opportunities and threats.

Equal employment opportunity (EEO) A broad concept holding that individuals should have equal treatment in all employment-related actions.

Ergonomics The study and design of the work environment to address physiological and physical demands a position.

Essay Describes an employee's performance during a given evaluation period.

Essential functions Job activities that are required for the job to be done satisfactorily.

Estimates Forecasting method used to determine how many emplyees might be needed in the future.

Exception-based reviews Employee reviews that shorten the performance process and recognize behaviors that either exceed the job standards or identify behaviors that can be improved.

Exit interview An interview of those who are leaving the organization to determine the reasons for their departure.

Extended illness banks Program that allows employees to accrue time to be used for longer-term illness or health-related care that does not result in a disability, such as maternity care.

F

401(k) and 403(b) plans Retirement plans that allow employees to elect to reduce their current pay by a certain percentage, which is then used to fund a retirement plan.

Federal Mediation and Conciliation Services (FMCS) An agency charged with mediating labor negotiations when asked by negotiating parties or assigned by the FMCS Director.

Feedback systems Three components of performance appraisal: collecting data, evaluating data, and taking action based on the data.

Field-review A review of manager's comments about each employee's performance.

Firm-choice option An approach recommended to encourage employees to seek help for their substance-abuse problems or face discipline.

Flexible benefits plan A flex or cafeteria plan, that allows employees to select the benefits they prefer from groups of benefits established by the employer.

Flexible spending accounts A plan that allows employees to contribute pre-tax dollars to buy additional benefits.

For-cause testing Drug test used to test employees suspected of being under the influence of drugs while at work.

Forced distribution Appraisal method of ranking employees and using statistics to sort all employees along a bell curve.

Forecasting Using information from the past and present to identify expected future conditions.

Formal appraisal process Performance appraisal system that defines and evaluates an employee's job performance.

Funeral or bereavement leave Time off to attend to the arrangements and funeral after the death of an immediate family member.

G

Gainsharing plans Group incentive where employee teams that meet certain goals share in the gains measured against performance targets.

Gap analysis Process that identifies the distance between where an organization is with its employee capabilities and where it needs to be.

Glass ceiling Discriminatory practices that have prevented women and other protected-class members from advancing to executive-level jobs.

Graphic-rating scale A scale that allows the rater to mark an emplyee's performance on a continuum.

Green-circled employee An incumbent who is paid below the range set for the job.

Grievance procedure A formal process used to resolve issues between managers and workers.

H

Halo effect Situation in the performance-review process when a manager rates an employee high or low on all job standards based on one characteristic.

Health A general state of physical, mental, and emotional well-being.

Health Insurance Portability and Accountability Act (HIPAA) Law that allows employees to switch their health insurance coverage from one employer to another regardless of pre-existing conditions.

Health promotion A supportive approach to facilitate and encourage employees to enhance healthy actions and lifestyles.

HR development Focuses on individuals gaining new capabilities useful for both current and future jobs.

HR management Refers to the strategies, tactics, plans, and programs that organizations utilize to accomplish the work of the organization through its employees.

HR metrics Methods used to measure HR activities.

HR planning Phase in which managers attempt to anticipate forces that will influence the future supply of and demand for employees.

HR strategic planning The process of analyzing and identifying the need for and availability of human resources in order to accomplish organizational objectives.

Human Resource Information system (HRIS) An integrated system designed to provide information used in HR decision making.

I

Immediate confirmation Training concept that people learn best if reinforcement and feedback are given as soon as possible after training.

Immigration Reform and Control Act of 1986 (IRCA) A law that requires that within seventy-two hours of hiring, an employer must determine whether a job applicant is eligible to work in the U.S.

Impasse Situation in which negotiating parties cannot come to an agreement.

Implied contract Unwritten agreements between employers and employees, which suggest that an employee will be employed indefinitely or as long as the employee performs the job satisfactorily.

Independent contractors Workers who perform specific services on a contract basis.

Individual incentives Pay given to reward the effort and performance of individuals.

Individual retirement account (IRA) A special account in which an employee can set aside funds that will not be taxed until the employee accesses the funds at retirement.

Informal appraisal process Performance appraisal system conducted at the manager's discretion to praise employees or motivate better behavior.

Informal training Training that occurs through interactions and feedback among employees.

Integrated disability management programs Integrating disability programs with workers' compensation programs to reduce costs and coordinate claim processing.

Interest-based bargaining A style of negotiating contracts based on identifying and meeting the parties' mutual interests.

Internal recruiting Focusing on recruiting current employees and others with previous contact with an employing organization.

J

Job A grouping of common tasks, duties, and responsibilities.

Job analysis A systematic way to gather and analyze information about the content and human requirements of jobs and the context in which jobs are performed.

Job board A Web site on which employers can post jobs or search for candidates.

Job description Summary of multiple criteria that defines a job.

Job design Organizing tasks, duties, and responsibilities into a productive unit of work.

Job evaluation A systematic basis for determining the relative worth of jobs within an organization.

Job posting and bidding Method for recruiting employees, whereby the employer provides notices of job openings and employees respond by applying for specific openings.

Job rotation Shifting an employee from job to job.

Job satisfaction A positive emotional state resulting from job experiences.

Job-site development Development process that occurs on the job.

Joint Commission on Accreditation of Healthcare Organizations (JCAHO) A quality accreditation organization whose members subscribe to a standard-based review process.

L

Labor force population All individuals who are available for selection if all possible recruitment strategies are used.

Labor markets The external sources from which employers attract employees.

Labor-management committees Committees that are jointly sponsored by management and the union. Their purpose is to identify common problems, interpret contract language, and resolve the issues.

Landrum-Griffin Act Act that was designed to curtail corrupt union practices, including officials misusing pension funds and threatening workers in order to retain power.

Law of effect People tend to repeat responses that give them some type of positive reward and avoid actions associated with negative consequences.

Leaves of absence Time off with or without pay.

Leniency raters Managers who in the performance-review process give most of their employees high ratings.

Lock-out/tag-out regulations OSHA rules that require safety locks and tags on machinery and power sources to prevent accidental start-up of a machine when it is defective.

M

Managed care Approaches that monitor and reduce medical costs through restrictions and market-system alternatives.

Management by objectives Specifies the performance goals that an employee and manager agree to complete within a defined period.

Management rights clauses Clauses that vary from contract to contract and give management the exclusive right to manage, direct, and control its business.

Mandated benefits Benefits required by law.

Mediation A dispute process in which a trained mediator assists the parties in reaching a settlement.

Mental ability tests Tests that measure reasoning capabilities.

Mentoring A relationship in which experienced managers aid individuals in the earlier stages of their careers.

N

Narrative performance-appraisal method Method that provides comments using essays, documentation of critical incidents, or field reviews.

National Labor Relations Act (NLRA) Also known as the Wagner Act, a 1935 act passed to provide more specific guidelines to govern the relationship between unions, organizations, and employees.

National Labor Relations Board (NLRB) Board created by the National Labor Relations Act that enforces the provisions of the NLRA for both unions and organizations.

Nominal group technique Forecasting method that requires experts to meet face to face as independent ideas are generated.

Non-compete provisions Contract provisions that specify that employees will not compete with the organization if they leave.

Non-contributory plan Pension plan in which the employer provides all the funds for pension benefits.

Nurse Practice Act Law that sets professional practice standards for registered nurses.

O

Off-site development Process that gives individuals opportunities to get away from the job and concentrate solely on education or development.

Ombudsman A staff employee who administers a program designed to resolve disputes between employees and employers.

On-the-job training Planned training that uses a supervisor or manager to teach and show the employee what to do.

Organization chart A chart that depicts the relationships among jobs in an organization.

Organizational commitment The degree to which employees believe in and accept organizational goals and desire to remain with the organization.

Organizational culture A pattern of shared values and beliefs giving members of an organization meaning and providing them with rules for behavior.

Organizational incentives Compensation given to reward people based on the performance results of the organization.

Orientation The planned introduction of new employees to their jobs, co-workers, and the organization.

Outside rater An appraisal method in which an outside expert evaluates the employee's performance.

Outsourcing Using external training firms, consultants, or other entities to perform HR functions.

P

Paid time-off plan A time off program that combines short-term leave, vacation, and holiday pay into one bank.

Panel interview Several interviewers interview the candidate at the same time.

Pay adjustment matrix A salary guide chart in which adjustments are based in part on the person's pay, divided by the midpoint of the pay range.

Pay compression Shrinking the pay differences among individuals with different levels of experience and performance.

Pay grade A grouping of individual jobs having approximately the same job worth.

Pay survey A collection of data on compensation rates for workers performing similar jobs in other organizations.

Peer-review panel An internal committee of employees who review employee complaints and make decisions about them.

Pension plans Retirement benefits established and funded by employers and employees.

Performance appraisal The process of evaluating how well employees perform their jobs when compared to a set of standards, and then communicating that information to employees.

Performance consulting A process in which a trainer and the organizational client work together to boost workplace performance in support of organizational goals.

Performance-improvement plan Plan based on information managers receive about an employee's performance, implemented when the manager and employee meet to discuss job expectations.

Phased retirement A program that helps employees retire in stages.

Placement Fitting a person to the right job.

Portability Ability to move pension funds from one company to another.

Position A job performed by one person.

Predictors Identifiable indicators of the selection criteria.

Pre-employment drug test A test used to avoid hiring individuals who use illegal drugs or abuse legal drugs.

Preferred provider organization (PPO) A healthcare provider that contracts with an employer or an employer group to provide healthcare services to employees at a competitive rate.

Privacy Act of 1974 Law that issues regulations that affect human resource record-keeping systems, policies, and procedures.

Productivity A measure of the quantity and quality of work done, considering the cost of the resources it took to do the work.

Progressive discipline Five-step discipline process that gets more strict at each step.

Protected class People having certain designated characteristics such as minority race, women, individuals over age 40, individuals with disabilities, those with military experience, or certain religious beliefs.

Psychological contract The unwritten expectations that employees and employers have about the nature of their work relationships.

Psychology of selection Useful way to think about the way a selection decision should be approached and made.

Psychomotor tests Test that measures a person's dexterity, hand-eye coordination, arm-hand steadiness, and other factors.

Public-policy violation A provision under which an employee can sue an employer if the employee was discharged for reasons that violate some public policy.

R

Random testing Drug testing done in a random fashion.

Ranking Appraisal method that compares employees, against each other.

Rater bias Situation in the performance-review process when a manager has a bias against a certain employee or employee group based on the manager's own values or prejudices.

Realistic job preview (RJP) Part of a job selection process that is designed to inform job candidates of the organizational realities of the job so they can evaluate their own job expectations.

Reasonable care Employer practice of establishing sexual harassment policies, communicating with and training employees on harassment issues, and investigating and taking action when complaints are voiced.

Recruiting Identifying where to recruit, whom to recruit, and what the job requirements will be.

Red-circled employee An incumbent who is at the maximum of the range set for the job.

Reengineering Rethinking and redesigning work to improve cost, service, and speed.

Reinforcement Concept of training based on the law of effect.

Resource pools (float pools) Workers specifically hired to be available (float) to various units when the needs are higher than core staff can meet.

Results-based criteria Process that identifies behavior based on results that are easy to identify and evaluate.

Retention Keeping employees who have been recruited, selected, and trained.

Retention agreement A contract agreement that is designed to retain key employees during mergers, consolidations, or changes in the organizational leadership.

Review and rescission rights Rights and responsibilities of a prospective employee.

Right-to-sue letter A letter that notifies a complainant that he or she has ninety days in which to file a personal suit in federal court.

Rules of thumb Forecasting method that relies on general guidelines applied to specific situations within the organization.

S

Sabbatical leave Paid time off the job to develop and rejuvenate oneself.

Safety Protecting the physical well-being of people.

Salary Compensation based on a fixed amount, regardless of hours worked.

Security Protecting employees, patients/ residents/clients, and visitors.

Security audit Conducting a comprehensive review of organizational security; sometimes called a vulnerability analysis.

Selection The process of choosing qualified individuals who have relevant qualifications to fill jobs in an organization.

Selection criterion a charactistic that a person must have to do the job successfully.

Self-rating Method of appraisal in which employees rate themselves.

Severance pay A security benefit voluntarily offered by employers to some employees who lose their jobs.

Shadowing programs Programs that provide an individual who is considering a position the opportunity to accompany a professional during a workday.

Sick-building syndrome A situation in which occupants experience acute health problems and discomfort that appear to be linked to time spent in a building.

Staffing Function of human resources designed to provide an adequate supply of qualified individuals to fill the jobs in an organization.

Statistical regression analysis Forecasting method that makes a statistical comparison of past relationships among various factors.

Statutory rights Existing laws, legislation, and evolving case law that protect employees' rights.

Step systems Pay system in which employees' wages are adjusted based on how long they have been with the organization.

Strategic HR management Use of employees to help an organization gain or keep a competitive advantage against its competitors.

Strategic training A process that focuses on efforts that develop individual worker competencies and produces ongoing value and competitive advantages for the organization.

Strict raters Managers who in the performance-review process, give all of their employees low ratings.

Strike contingency plans Plans that help assure communities that patients will receive continuous healthcare in the event of a strike.

Structured interview A set of standardized questions that are asked of all applicants so comparisons can be made among applicants.

Substance abuse The use of illicit substances or the misuse of controlled substances, alcohol, or other drugs.

Succession planning A process of identifying a longer-term plan for the orderly replacement of key employees.

T

360-degree appraisal Process of appraisal that involves getting performance evaluations from the full circle of individuals with whom the staff member has experience.

Taft-Hartley Act Act that equalized the effects of the NLRA by defining and prohibiting unfair labor practices by unions.

Task A distinct, identifiable work activity composed of motions.

Team or peer rating Performance-rating approach in which managers collect performance information by using teams and peers that the employee worked with during the evaluation period.

Temporary employees Workers who are hired on a rate-per-day or per-week basis as needed.

Ten-day strike notice Requirement that unions give healthcare organizations ten days' notice before striking against them.

Tentative agreement Situation in which union and management agree to move forward with a recommended contract.

Training A process whereby people acquire capabilities to aid in the achievement of organizational goals.

Training design Determining how the assessed needs are to be addressed, considering learning concepts, legal issues, and the types of training available.

Training needs assessment Considering employee and organizational performance issues to determine if training can be helpful.

Trait-based criteria Process that identifies subjective personal traits that may contribute to job success.

Transfer of training Process whereby trainees actually use on the job what was learned in training.

U

Unfair labor practices Actions defined by the National Labor Relations Act as illegal.

Union security clause Clause in union contracts that recognizes the exclusive right of a union to bargain on behalf of the employees.

Utilization review Review and audit of medical work, possibly including a second opinion, review of procedures used, or review of charges for procedures done.

V

Variable pay Compensation linked directly to individual, team, or organizational performance.

Vesting Assurance that employees have worked the minimum number of years to qualify for a pension plan.

Violence response team A group of security personnel, key managers, HR staff members, and selected employees who analyze, respond to, and investigate workplace violence situations.

W

Wages Compensation based on hourly pay.

Wellness programs Programs designed to maintain or improve employee health before problems arise by encouraging personal lifestyle changes.

Whistleblowers Employees who report employer public-policy violations.

Whole learning (Gestalt learning) As applied to job training, a training concept in which instructions should be divided into smaller elements after employees have had the opportunity to see how the elements fit together.

Work analysis A study of the workflow, activities, context, and output of a job.

Workers' compensation Benefits provided to a person injured on the job.

Wrongful discharge Termination of employee for reasons that are illegal, that are improper, or that don't follow organizational policies.

INDEX

Note: Human resource is abbreviated as HR in the index.

A

AAPs. *See* Affirmative Action Plans
Ability test, 125
Academic and credential requirements, 181
Accident investigation and evaluation, 318–319
Accident rates, 316
Accidents, reasons for, 316–317
Accountability, 10
Accreditation. *See* Joint Commission for Accreditation of Healthcare Organizations (JCAHO)
ACHE. *See* American College of Healthcare Executives
ADA. *See* Americans with Disabilities Act
Adoption benefits, 289
ADR. *See* Alternative dispute resolution
Adult learning, 165–166
Adverse events, serious, 31
Affirmative action, 63–67
  healthcare and, 65–66
  preemployment vs. after-hire inquiries, 58
  requirements, 63

and reverse discrimination, 62
tracking, 44
See also Affirmative Action Plans
Affirmative Action Plans (AAPs), 63–67
actions and reporting, 65
analyses and comparisons, 64–65
audit of, 65
healthcare and affirmative action, 65–66
internal background review, 63–64
policy statements, 63
voluntary, 63
Age discrimination, 57, 71–72, 280–281
Age Discrimination in Employment Act (1967), 57, 280
AHA. *See* American Hospital Association
Air quality in the workplace, 322
Alexandria Clinic (Minnesota), 230
Alternative dispute resolution (ADR), 212
Ambulatory healthcare services, 5, 12
American College of Healthcare Executives (ACHE), 65

American Hospital Association (AHA)
Commission on Workforce for Hospitals and Health Systems, 3
recommendations, 3
American Nurses Associations (ANA) Code of Ethics, 321
American Society for Training and Development (ASTD), 158, 173
Americans with Disabilities Act (ADA), 51, 57, 72–73
compliance, 72–73
emotional/mental health illness covered by, 321
job analysis and, 93–94
job evaluation and, 261–262
medical examinations and inquiries, 130
safety and, 306–307
and substance-abuse cases, 320
ANA. *See* American Nurses Associations (ANA) Code of Ethics
Applicant flow data, 77
Applicant pool, 108
Applicant population, 108
Application disclaimers and notices, 125
Appraisal. *See* Performance appraisal